FICHTE'S *FOUN* *NATURAL*

Fichte's *Foundations of Natural Right* (1796/97) was one of the most influential books in nineteenth-century philosophy. It was read carefully by Schelling, Hegel, and Marx, and initiated a tradition in German philosophy that considers human subjectivity to be relational and intersubjective, thus requiring relations of recognition between subjects. The essays in this volume highlight this little understood book's most important ideas and innovations. They offer discussions of Fichte's conception of freedom, self-consciousness, coercion, the summons, the body, and human rights, together with new analyses of his deduction of right, his views on the social contract, and his arguments for the separation of right from morality. The essays expand and deepen ongoing debates in the scholarship and chart new avenues of thought about Fichte's most enduring work of political philosophy. They will be essential reading for students and scholars of German Idealism, nineteenth-century philosophy, and the history of political thought.

GABRIEL GOTTLIEB is Associate Professor of Philosophy at Xavier University. He has published numerous articles on Fichte and the philosophy of action.

CAMBRIDGE CRITICAL GUIDES

Titles published in this series:

Hegel's *Phenomenology Of Spirit*
EDITED BY DEAN MOYAR AND MICHAEL QUANTE
Mill's *On Liberty*
EDITED BY C. L. TEN
Kant's *Idea For A Universal History With A Cosmopolitan Aim*
EDITED BY AMÉLIE OKSENBERG RORTY AND JAMES SCHMIDT
Kant's *Groundwork Of The Metaphysics Of Morals*
EDITED BY JENS TIMMERMANN
Kant's *Critique Of Practical Reason*
EDITED BY ANDREWS REATH AND JENS TIMMERMANN
Wittgenstein's *Philosophical Investigations*
EDITED BY ARIF AHMED
Kierkegaard's *Concluding Unscientific Postscript*
EDITED BY RICK ANTHONY FURTAK
Plato's *Republic*
EDITED BY MARK L. MCPHERRAN
Plato's *Laws*
EDITED BY CHRISTOPHER BOBONICH
Spinoza's *Theological-Political Treatise*
EDITED BY YITZHAK Y. MELAMED AND MICHAEL A. ROSENTHAL
Aristotle's *Nicomachean Ethics*
EDITED BY JON MILLER
Kant's *Metaphysics Of Morals*
EDITED BY LARA DENIS
Nietzsche's *On The Genealogy Of Morality*
EDITED BY SIMON MAY
Kant's *Observations And Remarks*
EDITED BY RICHARD VELKLEY AND SUSAN SHELL
Augustine's *City Of God*
EDITED BY JAMES WETZEL
Descartes' *Meditations*
EDITED BY KAREN DETLEFSEN
Kant's *Religion Within The Boundaries Of Mere Reason*
EDITED BY GORDON MICHALSON
Kant's *Lectures On Anthropology*
EDITED BY ALIX COHEN
Kierkegaard's *Fear And Trembling*
EDITED BY DANIEL CONWAY
Kant's *Lectures on Ethics*
EDITED BY LARA DENIS AND OLIVER SENSEN
Aristotle's *Physics*
EDITED BY MARISKA LEUNISSEN
Aristotle's *Politics*
EDITED BY THORNTON LOCKWOOD AND THANASSIS SAMARAS
Aquinas's *Disputed Questions on Evil*
EDITED BY M. V. DOUGHERTY

FICHTE'S *FOUNDATIONS OF NATURAL RIGHT*

A Critical Guide

EDITED BY

GABRIEL GOTTLIEB

CAMBRIDGE
UNIVERSITY PRESS

CAMBRIDGE
UNIVERSITY PRESS

University Printing House, Cambridge CB2 8BS, United Kingdom

One Liberty Plaza, 20th Floor, New York, NY 10006, USA

477 Williamstown Road, Port Melbourne, VIC 3207, Australia

314-321, 3rd Floor, Plot 3, Splendor Forum, Jasola District Centre, New Delhi - 110025, India

79 Anson Road, #06-04/06, Singapore 079906

Cambridge University Press is part of the University of Cambridge.

It furthers the University's mission by disseminating knowledge in the pursuit of education, learning and research at the highest international levels of excellence.

www.cambridge.org
Information on this title: www.cambridge.org/9781107435070

First published 2016
First paperback edition 2018

A catalogue record for this publication is available from the British Library

Library of Congress Cataloging in Publication data
Names: Gottlieb, Gabriel, editor.
Title: Fichte's *Foundations of natural right* : a critical guide /
edited by Gabriel Gottlieb, Xavier University.
Description: New York : Cambridge University Press, 2016. |
Series: Cambridge critical guides | Includes bibliographical references and index.
Identifiers: LCCN 2016023276| ISBN 9781107078147 (hardback) |
ISBN 9781107435070 (pbk.)
Subjects: LCSH: Fichte, Johann Gottlieb, 1762–1814.
Grundlage des Naturrechts nach Principien der Wissenschaftslehre. |
Natural law. | Political science. | State, The. Classification:
LCC JC181.F623 F53 2016 | DDC 320.01–dc23
LC record available at https://lccn.loc.gov/2016023276

ISBN 978-1-107-07814-7 Hardback
ISBN 978-1-107-43507-0 Paperback

Contents

Contributors

JAMES A. CLARKE is a lecturer in the Department of Philosophy at The University of York. He has published articles on Fichte in *Inquiry*, *British Journal for the History of Philosophy*, and *Review of Metaphysics*.

PAUL FRANKS is Professor of Philosophy at Yale University. His publications include: *All or Nothing: Systematicity, Transcendental Arguments, and Skepticism in German Idealism* (2005). He is the translator and editor (with Michael L. Morgan) of *Franz Rosenzweig: Philosophical and Theological Writings* (2000). He has published essays in the *Yearbook of German Idealism* and the *Cambridge Companion to Hegel and Nineteenth Century Philosophy* (2008).

GABRIEL GOTTLIEB is Associate Professor of Philosophy at Xavier University. He has published articles on Fichte and philosophy of action in the *International Philosophical Quarterly*, *Pacific Philosophical Quarterly*, *Phenomenology and the Cognitive Sciences*, and *The Nineteenth Century Philosophy Reader* (2015).

DAVID JAMES is Associate Professor of Philosophy at the University of Warwick. His publications include: *Fichte's Republic: Idealism, History and Nationalism* (2015), *Rousseau and German Idealism: Freedom, Dependence and Necessity* (2013), and *Fichte's Social and Political Philosophy: Property and Virtue* (2011). He is currently editing *Hegel's Elements of the Philosophy of Right: A Critical Guide* for Cambridge University Press and also co-editing (with Günter Zöller) *The Cambridge Companion to Fichte*.

WAYNE MARTIN is Professor of Philosophy at the University of Essex. His publications include: *Theories of Judgment: Psychology, Logic, Phenomenology* (2006) and *Idealism and Objectivity: Understanding Fichte's Jena Project* (1997). His work on Fichte has also appeared in the *European Journal of Philosophy*, *Ratio* and *Topoi*.

JEAN-CHRISTOPHE MERLE is Professor at Universität Vechta. His publications include: *Spheres of Global Justice* (2013) and *German Idealism and the Concept of Punishment* (2009). He is also editor of *Johann Gottlieb Fichte: Grundlage des Naturrechts* (2001) and with Andreas Schmidt, *Fichtes Das System der Sittenlehre: Ein kooperativer Kommentar* (2015).

DEAN MOYAR is Associate Professor of Philosophy at Johns Hopkins University. His publications include: *Hegel's Conscience* (2011). He is also the editor of *The Routledge Companion to Nineteenth Century Philosophy* (2010) and the co-editor (with Michael Quante) of *Hegel's Phenomenology of Spirit: A Critical Guide* (2008).

MICHAEL NANCE is Assistant Professor of Philosophy at the University of Maryland Baltimore County. His work on Fichte and Kant has been published in the *European Journal of Philosophy* and *International Journal of Philosophical Studies*.

FREDERICK NEUHOUSER is Professor of Philosophy and Viola Manderfeld Professor of German at Barnard College and Columbia University. His publications include: *Rousseau's Critique of Inequality: Reconstructing the Second Discourse* (2014), *Rousseau's Theodicy of Self-Love: Evil, Rationality, and the Drive for Recognition* (2008), *Actualizing Freedom: The Foundations of Hegel's Social Theory* (2000), and *Fichte's Theory of Subjectivity* (1990). He also edited Fichte's, *Foundations of Natural Right*, translated by Michael Baur (2000).

ANGELICA NUZZO is Professor of Philosophy at the City University of New York. Her publications include: *Memory, History, Justice in Hegel* (2012), *Ideal Embodiment: Kant's Theory of Sensibility* (2008), and *Kant and the Unity of Reason* (2005).

JOHN RUSSON is Professor of Philosophy at the University of Guelph. His publications include: *Bearing Witness to Epiphany: Persons, Things and the Nature of Erotic Life* (2009), *Reading Hegel's* Phenomenology (2004), *Human Experience: Philosophy, Neurosis and the Elements of Everyday Life* (2003), and *The Self and Its Body in Hegel's* Phenomenology of Spirit (1997).

ALLEN W. WOOD is the Ruth Norman Halls Professor in Philosophy at Indiana University. His publications include: *The Free Development of Each: Studies on Freedom, Right, and Ethics in Classical German Philosophy* (2014), *Kantian Ethics* (2008), *Kant* (2004), *Kant's Ethical Thought* (1999), and *Hegel's Ethical Thought* (1990). He is also editor of Fichte's *Attempt at a Critique of All Revelation*, translated by Garrett Green (2010) and with Songsuk Susan Hahn, *Cambridge History of Philosophy in the Nineteenth Century (1790–1870)* (2012).

Acknowledgments

The idea of organizing a volume on Fichte's philosophy began brewing in my mind while I was writing my dissertation. Like many other burgeoning Fichte scholars, I felt acutely the lacuna of high-quality scholarship on Fichte, especially when compared to the likes of Kant and Hegel. It took some time to find the right idea for the makings of an edited volume, and I finally hit upon the idea of a *Critical Guide* on the *Foundations of Natural Right* at the 2013 Pacific APA in San Francisco, where a conversation with Lara Denis about her work on the *Critical Guide* to Kant's *Metaphysics of Morals* prompted me to reach out to Cambridge and Hilary Gaskin. Much thanks to Lara for her initial advice. Many thanks are due to Hilary Gaskin for guiding me through the process of putting together the proposal and the book. Thanks also to her team at Cambridge and in particular Emma Collison and Christofere Fila.

The New York German Idealism Workshop was kind of enough to host a conference on the topic of the book on October 3–4, 2014. This allowed a number of contributors to present drafts of their papers and to receive critical feedback. The conference certainly would have been impossible without the support and guidance of Scott Shushan. Thanks so much, Scott. Thanks also to the other members of the organizing committee of the Workshop (Michael Becker, Borhane Blili Hamelin, Anna Katsman, and Thimo Heisenberg). Many thanks to the contributors who presented (and Wayne Martin who had the great idea to host a workshop), and everyone who participated in the conference, especially Jay Bernstein and Nedim Nomer. There is no doubt that the workshop improved the overall quality of the book.

I am thankful also to the support of the Philosophy Department at Xavier University, and in particular conversations with Richard Polt, Tim Brownlee, Dan Dwyer, Tim Quinn, and Steve Frankel. Thanks are due to a number of friends and colleagues whose support I am grateful for as well: Evan Strevell, James Wood, Rachel Chrastil, Zed Adams, Lori

Francis and Reggie Tarantino, and Adam Rossi. I am thankful for my conversations with James Dow as they positively shape practically all of my philosophical work. Kristen Renzi's support, comments, and advice helped me tremendously, and I am grateful for her love and dedication. Thanks to all the love and support of my family, especially my parents, Joel and Susan Gottlieb, as well as Kim, Matt, and Logan Brown.

Finally, thanks so much to all of the contributors for their hard work, support, and commitment to the volume.

Abbreviations

The following abbreviations are used throughout the volume. The *Foundations of Natural Right* is referred to either by its entire title or by the shortened title *Natural Right* in the body of the essays. In the case of citations, it is referred to as *FNR*. Citations to Fichte's work cite first an English translation, when available, and then his *Sämmtliche Werke*. In the instances when Fichte's German text is not published in the *Sämmtliche Werke*, another German edition is cited.

Fichte

ACR	Fichte, *Attempt at a Critique of All Revelation*. A. W. Wood (Ed.). Cambridge: Cambridge University Press, 2010.
CC	Fichte, "Crystal Clear Report to the General Public Concerning the Actual Essence of the Newest Philosophy: An Attempt to Force the Reader to Understand," trans. John Botterman and William Rasch, in *Philosophy of German Idealism*, Ernst Behler. New York: Continuum, 1987.
EPW	Fichte, *Fichte: Early Philosophical Writings*, trans. Daniel Breazeale. Ithaca: Cornell University Press, 1988.
FNR	Fichte, *Foundations of Natural Right*, trans. Michael Baur and ed. Frederick Neuhouser. Cambridge: Cambridge University Press, 2000.
GA	*J. G. Fichte: Gesamtausgabe der Bayerischen Akademie der Wissenschaften*, ed. E. Fuchs, R. Lauth, H. Jacobs, H. Gliwitsky, et. al. Stuttgart-Bad Cannstatt: Frommann-Holzboog, 1964–2012.
IW	Fichte, *Introductions to the Wissenschaftslehre*, ed. D. Breazeale. Indianapolis: Hackett, 1994.
K	Fichte, *Wissenschaftslehre nova methodo: Kollegnachschrift K. Chr. Fr. Krause 1798/99*, ed. Erich Fuchs. Hamburg: Meiner, 1994.

R Fichte, "Reclamation of the Freedom of Thought from the Princes of Europe, who have Oppressed it Until Now" in J. Schmidt (ed.) *What is Enlightenment? Eighteenth-Century Answers and Twentieth-Century Questions*, Berkeley: University of California Press, 1996: pp. 119–43.

RPP Fichte, "Review of Immanuel Kant, Perpetual Peace," trans. Daniel Breazeale, *The Philosophical Forum* 32: 311–22.

SE Fichte, *System of Ethics*, trans. and ed. Daniel Breazeale and Günter Zöller. Cambridge: Cambridge University Press, 2005.

SK Fichte, *Science of Knowledge (Wissenschaftslehre)*, trans. and ed. Peter Heath and John Lachs. Cambridge: Cambridge University Press, 1982. [Contains the "First and Second Introductions" and *Foundations of the Entire Wissenschaftslehre*.]

SW *Sämmtliche Werke*, ed. I. H. Fichte. Berlin: Walter de Gruyter, 1965.

VM Fichte, *The Vocation of Man*, trans. Peter Preuss. Indianapolis: Hackett, 1987.

WLnm Fichte, *Foundations of Transcendental Philosophy: Wissenschaftslehre nova methodo (1796/1799)*, trans. D. Breazeale. Ithaca: Cornell University Press, 1992.

Kant

C Kant, *Correspondence*, trans. Arnulf Zweig. Cambridge: Cambridge University Press, 1999.

CF *Conflict of the Faculties*, in A. Wood and G. diGiovanni (eds.) *Kant: Writings on Religion and Rational Theology*. New York: Cambridge University Press, 1996.

CJ Kant, *Critique of the Power of Judgment*, trans. Paul Guyer and Eric Matthews. Cambridge: Cambridge University Press, 2000.

CPR Kant, *Critique of Pure Reason*, trans. P. Guyer and A. Wood. Cambridge: Cambridge University Press, 1998.

CPrR Kant, *Critique of Practical Reason*, trans. Mary Gregor. Cambridge: Cambridge University Press, 1997.

GW Kant, *Groundwork of the Metaphysic of Morals*, trans. Mary Gregor. Cambridge: Cambridge University Press, 1997.

MM Kant, *Metaphysics of Morals*, trans. Mary Gregor. Cambridge: Cambridge University Press, 1996.

OT Kant, *What Does it Mean to Orient Oneself in Thinking?* in A.Wood and G. diGiovanni (eds.) *Kant: Writings on Religion and Rational Theology*. New York: Cambridge University Press, 1996.

P *Kant, Prolegomena to Any Future Metaphysics*, in H. Allison (ed.), *Theoretical Philosophy after 1781*. New York: Cambridge, 2002.

TPP Kant, *Toward Perpetual Peace*, in M. Gregor (ed.) *Kant: Practical Philosophy*. New York: Cambridge, 1996.

WE Kant, *An Answer to the Question: What is Enlightenment?*, in M. Gregor (ed.) *Kant: Practical Philosophy*. New York: Cambridge, 1996.

Introduction

Gabriel Gottlieb

I

During the 1790s, the literary world in Germany witnessed a veritable explosion of interest in the question of natural right and its foundations. In addition to the publication of Johann Gottlieb Fichte's *Foundations of Natural Right*, the first part of which appeared in 1796 and the second part in 1797, Schelling published his essay "New Deduction of Natural Right" in 1796, and in 1797 the *Doctrine of Right*, the first part of Kant's *The Metaphysics of Morals*, appeared. Prior to these important works, a number of works on natural right were published in the first half of the decade, including Gottlieb Hufeland's *Lehrsätze des Naturrechts* (1790), Theodor Schmalz's *Das Reine Naturrecht* (1792), Johann Benjamin Erhard's *Über das Recht des Volks zu einer Revolution* (1795) and "Apologie des Teufels" (1795), Maimon's "Ueber die ersten Gründe des Naturrecht" (1795), and Carl Christian Erhard Schmid's *Grundriss des Naturrechts* (1795). As Paul Johann Anselm Feuerbach would confirm in his *Kritik des natürlichen Rechte* (1796), "No science has found in our age so universal an interest or been met with so much zeal as the science of the right of man (*Rechte des Menschen*)."[1]

This flurry of activity was not accidental. The French and American Revolutions provoked a number of philosophers to seek out a philosophical grounding of right, and with the rise and growing influence of Kant's newly developed moral philosophy, many believed they could secure such a foundation by grounding right in the moral law. Fichte's own *Contribution to the Rectification of the Public's Judgment of the French Revolution* (1793) and his essay "Reclamation of the Freedom of Thought from the Princes of Europe" (1793) reflect such a pursuit. In the latter, Fichte provides a "short deduction of rights" that derives right from

[1] Feuerbach 1796: 3.

"conscience" (*Gewissen*), which commands "absolutely and unconditionally," as well as "*freely* and *autonomously*" (*R*, 124). One has a right, Fichte argues, to whatever the moral law of conscience commands as one's duty or does not prohibit.[2] In addition to Fichte, the Kantian jurists Hufeland and Schmalz ground natural right in similar Kantian moral considerations. Schmalz, for instance, who alludes to the French Revolution as the "great occurrences of our day" in his "Preface," grounds the principle of natural right in a version of Kant's categorical imperative.[3] He claims in §31 that "the supreme principle of natural right as the embodiment of external perfect right and duty is therefore: *Treat the humanity in others never as a mere means.*"[4]

Although Fichte's initial reflections on right largely presuppose Kantian moral philosophy, by late 1795 Fichte had developed a healthy dose of skepticism about basing right squarely on moral principles.[5] Spurred on by "excellent hints" found in Erhard's "Apologie des Teufels" and Maimon's essay on natural right, Fichte, as a self-identifying Kantian, developed a non-moral foundation of right, even when it remained unclear to him, given Kant's relative silence on the foundations of natural right at the time, whether or not "Kant derives the law of right from the moral law," as was "the usual way of doing things" for the Kantian jurists (*FNR*, 13; *SW*, III: 13).[6]

The summer of 1795 proved to be important in Fichte's move away from a morally based theory of right. In his August 29, 1795 letter to Reinhold, Fichte writes:

> I have been investigating natural rights this summer and have found that no deduction of the *reality* of the concept of right exists anywhere. All explanations of it are merely formal, semantic explanations, which already presuppose both the existence within us of such a concept (as a fact) as well as the meaning of this concept. Such explanations do not even adequately deduce this concept from the fact of the moral law (which fact I am equally unwilling to accept, unless it too is deduced). In this connection, I reread Kant's *Groundwork for the Metaphysics of Morals*, and found that *here* if anywhere the inadequacy of Kant's principles can be concretely demonstrated. (*EPW*, 407; *GA*, III, 2: 385)

If we take Fichte at his word, even his own previous analyses of right in the *Contribution* and "Reclamation," as well as the works of the Kantian

[2] James Clarke's contribution to the present volume considers this essay and argument.
[3] Schmalz 1792: 3.
[4] Schmalz 1792: 32.
[5] For his reasons why see Neuhouser's and Clarke's essays in this volume. See also, Nomer 2013.
[6] See Schottky 1995 for a discussion of Erhard's and Maimon's influence on Fichte's *Natural Right*. See also, Ferry 1987.

jurists, are "merely formal" and presuppose the "reality" and legitimacy of the concept of right.[7] Furthermore, by questioning the adequacy of Kant's deduction of the moral law, Fichte doubts the very legitimacy of the Kantian jurists' attempts to secure the foundations of right upon the categorical imperative. A transcendental deduction of the concept of right, then, is required, since such an argument would be capable of establishing its legitimacy, or, in other words, our social and political entitlement to this concept.[8] Fichte carries out such a deduction in *Natural Right* by arguing that the concept of right is a necessary condition of individual self-consciousness. Thereby, we are justified in asserting the reality of the concept independently of moral considerations.

Since his deduction does not proceed from Kantian principles of morality, Fichte must provide some other principles to ground the concept of right. The subtitle of his book and the deduction's "First Theorem" acknowledge that the deduction proceeds in accordance with the principles he established in the *Wissenschaftslehre*, an account of which he published as the *Foundations of the Entire Wissenschaftslehre* in 1794 and 1795.[9] At the center of his *Wissenschaftslehre* is the activity of the self-positing I, which, as Fichte characterizes it, posits itself as self-positing or as "an activity that reverts into itself" (*FNR*, 18; *SW*, III: 17). Although Fichte's deduction is not a moral deduction of right, it is nonetheless a practical deduction of right in that it proceeds from a premise about practical reason, since Fichte understands the I as requiring the practical activity of forming and willing the concept of an action's end. He, in fact, refers to the I as a "practical I," one he identifies with "the I of original self-consciousness" (*FNR*, 21; *SW*, III: 20).[10]

In the midst of this flurry of publications on right during the 1790s, Fichte's *Foundations of Natural Right* stands out, both in its influence, and, most certainly, in its philosophical originality. His book is responsible for initiating an intersubjective tradition in philosophy and social theory, particularly due to the profound influence Fichte's *Natural Right* exercised on Hegel's philosophy and especially his *Phenomenology of Spirit* and

7 At this point Fichte would not have read Kant's *Perpetual Peace*, which did not appear until Fall 1795. Fichte eventually published in January of 1796 an important review of Kant's essay (see *RPP*) and even intended to deliver a set of public lectures on Kant's work. See, Breazeale's "Appendix: Fichte's Lectures and Writings, 1792–1799" in *EPW*, 48, n. 106.

8 See Allen Wood's contribution in this volume for an account of his deductive method in *Natural Right*.

9 For helpful overviews of Fichte's *Wissenschaftslehre*, see Breazeale 2013b, Neuhouser 1990, and Wood 1991.

10 See Neuhouser 2001.

Philosophy of Right. In the process of deducing the concept of right from the subject's self-consciousness of itself as an efficacious being, Fichte deduces the sensible world, the summons, other rational beings, and mutual recognition. His theory of the summons as initiating the self-activity of individual self-consciousness and characterizing the interactions required for upbringing, as well as his account of the social contract, stand out as remarkable philosophical innovations. Additionally, in *Natural Right*, he offers a novel analysis of property that *transcendentally* deduces the right to property. Finally, Fichte's *Natural Right* offers an important meditation on the nature of social and political freedom, in contrast to the conception of moral freedom familiar from Kant's moral philosophy.

Fichte's influence on Hegel is of particular interest given both the extent of Fichte's influence and the important role Hegel's work has played in shaping the reception of Fichte's *Natural Right*. It is commonplace to consider Fichte's *Natural Right* as a significant work insofar as it sheds light on the transition from Kant to Hegel. As readings of Hegel's *Phenomenology of Spirit* emphasized the role of recognition in the achievement of self-consciousness, readings of Fichte's *Natural Right* have tended to focus on primarily his account of recognition.[11] There is good reason to closely examine Fichte's views on mutual recognition as they are central to his deduction of the concept of right from self-consciousness. However, from the standpoint of Hegel's philosophy, Fichte's theory of recognition appears to some as normatively limp and problematically "abstract." On this line of thought, Fichte's theory of recognition deserves Hegel's overcoming or *Aufhebung* of it in the *Phenomenology of Spirit* and the *Philosophy of Right*. Accounts of *Natural Right* that examine Fichte's philosophy, or more particularly his theory of recognition, with the purpose of understanding the genesis or nature of some aspect of Hegel's philosophy are essentially transitional readings focused on the *von Kant bis Hegel* story.

While transitional readings of Fichte's work are important for Hegel scholarship, they may nonetheless do a disservice to Hegel scholarship, while at the same time doing a disservice to Fichte scholarship in general. Transitional readings tend to find Hegel's own interpretation of Fichte to be largely sound, and they tend to use Hegel's interpretation as a reliable guide to Fichte's text and arguments.[12] The difficulty with the transitional

[11] Siep 1979a, Williams 1992, and Redding 1996 illustrate such readings.
[12] See for instance, Williams 2002. See Nance's critical analysis of Williams 2002 in the present volume.

reading is that it assumes we already understand correctly Fichte's philosophical motivations and aims, as well as the philosophical implications and tensions found in his views. By approaching Fichte as a transitional figure, certain features of his philosophy inevitably become salient precisely because these features help one understand the development of Hegel's own philosophy. When this occurs other features of Fichte's thought that are less relevant to the transition are more easily ignored, thereby distorting and limiting our understanding of Fichte's philosophy. Finally, since Hegel himself certainly did not initially read Fichte as a transitional figure, approaching Fichte's work with such an end in view potentially blinds us to aspects of his philosophy that might, regardless of Hegel's own explicit analysis of Fichte, shed light on the genesis of Hegel's views.

A notable feature of the present volume is that the essays attempt to discover what is philosophically promising and relevant in Fichte's work independent of the historical question about how one should understand the transition from Kant's philosophy to Hegel's. Certainly, the essays in the present volume will shed light on transitional questions, as they offer close and thoughtful examinations of a text Hegel himself considered carefully and returned to continually throughout his life. While some of the essays briefly examine aspects of Hegel's work, they all largely develop interpretations of Fichte's *Foundations of Natural Right* – examining it on its own right and independently of the transition question – by focusing on the most important themes and issues in *Natural Right*.

II

As part of Cambridge's series of *Critical Guides*, the purpose of the *Critical Guide to Fichte's Foundations of Natural Right* is not to offer a commentary on the entirety of the text or to serve as an introduction for first time readers, though, certainly, such readers will benefit from a careful reading of the *Guide*. Instead, the essays aim at developing new lines of interpretation, analyzing carefully Fichte's arguments and central concepts, and thoughtfully engaging the developing scholarship on *Natural Right*. There are, therefore, aspects of *Natural Right* that do not receive much attention in this volume (i.e. his remarks on the ephorate, cosmopolitian right or punishment).[13] The upshot of the volume's approach, however, is the

[13] For a discussion of these topics see Maus 2001, De Pascale 2001, and Merle 2009.

robust treatment of key concepts, themes, and issues in Fichte's work, a number of which are examined in multiple essays with each offering distinctive interpretations.

In the first essay, Angelica Nuzzo examines the relationship between Fichte's *Foundations of Natural Right* and Kant's idea of right and law as developed in the *Doctrine of Right* and his *Perpetual Peace.* Her concern is ultimately systematic: how, for the two philosophers, should we understand the place of right in their differing conceptions of the practical sphere? She argues that the different place each gives to right within the practical sphere results from their discrete methodological starting points. While Kant begins from a "metaphysical" starting point, one that is rational and a priori, and which does not take for granted a conception of human nature or a transcendental anthropology, Fichte begins his analysis of right from within the standpoint of a transcendental anthropology of individual self-consciousness. Nuzzo recognizes, as well, that Kant and Fichte develop varying views on the relationship between right and its derivability from the moral law.

The relationship between right and morality is the primary focus in the following two essays by Frederick Neuhouser and James Clarke. Both essays examine Fichte's separation of right and morality and compare his considered view in *Natural Right* with the view developed in the *Contribution*; however, the two essays take remarkably different approaches to the issue. Neuhouser argues that implicit in Fichte's view of the separation of right and morality in *Natural Right* is an appreciation of an end, the fostering of individual personhood, unique to the political realm and not reducible to or derivable from the value of moral autonomy. What drove Fichte to this separation, in Neuhouser's reading, is his eventual recognition that rights such as property rights cannot be fully justified rationally from within the moral sphere alone. In contrast, James Clarke employs deontic logic and a "Hohfeldian" analysis of rights to establish the significance of Fichte's claim that right and morality are independent, what Clarke calls the "independence thesis." Clarke first provides a deontic analysis of Fichte's views on right and morality in the *Contribution* and "Reclamation." By extending his deontic analysis of right to *Natural Right*, Clarke shows how Fichte's argument for the independence thesis exploits the nature of permissions. Finally, Clarke considers the position Fichte's *Natural Right* occupies with respect to natural law theory and legal positivism.

The contributions by Allen Wood, Paul Franks, and myself take as their focus Fichte's conception of the summons. Wood's contribution considers Fichte's deduction of the summons and other rational beings. While Kant provides a metaphysical and transcendental deduction of the conditions required for cognition and experience, he does not deduce the existence of others or our ability to cognize their mental states. Yet, such a deduction is required if the conditions for objective validity and reason require intersubjective communication as Kant suggests. On Wood's view, Fichte's deduction of the summons and others extends, in a sense, Kant's own transcendental argument by deducing an essential condition Kant seems to ignore or one he, at least, takes for granted. After a helpful analysis of Fichte's synthetic method, Wood reconstructs Fichte's deduction of others and explains Fichte's reason for positing the summons, a unique kind of constraint that limits one's action while allowing for freedom at the same time. Wood concludes by addressing the role of the summons in both upbringing and grounding Fichte's anti-Cartesian conception of individuality.

Paul Franks takes a markedly different approach to the summons, although, like Wood, he is interested in understanding how the nature of the summons functions as a limiting, constraining, or finitizing activity. In his contribution, Franks argues that Fichte's summons requires a form of realism that accounts for the possibility of the second-personal address the summons is meant to specify. The realism of the summons, what Franks terms Kabbalistic Realism, embodies the logic of *ẓimẓum*, a concept central to Jewish kabbalah. Franks understands Fichte to be responding to the threat of nihilism – the problem of "accommodating individuality" – in *Natural Right* by establishing how his view of the absolute I can, in fact, accommodate individuality. Franks's argument involves showing that Fichte accommodates individuality with his account of the summons. Of particular interest is Franks's claim that Fichte's appeal to the summons and his reason for introducing it employ a pattern of reasoning akin to the logic of the kabbalistic concept of *ẓimẓum*. While the kabbalist tradition is likely unfamiliar to many contemporary readers of Fichte, Franks identifies its influence on Jacobi and Fichte's reception of the very concerns motivating Jacobi. At issue in the kabbalist tradition and the German tradition within which Jacobi and Fichte both reside is accounting for the infinite without annihilating the finite. Fichte, on Franks view, develops the concept of the summons in a way that exhibits aspects of *ẓimẓum*, and thereby accounts for how the infinite and finite coincide.

In my own contribution, I argue that Fichte's concept of the summons as "upbringing" involves a distinctive form of recognition, elementary recognition, which must be distinguished from political recognition. Political recognition is the recognition of an individual's standing as a right-bearing agent, and thereby takes as its end or purpose the respect of individual rights. In contrast, elementary recognition does not take as its end respect for the rights of individuals, but instead is oriented toward the development of the child's capacity to act in a reasons-responsive manner. In my analysis of these two forms of recognition, I examine Fichte's concept of individuality. My claim is that there are two conceptions of the individual in *Natural Right*: the individual human being and the political individual. The individual human being is reasons responsive and elementary recognition is aimed at developing such individual human beings. The political individual is constituted by virtue of relations of political recognition and requires that an individual human being wills itself into relations of reciprocal recognition and community with others. In the final section of the paper, I examine Fichte's naturalistic grounding of the summons in the child–parent relationship.

Readers of Fichte's *Natural Right* can be easily flummoxed by his difficult reflections on the body and by the very idea that the body is in need of a deduction. John Russon's essay takes Fichte's remarks about the body as its theme. Russon claims that, for Fichte, the body is the site at which our intersubjectivity and free agency is enacted. The body, on this view, is not a possession used to indicate there is some free agent residing within it and so it is not an alien piece of matter. Rather, as Russon, argues, the body is an actualization of a form of living. The summons, which is expressed bodily by a linguistic or bodily gesture, constitutes the medium of freedom, since it is by virtue of summoning one another and responding to the summons that one is a rational being. Being a free individual I is, then, an intersubjective accomplishment that is performatively realized.

Wayne Martin's contribution examines Fichte's theory of property and shows how it overcomes the flaws associated with Locke's views on property. Similar to Fichte's suggestion that previous philosophers had taken for granted the reality of the concept of right, Martin sees that Locke's theory of property begs the question with respect to the justification of the institution of property. In response, Fichte offers a transcendental deduction of property, one that avoids the theological framework of Locke's theory of property. In his analysis of Fichte's argument, Martin pays close attention to both the concept of *wirken* ("to act efficaciously"), which he translates as simply "work," and Fichte's view of self-positing, which Martin accounts for as a kind of gambit or move in a game that one could potentially lose. Work is a necessary condition of self-positing and self-consciousness. Martin's suggestion is that the self-posting of the I involves work and work requires that one has property in which one exercises his or her work. In that case, property is a necessary condition of self-consciousness; hence, property can be transcendentally deduced independently of certain Lockean assumptions.

The contributions by David James and Michael Nance take up the concept of freedom in Fichte's *Natural Right*. James examines what appears to be an inconsistency or tension between 1) Fichte's commitment to a methodological assumption of universal egoism that involves indirectly respecting the freedom of others since doing so is a condition of one's own freedom, and 2) the view, following from his remarks about the summons, that one ought to have a direct concern for the freedom of others. James argues that the tension is merely apparent since, *pace* moralized readings of *Natural Right*, Fichte is not committed to the view that one has an obligation to be directly concerned with the freedom of others. James sees that abiding by this distinction allows for a more consistent reading of *Natural Right*. Throughout his analysis, James helpfully compares Fichte's views with those of Hobbes.

Another charge of inconsistency in *Natural Right* made, in this case, by Hegel and some contemporary Hegelians such as Robert Williams, receives careful scrutiny in Michael Nance's essay. This charge of inconsistency Nance calls the Hegelian objection: on the one hand, Fichte claims that free agents stand in free relations of reciprocal recognition and such reciprocal relations are a necessary condition of self-consciousness, yet, on the other hand, Fichte argues that the state requires legally state-sanctioned coercion which guarantees that individuals respect each other's freedom. How can relations of mutual recognition be free and "forced" by virtue of coercive threats? Nance works to dissolve the inconsistency by arguing that free reciprocal recognition operates in the Fichtean state because individuals freely enter the civil contract, the grounds of the state's authority. At the same time, however, the state does rely on coercion. Fichte can have it both ways, Nance suggests, if we understand rightful relations within the state not in terms of a non-interference theory of freedom, but in terms of a non-domination, or republican model of freedom.

Dean Moyar examines a related tension in Fichte's theory of freedom: the tension between a non-voluntary and interdependent conception of freedom as mutual recognition and the freedom involved in voluntarily willing entry into the social contract. The tension's resolution, Moyar argues, is found in Fichte's unification contract, an organic conception of the social contract that relies on a holistic conception of contractualism rather than an atomistic contractualism. On Moyar's view, Fichte's contractualism shows how an atomistic contractualism, the familiar liberal model of the social contract, is overcome in the unification contract, a holistic contractualism in which the individual becomes one with the whole by appreciating that one's own interests are entangled or identical with the interests of the community.

The concept of human rights in Fichte's work is examined in Jean-Christophe Merle's essay. Merle traces Fichte's analysis of human rights in the *Contribution* and his development of natural right in the *Foundations of Natural Right,* and he concludes that Fichte's conception is more original and elaborate than Kant's own theory. Merle also considers the human rights that follow from Fichte's theory of right. One important right Fichte defends is the right to live based on one's own labor. Additionally, Merle suggests that Fichte's model of rights grounds subsistence rights. Merle concludes by comparing Fichte's approach to human rights with contemporary models, both of which Merle takes to assert that human rights are ultimately grounded in some unique foundation. Merle expresses skepticism about providing such a unique foundation that could ground all the relevant human rights.

III

The immediate reception of Fichte's *Foundations Natural Right,* like with many philosophical works, was somewhat mixed. Although it was the work of Erhard, in part, that influenced Fichte's deduction of right, Erhard declared in a 1797 letter to Kant that while Fichte's *Foundations of Natural Right* "has much merit in half of it," the "beginning is total raving (*Radotage*)." Erhard continues, "it really is a pity that Fichte loses himself in nonsense so much, just to make himself look deeply profound."[14] The precise part of the book Erhard has in mind is not clear from his letter, although it is reasonable to conclude, since *Natural Right* was published in two parts, he has in mind the entire first part, including Fichte's claims that right and morality are independent, the concept of right is deducible from self-consciousness, mutual recognition is a necessary condition of self-consciousness, and the nature of human embodiment can be rationally derived from the conditions of reciprocal relations of recognition. Erhard may have been shortsighted as it is the first part of *Natural Right*

[14] Quoted from *C*, 545, n. 3.

that many have come to find "deeply profound," including the contributors to the present volume.

In contrast to Erhard, other philosophers concluded that Fichte's *Foundations of Natural Right* was indeed a significant work. Wilhelm von Humboldt concluded in an 1800 letter to Goethe that Fichte's "*Natural Right* is actually a great work," and Karl Leonhard Reinhold considered Fichte's *Natural Right* the monument or crowning achievement of his philosophy.[15] Fichte himself considered this work "undoubtedly better" than his *Foundations of the Entire Wissenschaftslehre*, which should not perhaps come as a surprise since the latter work was intended as a supplemental text to his lectures at the University of Jena, and not, as is the case with *Natural Right*, a self-standing book (*EPW*, 419; *GA*, III, 3, no. 359). Throughout the nineteenth century figures such Hegel and Marx found inspiration – as well as much to disagree with – in *Natural Right*, while in the twentieth century Ernst Bloch and Axel Honneth, for instance, carefully examined Fichte's social and political philosophy.[16] If the wide attention received by Stephen Darwall's appropriation of Fichte's conception of the summons and the growth of the English language scholarship since the new Cambridge translation of *Natural Right* in 2000 are any indication, the twenty-first century will likely prove to be the period in which Fichte's *Natural Right* exerts its greatest influence.[17]

The reception of Fichte's *Foundations of Natural Right* is, certainly, still ongoing. The growing revival of interest in Fichte's philosophy, and particularly, his social and practical philosophy, suggests we have much to gain from carefully studying his work. In this regard, the essays collected here aim to deepen and expand the reception of the *Foundations of Natural Right*.

[15] See Lauth and Jacob's "Vortwort" in *GA*, I, 3: 310.

[16] Bloch 1987, Honneth 1996, and Honneth 2001.

[17] Darwall 2005 and 2006. For two critical analyses of Darwall's analysis of Fichte see Ware 2010 and Breazeale 2008.

CHAPTER I

Fichte's Foundations of Natural Right *and its Relation to Kant*

Angelica Nuzzo

In this essay I address the *systematic* question of the different place and role that a theory of right – a "doctrine" of right as part of a Metaphysics of Morals and a transcendental "foundation" of natural right as part of the Doctrine of Science respectively – have within the practical philosophy of Kant and Fichte. This question frames my discussion of the relationship between Fichte's *Foundations of Natural Right* and Kant's *Doctrine of Right*. Ultimately, at stake is the very idea of the "practical" – of practical philosophy and of the practical use and activity of reason. The practical is conceived, traditionally, as the part of philosophy distinct from the theoretical; but it is also declared to retain, in Fichte's famous formulation, a "primacy" over all other functions of reason. However, what counts specifically as "practical," that is, how this sphere is internally articulated in the relationship between morality strictly conceived, right, politics, and the realm of all "technical" activity, is an open and, indeed, a developing question for both Kant and Fichte.

Kant's *Metaphysics of Morals* is based on the critical and transcendental foundation of the early *Groundwork of the Metaphysics of Morals* and *Critique of Practical Reason*: the concept of right belongs to a "metaphysics" of morals, and systematically presupposes the transcendental investigation of the previous works. In Fichte's case, the doctrine of right (its "foundation") takes place within the systematic and "transcendental" framework of the *Foundations of the Entire Wissenschaftslehre*. The idea of the *Wissenschaftslehre* is itself in transition from the 1794–95 *Foundations* to the 1798–99 *Wissenschaftslehre nova methodo*. The theory of Fichte's "Doctrine of Right" with the emergence of the central idea of intersubjectivity as constitutive of self-consciousness plays a crucial role in shaping this transition.

My central issue is the place and function that right has within the practical sphere. I begin by discussing the systematic nature of Fichte's concept of right and some aspects of his idea of a "deduction" of the concept of right in the introduction to the *Natural Right*. I consider this argument in the particular perspective of what Fichte explicitly takes to be the novelty and originality of his theory, namely, the separation of morality and right. Then, on this basis, I offer a reconstruction of Kant's idea of right – of its concept, principle, and the universal law of right – as exposed in the introduction to the *Doctrine of Right*. Kant's account will be finally confronted with Fichte's exposition. My central claim is that the crucial difference separating Kant's and Fichte's concept of right lies in the fundamentally different starting points of their respective theories. Fichte's theory of right is framed in terms of a transcendental anthropology whose starting point is the individuality of self-consciousness in its free action. Accordingly, right is deduced as the transcendental condition of this determination of self-consciousness. For Kant, the starting point is the metaphysical (i.e., rational and a priori) concept of right that as such implies an "application" of practical concepts to "human nature" but is itself fundamentally independent of the nature of the subject of right.

Fichte's Doctrine of Right and the Idea of the "Practical"

For Kant, the sphere of the "practical" in the proper sense is the sphere of the strictly moral (hence non-pathologically determined) rational activity. Ultimately, it is the sphere of moral freedom legislated by its law, that is, the categorical imperative. For Fichte, the practical covers the realm determined not only by reason's activity but also by sensibility. This is the case because not only pure reason but also the broad range of sensible functions of the mind such as impulses, drives, feelings, desires, sensations are constitutive of human self-conscious individuality. In the *Groundwork*, Kant famously insists on the need to give to practical philosophy a "pure" a priori foundation. The highest principle of morality can be obtained only by an inquiry that is transcendental and as such independent of all psychological and anthropological considerations (*GW*, 4: 389). The "subject" of Kant's pure practical philosophy, that is, the subject of the obligation expressed by the moral law, is the rational being as such. Fichte's starting point already differs from Kant's to the extent that the subject or the I that practically acts is not the "absolute" I but is the I that is always related to an external world which determines it as an individual finite human subject. Accordingly, the practical part of the *Foundations of the Entire Wissenschaftslehre* covers a broad range of psychological functions that determine subjectivity in its individuality in relation to the not-I. Significantly, it is not concerned with morality, right, or teleology, but is a transcendental theory of the psychological functions of the human mind. The concepts of *Streben* and *Trieb*, central to the practical part of the *Foundations*, are responsible for the actualization of the real activity of the I. The different starting point of the practical, which – unlike the foundational step of Kant's pure moral philosophy, but also unlike the metaphysical starting point of the theoretical part of the *Foundations* – is from the outset subjectively and anthropologically oriented, posits, at the same time, the specific problems of Fichte's theory. First and foremost: how do the *transition* between the absolute I and the individual I, on the one hand, and the transition between theoretical activity and practical activity, on the other hand, take place? For Fichte the practical or "real" activity is, in general, responsible for the transition between absolute and individual I.

In "On the Concept of the *Wissenschaftslehre*" (1794), Fichte presents the practical as the foundation of all the other parts of philosophy. Natural right and ethics, along with a theory of the beautiful and the sublime and of nature's teleology, constitute the practical insofar as their principles are not only formal but material (*EPW*, 135; *GA*, I, 2: 151). Thus, at this time, the practical sphere covers, in addition to right and ethics, approximately all the topics that belonged to the *Critique of Judgment*. The questions that Fichte programmatically assigns to this part of the "system" have hardly any relation to what for Kant is the properly moral question, namely, establishing the highest principle of morality (*GW*, 4: 392f., 432, 463) or proving that reason is practical (*CPrR*, 5: 16, 55). What Fichte seems to be after, however, is – just as Kant, in the *Critique of Judgment*, is – the problem of building a "transition" between the theoretical and the properly moral sphere. In this respect, the sensible-practical fulfills, for Fichte, a mediating function. At stake in the practical part of the *Foundations* is the "deduction" of the laws of the *Streben* of the I, the determination and limitation of the I through the action of the non-I on the subject's sensibility. At issue is not primarily moral freedom but rather the opposite, namely, the different modalities of necessitation and necessary limitation that operate on the I so as to make it into an individual. On Fichte's view, only after the deduction of the "sensible-practical" functions of the I has taken place can one move on to a "moral-practical" philosophy consistent with the theoretical part of the *Wissenschaftslehre* (*GA*, II, 3: 247). Thus, the systematic relation that articulates the practical realm seems to be the opposite for Fichte and for Kant. For Kant, a theory of the sensible incentives to action (for a *human* will) can be presented only after the moral principle has been secured in its utter purity (i.e., for a rational being in general).

In sum, the anthropological and unified perspective on the acting subject implied in Fichte's view of the practical in the *Foundations* leads him to expand the realm of the practical *transcendentally* (and not merely empirically) beyond the Kantian principle of pure morality and moral autonomy. Fichte assigns to the practical broadly construed an intermediary or transitional function. Within this systematic constellation in 1795, Fichte begins to tackle the problem of a scientific "deduction" of the concept of right. By the time of the *Natural Right* the science of the practical to which the theory of right belongs as its real, concrete part is a "transcendental anthropology" that aims at "describing the middle ground between thinking and willing"; or even, is a "phenomenology of the I"[1] in which the pre-conscious actions are exhibited in their necessity as conditions on which "the possibility of self-consciousness" depends (*FNR*, 4; *SW*, III: 2). Finally, after the *Natural Right*, Fichte restates the intermediary transitional function played by the theory of right in the appendix to the last part of the *Wissenschaftslehre nova methodo* (Deduction of the Partition of the *Wissenschaftslehre*). Herein Fichte proposes, yet again, the problem of the transition between theoretical and practical. Now he offers a twofold solution, according to whether the human being is considered in the "real" or in the "ideal" perspective. In the case of the former, the "middle point" between theoretical and practical is the "doctrine of right, i.e., natural right"; in the latter, the "middle point" is aesthetics (*GA*, IV, 2: 264).

In a 1795 letter to Jacobi, Fichte claims: "My absolute I is clearly not the individual … The individual, however, must be deduced from the absolute I. With this aim in view, the *Wissenschaftslehre* will transition … to natural right" (*EPW*, 411; *GA*, III, 2: 392). The transition that the *Foundations of the Entire Wissenschaftslehre* accomplished by means of its practical part conceived as a theory of the sensible-practical functions of the I is now considered the task of the doctrine of natural right. It is clear that a significant systematic difference separates Fichte's idea of right in 1795 from the "moralistic" (or morally grounded) concept of right he had offered in the 1793 *Contribution to the Rectification of the Public's Judgment of the French Revolution*. For, by the time of the exposition of the practical part of the *Foundations*, Fichte had already distanced himself from the Kantian conception of the practical as strictly moral from which, in 1793, he had derived his idea of right.

[1] See Cesa 1992: 115.

The "Deduction" of the Concept of Right and the Individuality of Self-Consciousness

In the *Natural Right* Fichte views the theory of natural right – just as the immediately following theory of ethics in the *System of Ethics* – as a "science" based on universal and necessary principles from which a deduction is developed that moves from the universal to the particular. The theory of right, however, is itself a "particular" science within the system of philosophical cognition. It is a "real philosophical science" (*FNR*, 8; *SW*, III: 7) in opposition to the "formal" knowledge and the merely formal and formalistic way of doing philosophy that, on Fichte's view, has dominated after Kant. The theory of right is a "real" philosophical science to the extent that its inquiry is properly "transcendental," that is, gives a genetic account of the possibility and reality of self-consciousness employing a procedure in which concept and object are always simultaneously present. To claim that a certain "determinate concept" such as the concept of right is a rational concept, i.e., is contained in or given by reason originally and essentially, means that the rational being as such "acts necessarily in a certain determinate way." The demonstrative task of the theory of right is to "show that this determinate action is a condition of self-consciousness" (*FNR*, 9; *SW*, III: 8). This is the aim of the "deduction." The proof of the "necessity of the concept" lies in its functioning as condition of self-consciousness. In the deduction, the "determinate action" (of self-consciousness) that the concept itself is, is described "with respect to its form" as well as with regard to "what emerges for reflection in this acting" (*FNR*, 9; *SW*, III: 8). The deduction simultaneously fulfills three objectives, which must be taken as a unity, Fichte warns, in order to provide the science of right with the "reality" which distinguishes it from a merely "formal philosophy" (in which one or the other of these moments are considered in isolation). The deduction proves, first, the *necessity* of the concept/action; *determines*, second, the concept/action; and finally "shows its *application*" (*FNR*, 9; *SW*, III: 8). In this formulation we already meet the starting point and the crucial perspective characterizing Fichte's theory of right – the *transcendental* perspective that distinguishes it from the *metaphysical* account offered by Kant's *Doctrine of Right* but also from a "transcendental deduction" taken in Kant's sense. The concept of right as condition of the possibility and actuality of self-consciousness in its "determinate action" is functional precisely to the *specific nature* of self-consciousness – or of the action of self-consciousness – of which it is, transcendentally, a necessary condition. For this is, Fichte explains, the necessary action not just of a rational being as such, but of a rational self-conscious being that posits itself "as an individual, as one among several rational beings that it assumes to exist outside itself, just as it takes itself to exist" (*FNR*, 9; *SW*, III: 8). This twofold specification, which posits, in one action, self-consciousness (i) in its *individuality* and (ii) as a necessary *plurality* set in a net of reciprocal relations (which will be brought back to the "relation of right"), is the crux of the matter in Fichte's deduction. At the basis of this twofold specification is the systematic task underscored above, namely, first, the task of making the transition from the absolute I to the "individual" I – which now can be expressed as the transition from the "absolute spontaneity" of the acting subject (*FNR*, 9; *SW*, III: 8) to the limitation of its freedom – and second, the issue of showing that the individual can become a self-conscious *individual* or a "person" (*FNR*, 9; *SW*, III: 9) only in a world of similar, interconnected acting individuals. This introduces the concept of intersubjectivity that appears for the first time and so prominently in Fichte's deduction of the concept of right (§4).

Fichte's argument leading to "right" conceived as "the concept of the necessary relation of free beings to one another" can be summed up as follows. By positing myself as a rational and free being I posit myself as an *individual* (hence as a being limited in its freedom); but I can do so only by positing, at the exact same time – or "in the same undivided action" – a plurality of other free rational beings like myself (*FNR*, 9; *SW*, III: 8). The concept of right is functional to – or, transcendentally, is the necessary condition of – a determinate activity of self-consciousness, that is, its self-positing action as an individual necessarily connected with and responding to an intersubjective plurality of other individuals (more precisely: to the extent that these individuals impinge on each other's external sphere of free action) (*FNR*, 9–10, 11, 43; *SW*, III: 9, 11, 46). And this means that right is possible only within the sphere of such activity. Similarly, in the review of Kant's *Perpetual Peace*, Fichte writes, presenting his own position: "One can talk of right only to the extent that human beings are considered in relationship to one another, and a right is nothing outside of a relationship of this sort" (*RPP*, 315; *SW*, VIII: 430). Thus, while the concept of right is the transcendental condition of individual self-consciousness, the free activity of the latter within an objective and intersubjective world constitutes the *ratio essendi* of right. For Kant, by contrast, at stake in the *Doctrine of Right* is directly the question of the possibility of right (or more precisely of "*merely rightful* (intelligible) *possession*") or rather of "a synthetic a priori proposition of right" (*MM*, 6: 249). At stake is not, in the first instance, the possibility of a certain determination of the acting personality. As we will see in the last section, right is possible for Kant only as a certain normative relation of the external freedom of one in relation to the external freedom of another. Thus, the starting point of Fichte's deduction is a determinate action and constitution of self-consciousness (namely, rational and free personality) from which the necessity, applicability, and application of right obtains; Kant's starting point is the concept of right itself – as a metaphysical concept that already entails an "application" (to human nature) – which leads to the idea of a certain normative relation of external freedom among human beings (or in relation to a "will in general" which is, explicitly, and differing significantly in this from Fichte, *not* "*your* own will" (*MM*, 6: 389)).

The task of moving from the absolute I to the individual I is also formulated as the task of showing how we transition from "absolute spontaneity," which is the formal freedom that rational beings analytically ascribe to themselves and to one another as a capacity to freely choose their ends (whatever these ends may be), to the conscious self-ascription of freedom that characterizes the rational *individual* or "person" as individualized locus of agency and causal efficacy in the world (*FNR*, 8–10, 39–41; *SW*, III: 8–9, 41–3). Fichte describes the "deduction" that, in this latter case, leads to the concept of right in terms that come close to the way in which Kant presents the task of the transcendental deduction of the categories in the first *Critique*; hence, in terms that come close to the genuinely theoretical context of the possibility of synthetic a priori judgments. For, Fichte argues that "the object in experience that is thought of through the concept of the person's efficacy [should] actually correspond to that concept; what is required, therefore, is that something in the world outside the rational individual follow from the thought of his activity" (*FNR*, 9; *SW*, III: 9).[2] The deduction is here a proof of correspondence between a claim of causal self-activity and an object given in experience and posited in the external world. Individual action is free only if it actually "corresponds" to a free state of affairs in the world. And this is ultimately a proof of the truth of the "thought" of one's self-ascribed freedom. More strongly, Fichte posits a "demand" (*Anforderung*) set on the rational being "to realize its free efficacy" (*FNR*, 33; *SW*, III: 34). Interestingly, this is precisely the kind of proof that Kant claimed is *not* required when at stake is reason's practical, that is, properly moral activity. For, in this case, the moral law as "fact of reason" (*Faktum der Vernunft*) *is* itself, directly

[2] See De Pascale 1995: 261f.

and immediately, that proof, namely, the proof *that* reason is indeed practical. That for Fichte the concept of right is independent, systematically, from the moral law is already reflected in this fundamentally different demonstrative strategy. Fichte's deduction of the concept of right, connected as it is with the proof of the reality of one's individual freedom, which is *not moral freedom*, comes closer to Kant's *theoretical* deduction of the understanding's concepts (indeed, in this case, just as for Fichte's concept of right, the proof of the categories' *quid iuris* is the proof of their necessity and applicability to objects or cases in experience).

On Fichte's view, at stake in the concept of right taken as the *limitation* of *individual* freedom is the concept not only of free acting individuality ("person") but also, at the same time, of a "world" that is always and necessarily thought along with and implied by self-consciousness' free individual activity. In order to act freely and be conscious of its freedom, the individual, through its free action, is set in necessary relation to a world. The world is, at the same time, the place in which the "effects" of individual free action or the "efficacy" of individual causality belong – it is the external "sphere" of one's freedom (*FNR*, 10; *SW*, III: 9). But the world is also a place that is itself constituted by the mutual intersection and interaction of many individual freedoms, and that limits each self-ascribed freedom conferring to it a determinate *individuality*. From this Fichte derives a first conclusion that bears some similarity to Kant's "universal law of right": all individuals "would have to have made it a law for themselves not to disturb the freedom of those with whom they stand in mutual interaction" (*FNR*, 10; *SW*, III: 9). The role played by the notion of intersubjectivity in the deduction is directly connected to this "world" and to the action of self-limitation through which individual freedom first arises. The world now appears as a "*community among free beings*" (*FNR*, 10; *SW*, III: 9). This community stands under two conditions characterized by a different modality. There is a strictly necessary condition, which is the very assumption of the existence of other rational free beings as ourselves. But there is also an arbitrariness attached to the very "thought of such a community and its realization," since it is not absolutely necessary that other rational beings actually "continue to exist" (or are permanently guaranteed to exist) together "*as free beings*" (*FNR*, 10; *SW*, III: 9). While the existence of other persons is a necessary condition of self-consciousness, the fact that they form a community of free beings is not. This confers to the normativity of the principle of right a hypothetical or conditional validity. *If* such a community is thought (at all), then it must be thought according to the principle of right. The latter is, accordingly and following here Kant's distinction among imperatives, "a merely technical-practical" concept (*FNR*, 10; *SW*, III: 10). It is first formulated in the "rule of right": "Limit your freedom through the concept of the freedom of all other persons with whom you come in contact" (*FNR*, 10; *SW*, III: 10).

This argument seems to be at odds with what Fichte declared at the outset to be the crucial idea of his deduction: if the concept of right is, transcendentally, a necessary condition of self-consciousness in its individuality, how then can it be said to stand under the "arbitrariness" of a merely hypothetical condition?[3] This turn can be understood if we realize that at this point – namely, after having presented as the chief objective of the deduction to establish the *transcendental and theoretical* necessity of the concept of right – Fichte's aim is to qualify the nature of this concept's *practical* validity. Indeed, this turn is accompanied by a corresponding shift in the meaning of self-consciousness' *individuality*, whereby a merely *theoretical* significance (individuality as the point of causal efficacy in the world) is now complemented with an additional properly *practical* validity (to be limited free agency in relation to others, to be realization of formal freedom). Key herein is the specification that presents the concept of right as "a merely technical-practical" concept. To stand in a relation of right (self-limiting and mutually limiting freedom) with other rational beings like myself is a necessary condition of my self-conscious and free individuality. However, there is no absolute, that is, unconditioned practical necessity – which here means no properly *moral* necessity in the Kantian sense – for me to be part of such a community. That is, there is no moral (i.e., categorical) imperative that tells me that I ought to be in a relation of right to other beings like myself (or that I ought to make my end to realize such a community) (*FNR*, 11; *SW*, III: 10). In fact, the normativity of the concept of right is the normativity of "a merely technical-practical" concept. In deducing the concept of right as a necessary condition of self-consciousness' free individuality, Fichte claims for it the theoretical necessity and universality that Kant had guaranteed to the understanding's categories through his transcendental deduction. However, when the specifically "practical" character of the concept of right is at issue ("this concept, if thought *as a practical concept*") (*FNR*, 10; *SW*, III: 10), Fichte uses first the Kantian language of hypothetical or technical-practical imperatives (the idea of imperatives

[3] In the space that separates that necessity from this arbitrariness Fichte locates the function of the state.

of skill from the *Groundwork*)[4] and then appeals to a strong argument separating right from the strictly moral sphere. As we will see below, while Kant agrees with Fichte on denying that right itself can impose a *moral* demand on the subject, he also denies that its validity is merely technical-practical.

Fichte declares the separation between morality and right to be the specific and most novel feature of his *Natural Right* as well as the necessary mark of the truth of its positions. The point had already been made in the review of *Perpetual Peace* (*RPP*, 314–15; *SW*, VIII: 429), and famously represents the most important point of departure of the *Natural Right* from Fichte's own earlier *Contribution*. The claim is often repeated, and alternatively phrased as a radical *separation* (and hence *independence*) of the sphere of right from the sphere of ethics or strict Kantian morality (*FNR*, 10–11; *SW*, III: 10); or as the denial that (the concept of) natural right can be "derived" from the moral law or categorical imperative (*FNR*, 10–11; *SW*, III: 10); or that the latter can ever be the "source" of the former (*RPP*, 315; *SW*, VIII: 429). Fichte notices that the evidence provided by his deduction of the concept of right replaces a refutation of the claim that right can be derived from the moral law. Moreover, while he does not explicitly name his targets with regard to the opposed, allegedly customary theory, it is evident that at stake herein is his own position in the *Contribution* as well as the position of many Kantians. The more interesting question is whether Fichte thought that Kant had embraced more or less explicitly this thesis. It is clear that in the *Natural Right*, as in his review of *Perpetual Peace*, Fichte is unwilling to express a dissent from Kant, and this, along with the fact that the latter essay is Kant's only publication on the topic to date,[5] may explain why he leaves the question open. It is, however, significant that he *does* raise the question. Fichte contends that on the basis of the 1795 essay, "it is not possible to see clearly whether Kant derives the law of right from the moral law (in accordance with the usual way of doing things) or whether he adopts another deduction of the law of right." He adds that Kant's remarks concerning the "concept of a permissive law" "makes it at least probable that his deduction agrees with the deduction given here" (*FNR*, 13; *SW*, III: 13).[6] How, then, do things stand in Kant's *Doctrine of Right*?

4 See *GW*, 4: 416–17.

5 However, Fichte seems to think that this essay contains "if not the complete grounds, then at least the complete results of the Kantian philosophy of right" (*RPP*, 313; *SW*, VIII: 427–8).

6 The argument would run as follows: given that a right follows from a merely permissive law, and given that a permissive law, being conditioned and limited, cannot be derived from the unconditional and unrestricted command of the moral law, right cannot be derived from the moral law.

I now turn to Kant's concept of right in the first part of the *Metaphysics of Morals* or *Doctrine of Right* published a year after Fichte's work. I first set my argument on the background of the systematic constellation I addressed above with regard to the idea of practical philosophy in Fichte's Jena work; and then discuss Kant's concept of right in connection with the thesis of the non-derivability of right from the moral law.[7]

Kant's Practical Philosophy: Transcendental Foundation and Metaphysical Application

In the *Groundwork* and the *Critique of Practical Reason* Kant is concerned with the *foundation* of moral philosophy, which requires the "supreme principle of morality" to be established on firm grounds (*GW*, 4: 392). The distinction between a formal and material part of philosophy, and the further separation of the pure from the empirical part of both natural and moral philosophy, must be read in light of that objective. For, if the task is to establish the highest principle of morality, the inquiry must be carried out entirely a priori: no appeal to empirical principles or observations is allowed at this stage. If the principle at stake is a law of morality (and not of nature), then it displays the normative validity of an "ought," that is, is legislative with regard to how "everything ought to happen" in the world of freedom (*GW*, 4: 388). It is for Kant a well-accepted axiom that no "ought" can be derived from nature and matters of fact; or that no truly universally binding principle can have its source in experience – this would indeed be a "practical rule" but never a "moral law" (*GW*, 4: 389). From Kant's claim, it follows that the foundation of moral philosophy must be free from all reference to empirical disciplines such as moral psychology and anthropology but should also not depend on metaphysical assumptions regarding human nature (*GW*, 4: 389, 409–10).

This objective leads to the peculiar double characterization of Kant's moral philosophy at its foundational stage, and confirms its distance from the starting point of Fichte's practical philosophy. Kant's ethics is not a *philosophia practica universalis* such as Wolff's but a "particular" moral philosophy – and herein Fichte may agree although for different reasons. For, it takes into consideration not the general conditions of willing as such but rather the conditions of a particular kind of willing, namely, the *pure* will, that is, the will insofar as it is (or can be) "completely determined from a

7 I must limit myself to some crucial passages of the introduction to Kant's *Doctrine of Right*.

priori principles without any empirical motives" (*GW*, 4: 390f.). On the other hand, to this restriction in the type of willing corresponds an extension with regard to the subject of the moral theory or the addressee of the principle of morality – and it is here that Fichte's position differs. If the principle of morality "must carry with it absolute necessity," and if it has to display true universality, then it must be a principle that cannot hold "only for human beings, as if other rational beings did not have to heed it" (*GW*, 4: 389). Hence, the ground of obligation must be sought "a priori simply in concepts of pure reason" (*GW*, 4: 389, 410, 411f.; *MM*, 5: 216). Both the restriction (to the pure will) and the extension (to all rational beings) of Kant's moral theory at this stage ultimately depend on the gesture that frees the foundation of morality from the reference to human nature. Such a foundation is rendered independent of both an *empirical* and a *metaphysical* reference to human nature. But it is also independent of a unified account of human nature (rational *cum* sensible) such as Fichte's *transcendental* account.

Kant introduces the reference to human nature through the idea of "application." Once the highest principle of morality is established as valid for all rational beings, one can proceed to its "*application* to human beings" – a task that involves "anthropology" (*GW*, 4: 412). Such an application is needed, first, because of the difference between laws of nature and laws of freedom. The former are "laws in accordance with which everything happens"; the latter are laws according to which "everything ought to happen, while still taking into account the conditions under which it very often does not happen" (*GW*, 4: 388). The application of the moral law to human nature gives an account precisely of why the law of freedom, despite its commanding with absolute necessity, is not "executed" (*GW*, 4: 410) with the same absolute necessity with which laws of nature are executed. This explanation connects to the more explicit systematic reason that emerges in the *Critique of Practical Reason*, which points toward the *Metaphysics of Morals*. Kant contends that the *Critique of Practical Reason* only gives a "complete account of the principles of its [duty in general] possibility, its extent and limits, without particular reference to human nature" (*CPrR*, 5: 8). However, when the division of the "system" of the practical sciences is at stake, then the concept of duty must be set in relation to and determined by the way in which the "subject" is known in her actual existence, namely, as *Mensch*. In this case, duties are specified as "human duties." Since for such a specification of the pure concept of duty its application to human nature is required, its application is functional to the construction of a "system" of ethics and to its completeness (*CPrR*, 5: 8; *GW*, 4: 388).

In the introduction to the *Metaphysics of Morals*, Kant presents the idea of a "metaphysics of morals" – metaphysics being "a system of a priori cognition from concepts alone" (*MM*, 6: 216). Such metaphysics "cannot dispense with *principles of application*" whereby the "*universal* moral principles" are referred to the "*particular* nature of human beings, which can be known only by experience" (*MM*, 6: 217; my emphasis). On the basis of the "principles of application," the metaphysics of morals "assumes as its object" the human being. Now, to apply the universal principles of morality to the particular nature of man amounts to showing "in such nature" the concrete "implications" of those universal principles. Kant stresses that this principled application does not revoke the pure a priori character of those principles with regard to their "origin," and concludes, "this is to say, in effect, that a metaphysics of morals cannot be based upon anthropology but can still be applied to it" (*MM*, 6: 217). When Kant stresses that the doctrine of morals is normative "for everyone," he means *for all human beings* insofar as they are free agents endowed with practical reason, without taking into account particular inclinations, man's "animal nature," or "the ways of the world" (*MM*, 6: 216). At this stage also, then, Kant's position differs from Fichte's view of the subject of practical philosophy despite his more pointed focus on the human being. With regard to the source of the normativity of practical laws, Kant's position in 1797 is fundamentally unchanged. Now, however, the human being is placed from the outset at the center. Kant refers to a "moral anthropology" as the "counterpart" of the metaphysics of morals and as the "other member of the division of practical philosophy." This moral anthropology addresses "the subjective conditions in human nature that hinder or help people in fulfilling the laws of the metaphysics of morals." Significantly, the "application" of moral principles to human nature reveals how moral laws are actually carried out or implemented by human beings.[8]

The Universal Law of Right and the Highest Principle of Morality

In the introduction to the *Doctrine of Right*, Kant elaborates on the distinction between laws of nature and laws of freedom so as to introduce the

[8] See O'Neill 2007: 161, and Nuzzo 2011.

concept of right. Laws of freedom are called "moral" (*moralisch*): "As they are directed merely to external actions and their conformity to law, they are called juridical laws (*juridisch*); but if they *also* require that they themselves be determining grounds of action, they are ethical laws (*ethisch*)" (*MM*, 6: 214). The freedom to which juridical laws refer can only be freedom "in the external use of choice"; while moral freedom is freedom "*in both* the external and the internal use of choice" (*MM*, 6: 214; my emphasis). If we look at the way in which Kant presents the principle of autonomy in the *Critique of Practical Reason* as the "sole principle *of all moral laws* and of the duties in keeping with them" (*CPrR*, 5: 33; my emphasis), the question now is whether this unique principle governs the *entire* sphere of morality of which right is part next to ethics; or rather is the highest principle of "ethics" *only*. This seems to be, expressed in Kantian terms, the issue somehow corresponding to the one raised by Fichte and concerning the relation between morality and right.

For Kant, the sphere of ethics is broader than the sphere of right. Juridical laws concern "external" actions and external actions *only*; ethical laws, instead, require *in addition* that the law itself be the "determining ground" of action (properly, of the will). Right concerns freedom "in the external use of choice" *only*; ethics concerns freedom "*in both* the external *and* the internal use of choice" (*MM*, 6: 214). Kant further discusses the difference between juridical and ethical with regard to the idea of "legislation." To all legislation belong two elements, which are responsible, respectively, for the objective and subjective necessity proper to the "obligation" built into it: first, a "law" that represents that which ought to happen as "objectively necessary" or as a duty; second, an "incentive," which subjectively connects the determination of the will to action with the representation of the law (*MM*, 6: 218). While ethical law makes an action one's duty, and, at the same time, makes this duty the incentive to action (whereby objective and subjective necessity overlap), juridical law does not include the incentive as a determining ground in the law itself (i.e., it only concerns *external* action and the *external* use of choice), thereby allowing for a possible multiplicity of incentives and motivations other than the idea of duty. Being other than duty, these incentives must be taken from the sphere of "pathological" (i.e., sensibly determined) motives, inclinations, and particularly aversions – which explains why the lawgiving proper to right is one that constrains (*MM*, 6: 219). If we recall Fichte's investigation in the practical part of the 1794–95 *Wissenschaftslehre*, it is clear that he works on this Kantian paradigm (already in place in the second *Critique* although not yet including juridical law), fundamentally shifting the focus from the idea of duty to a doctrine of the incentives – hence, emphasizing the *subjective* and *pathological* aspect of the will, and integrating it into a unified conception of practical reason. Accordingly, it is also no surprise that after 1795 the function of producing the transition to individual self-consciousness generally belonging to the practical passes on to the theory of right. The systematic connection between right and the subjectivity of the will, however, has an opposite direction for Kant and Fichte. While Kant makes room for the anthropological characterization of the will on the basis of the metaphysical definition of juridical law, Fichte obtains the idea of right from the idea of self-consciousness as its transcendental condition.

Kant opens the introduction to the *Doctrine of Right* (§B) by asking the question: "What is right?" in the same way in which, in the Transcendental Logic of the first *Critique*, he asked: "What is truth?" (*MM*, 6: 229; *CPR*, A 58/B 82). The problem is formally very similar at least to the extent that the question embarrasses the jurist just as it embarrasses the logician by putting them in the position of answering either with an empty tautology or by providing empirical cases that as such do not answer the question. The point – and here Fichte agrees with Kant – is that the concept of right is a rational concept that has its origin a priori in reason but it is also a rational concept that does have an objective content (although not an empirical one). This is, for Fichte, the fundamental motivation for the "deduction."

Kant first introduces (i) the idea of right in its *subjective* or "moral concept" with the following formulation: "The concept of right, insofar as it is related to a corresponding obligation (i.e., the *moral* concept of right), concerns, first, only the external … relation of one person to another, insofar as their actions, as deeds (*Facta*), can have … influence on each other" (*MM*, 6: 230). The concept of right expresses for Kant a normative and reciprocal relation among persons with regard to their capacity of choice taken in its formality, that is, as free choice (and not in relation to the actually chosen matter or end) (*MM*, 6: 230). One person has (subjectively) a right toward another when she can impose on the other an obligation to refrain from a certain external use of freedom which is incompatible with her own external freedom; or, alternatively, when she can put the second person under the obligation to perform a determinate external action which is necessary to the preservation of her own (i.e., the first person's) external freedom. All this is comprised under a universal law of freedom that "unifies" the free "choice" of one with the free "choice" of another in their reciprocal limiting relation. The concept of right is said to be "moral" insofar as it is related to a corresponding "obligation" connected to some determining ground or other in the subject – a determining ground that is not necessarily the idea of duty itself (in which case it would be an "ethical" and not a "juridical" concept) (*MM*, 6: 218).

This *subjective* concept of right, however, has validity only on the basis of (ii) the *objective* concept of right, which Kant formulates as follows: "Right is … the sum total of the conditions under which the choice of one can be united with the choice of another in accordance with a universal law of freedom" (*MM*, 6: 230). This definition presupposes the idea of external freedom specific to the sphere of right and distinct from the freedom of internal determination and self-determination in one's choice of maxims and ends proper to ethics.[9] From the objective concept of right (iii) the "universal principle of right" (§C) follows analytically. This principle offers the answer to the question posed at the outset ("What is right?"): " 'Any action is right if it can coexist with everyone's freedom in accordance with a universal law, or if on its maxim the freedom of choice of each can coexist with everyone's freedom in accordance with a universal law' " (*MM*, 6: 230).[10] Again, this is an *objective* principle for the assessment of *external* actions (as *Facta*), which are chosen, as all rational actions are, on the basis of maxims. It is not a principle for the *internal* choice of these maxims themselves (namely, a principle that motivates the choice of maxims, which would make it into an ethical principle). The universal principle of right concerns the compatibility or incompatibility of one's external actions with the freedom of others *according to a universal law of freedom* (and not, for example, according to luck, contingent circumstances, or the like). Accordingly, insisting on setting the specifically juridical nature of this principle apart from ethical ones, Kant remarks that from the universal principle of right follows that "it cannot be required that this principle of all maxims be in turn my maxim, that is, it cannot be required that *I make it the maxim* of my action" (*MM*, 6: 231). The universal principle of right is indeed a "principle of all maxims" since all actions as instances of maxims, to the extent that they are externally setting me in relation to the freedom of other persons, fall under it. There is, however, no practical necessity that imposes this principle on me as my maxim, that is, as internal determining ground for my choice. This follows precisely from

[9] See Uleman 2004.

[10] At stake here is the "universal law" of freedom and the "universal law of right" (see (iv) below); see below for the difference between the universal law of right and the categorical imperative.

the distinction between juridical and ethical law, legislation, and freedom. Having Fichte's concern in mind, we should stress that Kant's universal law of right is not only different from but also independent of the ethical law in its normative validity and in the obligation and demand it sets on the subject (see (i) the subjective or "moral concept" of right). The universal law of right may be additionally connected to the ethical law (and compatible with it), not, however, in order to be the law of right that it already and independently is – there is in fact no "derivation" of right from the moral law. The universal law of right can be connected to the ethical law (i.e., the ethical law can make it a duty to endorse the maxim of acting according to right) precisely because the principle of right is fundamentally distinct from and independent of the ethical law both with regard to its normativity and with regard the realm on which it legislates.[11] Thus Kant adds, "That I make my maxim to act rightly is a demand that ethics makes on me" (*MM*, 6: 231). It is precisely because the universal law of right cannot impose on me an ethical obligation to act rightly (or cannot be made into the maxim to act rightly without becoming an *ethical* maxim), that ethics can make that demand on me.

Thereby Kant arrives at (iv) the "universal law of right": "so act externally that the free use of your choice can coexist with the freedom of everyone in accordance with a universal law" (*MM*, 6: 231). Kant's universal law of right does impose an obligation (it commands with regard to the external use of choice *in accordance with a universal law of freedom*) but this is not a moral obligation: it only concerns my external freedom and action and not the motivation on which I choose to limit my freedom. The universal law of right "does not at all expect, far less demand that I *myself should* (*solle*) limit my freedom to those conditions *just for the sake of this obligation*" (*MM*, 6: 231; my emphasis). There is no *ethical Sollen* expressed by the universal law of right. Nor, most importantly, does this law concern the ground determining my choice: it does not say that *I should* limit my freedom *on the ground* of those "conditions" that define (ii) the objective concept of right (namely, "the conditions under which the choice of one can be united with the choice of another in accordance with a universal law of freedom" (*MM*, 6: 230)). In other words, I may limit my external freedom for whatever internal reason or motivation (fear of punishment, self-interest, etc.) as long as my action is *Rechthandeln*, that is, can be united with the free choice of others

[11] And this explains Kant's claim that the ethical domain encompasses external actions as well (*MM*, 6: 214).

according to a universal law of freedom. In the universal law of right the ethical *Sollen* is replaced with a "factual" juridical "*is*." With this law, "reason says only that my freedom *is* limited to those conditions" – of lawful coexistence with the external freedom of others – "in conformity with the idea [of objective right] and that *it may also be actively limited* by others" (*MM*, 6: 231). In the universal law of right reason informs me of a twofold practical-juridical "fact": first, that my external freedom *is* indeed limited to the conditions of lawful coexistence with the freedom of others; and, second, that others *may in actual fact limit* my freedom according to those conditions. Importantly, reason says this "as a postulate that is incapable of further proof" (*MM*, 6: 231). There is no issue of derivation or even deduction here for Kant. In fact, the universal law of right is a "postulate" or an axiom for which as such no proof can be produced. In other words, neither the notion that my external freedom *is* limited to the conditions set by the objective concept of right nor the subjective right of others to actively limit my external freedom to these conditions can be derived or deduced from a higher principle – a principle, which could only be the moral imperative. Thus, with this claim, Kant excludes the possibility of deriving the law of right from the moral law.

Significantly, Kant does not present the universal law of right in terms of a "categorical imperative," even though his minimal definition of a "categorical imperative" in the *Doctrine of Right* as simply connected to the idea of "obligation" could allow for it. "The categorical imperative, which in general only expresses what obligation is, is: 'Act according to a maxim that can at the same time be valid as a universal law'" (*MM*, 6: 225). And "obligation," Kant claims, "is the necessity of a free action under a categorical imperative of reason" (*MM*, 6: 222). Now *this* definition of the categorical imperative applies broadly to both ethical and juridical laws.[12] Moreover, "examples" of categorical imperatives can be presented only in that "practical doctrine" that deals with obligation, that is, the doctrine – or the metaphysics – of "morals" (*Sitten*) in its two parts. Categorical imperatives are distinguished from all the others that are merely "technical" and conditioned (*MM*, 6: 222). Clearly, for Kant, the law of right while not a moral-ethical law is also not, as it is for Fichte, a technical imperative.

[12] See Baum 2013: 91.

However, the definition of a categorical imperative provided in the *Doctrine of Right* is very different from the one offered in the *Groundwork* and the *Critique of Practical Reason*, where Kant claims that:

> the *formal practical principle* of pure reason (in accordance with which the mere form of a possible universal law through our maxims must constitute the supreme and immediate determining ground of the will – *is the sole principle* that can *possibly* be fit for categorical imperatives, that is, practical laws (which make actions duties), and in general under the principle of morality (*Sittlichkeit*). (CPrR, 5: 41; my emphasis)

This definition *excludes* the sphere of right from the legislation of the categorical imperative, that is, from the principle of autonomy of the will as the foundational and unique principle of morality, since the principle of right allows for other determining grounds or incentives of the will than the purely formal idea of duty (*MM*, 6: 219). The principle of right is neither a principle of the morality of the will nor of the morality of maxims since it legislates merely on *external* actions and their freedom.[13]

Thus, with regard to Fichte's concern for the relation between the concept of right and the moral law we can conclude, first, that Kant does keep at the foundational stage of his moral philosophy the concept – and the principle and the universal law – of right (i–iv) separate from and independent of the moral-ethical law or categorical imperative/principle of autonomy as defined in the *Groundwork* and second *Critique*; and second, that there is, for him, no possible derivation of the former from the latter. Unlike Fichte, however, Kant claims that the universal law of right is a "postulate" that, as such, cannot be proved at all: it cannot be derived from a higher principle, for this could only be the moral-ethical principle of autonomy. Similarly maintaining the separation between ethics and right, Fichte sees instead the "deduction" of the concept of right as the chief task of his *Natural Right* (and as the indirect proof that the claim deriving right from the moral law is wrong). This is the case because of the fundamentally different starting point of Kant's and Fichte's respective theory of right. Fichte's theory of right is framed in terms of a transcendental anthropology the starting point of which is the individuality of self-consciousness in its free action. The concept of right is deduced as the transcendental condition of this determination of self-consciousness. For Kant, the starting point is the metaphysical concept of right as a

[13] By contrast, the highest principle of the "doctrine of virtue" is explicitly indicated as a "categorical imperative" and distinguished from the principle of right (*MM*, 6: 389). See Baum 2013: 88.

concept inscribed in his idea of a "metaphysics of morals" that follows the properly critical and transcendental foundation of morality and implies an "application" of practical concepts to "human nature" but is fundamentally independent of the nature of the subject of right. Kant, however, is interested in a problem that Fichte does not seem to pose, namely, the way in which ethics can turn the juridical obligation entailed in the universal law of right into an ethical one. Fichte, by contrast, having severed the relation of the two spheres in a more radical way, must still address the problem of how the individual can be obligated to limit her external freedom according to the law of right but must shift the problem to the realm of the application of a law that remains for him "merely formal" and as such "not capable of being applied" without additional political conditions, that is, ultimately, without recurring to the external intervention of the state (*FNR*, 15; *SW*, III: 15).

CHAPTER 2

Fichte's Separation of Right from Morality

Frederick Neuhouser

Between 1793 and 1796, Fichte's theory of right underwent a fundamental transformation: whereas his earlier position regarded political philosophy as one part of a more comprehensive moral theory, his position in *Foundations of Natural Right* insists on a "complete separation" of the two.[1] My aim in this paper is to explain what this separation amounts to and why it is philosophically significant. I hope to show that Fichte's separation of right (or political philosophy) from morality was a response to his realization of the impossibility of understanding the rational significance of the sphere of right, including private property, solely in terms of its relation to moral autonomy. Implicit in Fichte's later position is the view that the political realm has its own distinctive end, the creation of a community in which *individual personhood* (including personal freedom) is promoted (and respected), where the value of personhood is not simply derivative of that of moral autonomy. Alternatively, one could describe the separation between right and morality as the claim that these two branches of practical philosophy are grounded in distinct conceptions of subjectivity, moral autonomy in the one case and free personhood in the other.

In his 1793 defense of the French Revolution, *Contribution to the Rectification of the Public's Judgment of the French Revolution*, Fichte grounds political theory in moral philosophy in the following sense: he looks to the moral law (as understood by Kant) for an account of the inalienable "natural rights" that any legitimate state must preserve for all citizens. These rights are derived directly from one's duty to follow the moral law: natural rights are restrictions on the actions of others that

[1] This phrase comes from Siep 1979b: 122. Another excellent paper on this topic is Nomer 2013.

This is a thoroughly revised version of Neuhouser 1994. The views expressed here differ importantly from those of the earlier paper. Some translations of *Natural Right* have been modified. I am especially grateful to Allen Wood, Jake McNulty, Laura Martin, David Hills, and Thimo Heisenberg for discussion of many of the issues covered here.

safeguard the freedoms individuals need if they are to realize moral autonomy and to fulfill their moral duties. If, for example, morality requires me to perfect my capacities and talents, then I have an inalienable natural right to the freedoms that the development of those capacities and talents requires, and it is this feature of natural rights – that they are necessary for fulfilling the requirements of morality – that accounts for their inalienability. To relinquish those freedoms would be to forsake one's vocation as a moral being. Moreover, our obligation to respect the natural rights of others follows directly from our (involuntary) subjection to the moral law: it depends not on consent but on our nature as rational beings capable of moral autonomy. Although a rational state will provide non-moral incentives for respecting others' natural rights, our moral obligation to respect those rights remains in force even in the absence of political rule.

There is a further respect in which Fichte's early position derives right from moral theory: morality places *positive* requirements on the state that go beyond safeguarding natural rights. In addition to this, the state is charged with achieving a certain *end*, that of cultivating its citizens into morally autonomous beings. This cultivation (*Bildung*) consists primarily in the re-forming of citizens' natural sensibilities such that their reformed desires promote morality's ends rather than conflict with them. What unites these two aspects of Fichte's early theory of right is the view that the state's task is to promote the moral autonomy of its citizens; indeed, this is the state's *only* task, which implies that political community has no ends of its own, distinct from those of morality. This position could also be formulated as the view that moral and political philosophy are grounded in a single conception of subjectivity (or freedom) – moral autonomy – and that the principles of right are derived by thinking about how political community must be organized in order to create the social conditions necessary for moral agency to be realized by all citizens. In any case, Fichte's theory of right in 1793 is grounded in morality in the sense that it takes moral autonomy – both the capacity for moral agency and the actual achievement of moral virtue – as an *end* (and the only end) that rational political institutions are to strive to realize. As we will see below, Fichte's position of 1796 has at least this much in common with his earlier position: rational political institutions are justified by reference to their capacity to create a community in which a certain conception of free subjectivity is realized, that is, both respected and *promoted as their end*.[2]

[2] Claiming that the principal end of right is to promote personhood implies that his political theory is largely *teleological*: political community is justified by its ability to bring about a certain end in

What distinguishes the two positions is the specific conception of freedom that each regards as the principal value underlying political community.

In 1796 Fichte begins his theory of right with an explicit rejection of his earlier conception of the relation between right and morality: it is misguided, he now claims, to attempt to derive a theory of right from the moral law; right is not merely a "chapter" within moral theory but "a separate science standing on its own" (*FNR*, 11; *SW*, III: 10). Statements such as these make clear that Fichte intended to draw a sharper boundary between right and morality than he did in 1793, but they do not yet provide a precise picture of the nature and import of the intended distinction. Fichte has a number of ways of formulating the point he means to be making, but, as suggested above, the best way of understanding this transformation is to see it as a change in the conception of the subject that grounds the theory of right. In the *Natural Right,* it is no longer the concept of a morally autonomous subject from which the principles of right are derived but a new conception of free subjectivity that Fichte calls *personhood.* In order to understand Fichte's theory of 1796, then, we must first inquire into his conception of personhood and, after that, into how he uses that idea to ground a theory of right.

Personhood

At the beginning of the *Natural Right* Fichte articulates the fundamental thought of his theory of right as follows: "The rational being cannot posit itself as a rational being with self-consciousness without positing itself as an *individual,* as one among several rational beings" (*FNR*, 9; *SW*, III: 8). Fichte's emphasis on the term "individual" indicates that individuality is to play a central role in his conception of the person and therefore in his new theory of right as well. This alone suggests a preliminary formulation of the main difference between the positions of 1793 and 1796: principles of right will no longer be justified in terms of the role they play in fostering moral autonomy; rather, the political realm will be understood as a sphere the main purpose of which is to promote (and respect) its members' *individuality*, including (since "self-positing" is involved)[3] their *consciousness* of

the world, the realization of personhood. Some commentators deny that this is Fichte's view, most notably Allen Wood in his book *Fichte's Ethical Thought.*

[3] To say that the subject posits itself as X is to say that it is conscious of itself as X and that this self-consciousness is (at least partly) constitutive of its being X. In the case at hand: being aware of oneself as an individual is a necessary part of being one. For more on the concept of self-positing, see my 1990: Chapter 3.

themselves as individuals. And, since being an individual involves distinguishing oneself from other individuals (positing oneself as one individual among others), it is not difficult to see in general how a liberal political order – one committed to safeguarding a private sphere demarcated by a set of individual rights – might be taken to promote its members' individuality. Although some version of this idea lies at the bottom of Fichte's theory of right in 1796, there is more to be said about how he construes individuality and makes it into the main value underlying political community.

In order to understand how Fichte understands personhood (including individuality) it is necessary to bring together the various remarks he makes about it in the Introduction and §§1–7 of the *Natural Right*. The first thing to note is that he uses "person" interchangeably with "rational individual" (*FNR*, 9, 53; *SW*, III: 9, 56), which should lead us to ask in what sense the person is a *rational* individual, as well as how the rationality that defines personhood differs from that of the moral subject, which is bound by *universal laws* that come from "itself" (from the laws governing self-determined agency). For Fichte – as for German Idealism more generally – "rational," when predicated of a subject, refers to three interrelated ideas. First, to be rational is to be *determined by concepts* (rather than by causes), and the rationality of persons consists in their capacity for conscious, goal-directed activity, that is, in their ability to act in accordance with a concept of an end (*Zweckbegriff*) (*FNR*, 20; *SW*, III: 19). Second, "rational" implies "free," or "self-determined," and, as we will see below, the freedom characteristic of persons is bound up with their capacity "spontaneously" to form *Zweckbegriffe* and to act on their basis. Third, rationality is associated with *self-consciousness*, as evidenced by the central role that "self-positing" plays in his definition of the person. Persons posit themselves as such only insofar as they are self-conscious, where this implies knowing oneself as a being of a certain general type (a "person," or "free individual") that one takes other beings to instantiate as well. Finally, if we add to these aspects of rationality the consideration that *finitude* is essential to subjectivity (*FNR*, 18; *SW*, III: 17) – that a subject's activity is always limited by constraints that do not come from itself (*FNR*, 20; *SW*, III: 19) – then we can say, as a first approximation, that persons are self-conscious, finite individuals who are capable of determining themselves to act in accordance with their own concepts of ends and are conscious of themselves as such.

Let us expand on this characterization of persons by examining the sense in which Fichte regards them as free. The type of freedom relevant to personhood is "formal freedom" (*FNR*, 41, 102; *SW*, III: 43, 112), in contrast to the "material freedom" that belongs to the autonomous moral subject and constitutes the central concept of the *System of Ethics* (*SE*, 132, 153; *SW*, IV: 139, 161). Formal freedom is a capacity for "absolute spontaneity" (*FNR*, 9; *SW*, III: 8) in "the *forming* of the concept of an intended efficacy outside us, or the concept of an *end*" (*FNR*, 20; *SW*, III: 19).[4] To be formally free, then, is to be "the absolute and final ground" of one's *Zweckbegriffe* (*FNR*, 103; *SW*, III: 113), that is, the self-determined author of the concepts of the ends in accordance with which one acts. Another way of putting Fichte's point is to say that the freedom of persons consists in free choice; persons *choose* among a set of possible actions open to them, and they choose freely because their choices are carried out in accordance with concepts of ends that they spontaneously "project" (*entwerfen*) (*FNR*, 39–41; *SW*, III: 41–3).

The formal freedom of persons, then, is considerably broader than the material freedom at issue in moral autonomy. The latter, more complete form of self-determination requires the subject to determine its ends in accordance with its conception of its own essential nature as a rational being, whereas the former requires merely that the subject determines its ends in the sense of choosing how to act from among a range of given possibilities, where conformity with the moral law is not a condition of choosing freely. Hence, material freedom depends on the content of the ends one sets for oneself, on whether those ends are consistent with or determined by one's essential nature. Formal freedom, in contrast, does not require that ends be chosen in accordance with principles deriving from one's essential nature; what is required is only that one's ends be freely "projected." Although the autonomous moral subject must possess formal freedom (it must be capable of choosing), to be materially free it must exercise that freedom as the moral law dictates.

Thus far my discussion of formal freedom has made reference only to capacities internal to the subject, those involved in spontaneously projecting ends. If this were all there were to personal freedom, however, it would be unsuited to ground a political theory, since the external world with its potential hindrances to effective action would be irrelevant to the person's freedom. But interacting with the world – carrying out one's freely projected ends in action – is essential to completing the freedom of personhood:

> What is contained first and foremost in the concept of freedom is nothing but the capacity to project, through absolute spontaneity, concepts of our possible efficacy … But if a rational individual, or a person, is to find

[4] This conception of formal freedom also appears in the *System of Ethics*. For more on formal and material freedom see Neuhouser 1990: Chapter 4, and Kosch 2013.

> himself as free, then something more is required, namely, that the object thought through the concept of the person's efficacy actually correspond to that concept in experience … [or] that something in the world outside the rational individual follow from the thought of his activity. (*FNR*, 9; *SW*, III: 8–9)

This passage shows that it is not enough to characterize the person merely as a free chooser of ends. Persons, in order to "find" themselves as such, must also be causally efficacious. Real efficacy is essential to personhood for two reasons. First, the *freedom* of personhood is not exhausted by the spontaneous projection of ends. To be completely free (even in the formal sense) persons must also translate their ends into real action in the world: a subject that projected its own ends but failed to realize them would not *complete* its willing and achieve the full measure of freedom appropriate to the person.[5] This aspect of formal freedom has important implications for the theory of right, for it grounds Fichte's claim that persons are necessarily *embodied*: if persons are to be causally efficacious, they must be more than merely subjects of consciousness; they must also have bodies that enable them to interact with other objects in the world.[6]

The second reason efficacy is essential to personhood finds expression in the passage cited above. There Fichte first characterizes personal freedom in terms of the spontaneous projection of ends and then introduces causal efficacy as a condition of persons' ability to "find" themselves as free. His point is that real efficacy is essential to personhood not only because it constitutes one element of complete formal freedom but also because such efficacy is required for persons to be *self-conscious* with respect to their freedom. The general idea is that persons find themselves as free only by somehow encountering their freedom as an object of experience. It is difficult, however, to determine exactly what the content of the relevant self-consciousness of freedom is and what kind of experience counts as finding oneself as free. I will return to this issue in the following section when discussing the relation between right and the self-consciousness of persons.

Before proceeding to the topic of right it is important to recall that persons are not only free but also *individuals*, and as self-positing subjects they must be conscious of themselves as such. As the following passages

5 "What does *being free* mean? Evidently, it means being able to carry out the concepts I have made of my actions" (*FNR*, 9; *SW*, III: 51).

6 *FNR*, §§5, 11.

demonstrate, Fichte holds that persons' individuality, including their awareness of themselves as individuals, is also conditioned by the real exercise of their formal freedom:

> Within the sphere [of activity] allotted to it, the subject has freely chosen; it has absolutely given to itself the final determination of its own activity; and the ground of the final determination of its efficacy lies entirely *within the subject alone*. Only in this way can the subject posit itself ... as the sole ground of something; only in this way can it distinguish itself completely from the free being outside it and ascribe its efficacy to itself alone. (*FNR*, 40; *SW*, III: 41)

> That which alone made a choice within this sphere is ... the individual, the rational being that becomes determinate through opposition to another rational being; and this individual is characterized by a determinate expression of freedom belonging exclusively to it. (*FNR*, 40; *SW*, III: 42)

The most obvious aspect of individuality referred to in these passages is being, and being aware of oneself as, a single locus of agency, a discrete unit of formally free efficacy. The individual alone is the causal ground of her actions in the world, and her awareness of this constitutes (in part) her consciousness of herself as formally free. Her actions are not the results of a collective or alien will, nor the products of some more amorphously defined agent, and this fact is known to her. The individual and exclusive nature of the choosing involved in formal freedom makes it possible for her to say with respect to her freely chosen actions: "*I* did this; it was I, not some other being, who initiated these deeds, and (some of) the features of the world I see before me are due to my agency alone." It is the exercise of formal freedom, then, the choosing of a particular course of action from among a range of possibilities, that *individuates* persons, allowing them to be aware of themselves as discrete units of free agency.

At the same time, acting on their specific choices gives *particular determinacy* – real, distinguishable characteristics – to the individuals who have made those choices, and this makes individuals *qualitatively* distinct from others, who have made their own specific choices and acted on them. In projecting a particular end and acting on it, I acquire determinate qualities that distinguish me from other beings who have made different choices. As Fichte puts it in the second passage above, the formally free agent "becomes determinate," or comes to be "characterized by a determinate expression of freedom that belongs exclusively" to that individual. The point here is that the individuation of beings of the same general type ("formally free beings") – their realizing themselves as discrete units of agency – brings with it *particularization*, the acquisition of determinate qualities that make them qualitatively distinct. It seems likely, however, that Fichte is making a further point as well, namely, that particularization is a necessary condition of persons' *consciousness* of themselves as individuated units of free efficacy. In other words, particularization is not merely a *result* of persons' having made choices and initiated actions that come from them alone; persons also become *aware* of themselves as individual loci of causal efficacy only by seeing in the world the qualitatively distinct results of their choices.

Given the crucial role that individuality plays in the *Natural Right*, it is worth emphasizing the connection Fichte draws between individuality and formal freedom. The freedom on which moral theory is grounded – autonomous (or material) self-determination – does not *particularize* the subjects that exercise it. For moral self-determination requires subjects to determine their ends in accordance with what they *share* with other subjects: their essence as rational beings bound by the moral law. This is not to say that morality is inimical to the realization of agents' particularity but merely that moral self-determination alone, bound by universal laws applicable to rational beings in general, does not make the agents that exercise it into qualitatively distinct individuals.[7] One might say that the *arbitrary* character of formal freedom (that it places no constraints on the content of persons' choices) is precisely what explains its distinctive importance and the need for a branch of practical philosophy – and for a set of real practices, those of right – that supplements moral philosophy with its concern for non-arbitrary, material self-determination.

The final element of Fichte's conception of individuality comes to light in his claim that "there can be no opposition unless … the sides that are opposed are also posited as equal, related to, and compared with each other" (*FNR*, 40; *SW*, III: 42). The point here is that individuality involves not only distinguishing oneself from others but also seeing those one distinguishes oneself from as similar to oneself. More precisely, to be aware of oneself as a free being is to apply the concept "free being" to oneself, but this requires being able to apply the same concept to other free beings that one takes to be distinct from oneself and yet like oneself in the specific respect that justifies the application of the concept. Being aware of oneself as a being of a certain general type requires the awareness of some others as belonging to the same genus. When Fichte claims at the

[7] *SE*, 243; *SW*, IV: 254.

beginning of the *Natural Right* that to posit oneself as an individual is to be aware of oneself as "one among several rational beings" (*FNR*, 9; *SW*, III: 8), he is anticipating his argument in §4 that consciousness of oneself as "*one*" (as an individual) goes hand in hand with consciousness of oneself as "one *among*" others of the same type. In other words, the subject that Fichte calls an "individual" shares with other individuals the capacity for formal freedom and is *aware* of this commonality, and it is this awareness that enables it to apply the concept "individual" to itself. Adding this aspect of individuality to those discussed earlier, Fichte's position can be summarized as follows: positing oneself as an individual involves knowing oneself, first, as a numerically distinct agent; second, as qualitatively distinct from others (with particular determinate qualities); and, third, as a being of a certain general type – a formally free subject – to which other beings also belong.

Personhood as the Foundation of Right

Let us now turn to how the *Foundations of Natural Right* grounds a theory of right on the conception of the person. For simplicity's sake, I will restrict myself to the part of Fichte's theory that corresponds to his earlier doctrine of natural rights. In 1796 Fichte calls these rights "original rights" (*Urrechte*), but they are functionally akin to the natural rights of 1793 insofar as both help to define, prior to all positive right, the specific rights that rational political institutions must safeguard for individuals. Original rights are introduced in the *Natural Right* as "the conditions of personhood" (*FNR*, 102; *SW*, III: 112), as rights that "are contained in the mere concept of the person" (*FNR*, 87; *SW*, III: 94) and "that should belong absolutely to every person as such" (*FNR*, 102; *SW*, III: 113).

Two preliminary points must be noted if the connection between original rights and personhood is to be understood. First, rights govern relations *among persons* and come into play only insofar as a plurality of persons exists together. This relational character is essential to the very concept of right, the core of which Fichte locates in the conditions "of possibility of the coexistence of free beings" (*FNR*, 87; *SW*, III: 94). (In truth, Fichte's position is stronger than these statements suggest: insofar as being recognized by others is essential to personhood, persons can exist *only* as a plurality.) Second, original rights concern only those aspects of personhood that "appear in the sensible world" and are therefore subject to interference by other individuals (*FNR*, 87, 102; *SW*, III: 94, 112). The spontaneous projection of ends is essential to personhood, but since this internal aspect of willing is unaffected by others' actions, it does not enter into an account of the *rights* a rational political order must secure (*FNR*, 103; *SW*, III: 113). Thus, the aspect of formal freedom of concern to a theory of right is not the setting of ends but translating one's ends into actions, and original rights restrict others' actions so as to create for each person an exclusive, external sphere within which formal freedom can be exercised (*FNR*, 43, 48, 53; *SW*, III: 46, 51, 56). Original rights translate into the demand that individuals be treated by others in a manner consistent with their status as persons, and their underlying principle is: "no one has a right to an action that makes the freedom and personhood of another impossible" (*FNR*, 86–7; *SW*, III: 93–4).

Original rights fall into two broad classes: those concerning the inviolability of the body and those guaranteeing individuals a sphere of "free influence in the ... sensible world" (*FNR*, 108; *SW*, III: 119), where the latter includes rights to both self-preservation and private property.[8] I will not examine here what specifically these rights entail or whether they are in fact derivable from Fichte's conception of the person. For present purposes it is more important to consider the role that the sphere of right plays in realizing personhood.

It is relatively easy to see how safeguarding original rights realizes persons' freedom and individuality: by creating an exclusive sphere of free action for all, protected from the interference of others, the state allows persons both to exercise their formal freedom and, in so acting, to constitute themselves as particular individuals with real, determinate characteristics (the doer of X and Y). The more difficult task is understanding how the safeguarding of rights relates to persons' *self-consciousness*, and this will be my concern in the remainder of this section. Fichte's language strongly suggests that "the relation of right" – "that each is to limit his freedom through the concept of the possibility of the other's freedom" – is a condition of the possibility of persons' consciousness of themselves as free (*FNR*, 49; *SW*, III: 52). But if we understand this self-consciousness as simply an awareness of oneself as freely efficacious – as capable of initiating effects in the world through freely chosen actions – then the transcendental claim that relations of right make persons' self-consciousness possible appears to be implausibly strong, for surely even individuals who do not live in societies ordered by principles of right can be aware of themselves as free in this minimal sense.

[8] See *SE*, 243; *SW*, IV: 282f. See also James 2010.

The central role that self-consciousness plays in the *Natural Right* leaves little room for doubt, however, that Fichte regards *some* aspect of right as a necessary condition of persons' self-consciousness as such. The question is how to understand this transcendental claim such that it is both plausible and generally consistent with his text. The key to doing so is to emphasize three features of Fichte's argument that are not stated as clearly (or consistently) as they should be. The first of these features is that Fichte uses "the relation of right" interchangeably with "the concept of right." This can be confusing because the former most naturally refers to a *real* relation (of right) among subjects, which would distinguish it from the mere concept of such a relation, just as a "relation of love" is something more than the concept of that relation. Perhaps the reason Fichte uses these terms interchangeably is that the *concept* of right is inherently *relational*: to have that concept is to conceive of persons as standing in a certain relation to one another, but it is not necessarily to *be* in such a relation or to suppose that any beings are. If the relation of right is equivalent to the concept of right, it must be *having* the concept of right, not living in a right-governed society, that is "a condition of self-consciousness" (*FNR*, 49; *SW*, III: 52). This is what Fichte seems to mean when he says that the concept of right is "an original concept of pure reason," a necessary a priori concept in the sense that having it is a condition of self-consciousness (*FNR*, 4, 9; *SW*, III: 2, 8): "no finite rational being is possible if this concept is not present within it" (*FNR*, 49; *SW*, III: 53).[9] Showing that the concept of right must be "present within" any finite rational being corresponds to what Kant would have called its *metaphysical* deduction, but the strategy behind Fichte's deduction borrows from Kant's *transcendental* deduction insofar as it purports to show that the concept of right is necessary for self-consciousness.

The second feature of Fichte's argument to be noted is that the relation (or concept) of right that he claims to have deduced in this phase of his argument (before original rights have been introduced) most plausibly refers to a general pattern of reciprocal recognition – individuals mutually constraining their own freedom in some way by the idea of others' freedom (*FNR*, 42; *SW*, III: 44) – that can be instantiated in the world in a variety of ways. Respecting persons' original rights is one way of recognizing others as free – and the way most relevant to a theory of right – but other forms of such recognition

[9] As I argue below, for Fichte there is no instance of having a concept that is not also an application of that concept (in experience) of some kind.

are imaginable, too.[10] As Fichte says, the concept of right "must be operative *wherever human beings live together*," not only when they live together in a right-governed state *(FNR*, 50; *SW*, III: 53; emphasis added).[11] It appears that Fichte has this broad sense of recognition in mind when he says that "at the basis of all voluntarily chosen reciprocal interaction among free beings there lies an *original and necessary reciprocal interaction* among them, which is this: the free being, by his mere presence in the sensible world, compels every other free being, without qualification, to recognize him as a person" (*FNR*, 79; *SW*, III: 85; emphasis added). On this interpretation, what Fichte claims to be a condition of self-consciousness is (having the concept of) the relation of right in its "original and necessary" generic form, not in its specifically political form.

Third, it is not completely clear what it is for a subject to *have* the concept of right or, equivalently, for that concept to be "present within" us and "operative" (wherever humans live together). It seems important, however, that when Fichte speaks about right in its generic form, he treats having that concept as including a consciousness of others' freedom that is accompanied by an awareness of being subject to normative demands concerning how those others are to be treated, together with the corresponding "expectation" that others will treat one in accordance with those same demands (*FNR*, 43, 49; *SW*, III: 45, 52). In other words, having the concept of right seems to imply actually applying it in at least the limited sense of recognizing the validity of certain normative constraints on persons' practical freedom, and it appears to be this normative awareness that Fichte takes to be a condition of the possibility of persons' self-consciousness. This makes having the concept of right look more like a *real* relation of sorts (I take myself to stand under normative constraints in relation to others) than a commonsense understanding of concepts typically implies. The basic idea, however, is familiar enough from Kant: to have a concept in the theoretical realm is to recognize the validity of certain norms that govern its application in experience. In the practical realm, where concepts are action-guiding, to have a concept is to recognize the validity of norms that constrain one's freedom as, for example, the concept of a person (for Kant) imposes normative constraints on how

10 For example, in playing games with others, or in non- or pre-political communities in which individuals have some kind of recognized status as such.

11 Fichte notes that "right" is used here in a technical and general sense – as "the [general] concept of a relation [of recognition] among rational beings" (*FNR*, 51; *SW*, III: 55) – that need not correspond to what we ordinarily think of as political rights. See also *FNR*, 79–80; *SW*, III: 85–6.

one may act.[12] The "real relation" involved in having the concept of right, however, is not an external, political condition but a normative orientation to the freedom of others. If this is correct, then Fichte is best understood as deducing the necessity of some general normative understanding of the practical implications of individuals' formal freedom as a condition of the possibility of persons' self-consciousness: "*I must expect that all rational beings outside me recognize me as a rational being*. The necessity of this universal, ongoing expectation must be shown to be the condition of the possibility of self-consciousness" (*FNR*, 43; *SW*, III: 45–6). (I will argue below that sometimes §4 appears to claim that *actual recognition* by others, not merely an awareness of practical norms, is required for self-consciousness. This complicates the interpretive claims I have made here, but it does not nullify them.)

There is a further ambiguity in Fichte's argument that cannot be ignored. As I have formulated it here, his argument asserts that awareness of others as free individuals, and of being bound by general norms of mutual respect appropriate to the treatment of such beings, is necessary if persons are to be self-conscious. The ambiguity here concerns whether this transcendental claim is to be understood *genetically* or *constitutively*. An example of a genetic claim is Fichte's argument in §3, immediately prior to his deduction of the relation of right in §4, that a summons issued by another subject – a call to "resolve to exercise [one's] efficacy" – is a necessary condition of ascribing to oneself free efficacy in the sensible world (*FNR*, 31; *SW*, III: 33).[13] We know that this is at least in part a genetic claim because one conclusion Fichte draws from it is the necessity of initially unformed subjects, if they are to acquire an awareness of themselves as free individuals, to be *erzogen* – "brought up" – by beings already constituted as free subjects (*FNR*, 38; *SW*, III: 39). And as the Corollary makes clear, Fichte conceives of the *Erziehung* that he has shown to be necessary as a temporal, developmental process at the end of which individuals acquire something they previously lacked (consciousness of their free efficacy) and which, once acquired, does not require the continuation of what made it possible (their *Erziehung*). (Compare this with an example of a constitutive transcendental claim: Kant's argument that

[12] An important difference between Kant's moral philosophy and Fichte's political theory with respect to the norms implicit in practical concepts is that for Fichte principles of right on their own command only hypothetically, not categorically: they bind my *actions* only on the condition that I "arbitrarily" choose to live in a community of free beings (*FNR*, 11–12, 81; *SW*, III: 11, 87–8) and that others are committed to following those principles (*FNR*, 83; *SW*, III: 89).

[13] See Wood 2006.

applying the categories of the understanding to the manifold of intuition is a necessary condition of theoretical self-consciousness (and vice versa). Clearly, neither the application of the categories nor self-consciousness is a temporally prior, *genetic* condition of the other. Kant's claim, rather, is that a subject cannot be self-conscious without, in the very same act of consciousness, applying the categories to the manifold of experience. In the case of a constitutive relation, neither *relatum* precedes the other temporally, and neither can be present without the other.)

As I have interpreted Fichte's deduction of the relation of right in §4, it asserts that having the generic concept of right (including the normative awareness that accompanies it) is a *constitutive* condition of being aware of oneself as a formally free individual: being aware of norms of mutual respect as appropriate to the treatment of persons is part of what it is to be a self-conscious person. Even if this interpretation makes the best sense of §4, it raises a serious question about the cogency of the *Natural Right's* argument as a whole: how can what purports to be an unbroken string of transcendental arguments mix genetic (in §3) with constitutive claims (in §4) about the conditions of self-consciousness? Rather than attempt to solve this problem here,[14] however, I want to consider an issue more directly relevant to my topic, namely, whether Fichte means to claim that right *in the specifically political sense* – actually living in a society where principles of right are realized – has some important relation to the self-consciousness of persons.

I have already argued that the political realization of right cannot plausibly be understood as a *genetic* condition of individuals' consciousness of themselves as formally free. It is no more plausible to think that actually living in a right-governed society is a *constitutive* condition of such self-consciousness, and, as we have seen, Fichte himself says that the concept of right "must be operative" wherever humans live together (*FNR*, 50; *SW*, III: 53), not merely when they inhabit a certain type of political community. There are, nevertheless, resources in the *Natural Right* for arguing that Fichte is committed to thinking of living in a society governed by right as having *some* (actual, empirical) relation to individuals' consciousness of themselves as persons. Figuring out what this relation is essential to appreciating the distinctive philosophical significance of Fichte's text, as well as to seeing how it influenced Hegel's later conception of personhood and "abstract right."

[14] Michael Nance tackles this problem in Nance 2015: 618–24.

The basis for thinking that politically realized relations of right must have some important connection to persons' self-consciousness is found in the strand of Fichte's argument in §4 that makes others' *actual recognition* (not merely an awareness of the norms governing recognition) essential to a free individual's self-consciousness. Throughout §4, Fichte distinguishes between a "problematic" and a "categorical" knowledge of other free subjects (*FNR*, 41; *SW*, III: 43). Strictly speaking, it is only the former – where I *assume* that the other before me is a formally free subject and I know what general norms ought to govern interactions among free beings – that he claims to be a condition of persons' self-consciousness. In order to *know* (categorically) that the other being before me is free, however, I must actually *be treated* as free by it:

> [O]ne individual's knowledge of the other is conditioned by the fact that the other treats the first as a free being (i.e., limits its freedom through the concept of the freedom of the first). But this manner of treatment is conditioned by the first's treatment of the other; and the first's treatment of the other is conditioned by the other's treatment and knowledge of the first, and so on. (*FNR*, 41; *SW*, III: 43)[15]

Given that the *Natural Right* sets out to uncover the conditions of *finding* oneself as a free individual (*FNR*, 9; *SW*, III: 9) – in the world and not merely in consciousness – the actual recognition of others cannot be merely incidental to its argument. As Fichte recognized in §3, in order to *find* myself as freely efficacious, my freedom must be present to me as more than merely my idea of it; it must also lie before me as an object of my experience, which is why he claimed that an (actual) summons is required if I am to be conscious of myself as free. Similarly, if §4 inquires into the conditions of self-consciously free *individuals*, then finding oneself (actually) treated in accordance with the norms governing the interaction of free individuals would seem to be a necessary condition of finding oneself as an individual. The idea behind the requirement that one find oneself as free (in the world) if one is to be conscious of oneself as such – an idea central to Hegel's conception of *Geist* – is that actually to *know* oneself as X involves finding confirmatory evidence in the real world of one's conception of oneself as X.

If, as his talk of "finding" oneself implies, Fichte's aim is to elaborate the conditions of complete, objectively confirmed self-consciousness, then the existence of real relations among persons in which their free

[15] Similar language is found throughout *FNR*, 42–5; *SW*, III: 45–8.

individuality is actually recognized by others cannot be a matter left to the "arbitrary decision" of subjects as to whether or not to "live in community with others" (*FNR*, 11–12; *SW*, III: 11).[16] Fichte seems to admit as much sometimes – for example, in claiming that "if the subject had no [categorical] knowledge of a free being outside itself, then something that ought to have occurred, according to the laws of reason, would not have occurred" (*FNR*, 41–2; *SW*, III: 43–4). "If reason is to be realized at all in the sensible world" (*FNR*, 85; *SW*, III: 92) – if actually *finding* oneself as a free individual is to occur – then it would seem that some realization of the relation of right is required, even if it is difficult to reconcile this claim with Fichte's insistence that the establishment of a right-governed political order is a matter of arbitrary choice.[17] One possibility left open by my reading of §4 is that *some* kind of real recognition is rationally required but not necessarily recognition in its specifically political form. This option, however, looks less appealing the farther one advances in Fichte's text. For many of the claims of later sections – regarding the centrality of *bodies* and the manipulation of *things* to the exercise of formal freedom – constitute an argument for the *unique* importance of original (political) rights to the realization of free individuality, especially those that secure the body's inviolability and the existence of private property.

It is hard to avoid concluding that the *Foundations of Natural Right* offers an imperfectly articulated but still powerful argument for the claim that part of the rational significance of political right lies in its consequences for the actual self-consciousness of its members: living in a right-governed political order not only provides persons with a secure social space within which they are free to exercise their formal freedom, but also *shapes* (gives determinacy to), *confirms*, and *allows for the expression* of its members' *self-conscious identities* as persons. This constitutes a further sense in which right realizes personhood.

The Significance of Separating Right from Morality

How are we to assess the philosophical significance of Fichte's separation of right from morality? The best approach to this topic is to ask what

[16] Paradoxically, Fichte's separation of right from morality may be precisely what leads him to assert the arbitrary character of our decision to live in community with others: if categorical imperatives belong exclusively to morality, then right, one might think, can be based only on hypothetical imperatives.

[17] See Ware 2010; Breazeale 2008: 272–4.

considerations led him to replace moral subjectivity as the basis of right with his conception of the person.[18] In 1796, Fichte argues that political theory cannot be derived from morality by appealing to a conceptual distinction between rights and (moral) duties. Principles that ascribe rights are of a distinct logical type from those that prescribe duties, and this difference shows that a theory of right must be independent of moral theory. The main point is that while moral laws command categorically – they tell us what we *must* and *may not* do – rights merely *permit*: "a right is something one can avail oneself of or not" (*FNR*, 13; *SW*, III: 13); "right only permits but never commands that one exercise one's right" (*FNR*, 50; *SW*, III: 54). Fichte's claim cannot be that it is impossible to derive permissibility from a categorical ought. Such a claim would be mistaken since permissibility can be inferred in instances where the moral law is silent.[19] His point, rather, is that asserting a politically enforceable *right* to a certain action goes beyond claiming that the action is morally permissible: it claims that the possibility of that action must be *guaranteed* to individuals by placing constraints on the actions of others. Fichte's argument, then, is that while a moral law can say "you must" and "you may not" (and therefore also "you may"), it lacks the logical resources to pronounce the very different assertion "you have a right."

While Fichte is correct to distinguish rights from both duties and morally permissible actions, this alone does not imply that rights cannot be derived from moral theory. To illustrate this we need only recall Fichte's earlier account of natural rights. In 1793 Fichte generated a set of necessary constraints on the actions of others by considering what kinds of practical possibilities must be available to individuals if they are to be able to exercise and fulfill the demands of moral autonomy. Fichte's claim in 1796, however, is that this way of proceeding does not yield rights at all for the following reason: "The moral law very often forbids the exercise of a right, and yet [it] … does not therefore cease to be a right. In such a case one judges that the person surely had a right … but that he ought not to have exercised it" (*FNR*, 50; *SW*, III: 54). The point here is that rights can permit actions that morality prohibits: although I have the right to dispose of my property as I will, morality may require me to buy my jobless neighbor a meal rather than betting my money at the races. But if I have the

[18] Many commentators have found Fichte's explanations puzzling, see Ferry 1987: 183 and Verweyen 1975: 94–5.

[19] In early writings Fichte acknowledges this point (*SW*, VI: 58, 60, 318–19) but later holds that from the moral perspective there are no merely permissible actions (*SE*, 253; *SW*, IV: 264). This does not affect the conceptual point I make here.

right to dispose of my property in ways that conflict with moral demands, that right must be grounded in some principle other than the moral law. Our rights to act in ways that morality condemns must be understood as deriving from a value other than moral autonomy, and it is an account of this value that Fichte's conception of the person provides: the justification of a political order that safeguards original rights is based on the fact that it guarantees citizens an exclusive sphere of free activity that is necessary for them to realize themselves as formally free, qualitatively distinct individuals. The principles that govern the political realm, then, have a foundation distinct from that of morality, insofar as they aim to promote not moral autonomy but free, self-conscious individuality.[20]

Grounding the theory of right in personhood enables Fichte to explain how rights can permit actions ruled out by the moral law. But there is reason to believe that a second consideration also motivated this development: deriving original rights from personhood enabled Fichte to provide a firmer grounding of the right to private property than was available from his earlier perspective. It is difficult to see how a theory that derived natural rights from the requirements of a morally autonomous will could establish, without the concept of personhood, an inalienable right to private property.[21] Fichte admitted as much in 1793 in arguing that the right to property could be alienated both in part and as a whole (*SW*, VI: 177). By 1796, however, he had come to view individually owned property as essential to the realization of freedom and as a central concern of a theory of right.[22]

If we conceive of private property as part of the sensible world that is "subordinated to [one's] ends" and "appropriated exclusively as the sphere of [one's] interaction" with that world (*FNR*, 106, 103; III, 116, 210), then it is not difficult to see how the idea of personhood opens up the way to understanding private property as a necessary, inalienable right: if formal freedom is completed only in real, causally efficacious action, then the subjection of (a part of) the external world to one's subjective ends is necessary for the realization of personhood. Moreover, if the person is to be an individual, the part of the world subject to its ends must be exclusively its own, a sphere in which other individuals are prohibited from carrying

20 See note 17.

21 The *System of Ethics* establishes a moral duty to acquire property but only via the concept of personhood and the moral duty to realize formal freedom (*SE*, §23).

22 We find this view, along with Fichte's new conception of the tasks of political theory, in notes from 1795: "Property, contract and the synthesis of both, civil society, are the principal objects of the theory of right ... What belongs to a deduction of property?" (*GA*, II, 3: 406).

out their own ends. Surrendering one's right to property or living in a social order where no provisions for it existed would preclude not the realization of moral autonomy but one's existence as a self-conscious, formally free individual.[23]

It is now clear how to understand Fichte's assertion in 1796 that right is separate from morality: the two "sciences" are grounded in different first principles, or, more precisely, the two realms aim at realizing different conceptions of subjectivity – the person with its formal freedom and the autonomous will that is materially free. This, however, raises the question of the status of the principal value realized in the political realm (personhood, or free individuality) with respect to the value of moral autonomy. Is personhood (and the community that makes it possible) valuable in itself apart from its relation to morality, or does it have value only because it contributes in some way to moral self-determination? In my view, the most compelling reading of Fichte's position holds that personhood (and its realization in the world in a community ruled by right) is an end in itself,[24] valuable independently of its relation to morality.[25] For the reasons suggested above this interpretation makes most sense of the importance Fichte's theory of 1796 ascribes to private property. It is also suggested by his insistence that the concept of right "has nothing to do with the moral law" and "is deduced without it" (*FNR*, 50; *SW*, III: 54). This interpretation does not exclude the possibility that some of the principles of right are deducible from the standpoint of morality as well.[26] What it asserts is that any such connection is irrelevant from the perspective of a theory of right and unnecessary for a *political* justification of such principles. Such a reading is required if we are to take seriously Fichte's repeated claim that the rationality of right can be grasped without the moral law and with reference solely to the principle on which the independent science of right is founded: the idea of personhood.

One question this raises is whether Fichte's system can accommodate a species of value that is not derivative of moral autonomy. I believe that it can and that this becomes apparent if we recall that the highest principle

[23] This defense of private property is not a defense of *capitalism*. This part of Fichte's doctrine does not address what kinds of things may be owned by individuals; it does not determine whether the means of production are among them.

[24] There is no conflict in maintaining both that individual personhood is the highest value recognized by a theory of right and that a *community* of free persons is its ultimate end. Since personhood can be realized only within such a community, the two ends necessarily converge.

[25] For an alternate view, see Renaut 1986: 250.

[26] Belonging to a state and acquiring property are also moral duties (*SE*, 279, 285; *SW*, IV: 292, 299).

of Fichte's philosophy is not the materially self-determining will of morality but self-positing subjectivity more generally. Moral autonomy is one form of self-positing subjectivity, even the highest form of practical subjectivity (since it embodies material and not merely formal freedom), and it therefore counts as the supreme value for Fichte. It does not follow from this, however, that there are no values independent of moral autonomy, or that other forms of subjectivity have value only insofar as they further it. Personhood is also a form of self-positing subjectivity and is for that reason valuable in itself, even if it is not self-determination in its most complete form. Personhood is valuable in itself because it involves a type of self-determination (formal freedom) that, though less complete than moral autonomy, remains nonetheless a species of freedom. One could object that this interpretation of the relation between the values of personhood and moral autonomy misreads Fichte through Hegelian lenses. I believe it would be more accurate to say that on this issue Hegel was an especially acute reader of his predecessor who realized, perhaps more clearly than Fichte himself, the implications of one of Fichte's most important contributions to practical philosophy: the separation of right from morality.

CHAPTER 3

Fichte's Independence Thesis

James A. Clarke

One of the most striking theses of Fichte's *Foundations of Natural Right* is the thesis that legal and political philosophy (the "science of right" or "law" [*Recht*]) is independent from moral theory (the "science of morality," where "morality" denotes Kantian moral theory).[1] In advancing this "independence thesis,"[2] Fichte rejects the claim, which he advanced in his first works on the philosophy of right, that the fundamental principles of legal and political philosophy are dependent on, and derivable from, the moral law (call this the "dependence thesis").

An adequate understanding of the independence thesis is crucial for an understanding of Fichte's philosophy of right as outlined in the *Natural Right*. However, it merits scrutiny for a further reason – namely, that it addresses, and illuminates, fundamental issues in legal and political philosophy. In this chapter, I provide an interpretation of Fichte's independence thesis that focuses on the manner in which Fichte explores the nature of legal and moral concepts and principles and the conceptual relations between them. In so doing, I hope to demonstrate the relevance of Fichte's independence thesis for contemporary legal philosophy.

The independence thesis requires a rejection of the dependence thesis and is only fully intelligible in relation to it. Consequently, the first section of this chapter reconstructs and discusses the dependence thesis. To elucidate the dependence thesis, I draw upon deontic logic and

[1] "[T]he philosophical doctrine of right ... ought to be a separate science standing on its own" (*FNR*, 11; *SW*, III: 10). See also *FNR*, 50–1; *SW*, III: 54–5; *GA*, II, 3: 404.

[2] Nomer 2013 uses the term "separation thesis." I use the term "independence thesis" to avoid confusion with the "separation thesis" that is associated with the legal positivism of H. L. A. Hart. I consider the relationship between the independence thesis and the separation thesis in the third section of this chapter.

I am grateful to Sophie Gibb, Gabe Gottlieb, Chris Jay, and the participants in the New York German Idealism Workshop for their helpful comments, advice, and criticisms.

the "Hohfeldian" analysis of rights.[3] The second section of this chapter explains the independence thesis and reconstructs and evaluates Fichte's arguments in support of rejecting the dependence thesis. In the third, and final section, I briefly attempt to situate Fichte's independence thesis in relationship to a fundamental debate in the philosophy of law – the debate between natural law theory and legal positivism.

The Dependence Thesis

Fichte's independence thesis constitutes a break with his first works in legal and political philosophy, the 1793/4 *Contribution to the Rectification of the Public's Judgment of the French Revolution* (hereafter, *Contribution*) and the 1793 "Reclamation of the Freedom of Thought from the Princes of Europe, who have Oppressed it Until Now" (hereafter, "Reclamation"). In these works, Fichte follows Kantian theorists of right such as Hufeland and Schmalz in arguing that the science of right is dependent upon, and derivable from, the science of morality.[4]

Both the *Contribution* and the "Reclamation" attempt to derive the basic concepts of the philosophy of right from the basic concepts of Kant's moral theory. More specifically, both attempt to deduce natural rights or inalienable rights (I will use these terms interchangeably)[5] and certain obligations of the state from the "moral law" or "categorical imperative."[6] These deductions are intended to justify the claim that we possess natural rights and the claim that the state has certain obligations towards us. I shall concentrate solely on Fichte's attempt to deduce natural rights from the moral law since it is this attempt that he rejects in the *Natural Right.*

Fichte's deduction proceeds in two steps. First, he derives the concept of a right in general from the moral law. Second, he derives the distinction between inalienable and alienable rights from the moral law. I will discuss each step in turn.

[3] This is the analysis of rights that was first developed by W. N. Hohfeld. For a helpful summary of this analysis, see Wenar 2010.

[4] See Renaut 1986: 227–8 and Philonenko 1988: 115.

[5] Fichte considers all natural rights to be inalienable in both the "Reclamation" (*R*, 129–30, 132; *SW*, VI: 19, 23) and the *Contribution* (*SW*, VI: 66, 70, 111, 175, 178, 214).

[6] As Neuhouser notes, in the *Contribution* Fichte does not attempt to derive all of the science of right from morality. He does not attempt to derive the "foundation of a state" or "civil legislation" from morality. Fichte only attempts to derive natural rights and certain obligations of the state from the moral law. Neuhouser 1994: 159, 161. See *SW*, VI: 83.

The Derivation of the Concept of a Right in General

Fichte's derivation of the concept of a right in general is best understood in terms of three claims about the moral law. The first claim is the (trivial) claim that the moral law determines the rightness or wrongness of actions and hence their deontic modality – that is, whether they are obligatory, prohibited (or forbidden), or indifferent. Fichte's derivation exploits this feature of the moral law and this has led Wolfgang Kersting to dub the approach it exemplifies (which can be traced back to Christian Wolff)[7] the "deontic deduction of right."[8] Since Fichte's derivation relies on the relationships between the deontic concepts of the obligatory, prohibited, permitted, and indifferent, we should state those relationships. Taking the concept of permission as primitive, we can define the other deontic concepts as follows: an action or state of affairs, *p*, is prohibited just in case *p* is not permitted; *p* is obligatory just in case *not-p* is not permitted; *p* is indifferent just in case *p* is permitted and *not-p* is permitted. While everything that is indifferent is permitted, not everything that is permitted is indifferent: obligatory actions or states of affairs are permitted but not indifferent (if *p* is obligatory, then *p* is permitted but *not-p* is not permitted).[9]

The second claim is that the moral law is our only law: it is the sole and ultimate arbiter of the rightness or wrongness of our actions. This means that the deontic modality of our actions – whether they are obligatory, prohibited, or indifferent – is determined ultimately by the moral law (*R*, 125; *SW*, VI: 12; *SW*, VI: 60, 81). There is no competing "tribunal" (*Richterstuhl*) or legislative authority that could countermand or override the moral law by prohibiting an action that it permits or permitting an action that it prohibits.[10] Consequently, if the moral law does not prohibit an action, then that action is not prohibited and we are permitted to perform it.

The third claim is that if an action is permitted by the moral law, then I have a right to perform it. On the basis of these claims, Fichte claims that we have a right to everything that the moral law permits:

[7] Renaut 1986: 230.

[8] Kersting 2001: 22, 27. My understanding of Fichte's derivation is indebted to Kersting's paper.

[9] Von Wright 1951: 4.

[10] It is important to stress that Fichte is not claiming that there are no other "tribunals" (*Richterstühle*) for the appraisal of human action. He is simply claiming that the judgments or "sentences" (*Aussprüche*) of any such tribunal will always be subordinate to and – in cases of conflict – overridden by the sentences of the tribunal of morality. See Fichte's discussion of the relationship between the tribunals of morality and prudence in the Introduction to the *Contribution* (*SW*, VI: 73–5).

> If this law is his only law, then he may do as he wishes wherever this law does not speak; he has *a right* to all that is *not prohibited* (*nicht verboten*) by this exclusive law. (*R*, 125; *SW*, VI: 12)

> If we, as rational beings, stand under this law absolutely and without any exception we cannot, *as such beings, stand under any other law*. Consequently, where this law is silent, we are under no law, we *are permitted* (*wir dürfen*). Everything that the law does not prohibit, we are permitted to do. What we are permitted to do, we have – because this permission *is lawful* – *a right* to do. (*SW*, VI: 60)

Here "everything" should be understood to include states and capacities of the agent as well as actions. Although Fichte speaks of "*a right*" in the singular, he thinks that we have *rights* to those actions, capacities, or states that are permitted by the moral law, and that these rights are individuated by the types of actions, capacities, or states that they are rights to. Rights in general (both alienable and inalienable) are rights to actions, capacities, or states that are permitted by the moral law, and the domain of right is thus, as Frederick Neuhouser and Kersting note, coextensive with the domain of the morally permissible.[11]

At first glance, Fichte's definition of a right in terms of permission might not seem very compelling. There are two closely related concerns that one might have here. First, one might object that we typically conceive of a right as something *more* than a permission, even a moral permission. More specifically, one might object that to say that I have a right to do or to enjoy something is to say, not simply that I am *permitted* to do or to enjoy that thing, but that I am *entitled* that others refrain from interfering with my doing or enjoying it.[12] What is missing from Fichte's definition, it seems, is the idea that a right is an entitlement that other people refrain from interfering.[13]

Second, one might think that Fichte's definition of a right in terms of permission commits him to conceiving of rights as consisting of nothing more than what modern theorists of rights call "liberties" or "privileges." In the Hohfeldian analysis of rights, an agent, *S*, has a liberty to φ (or *not*-φ) just in case *S* has no duty not to φ (or *not*-φ). Now, such

[11] See Neuhouser 1994: 160. Kersting claims that the domain of right is "coextensive with the domain of the morally possible" (Kersting 2001: 28).

[12] This is recognized by Hufeland, who argues that the concept of a right includes, in addition to the concept of permission, the concept of an "entitlement [or authorization – *Befugnis*] to do something." Hufeland defines a *Befugnis* as "the property of an action in virtue of which others are obligated not to hinder me in the exercise of that action." Hufeland 1785: 34. See also Hufeland 1790: §§3–4.

[13] Here, I focus solely on "negative" claim rights. In the case of so-called positive claim rights, a right is an entitlement to the "provision of some good or service" (Wenar 2010: §2.1.8).

a conception of a right would not be unprecedented: it is sometimes claimed that Hobbes conceives of natural rights in this way.[14] However, as Hart points out, conceiving of rights as "naked liberties" is problematic insofar as such "rights" are consistent with extensive interference by other agents.[15] Such a conception fails to do justice to the idea that rights impose "normative constraints"[16] on the behavior of other agents. To do justice to this idea, it seems that rights must also, at a minimum, involve Hohfeldian "claims," where *S* has a claim that another agent, *O*, φ (or *not*-φ), just in case *O* has a duty to *S* to φ (or *not*-φ). The claim (or several claims) protects the liberty against interference from other agents.

We can address these concerns by unpacking Fichte's claim that we have a right to do what the moral law permits us to do because "this permission *is lawful*." To say that the permission is "lawful" (*gesetzlich*) implies that the permission can be justified or warranted with reference to the moral law. Hence, if someone attempts to prevent me from performing an action that the moral law permits, I can respond by claiming that I am *entitled* to perform the action *because the moral law permits it*. Moreover, to say that the permission is lawful is also to claim that the permission (where the action permitted may be obligatory or indifferent) is protected by a prohibition against interference. Fichte's argument for this claim relies on the claim that the moral law is the sole and ultimate arbiter of the rightness and wrongness of our actions. If the moral law's judgment regarding the deontic modality of our actions is definitive, then it must – on pain of contradiction – judge any action that would effectively countermand or override its judgment to be impermissible. Thus, actions that aim to prevent or interfere with the realization of permissions of the moral law (thereby effectively "revoking" those permissions) are prohibited by the moral law, and Fichte can therefore say that a permission invoked by me is a "*prohibition*" (*Verbot*) for you (and, indeed, for all rational agents) (*SW*, VI: 75–6; see also 73, 81). Since a prohibition against interference is equivalent to an obligation *not* to interfere, lawful permissions – and hence rights – impose obligations of non-interference on other agents. Putting all of this together, we can say that Fichte's definition of a right in general captures the sense in which a right is an entitlement that imposes normative constraints on the behavior of other agents.

[14] See Hart 1982: 173 and Rainbolt 2006: 29.
[15] Hart 1982: 173.
[16] See Rainbolt 2006: Ch. 2.

The Derivation of the Distinction between Inalienable and Alienable Rights

Having derived the concept of a right in general from the moral law, Fichte proceeds to derive the distinction between inalienable (or natural) and alienable rights. This derivation turns upon the fact that the category of the permitted comprises the categories of the obligatory and the indifferent. Fichte uses the locutions "that which is not-prohibited" (*Nicht-Verbotenen*) and "that which is merely permitted" (or "merely allowed" – *bloss Erlaubten*) to denote, respectively, the permitted and the indifferent.

Fichte claims that those items (actions, capacities, or states of the agent) that fall under the "idea" (*Inbegriff*) of that which is not prohibited by the moral law admit of a tripartite classification:

> That in our nature without which the law in it would not at all be possible, as well as that which the law actually commands, belong with that which is merely permitted (*bloss Erlaubten*) by the law under the idea of that which is *not-prohibited* (*Nicht-Verbotenen*) by the law. Consequently, we can just as well say: we have a right to be rational beings – we have a right to do our duty; as we can say: we have a right to do what the moral law permits. (SW, VI: 60)

In the first class are those features of our "nature" which are necessary conditions of the possibility of moral agency: "the conditions under which alone" we are "able to act according to duty" (*R*, 125; *SW*, VI: 12). In the "Reclamation," Fichte tells us that these conditions include "*freedom*" and "*personality* (*Persönlichkeit*)" (*R*, 125; *SW*, VI: 12). The moral law commands that we possess these conditions and it is therefore obligatory that we possess them. Since obligation entails permission, we are permitted to possess them. In the second class are those actions the performance of which is commanded by the moral law. Again, since obligation entails permission, we are permitted to perform these actions. In the third class are those actions that are "merely permitted." These actions are neither prohibited nor commanded by the moral law.

We have rights to all of the items belonging to all three classes, because we have rights to all that is permitted or "not-prohibited" by the moral law. However, Fichte notes that there is an "essential distinction" between the first two classes and the third, a distinction that is "infinitely important for its consequences" (*SW*, VI: 60–1).

The distinction concerns the nature of the permission involved. In the case of the first two classes, it is morally obligatory that I possess the relevant capacities or perform the relevant actions. But to say this is to say that I am forbidden – that is, not permitted – not to possess these capacities or not to perform these actions. I am thus permitted to possess the capacity or to perform the action and *not* permitted not to possess the capacity or not to perform the action. I therefore possess a unilateral permission. In the case of the third class, performance of the relevant actions is "merely permitted" or indifferent: I am permitted to perform the action *and* permitted not to perform it.[17] I therefore possess a bilateral permission. In the case of the first two classes, the permission flows from a command of the law. In the case of the third class, the permission flows from the "silence" of the law, and whether I perform these actions or not is a matter for my "arbitrary will" (*Willkür*), where "arbitrary will" is the bare capacity to choose from among several possible actions.[18]

The consequences of this distinction are "infinitely important" because it serves as the basis for a distinction between inalienable (natural) and alienable rights. Rights belonging to the first two classes are inalienable, and rights belonging to the third class are alienable. As Fichte puts it in the "Reclamation":

> One can say therefore that man has a right to the conditions under which alone he is able to act according to duty, and to the actions that his duty commands. Such rights can never be given up; they are *inalienable*. We have no right to alienate them.
>
> I have a right to the actions that the [moral] law merely permits (*bloss erlaubt*): but I can also not avail myself of this permission. Then I do not avail myself of my right; I surrender it. Rights of this second type are therefore *alienable*; however, man must surrender them *voluntarily*, he must never *have* to surrender them. Otherwise he would be compelled by a law other than the law in him, and this is unjust for the one who does it, and for the one who endures it when he can change it. (R, 125; SW, VI: 12, translation modified)

Fichte thus claims to have deduced the concept of a right in general and the distinction between alienable and inalienable rights from the moral law.

Fichte's deduction also furnishes us with a principle for deriving and justifying inalienable rights: if the moral law commands us to perform

[17] Kersting 2001: 28.
[18] See Neuhouser 1990: 123.

an action then we have an inalienable right to that action; if the possession and exercise of a capacity is necessary for acting in accordance with the moral law, then we have an inalienable right to possess and exercise that capacity. Hence, in the *Contribution* and the "Reclamation," Fichte derives the following inalienable rights from the moral law: the right to life,[19] the right to liberty,[20] the right to freedom of thought,[21] and the right to communicate one's convictions.[22] Having discussed Fichte's deduction of rights from morality in the *Contribution* and the "Reclamation," I now turn to the independence thesis.

The Independence Thesis

The *Foundations of Natural Right* is a treatise on the science of right or law. The task of the science of right, as Fichte conceives of it, is threefold: it must i) deduce its fundamental concept (the "concept of right"); ii) demonstrate that that concept is "applicable" to experience; iii) deduce the necessary conditions for the instantiation or "realization" of that concept in experience (where these include legal and political institutions) (*FNR*, 12; *SW*, III: 11).

To claim that the science of right is independent of the science of morality (i.e., to maintain the independence thesis) is to claim that its task can be fulfilled without appeal, either explicit or implicit, to moral concepts or principles (where these are Kantian moral concepts and principles). It is also to claim that the concepts and principles of the science of right are intelligible without reference to moral concepts or principles.

Fichte places considerable emphasis on demonstrating the independence of the "concept of right" from moral concepts or principles. This is because the concept of right plays a foundational role in the science of right, the latter constituting the "analysis" of the former (*GA*, II, 3: 404–5). Given this emphasis, my discussion will focus on Fichte's attempt to demonstrate the independence of the concept of right by providing a deduction of it that does not refer, or appeal, to moral concepts or principles. This deduction is discussed in section 2.1.

Fichte thinks that the deduction of the concept of right in the *Natural Right* entails a rejection of the deduction of right provided in the

[19] *SW*, VI: 178.
[20] *R*, 124–5; *SW*, VI: 10–11.
[21] *R*, 126; *SW*, VI: 14.
[22] *R*, 127–8; *SW*, VI: 15–17.

Contribution and "Reclamation." Although Fichte does not refer to his earlier position by name – he prefers the epithet the "usual way of dealing with natural right" – he rejects it and provides two arguments in support of this rejection (*FNR*, 13; *SW*, III: 12). These arguments are examined in section 2.2.

The Deduction of the Concept of Right

In the first section of the *Natural Right*, Fichte provides a "Deduction of the concept of right." In a radical departure from his earlier position, he now uses the term "deduction" to denote a transcendental argument. The deduction of the concept of right aims to demonstrate that the concept of right, where this denotes a specific kind of intersubjective relationship, is a necessary condition of self-consciousness. If successful, Fichte's deduction will provide a justification of the claim that we possess the concept of right.

The argument of Fichte's deduction can be briefly stated as follows. The deduction opens with the claim that self-consciousness involves the self-ascription of "free efficacy," where this is the capacity to freely form concepts of ends and to will to realize them in the world. Free efficacy, Fichte claims, is an activity whose "ultimate ground" lies in the subject and which the subject can ascribe solely to itself (*FNR*, 18–21; *SW*, III: 17–20).

As is well known, Fichte argues that the subject can self-ascribe free efficacy (and hence attain self-consciousness) only if it is summoned to manifest its free efficacy by another rational being. In issuing the summons, the other subject limits its freedom so that the subject may possess a sphere of freedom in which to act. In responding to the summons, the subject manifests its capacity for free efficacy and ascribes it to itself. Having deduced the summons, Fichte argues that the subject must "posit" itself as an "individual" or "person" (*FNR*, §4). To posit oneself as an individual is to ascribe to oneself an exclusive sphere of freedom – that is, a sphere from which other subjects are excluded. It is not entirely clear why the self-ascription of an *exclusive* sphere of freedom should be a necessary condition of self-consciousness, and one might think that there is a lacuna here. However, as I understand Fichte's argument, this self-ascription is necessary because the summons, although it elicits the manifestation of free efficacy that is necessary for self-consciousness, conflicts with the requirement that the subject ascribe to itself an activity whose "ultimate ground" is located in the subject (*FNR*, 18, 39; *SW*, III: 17, 41). This is so because the subject's awareness that its manifestation of its free efficacy is a response to, and dependent upon, the free activity of the summoner, leads it to locate the ultimate ground of its free efficacy in the other subject as well as in itself. If the subject is to regard itself as the ultimate ground of its free efficacy, it must separate its free activity from that of the summoner. The subject does this, Fichte claims, by self-ascribing a sphere of freedom in which it alone can act (*FNR*, 40; *SW*, III: 41–2).

The subject can ascribe an exclusive sphere of freedom to itself only if it possesses such a sphere, and this is possible only if the other subject undertakes not to overstep the limits of its sphere. That is, the subject's self-ascription of an exclusive sphere of freedom is directly dependent on the free activity of the other subject. This means that the subject's positing of itself as an individual is not simply an act of "theoretical" awareness in which the subject apprehends a pre-existing characteristic of itself. Because the subject's possession of an exclusive sphere is dependent on the will of the other subject, the subject's positing of itself as an individual contains a normative "demand" (*Anforderung*) addressed to the other subject: the demand that it limit its freedom in accordance with its concept of the subject's freedom. As Fichte puts it, "This demand upon the other is contained in the act of positing myself as an individual" (*FNR*, 48; *SW*, III: 52). This demand (which could be regarded as a prototypical rights-claim) will be addressed to any other subject whom the subject might encounter.

The individual demands that the other subject limit its freedom so that it can possess an exclusive sphere of freedom. The other subject issued the summons – and limited its freedom so that the subject might act – because it "recognized" the subject to be a *potentially* rational being. It will be rationally compelled to continue to treat the subject as a rational being only if the subject acts in a way that demonstrates that it *actually* is a rational being. But a rational being is a being that limits its freedom in consequence of recognizing another rational being (*FNR*, 42; *SW*, III: 44). Consequently, if the subject does not limit its freedom, the other subject will be warranted in encroaching on its sphere of freedom (because it will have no conclusive evidence for thinking that the first subject is a rational being and should be treated accordingly). Similarly, if the other subject should cease to restrict its freedom, the first subject will be warranted in encroaching on its sphere of freedom. A subject will recognize another subject and treat it accordingly only if it is recognized by that other subject and treated accordingly; consequently, recognition, if it is to occur at all, must be mutual.

The upshot of Fichte's transcendental argument is that any subject who interacts with other subjects necessarily posits itself as an individual, and thereby implicitly demands of any subject with whom it interacts that it recognize it by restricting its freedom. The other subject will accede to this demand only if the first subject recognizes it, and vice versa. If the demands of individuals are to be satisfied, they must stand in a relationship of mutual recognition. This relationship of mutual recognition is the concept of right. From it, Fichte derives the law of right: "limit your freedom through the concept of the freedom of all other persons with whom you come in contact" (*FNR*, 10; *SW*, III: 10; see also *FNR*, 14, 49, 82, 102, 109; *SW*, III: 14, 52, 89, 112, 120). As Alain Renaut points out, the law of right merely makes explicit what is implicit in the concept of right.[23]

Now, it is not immediately obvious how the concept of right is related to the concept of a natural right. Fichte appears to have deduced something very different from the natural or inalienable rights that he deduced in the *Contribution* and the "Reclamation." And if that is the case, one might think, *pace* Fichte, that there is no real conflict between the two deductions. How, then, is the concept of right related to the concept of a natural right? The answer to this question is provided by Fichte's account of "original rights" in the "Deduction of Original Right." There, Fichte deduces a set of "original rights" as necessary conditions of "personality" or "individuality." His argument, very roughly, is that original rights protect the perimeter of an individual's sphere of freedom (thereby guaranteeing the individual's exclusive possession of it) and enable it to effectively realize its freely chosen ends. Fichte's original rights are the right to the "continued existence of the absolute freedom and inviolability" of one's body and the "right to the continued existence of our free influence within the entire sensible world" (*FNR*, 108; *SW*, III: 119). These rights are clearly similar in kind to the natural rights derived in the *Contribution* and the "Reclamation." However, as we shall see in the next section, they differ from them in one crucial respect.

Fichte claims to have deduced the concept of right independently of the concept of the moral law or any moral concepts (*FNR*, 50; *SW*, III: 54). This claim seems plausible. The concept of free efficacy is not a moral concept; it denotes simply the human being's capacity to choose and will freely, a capacity which, while it may result in moral or immoral volitions or actions, is itself morally neutral. The concept of right is concerned

[23] Renaut 1986: 351.

solely with the publicly observable behavior of agents and not with the quality of their motivation (*FNR*, 42–3, 51; *SW*, III: 44–5, 55). Although one might be tempted to interpret the relation of recognition as a moral relationship (perhaps in terms of Kant's "Formula of Humanity"), Fichte argues that within the domain of right the requirement that subjects recognize one another is a requirement, not of morality, but of "theoretical consistency" (where theoretical consistency governs both thought and action). In other words, having identified something as a member of the class rational being, and knowing (in my own case) that members of this class are to be treated in a certain way, I am rationally compelled – on pain of contradiction – to treat that being in a certain way (*FNR*, 69, 79–80; *SW*, III: 74, 86). Of course, in Kantian ethics there is an intimate connection between consistency and morality. However, as Fichte rightly points out, although consistency is a necessary condition of morality, it is not sufficient: one might be a "thoroughly consistent villain" (*FNR*, 11, n. f. *SW*, III: 11, n. *).

The Rejection of the Dependence Thesis

Fichte's claim that the concept of right (and the law of right deriving from it) is derivable without recourse to moral concepts or principles seems plausible. However, he now needs to rule out the competing "deontic" deduction of right which he advanced in his earlier works (i.e., he needs to rule out the "dependence thesis"). His two arguments in support of the claim that the concept of right is *not* derivable from the concept of the moral law rely on the claim that the "law of right" and the moral law possess characteristics which make such a deduction impossible. To understand Fichte's arguments, a discussion of these characteristics is necessary.

Fichte claims that the law of right tells an agent what she ought to do ("limit your freedom," etc.) if she wishes to live in a community with other free beings. It specifies the means to an end and obligates an agent *only if* she wills that end. It does not itself command the agent to will that end; that, Fichte claims, is a matter for the individual's "arbitrary will." The law of right is clearly, although Fichte does not say so explicitly, a hypothetical imperative.[24] But that means that the law of right cannot be the moral law, because the moral law is a categorical imperative – an

[24] See Druet 1975: 62. Fichte does say that the law of right has "hypothetical validity" (*FNR*, 82; *SW*, III: 89).

imperative that binds unconditionally, irrespective of whether an agent wills the relevant end.

Fichte also claims that the law of right, unlike the moral law, is a "permissive law" (*FNR*, 13–14, 83, n. a; *SW*, III: 13, 90, n. *). This characteristic is closely related to the first. Fichte borrows the term "permissive law" from Kant, but alters its meaning. A permissive law, as Fichte defines it, is a law that has restricted validity, it is "limited only to a certain sphere." A permissive law determines the restricted sphere to which it applies and, in so doing, "simultaneously determines the sphere to which it does not apply; it explicitly holds itself back from saying anything about this sphere and making prescriptions with respect to it" (*FNR*, 82–3; *SW*, III: 89–90). Actions falling within this latter sphere are indifferent or merely permitted: we are permitted to perform them and permitted not to perform them. Within this latter sphere we may act – absenting any other law – according to the dictates of our arbitrary will. Fichte claims that the limited character of a permissive law "manifests itself in the fact that it is conditioned" (*FNR*, 13–14; *SW*, III: 13). A permissive law is limited because it holds only under certain conditions – it has only "hypothetical validity." A permissive law, in other words, is a hypothetical imperative.

The law of right is a permissive law. It prohibits only those actions that might interfere with the freedom of others and make peaceful coexistence impossible. It permits us to perform and not to perform any action that does not violate the freedom of others.[25] Fichte claims that a right "follows from a merely permissive law" because a right is "clearly something that one can avail oneself of or not" (*FNR*, 13; *SW*, III: 13).[26] This is because a right contains a bilateral permission (i.e., one can "avail oneself or not" of a right because it contains a permission to φ and a permission to *not*-φ). By contrast, Fichte claims that the moral law is not a permissive law:

> The moral law is not of this kind. It does not posit a particular sphere for itself, but governs (*gebietet über*) all acts of rational spirits. (*FNR*, 83, n. a; *SW*, III: 90, n. *)

Fichte's claims about the characteristics of the law of right and the moral law represent a departure from his early position in two respects. First, Fichte's claim that a "right is clearly something of which one can avail

[25] "According to the law of right, the person's freedom is limited by nothing but the possibility that others outside him can also be free and have rights. According to that law, a person is supposed to be permitted to do anything that does not infringe upon the rights of another, for the person's right consists precisely in this permission" (*FNR*, 94; *SW*, III: 101).

[26] See also *RPP*, 314–15; *SW*, VIII: 429.

oneself or not" is a rejection of his earlier account of the concept of a right and of the distinction between alienable and inalienable rights. As we saw, Fichte distinguished between alienable and inalienable rights in terms of the permission involved: alienable rights contained a bilateral permission; inalienable rights contained a unilateral permission. Fichte now claims that *all* rights – whether alienable or inalienable – contain a bilateral permission.[27]

Second, Fichte's concept of the moral law has undergone considerable revision. In the *Contribution* and the "Reclamation," the moral law *is* a permissive law. It is a law with a restricted sphere of applicability insofar as some actions are morally indifferent. It is "silent" about these actions and it is in virtue of this silence that agents possess a bilateral permission to perform them and not to perform them. Fichte now claims that the moral law is never silent: the moral law "governs *all* acts of rational spirits" (my emphasis); it "commands unconditionally and thereby extends its reach to everything" (*FNR*, 13–14; SW, III: 13). This is equivalent to the assertion that there are no morally indifferent actions. This conception of the moral law is not a momentary aberration on Fichte's part: he explicitly endorses it in the 1798 *System of Ethics*.[28] On the basis of these revised characterizations of the concept of a right and of the moral law, Fichte argues that the law of right cannot be derived from the moral law:

> A right is clearly something that one can avail oneself of or not. Thus a right follows from a merely permissive law, and it is a permissive law because it is limited only to a certain sphere, from which it can be inferred that outside the sphere of the law one is free from it, and if there is no other law concerning the object, one is generally left solely to one's own arbitrary choice (*Willkür*). This permission is not explicitly contained in the law; it is merely inferred from an interpretation of the law, from its limited character. The limited character of a law manifests itself in the fact that it is conditioned. It is absolutely impossible to see how a permissive law should be derivable from the moral law, which commands unconditionally and thereby extends its reach to everything. (*FNR*, 13–14; *SW*, III: 13)[29]

What are we to make of this argument? According to Neuhouser, Fichte's claim cannot be that it is "conceptually impossible to derive permissibility

[27] In the *Natural Right*, our "original rights" are inalienable since they are the conditions of personality. Neuhouser in *FNR*: xix–xx.

[28] *SE*, 148, 253; SW, IV: 155–6, 264. Fichte also endorses this conception of the moral law in the 1795 draft of a review of recent theories of natural right. See *GA*, II, 3: 405. See Neuhouser 1994: 179–80, n. 28.

[29] See also *FNR*, 83, n. a; *SW*, III: 90, n. * and *RPP*: 314–15; *SW*, VIII: 429.

as such from a categorical ought" since such a derivation is possible.[30] This is so, Neuhouser contends, even on Fichte's revised conception of the moral law, according to which "morally speaking, there are no merely permissible actions," since "it is logically possible to derive mere permissibility from a categorical ought."[31] If Neuhouser is using the term "mere permissibility" to denote "indifference,"[32] I would suggest that he is mistaken. On Fichte's revised conception of the moral law, every action is either obligatory or prohibited (this is equivalent to the claim that there are no morally indifferent actions). To say that an action or state of affairs, *p*, is "merely permitted" or indifferent is to say that *p* is permitted and *not-p* is permitted. Now, if *p* is obligatory, then *p* is permitted but *not-p* is *not* permitted. Consequently, if *p* is obligatory, it cannot – on pain of contradiction – be indifferent.

Fichte's claim, stated precisely, is that it is impossible to derive a law that declares some actions to be indifferent – a permissive law – from a law that declares no actions to be indifferent (because it declares every action to be either obligatory or prohibited). Put differently, but equivalently, Fichte's claim is that it is not possible to derive a law that furnishes bilateral permissions from a law that furnishes only unilateral permissions. This claim seems highly plausible. Consequently, Fichte's conclusion that the derivation of the law of right from the moral law is impossible is warranted.

However, one might think that this conclusion is purchased at the price of plausibility. For, as we have seen, it relies upon the claim that the moral law is "never silent," that is, that there are no morally indifferent actions. This means that the moral law declares every action that I (intentionally) perform to be either obligatory or prohibited. At first glance, this claim might be thought implausible on the grounds that it requires us to consider actions which we ordinarily regard as too trivial to warrant moral appraisal (e.g., brushing one's teeth; combing one's hair) to be obligatory or prohibited. The appearance of implausibility is not removed by citing contexts or situations in which these actions would be judged to be obligatory or prohibited (e.g., the situation in which I blithely continue to brush my teeth while someone chokes to death in the next room).[33] This is

[30] Neuhouser 1994: 172.
[31] Neuhouser 1994: 179–80, n. 28.
[32] That Neuhouser is using the term in this way is suggested by his reference to Fichte's *System of Ethics*. See Neuhouser 1994: 180, n. 28. See also *SE*, 253; *SW*, IV: 264.
[33] The example is from Scheffler, who uses it to argue for the claim that the assessment involved in judgments of triviality is indistinguishable from moral assessment. Scheffler 1994: 23, 24. Scheffler's argument does not affect the point made here.

because Fichte's position seems to require, not merely that certain actions *would* be judged to be obligatory or prohibited in certain extraordinary contexts, but that they *are* judged to be obligatory or prohibited as they occur in the circumstances of ordinary life. And this will strike many of us as implausible. A complete defense of Fichte's argument would have to show either that this is not a requirement of his position or, if it is, that it is not as implausible as it seems.[34]

Because it relies on the claim that there are no morally indifferent actions, Fichte's argument is problematic. However, it is not, *pace* Kersting,[35] his only argument in support of the claim that the law of right is not derivable from the moral law. Fichte also argues that the law of right cannot be derived from the moral law because the former often permits actions that the latter prohibits (*FNR*, 50; *SW*, III: 54). This argument relies upon the uncontroversial observation that there is often a conflict between the legitimate exercise of a right and what morality demands. Thus, I am quite within my rights to reduce someone to penury by insisting on the repayment of a loan, even though doing so is prohibited by the moral law.[36] In such cases, the law of right declares an action to be indifferent that the moral law prohibits. Now, if we were to derive the law of right from the moral law, we would be committed to the claim that the moral law could both prohibit an action and declare it to be indifferent. In other words, we would be committed to the claim that the moral law could legislate *inconsistently*. Since Fichte considers consistency to be a necessary (albeit, not sufficient) condition of morality, the moral law would not be a moral law. We can avoid thinking of the moral law as "at odds with itself" if we attribute the conflicting demands to independent legislative authorities: the moral law, on the one hand, and the law of right, on the other.[37]

This second argument does not rely upon the problematic claim that the moral law determines all actions to be either obligatory or prohibited. It is therefore a good deal more plausible than the first argument.

[34] For an interesting discussion of the relevant issues, see Nease 2002.

[35] Kersting 2001: 29.

[36] For a different example, see Neuhouser 1994: 173.

[37] It is perhaps worth noting that this argumentative strategy is anticipated in the *Contribution*. There, Fichte argues from the claim that there can be a conflict between the "advice" (*Rath*) of prudence and the demands of morality – one commanding or merely permitting what the other prohibits – to the claim that the "tribunals" of prudence and morality are independent of each other. See *SW*, VI: 73.

The Independence Thesis and the Separation Thesis

I have reconstructed Fichte's independence thesis and his arguments in support of it using the language of analytic jurisprudence and deontic logic. In doing so, I hoped to reveal the sophistication of Fichte's reflections on the nature of legal and moral concepts and principles and on the conceptual relationships between them. In this concluding section, I would like to take a broader view of Fichte's independence thesis by considering it in relation to a fundamental debate within legal theory – the debate between natural law theory and legal positivism. I hope to show that Fichte's independence thesis occupies a distinctive position in that debate.

Several commentators have attempted to situate Fichte's philosophy of right in relationship to the debate between natural law theory and legal positivism. Hence, Michel Villey and Christophe Laudou both argue that Fichte is a seminal figure in the development of legal positivism.[38] Renaut disagrees, arguing that, despite the striking affinities between Fichte's conception of an autonomous science of right and the positivist Hans Kelsen's project of a "pure theory of law" (*reine Rechtslehre*), Fichte's account of the "legal sphere" is free "from any positivism."[39]

One obvious difficulty facing any attempt to situate Fichte's independence thesis in the legal positivism–natural law debate is that characterizations of the competing positions diverge widely. To steer a course through this debate, I will focus on a thesis the endorsement and rejection of which are often taken to be definitive, respectively, of legal positivism and natural law theory: the "Separation Thesis."[40] This thesis, which is associated with the legal positivism of Hart, contends that there is no "necessary connection" between law and morals.[41]

The separation thesis appears to be fairly straightforward. However, this appearance is deceptive. As Klaus Füßer has argued, discussions of the separation thesis have tended to vacillate between, or run together, two distinct separation theses. The first is a "meta-level" thesis, which concerns legal *concepts* and *theories*. This thesis – which Füßer calls the "Neutrality Thesis" – stipulates that "the definition of the concept of law should be

[38] For a brief account of Villey's interpretation, see Renaut 1986: 120, n. 13, 227. Laudou 2008: §§4–5.

[39] Renaut 1986: 250.

[40] Alexy 2002: 3: "All positivistic theories defend the *separation thesis*"; Beyleveld and Brownsword 1986: 8: "rejection of the Separation Thesis defines Natural-Law Theory."

[41] Hart 1958: 593.

morality-free," that is, that moral concepts or principles should play no role in the definition of the concept of law and cognate concepts.[42] The second thesis is an "object-level" thesis which concerns the *objects* picked out by the definition of the concept of law, namely, laws, legal systems, and legal institutions. This thesis – which Füßer calls the "Fallibility Thesis" – holds that there is no necessary connection between the objects of a legal theory and "moral values" or requirements. It is encapsulated by Hart's claim that "it is in no sense a necessary truth that laws reproduce or satisfy certain demands of morality."[43]

The decisive issue in the dispute between legal positivists and natural lawyers concerns whether the Fallibility Thesis is true. However, the Neutrality Thesis has played an important role in the debate because, as Füßer points out, positivists such as Kelsen and Hart have tended to regard the Fallibility Thesis as a "corollary" of the Neutrality Thesis.[44] Although this might seem a reasonable assumption, Füßer argues that it is incorrect. If one endorses the Neutrality Thesis, then the objects picked out by one's morality-free concept of law will be "amoral" insofar as the properties that are essential to them *qua* legal objects are not moral. However, this need not entail a commitment to the Fallibility Thesis. For one might argue that the relevant properties necessarily possess moral value "in the light of a moral principle," where this is a necessarily binding "ultimate moral principle" (candidates for such a principle would presumably include Kant's categorical imperative).[45] Such a moral principle would "[link] positive moral conclusions to the set (or a subset) of necessary amoral features of legal objects."[46] The upshot of this is that a commitment to the Neutrality Thesis need not entail a commitment to the Fallibility Thesis; in other words, one could be a "meta-level" legal positivist *and* an "object-level" natural lawyer.

Füßer's analysis provides an illuminating map of the debate between legal positivism and natural law theory. Where should we locate Fichte on this map? As we have seen, Fichte claims that the fundamental concepts and principles of the science of right should be derived independently of moral concepts or principles; he also claims, plausibly, to provide such a derivation. Indeed, it is interesting to note, in this connection, that Kersting uses the very same term to describe Fichte's method as Füßer uses

[42] Füßer 1999: 121.
[43] Hart cited in Füßer 1999: 121.
[44] Ibid. 121, n. 10.
[45] Ibid. 124.
[46] Ibid. 123.

to describe the Neutrality Thesis: "morality-free."[47] The content of the concepts and principles derived by Fichte's arguments is also "morality-free": the concept of right is not a moral concept; the law of right is not a moral principle; the criterion for evaluating action and the principle of obligation in the domain of natural right is not the categorical imperative, but "theoretical consistency" (*FNR*, 44–5, 69; *SW*, III: 47–8, 74). It therefore seems that Fichte endorses the Neutrality Thesis. If this is correct, he can be described as a "meta-level" legal positivist.

What is Fichte's position on the "object-level"? Does he accept the Fallibility Thesis? Although I think that there are several considerations in favor of a negative answer to the latter question, I will restrict myself to two related points. The first point is that although the laws and institutions derived by Fichte's theory of right (and consequently the laws and institutions that are picked out by that theory) do not derive their legal legitimacy or validity from the moral law and do not rely on the "good will" of participants in the legal system, they function in a way that satisfies certain moral requirements (*FNR*, 50; *SW*, III: 54). Thus, Fichte says that the law of coercion and the institutions that support it function to ensure that agents perform actions that they would perform if they had "thoroughly good will[s]" (*FNR*, 125, 127; *SW*, III: 140, 142). The second point concerns the relationship between the moral duties derived in Fichte's moral theory (as outlined in the *System of Ethics*) and the legal rules and institutions derived in his theory of right. What is noteworthy about this relationship is that the *System of Ethics* derives duties which either correspond to, or require us to establish and act in accordance with, several of the rights, rules, and institutions that are derived in the *Natural Right*. Thus, to take but one example, the *System of Ethics* derives the duty to institute the right to private property (*SE*, 279; *SW*, IV: 292). Moreover – and this is crucial – the *System of Ethics* derives the moral duty to live in a community and thus to act in accordance with the law of right (it therefore provides a "new sanction" for the law of right) (*SE*, 223; *SW*, IV: 234–5; *FNR*, 10–11, 50; *SW*, III: 10, 54). In light of these two points, we can say that although the rules and institutions belonging to the domain of right might be described as "amoral" insofar as they are not moral rules or institutions and do not presuppose or rely on the capacity of agents to act morally, they satisfy certain requirements of morality and have, to use Füßer's phrase, moral value "in the light of a moral principle."

[47] Kersting 2001: 25.

This suggests that there is an intimate connection between law and morality as Fichte conceives of them. But is this connection a "necessary" one? According to Hart, legal positivism can accommodate certain kinds of necessary connection between the rules of a legal system and moral requirements.[48] What is needed to defeat the Fallibility Thesis is a connection that is "metaphysically necessary" – that is, which obtains in every possible world in which there are human beings.[49] Now, I think that one can interpret Fichte as attempting to establish this kind of necessary connection. The *Natural Right* and the *System of Ethics* use transcendental arguments to derive the requirements of right and the requirements of morality as necessary conditions of human subjectivity. Since it is often thought that the necessity transcendental arguments seek to establish is "metaphysical necessity" (i.e., they seek to show that X is a necessary condition of the possibility of Y in every possible world),[50] we can interpret Fichte as attempting to show that these two sets of requirements and any connections between them will obtain in any possible world in which there is human subjectivity.

If these considerations are plausible, we can tentatively conclude that Fichte rejects the Fallibility Thesis and is a natural lawyer at the object-level. But this would mean that Fichte occupies a distinctive position in the jurisprudential landscape: he is a "metal-level" legal positivist and an "object-level" natural lawyer. This position is intriguing because it argues from premises that are congenial to legal positivism to a conclusion that is congenial to natural law theory. Whether it is also viable is a topic for another paper.

[48] See his comments on the "minimum content" of natural law in Hart 1961: Ch. 6, Sec. 2.

[49] Füßer 1999: 128.

[50] Stern 1993: 3.

CHAPTER 4

Deduction of the Summons and the Existence of Other Rational Beings

Allen W. Wood

> The most striking demonstration of the incompleteness of Kant's critical philosophy is that Kant never provided an explanation of how I come to assume that there are rational beings outside of me.
> – J. G. Fichte (*WLnm*, 303; *GA*, IV, 2: 142)

In the *Critique of Pure Reason*, Kant attempts to provide a transcendental grounding for a number of different claims he regards as essential to the cognition of empirical common sense and natural science, for example, the existence of empirical objects that are material substances, whose states are related by necessary connections of cause and effect, and whose existence is distinct from that of our subjective representations through which they are cognized (*CPR*, A 176–218/B 218–65, B 274–9, cf. B xxxix–xli n). More specifically, Kant provides a complex argument in several stages regarding the concepts involved in such objects. First, he provides a *metaphysical deduction* of these concepts, showing their source: their a priori origin in the judging activity of our understanding (*CPR*, A 66–83/B 91–116). Next he provides a *transcendental deduction* of these concepts, answering the *quaestio quid iuris* about them by showing that we *have the right* to apply them to empirical objects: that they necessarily apply to any objects that come before our senses (*CPR*, A 92–130/B 124–69). Third, he offers a *schematism* of them, indicating how their instances may be recognized in experience (*CPR*, A 137–47/B 176–87). And finally, he shows how these concepts apply to empirical objects, offering proofs of the principles already cited above, grounded on the necessity of time-determination (of their being an objective fact of the matter about the duration, succession, and simultaneity of events occurring in time).

However, Kant never offers any *transcendental* argument concerning the existence or cognizability of the mental states of other rational beings. It is not that the existence of a plurality of rational beings, or the possibility of their mutual interaction, is not important to the critical philosophy. On the contrary, Kant frequently stresses the importance of the free rational communication of a learned public as the condition for the very existence of reason itself (*CPR*, A xi n., A 738/B 766; *WE*, 8: 33–42; *OT*, 8: 143–6; *CF*, 7: 27–9); the concept of a community of rational beings, a "realm of ends," is fundamental to his moral philosophy (*GW*, 4: 433–5), as well as to his conception of reflective judgment and aesthetic experience (*CJ*, 5: 291–303). Kant appears to regard the necessity of rational communication as a merely empirical condition of reason, just as our cognition of the existence and mental states of others is grounded merely on experience and lacks any transcendental necessity.

But is Kant's position self-consistent? That is what Fichte means to call in question. Kant holds that "objective validity and necessary universal validity (for everyone) are therefore interchangeable concepts; and although we do not know the object in itself, nonetheless, if we regard a judgment as universally valid and hence necessary, objective validity is understood to be included" (*P*, 4: 298). If this is so, then transcendental proof of the objective validity of the concepts of empirical object, substance, and cause should also include a transcendental proof of the intersubjective validity of these concepts, just as the *a priori* validity of morality and aesthetic judgment would seem to make the same demand. Fichte also argues that Kant's transcendental unity of apperception, which appears to be both a transcendental condition for the possibility of experience and the thought of an individual I, must rest on a confusion if so understood: "Nor can Kant understand by this pure apperception the consciousness of our individuality, or confuse the one with the other; for consciousness of individuality is necessarily accompanied by another consciousness, that of a *Thou* (*du*), and is possible only on this condition" (*SK*, 49; *SW*, 1: 476).

It is clear from early on that Fichte intends his *Wissenschaftslehre* to include a demonstration of the existence of other I's as a transcendental condition for the self-positing of the I. As he puts it in the *Foundations of the Entire Wissenschaftslehre* of 1794, "No Thou (*du*), no I; no I, no Thou" (*SK*, 172–73; *SW*, I: 189). In the popular lectures Fichte gave at the same time, the intent of giving a transcendental (not merely an empirical) justification for the existence of other I's – supplying an answer to the *quaestio quid iuris* – is even clearer:

> The most experience can teach is that there are effects, which resemble the effects of rational causes. It cannot, however, teach us that the causes in

> question actually exist as rational beings in themselves. For a being in itself is no object of experience.
>
> We ourselves first introduce such beings into experience. It is we who explain certain experiences by appealing to the existence of rational beings outside ourselves. But *with what right* do we offer this explanation? The *justification* needs to be better demonstrated before we can use this explanation. (*EPW*, 154; *SW*, VI: 303)

Fichte's Synthetic Method of Transcendental Philosophy

In order to see how Fichte intends to provide a transcendental argument for the existence of other I's, we need first to understand his creative transformation of the method of transcendental philosophy he inherited from Kant. Although Fichte's *Wissenschaftslehre* went through many transformations during the twenty or so years he devoted to it, and seems never to have reached a final or complete form, there are certain features of his transcendental philosophy developed during his Jena period that seem particularly striking, and especially applicable to the transcendental deduction of the existence of other rational beings.

The *Wissenschaftslehre* is conceived by Fichte as a science, and even as the science which is fundamental to all the others: the science of science as such (*EPW*, 106; *SW*, I: 45). Every science, Fichte claims, is grounded on a single first principle; every science other than the *Wissenschaftslehre* derives its first principle from the *Wissenschaftslehre* (*EPW*, 104; *SW*, I: 41–2). As for the first principle of the *Wissenschaftslehre* itself, Fichte's position seems to have altered somewhat during his Jena period (and even more afterward, though here these further developments will not concern us). In 1793–4, he seems to have thought that it was (that the very concept of science requires that it be) entirely self-evident and beyond doubt. It must be known with certainty if anything is known (*EPW*, 107–10; *SW*, I: 47–50). Fichte seems to have thought at that time that this standard is met by the principle: "I am," or "The I posits itself absolutely" (*EPW*, 73; *SW*, I: 20; *SK*, 99, 119, 222; *SW*, I: 98, 122, 251). Yet because this principle involves absolute freedom, Fichte came to regard it as something that could be denied by the species of philosophers he calls "dogmatists," and came to see it as resting on a faith involving a moral commitment (*SK*, 8–20; *SW*, I: 425–40; *SE*, 30–3; *SW*, IV: 25–7). But the situation is complex: Fichte maintains that dogmatism cannot, as a philosophy, be held self-consistently; but the way this inconsistency favors the assertion of freedom does not permit us to regard freedom as having been proven theoretically. Belief in freedom remains a "faith," even though we have no rational alternative to it.[1]

Whatever the status of the first principle, the method of the *Wissenschaftslehre* is to proceed from it to other propositions that are known because the first principle communicates its certainty to them; these propositions, moreover, constitute a determinate series, so that the *Wissenschaftslehre* derives them in a determinate order (*EPW*, 110–11; *SW*, I: 50–1). If there are variations in this order, then they depend on the way the first principle is considered – differently in the fundamental science itself, but with variations in sciences such as natural right and ethics (*EPW*, 119–22; *SW*, I: 62–6; *FNR*, 8–10; *SW*, III: 7–9; *SE*, 20–3; *SW*, IV: 15–18; *WLnm*, 182, 295, 467–74; *GA*, IV, 3: 72, 145, 240–4).

What is most interesting, original, and important for our present topic, however, is the method Fichte developed during his Jena period for moving beyond the first principle, and providing a transcendental proof of other propositions: in particular, the existence of other rational beings. This was what he came to call the "synthetic method" (*SK*, 111; *SW*, I: 113; *FNR*, 92; *SW*, III: 99, 116–17; *SE*, 100; *SW*, IV: 104; *WLnm*, 248–9, 285, 309, 449; *GA*, IV, 2: 107–8, IV, 3: 138, 153, 228–9).

This method is based on the strategy adopted by Kant in his transcendental arguments. These arguments may be seen as showing a kind of incoherence in a conception of experience that may seem initially plausible, but is too simple or impoverished to be maintained consistently. The Transcendental Deduction of the Categories argues, in effect, that an experience that does not include objects cognized under the categories lacks the conditions of objective judgment that are necessary for the unity of apperception. The three Analogies and Refutation of Idealism depend on the idea that if we try to conceive the experienced world as one without substances whose states are necessarily connected by causal laws, then we cannot account for there being determinate facts about the temporal duration, succession, and simultaneity of events in this world. Fichte's *Wissenschaftslehre* proceeds from the self-positing and self-awareness of the I, but argues that a whole series of conditions must be met if we are to obtain a coherent conception of the I's free action. The first of these is that for the I to form a coherent self-conception, it must contrast itself with a not-I, a real world of things or objects distinct from and opposed to itself, against which its action is directed (*SK*, 102–5; *SW*, I: 101–5; *FNR*, 23–9;

[1] See Wood 2011; reprinted with minor revisions as Chapter 7 of Wood 2014.

SW, III: 23–9; *SE*, 81–2, 87–91; *SW*, IV: 81–3, 89–93; *WLnm*, 66–7, 121–38; *GA*, IV, 3: 35–46). From this point on, Fichte argues that we are threatened with a series of contradictions or incoherences that can be avoided only through the introduction of a series of concepts whose objects are required to make possible the self-awareness of the I's activity.

Apparent contradictions easily arise if we think in terms that are (as we might say) conceptually impoverished. We see this in the first move Fichte typically makes after asserting the first principle – the I's activity – and then the second, the existence of a not-I against which it acts. The I and the not-I are each required for the other, but they are opposites. The activity of the I negates that of the not-I, and vice versa. If we have only the conception of negating activity, the activity of each seems to contradict the existence (and the activity) of the other, but since these activities reciprocally condition each other, each of them seems to negate a condition of its own possibility and that yields a contradiction – the I acts, but a condition of its action (the counter-action of the not-I) renders the I's acting impossible. The contradiction is easily avoided, however, if we introduce a new concept – that of limited, partial, or divisible activity or negation (*SK*, 105–10; *SW*, I: 105–10). We can avoid the contradiction if we say that the I and the not-I limit each other by *partially* negating each other, abolishing each other's activity only in part. Each is therefore partly compatible with the other, and this compatibility offers us a common *ground* for their synthesis or reciprocal dependency. The new concept thus generated is therefore the concept of ground (*SK*, 110–19; *SW*, I: 110–22). The concept of the I's *positing* required the concept of *negation*, and the compatibility of these two concepts requires the concept of *ground*.

Fichte's synthetic method consists in generating a series of apparent contradictions or incoherences, each of which is then avoided or resolved by the introduction of a new concept that enables us to make coherent sense of what we are trying to assert. Sometimes Fichte presents the apparent contradiction as an antinomy: "thesis vs. antithesis" and considers the new concept required to avoid the antinomy as the "synthesis" of the two opposites (*EPW*, 62–3, 249; *SW*, I: 7, 337; *SK*, 112–14; *SW*, I: 114–15; *FNR*, 94; *SW*, III: 101–2; *SE*, 98–100; *SW*, IV: 102–5). It was Fichte, therefore, who invented this particular jargon: "thesis–antithesis–synthesis," which was sometimes also used by Schelling;[2] but it was studiously avoided by

[2] Fichte's actual use of the synthetic method predates its formulation as a method (or in the jargon of "thesis–antithesis–synthesis"). It is to be found already in *Attempt at a Critique of All Revelation*, where it is used to resolve threatened conflicts, for example, between moral vs. non-moral volition,

Hegel.[3] In fact, as we shall see in the deduction of other rational beings, the incoherence often does not take the form of a contradiction, but rather of a circular explanation, infinite regress, an unsolved problem, aporia, or paradox that demands a resolution; and what threatens us with a *contradiction* is then sometimes the initial (abstract) statement of the new concept needed to avoid the problem or escape the aporia. Then the resolution of the contradiction takes the form of an explanation of the paradox (the apparent contradiction) that removes the appearance of contradiction through the use of the new concept, which makes the situation at last intelligible.[4]

Any new concept that is introduced in this way, and shown to be necessary to avoid a contradiction, is thereby given (in Kantian terminology) both a *metaphysical deduction* – its transcendental origin and function has been displayed – and also a *transcendental deduction* – its objective application has been shown to be necessary, as a requirement for coherently conceiving the conditions under which the I can be aware of itself as active. The series of such concepts, and their deductions through the synthetic method, is supposed to constitute the *Wissenschaftslehre*, and also constitutes the other sciences (such as that of right and ethics) that are grounded on the *Wissenschaftslehre*. Our task here is to understand how Fichte proposes to provide a deduction of the existence of other rational beings.

The Starting Point of the Deduction

Fichte's first, most elaborate and best-known deduction of other rational beings in any of his published writings is in §3 of the *Foundations of*

impulse vs. the moral law, the law as objective vs. legislated by our own will, and moral vs. sensuous incentives in divine revelation (*ACR*, 23, 24–6, 26–7, 29–32, 39–42, 64–5; *SW*, V: 33, 35–6, 36–8, 40–2, 52–6, 79–80).

3 Fichte's synthetic method was clearly the original model for Hegel's dialectic, but Hegel deliberately avoids using the same triadic terminology, obviously in order to avoid having his dialectic associated with Fichte's method, and with Fichtean transcendental philosophy, which he does not accept in an unmodified form. Marx's only use of this jargon is in *The Poverty of Philosophy*, where he associates it with Pierre Proudhon's attempts to appropriate Hegelian philosophy; Marx intends its use to express ridicule of Proudhon's poor understanding of German idealism. All expositors of Hegel or Marx who use this jargon to present their "dialectic" are therefore telling you (without intending to) something quite significant: namely, that they are not all that familiar with the original works of Hegel and Marx, and basically, they do not know what they are talking about.

4 For example: Fichte argues that the I must act negatively on the not-I but can never abolish it. This activity, he argues, must therefore be conceived as "a causality that is not a causality"; Fichte explains the meaning of this concept by saying that it refers to a striving (*EPW*, 75–6; *SW*, I: 23–4, *ACR*, 25–6; *SW*, V: 34–7; *SK*, 230; *SW*, I: 261, *SE*, 38, 74, 116; *SW*, IV: 34, 73, 121). In this way, Fichte appropriates Spinoza's conception of conatus (striving or endeavor) (Spinoza, *Ethics*, II: P6).

Natural Right (*FNR*, 29–39; *SW*, III: 30–40). It occurs as part of the deduction of the concept of right, and its starting point is that the original I of self-consciousness is the practical I, or the I as will (*FNR*, 21; *SW*, III: 20). Fichte's First Theorem (§1) is: "*A finite rational being cannot posit itself without ascribing a free efficacy to itself*" (*FNR*, 18; *SW*, III: 17). The I is a free, self-positing act, not a thing or substance of any sort. This act, of course, does require a natural agent – the human body. Fichte regards a disembodied I (a Cartesian *res cogitans*) as incoherent, and the I's embodiment as knowable *a priori*.[5] The deduction of the concept of the body (§5), however, occurs a bit later (*FNR*, 53–8; *SW*, III: 56–61). It follows from the fact that the activity of the I must be directed against a natural or material world (§2), which must be posited along with the I (*FNR*, 24; *SW*, III: 23–4), and therefore must have a natural or material vehicle of its activity.

The I's relation to the material world is that of reciprocal interaction, it is simultaneously an acting and a being acted upon (*FNR*, 23; *SW*, III: 23). Every act of the I thus relates it to an *object* that is external to it and constrains it. This is also simultaneously a practical relation and a theoretical relation (*FNR*, 26–7; *SW*, III: 26–8). Willing and representing stand in constant, necessary reciprocal interaction (*FNR*, 22; *SW*, III: 21–2). The I's cognition of the world is a cognition of something objective, that constrains or binds it; the I's opposed activity is intuited as free, as the capacity to act in a variety of ways within these objective constraints of the material world (*FNR*, 19–20; *SW*, III: 18–19).

The I's consciousness of its activity is not merely consciousness of acts that have occurred, or are presently occurring – as though these acts took place somewhere outside the I, and it merely observed them taking place. On the contrary, they are acts of the I itself, whether it is immediately conscious of them, or they must be inferred as necessary for those acts of which the I is aware in performing them. The I must think of itself as presently performing its acts, not merely observing them. Thus we would do better to think of the I's *present* consciousness of its action as the thought not of something that has been done or is being done, but rather the thought of something that is *to be done*. This is the meaning of Fichte's important claim that the I's activity is "the *act of forming* the concept of an intended

[5] "Apart from connection with a body, [the rational being or I] would not be a person at all, but would be something quite inconceivable" (*EPW*, 147; *SW*, VI: 295.) "Experience could never teach us that we have a body. That we have a body and that it is ours is something we have to know in advance, as a condition for the possibility of experience and of all acquisition of knowledge" (*WLnm*, 340; *GA*, IV, 3: 171; cf. *SK*, 66; *SW*, I: 495; *SE*, 204; *SW*, IV: 215–16).

efficacy outside us, or the concept of an *end* (*Zweck*). At the same time, its activity is to be *related* to – i.e. posited as identical to – the intuiting [of its own activity]" (*FNR*, 20; *SW* III: 19–20). As a result, the I's activity contrasts with the objective existence of the world by perpetually changing, while the world, in contrast to its activity, is fixed and unchanging: "The I is what it is in acting, the object in being. The I exists in a state of endless becoming, there is nothing permanent in it at all; the object is as it is forever: it is what it was and what it will be" (*FNR*, 27–8; *SW*, III: 28). The claim here is not that the world is unchanging (or more unchanging than the human self), but rather that the world on which we act simply has been, is, and will be whatever it is, while by contrast the human agent must at every moment make (or re-make) itself into what it is through its free action, which could always be other that what it is, and other than what it could be. The not-I, whether undergoing change or not, is permanent in the sense that it is *inactive*; the I, however, is always active, and therefore, even when it chooses to remain in its current state, it is always in transition – always in opposition to what it is or has been, simply because, even in choosing to remain where it was, it is in a state of endless becoming, because it must at each moment make that choice anew.[6]

The freedom of the I thus also constitutes its temporality: "Since the object is posited as nullifying the I's efficacy, yet the efficacy is supposed to persist along with the object, there is a conflict here that can be mediated only through a wavering of the imagination between both these moments, a wavering through which time comes to be" (*FNR*, 28; *SW*, III: 28–9). In the present moment, the material world resists the I's activity, and yet the I's effective agency exists along with this and involves a consciousness of different possibilities regarding what is to be done. The past is fixed, but the future is always something that could be either this or that, depending on the choice of the I and on the way the world reacts to that choice. Imagination, for Fichte, is the faculty that represents a wavering between, or hovering over, alternative possibilities. Imagination is therefore the faculty through which we experience the passing of time, the difference between the fixed past, the present of what we are freely and contingently doing, and the future, which is always open to multiple alternative possibilities.[7]

[6] Compare the famous assertion of this same point by the most Fichtean of all later philosophers: "[The in itself] is what it is … Human reality [is] a being which is what it is not and is not what it is" (Sartre 1956: lxv, 59).

[7] Fichte here adopts from Spinoza (*Ethics*, II: P44S) the doctrine that temporality, freedom, and contingency are created through the "wavering" (German *Schweben*, Latin *fluctuatio*) of the

The objectivity and temporality of consciousness, together with the present moment as that in which our free agency consists in the awareness of an action as *to be done*, turn out to be the crucial premises in Fichte's deduction of the existence of other rational beings.

Deduction of the Object of Present Free Action

Every act of the I is at the same time a relation to an object and involves cognition of the object, and vice versa: every cognition of an object involves efficacious action. This is the starting point of Fichte's deduction (§3): "The rational being cannot posit (perceive and comprehend) an object without simultaneously – in the same undivided synthesis – ascribing efficacy to itself" (*FNR*, 29; *SW*, III: 30). So what is the object of the present act – the act *to be done* that takes the form of forming the concept of an end? It might seem that the answer is obvious: it is whatever material thing or complex of things one is proposing to alter by the action. Fichte's first task is to reject this answer, as based on a confusion. For the object just referred to is something that already exists, and that stands fixed and opposed to one's act, rather than being posited along with the free act "in the same undivided synthesis": "[The rational being] cannot ascribe an efficacy to itself without having posited an object upon which such efficacy is supposed to be exercised" (*FNR*, 29; *SW*, III: 30).

The fixed and existent material object on which we exercise efficacy has always arisen in a temporally prior act of consciousness, not in an act which is present and now to be done. The kind of object we are looking for must have been present then too, of course, but at an earlier moment, not at the present one. If we again think of this as an existent material object, we therefore make reference to yet another preceding moment, in which consciousness of action is presupposed, but not yet explained. The activity of consciousness at the present moment, from this point of view, is "only possible under the condition of [yet another] preceding moment, and so on *ad infinitum*. We have not found any possible moment in which we might attach the thread of self-consciousness (through which alone all consciousness is possible), and thus our task is not solved" (*FNR*, 30; *SW*, III: 31). Here Fichte

imagination. The difference, of course, is that Spinoza considers freedom and contingency to be errors of the imagination, dependent on the illusion of time as passing, whereas Fichte takes our experience of the passing of time, and along with this of freedom and contingency, as transcendental conditions of the possibility of our experience of an objective world.

seems to be using a metaphor from sewing: if we do not put a knot in the thread, it pulls through the material and no attachment occurs by means of it. Analogously, if we do not introduce the concept of a new kind of object, synthetically combined with our act to be done in the same moment, no satisfactory account of consciousness is possible. We presuppose what we are trying to explain, deferring our explanation to a previous moment, and thus to go in a vicious circle, like a needle and thread passing over and over through the cloth without ever attaching itself. Unless we introduce a new and different concept of an object, therefore, "consciousness can be explained only circularly; thus it cannot be explained at all, and so it appears to be impossible" (*FNR*, 30; *SW*, III: 30). This is the sort of *aporia* or "contradiction" that drives Fichte's synthetic method. So Fichte now introduces the abstract formula for the new concept of an object which is needed to resolve the problem:

> The reason for the impossibility of explaining self-consciousness must be canceled. But it can be canceled only if it is assumed that the subject's efficacy is synthetically unified with the *object* in one and the same moment, that the subject's efficacy is itself the object that is perceived and comprehended, and that the object is nothing other than the subject's efficacy (and thus that the two are the same). Only with such a synthesis can we avoid being driven to a preceding one; this synthesis alone contains within itself everything that conditions self-consciousness and provides a point at which the thread of self-consciousness can be attached. (*FNR*, 31; *SW*, III: 32)

We might also put it this way: The concept of an object that we need is merely the objective side of the subject's free act itself. It goes with Fichte's transcendental idealism that objects of consciousness must be viewed as necessitated by the subjective conditions of the I's action on and cognition of them: in other words, we must gain insight into the subjective aspect of the object, rather than thinking of it as a "thing in itself" (after the manner of dogmatism), something about which we can theorize and obtain cognition without considering the transcendental conditions of this cognition. But it is equally true for transcendental idealism that every subjective act must also have an objective side or aspect.

Fichtean criticism or idealism sometimes sounds like the assertion of an "I in itself," which is supposed to be as one-sided as the dogmatist's assertion of a thing in itself (*SK*, 8–12; SW, I: 425–9). But this is misleading. The transcendental idealist's assertion is not that there is an "I in itself" that has only subjectivity, but rather that we must reject the dogmatic assertion of a thing in itself that excludes subjectivity and freedom. Transcendental idealism seeks to grasp the subjective conditions of objectivity and also the objective conditions of subjectivity: "The I is by no means a subject; instead, it is a subject-object. If it were a mere subject, then consciousness would be incomprehensible. If it were a mere object, then we would be driven to seek a subject outside it – which one will never find" (*WLnm*, 114; *GA*, IV, 3: 31). What is needed to resolve the present problem is the concept of the objective side of the I's free action. But objectivity consists in being external to the subject and constraining the subject. To be free, on its objective side, is always to be limited: "There can be no expression of freedom without some expression of limitation" (*WLnm*, 287; *GA*, IV, 2: 131). What we are looking for is the concept of an object that has these features – externality and constraint – limiting the subject, while at the same time being united directly with the subject's free exercise of efficacy. What concept could this be?

Deduction of the Summons

The concept as deduced might indeed seem self-contradictory, as Fichte observes (*FNR*, 31; *SW*, III: 32). For it demands the synthetic unity – in effect, the identity – of the free *efficacy* of the rational being with some *object* of that efficacy; but an object is something that is both external to the subject and constrains it. How can this object be external to the subject's efficacy while being synthetically united with it? How could the subject's efficacy be unified with the object and also be the object? And how can it leave the subject free if it constrains the subject?

Fichte answers these questions by explaining what the deduced concept "mean[s], what is to be understood by it" (*FNR*, 31; *SW*, III: 32). This explanation introduces the concept of the summons: "The subject's free activity is posited as constrained. But this object is supposed to be the subject's free efficacy ... Both are completely unified if we think of the subject's being-determined as *its being-determined to be self-determining*, i.e. as a summons (*Aufforderung*) to the subject, calling upon it to resolve to exercise its efficacy" (*FNR*, 31; *SW*, III: 32–3).

The German word *Aufforderung* has a very broad meaning, ranging from *bitten* (to request or beg) all the way to *verlangen* (to demand or require). Somewhere in the middle is its meaning in the title of Carl Maria von Weber's *Aufforderung zum Tanz*, op. 46 (best known in its orchestration by Hector Berlioz), usually translated as "Invitation to the Dance." An *Aufforderung* is any representation of a free action, addressed to one who might choose to perform it, that in some way suggests the possible performance of this action, yet without necessitating it, since that would contradict the concept of free action. This occurs equally when we *ask* that something be done, *invite* its being done, and *demand* or *require* that it be done (so long as our demand does not carry with it a causal force that excludes its not being done).

In the *Foundations of Natural Right*, Fichte is using *Aufforderung* to introduce the concept of a specific "summons," which is a demand (*Anforderung*) to limit one's own freedom in such a way as to respect the external sphere of freedom of another. The concept of the relation between two rational beings where they mutually make this demand on each other is the concept of the "relation of right" (*FNR*, 33, 39–45; *SW*, III: 34, 41–7). But what is crucial merely to the concept of the *summons* is that it *constrains* action, yet only in such a way that the being to which it is addressed may still nevertheless choose either to act according to it or not act according to it. "Either I act in accordance with the summons or I do not act in accordance with it. If I have understood this summons, I can, of course, still decide not to act [as the summons represents]" (*GA*, IV, 2: 179; cf. *WLnm*, 355; *GA*, IV, 3: 179; *FNR*, 33; *SW*, III: 34).

Yet the summons in some way *constrains* the free action. What is the nature of a constraint on action that still leaves the agent free either to do or not do as it is constrained? I submit that a summons, in the precise sense in which this concept answers to the needs of Fichte's synthetic method at this point, is the concept of a *ground* or *reason* for doing something (for doing what we are summoned – asked, invited, required – to do). We speak of "compelling reasons," but this is hyperbole, and misleading at that. Reasons do not compel or necessitate. Leibniz was right: reasons always incline, yet without necessitating. Being asked or invited to do something gives us a *prima facie* reason to do it; if we are required to do something for a reason the element of constraint is still stronger. But we are still free to do it or not to do it, and we may or may not be inclined to do it. It constrains in a way that still leaves us free – "by determining us to be self-determining." The summons, understood as a reason or ground for an action, is united with the action that is done for it as a reason: the reason informs the action itself, and in that sense becomes identical with it. Yet the reason is also objective in the sense of being external to the action, standing over it as that which summons it. Something seen as a genuine and good reason is always experienced as outside (and in some manner authoritative over) the act with which it is also united as the reason for that act. This is also the way it constrains: a reason gives us a *ground* for a free action, but never prevents us from doing otherwise. It constrains by summoning us to determine ourselves to do the action. Even if we do not act as we are summoned, if the summons offers us a *prima facie* reason, it exercises a kind of constraint on us.

Fichte does not often explicitly describe the summons as a reason or ground, but sometimes he does: "The summons would thus contain within itself the real ground of a free decision; i.e. it would be the determining agency that intervenes between what is determinable and what is determinate" (*WLnm*, 356; *GA*, IV, 3: 180; cf. *GA*, IV, 2: 179). Will, according to Fichte, is the conscious transition from indeterminacy to determinacy – from what I could do but need not do to what I choose to do. The summons, regarded as a ground or reason for action, is the kind of constraint that can effect this transition.

In this way, the summons also serves as the ground of an *end*: "How is the concept of an end possible?" (*WLnm*, 346, *GA*, IV, 3: 174; cf. *GA* IV, 2: 173). "The end is given to us along with the summons" (*GA*, IV, 2: 177). But forming the concept of an *end* (forming an intention) is fundamental to "finding oneself," being conscious of oneself as a free agent. In this way, the summons is a necessary condition for the self-consciousness of the I: "I never find myself except insofar as I find myself summoned to act freely" (*GA*, IV, 2: 184). Therefore, "consciousness begins with consciousness of a summons" (*WLnm*, 370; *GA*, IV, 3: cf. *GA*, IV, 2: 189).

Inference to Other Rational Beings as the Cause of the Summons

Fichte explicitly distinguishes three stages of the present deduction, the first two expository and the third inferential: (1) the deduction of the concept of an object synthetically united with the rational being's free agency, the abstract concept needed to provide the objective side of free activity; (2) the determination of the meaning of this concept, as the summons; and (3) the *inference* to the *cause* of the object whose concept has been deduced, as well as to other consequences concerning this cause (*FNR*, 34; *SW*, III: 35). It is in this third stage of the argument that Fichte proposes to establish that a rational being must employ the concept of *other* rational beings, and discover such beings in its experience as a condition of the possibility of its own self-consciousness.

Before entering explicitly into this third stage, however, Fichte has also taken steps in its direction, which are indispensable to his argument. First, he has argued that the object in question must be "given in sensation, and in outer sensation, for all inner sensation arises only through the reproduction of inner sensation" – and in any case, if one were to presuppose it in inner sensation, this would again presuppose self-consciousness as actual, which would take us in the same circle from which we have just escaped (*FNR*, 32; *SW*, III: 33). And second, he insists that the objectivity of what has been deduced must have in common with all objectivity that it constitutes an *external check* (*Anstoß*) on the subject's activity (*FNR*, 32; *SW*, III: 33; cf. *SK*, 195, 203–6; *SW*, I: 218, 228–31; *EPW*, 244; *SW*, I: 331). Fichte even thinks that once we recognize the summons as a condition of self-consciousness, we must regard the object it represents as fundamental even to our experience of other objects: "The thread of consciousness can be attached only to something like this, and then this thread might well extend without difficulty to other objects as well" (*FNR*, 33; *SW*, III: 35).

We might well pause over these points. For if the summons is supposed to give us something like the concept of a reason or ground for doing something, we need to face the fact that some standard (empiricist) theories of practical reason trace all such reasons back to merely subjective or internal states of the agent – its desires, preferences, or feelings of pleasure and displeasure. Fichte's argument clearly intends to challenge these theories. Reasons must come to us from outside, often even from outside our bodies – as when the needs of another give me a moral reason to help. Mere urges welling up from our body's vitality, or conscious expressions of these in feelings are not reasons until they are taken up by me as possible grounds for action. On the contrary, reasons must be experienced as a check or constraint on such urges or feelings.

A view of reasons as external to us is, however, quite defensible. For no desire or feeling, simply as such, constitutes a reason for doing anything: it does not even possess the form of a reason. Some desires (so-called "motivated desires")[8] are themselves expressions of reasons, or responses to them; in such cases, it is these reasons, and not the desire that is properly the reason for acting. Unmotivated desires, on the other hand, naturally raise the question whether we ought to satisfy them – whether their objects are good or bad, whether the resources we have available for their satisfaction ought to be employed in that way, or in short, whether the actions we might take to satisfy them are actions we have *reason* to do. Fichte shares with some recent theories of practical reason the idea that reasons for action are properly regarded as objective facts, that all genuine reasons are "object-given."[9]

[8] This term was introduced by Thomas Nagel in his 1970 work *The Possibility of Altruism*.

[9] I am thinking of theories such as those of Joseph Raz and Derek Parfit. See, for example, Raz 1999 and Parfit 2011, esp. Volume 2. I do not mean to say that these theories agree in all respects with

The summons, however, is not merely an external fact that offers us a reason; it is a *representation* of a specific way the subject may (or may not) *act*. It is this that constitutes the basis for further inferences about the external source of the summons. The summons is a purposive action by another agent: it aims at giving a rational being a possible reason to act freely in the manner represented by the summons. Only a being with an understanding, a being itself capable of free activity for reasons, could be capable of such purposive activity: "The purposiveness of the summons is conditional on the understanding and freedom of the being to whom it is addressed. Therefore, the cause of the summons must necessarily possess the concept of reason and freedom ... it must be a free and thus a rational being, and must be posited as such" (*FNR*, 35; *SW*, III: 36). The summons requires a concept of the way I am summoned to act, and also a concept of my awareness of this, or as Fichte puts it later in the *System of Ethics*, "the concept of a concept": "I cannot comprehend the summons to self-activity without ascribing it to an actual being outside myself, a being that willed to communicate to me a concept: namely, the concept of the action that is demanded (*gefordert*), and hence a being capable of the concept of a concept" (*SE*, 209; *SW*, IV: 220–1). "Concept" is a term Fichte often uses for a *normative* representation. His point in the above claim is that when I am summoned, I am provided a possible reason – a normative representation – for doing something, in such a way that its source or cause must also be in possession of such a normative representation.

The deduction of the summons, as just presented, is at the same time both a metaphysical deduction and a transcendental deduction of the concept of *another rational being*: it shows where this concept has its transcendental origin – namely, in the synthesis required to solve the problem of the objective side of a free action – and it also shows that this concept must be applied to empirical objects – namely, in order to attach the thread of self-consciousness to the object that makes possible the formation of the concept of an end, a present intention of an action as something to be done for a reason. The remaining task is that of providing something like a Kantian *schematism* of this concept: that is, a way of applying the concept empirically. The task of determining which effects can be explained only by a rational cause is seen by Fichte as an instance of what Kant (in the third Critique) calls "reflective judgment" (*FNR*, 35; *SW*, III: 37). *Determining judgment* for Kant applies a given concept to

Fichte (far from it), but only that they also represent a rejection of the view that reasons are always constituted fundamentally by subjective facts such as desires or preferences.

its instances; reflective judgment proceeds from experiential data to form a concept that is suited to express the systematicity found in them (*CJ*, 5: 179). It is the activity of reflective judgment that leads us to form the concept of a plant or animal organism, and the inner purposiveness it exhibits (*CJ*, 5: 377–83). Analogously, we apply the concept of an embodied being whose behavior can best be comprehended by positing in it rational representations, such as the representation of a manner of acting, and that of the purposive intention of summoning another to act in that manner (*FNR*, 37; *SW*, III: 38–9).

We might think that the use of language, or at least communication, would play a role here, and it apparently does, when Fichte distinguishes the different ways that persons can influence one another (§6). Here he employs Spinoza's distinction between harder and softer, or coarser and subtler matter to draw the distinction between coercing someone and communicating with them (*FNR*, 58–68; *SW*, III: 61–72; cf. Spinoza, *Ethics*, II: P13, Post. 2, Post. 5, P40S2). A bit later in the *Foundations of Natural Right*, however, Fichte provides a more detailed schematism of the concept of a rational being, by describing a variety of characteristics which lead us to judge that something is a rational being: (1) action not governed solely by instinct, (2) the use of clothing, (3) upright gait, and acquired skills using the hand with an opposed thumb, (4) an expressive face, especially of the eye that looks back actively rather than merely passively receiving its world (*FNR*, 75–9; *SW*, III: 81–6). This list of items may at first seem whimsical, but on reflection I think we can recognize in them some deep insights. These items plainly display the influence of Kant's anthropology, and Herder's *Ideas for the Philosophy of History of Humanity*; they also anticipate the insights of later philosophers in the continental tradition, notably of Emmanuel Lévinas.

The Summons to Rational Activity as Education or Upbringing (*Erziehung*)

Fichte's deduction might seem to have proven far too much. It might seem to have the consequence that it is impossible for a rational being to act at all except in the presence of another rational being who summons it so to act. But this reaction displays a misunderstanding of the role that a transcendental condition plays in explaining how consciousness is possible. It confuses what Kant would call the *quaestio quid iuris* – our right to employ certain concepts – with the *quaestio quid facti* – how empirically we come to acquire them and be acquainted with the objects to which they apply. The summons offers us the condition for being conscious of the objective side of a free action as something we are about to perform; the claim that the summons is what makes this possible is not the claim that empirically, every free action must be accompanied by a summons.

Moreover, Fichte draws further inferences about the cause of the summons that are intended to correct this misunderstanding, and also to determine the way in which the summons, as a condition of free efficacy and self-consciousness, makes possible the experience of the I. The summons, as it issues from other rational beings, is not necessarily some particular act that must accompany each free action of a given rational being. To say that the summons must have its source in another rational being is not to say how it does so, and it leaves open the possibility that I can be summoned by others in different ways. In the *Foundations of Natural Right*, Fichte argues that each rational being, simply by recognizing every other as itself a rational agent, summons every other to restrict its free activity in such a way as to leave the one who summons an external sphere in which to exercise its freedom (*FNR*, 39–45; *SW*, III: 41–7). This mutual summoning constitutes the relation of right (*Rechtsverhältnis*) (*FNR*, 39; *SW*, III: 41). But Fichte argues that the more pervasive form taken by the summons is that influence of other rational beings by which each rational being becomes a rational being in the first place. "The summons to engage in free self-activity is what we call upbringing (*Erziehung*)" (*FNR*, 38; *SW*, III: 39). It is this that makes me into a rational being: "I become a rational being – *actually*, not merely *potentially* – only by being *made* into one; if the other rational being's action did not occur, I would never have become rational. Thus my rationality depends on the free choice, on the good will, of another; it depends on chance, as does all rationality" (*FNR*, 69; *SW*, III: 74). Fichte concludes: "It can thus be proven strictly *a priori* that a rational being does not become rational in an isolated state ... My I-hood, along with my self-sufficiency in general, is conditioned by the freedom of the other" (*SE*, 210; *SW*, IV: 221). Between rational beings who have been brought up or educated to be rational, the summons can then show itself on particular occasions, in the form of free, rational communication (*FNR*, 38; *SW*, III: 40; cf. *EPW*, 158; *SW*, VI: 308–11; *SE*, 219–22; *SW*, IV: 230–3). There can then also be reasoning to oneself, but only on the basis of capacities developed through the rational influence of others. Giving oneself a reason for acting is therefore derivative from being given a reason by others and from giving others a reason. Giving others a reason is a response to being given a reason by another, and giving oneself a reason is only an internalization, or application to oneself, of giving others a reason.

Fichte's argument here depends on something striking, and perhaps questionable: a genetic application of the transcendental deduction. Fichte is arguing that it is an *a priori* necessary condition of our self-conscious exercise of free efficacy that our actual capacity for this should have been acquired in a certain way, namely through being summoned to free activity by others. This idea may be questionable, but it is also worth taking seriously. For more generally, the concept of *education*, and of acquiring certain capacities (intellectual and moral) by being *educated*, might be held to be a necessary process of this sort. It may seem logically possible – in the thoughts of philosophers who like science fiction – that someone might acquire the capacity to speak French, or do mathematics or historiography, or to acquire the character of a wise and benevolent person, not by being taught these things through a process of communicative interaction with other human beings (through speech or writing), but rather only by taking a pill, being injected with a serum, or having one's brain stimulated in certain ways by electrodes. But the coherence of such fancies is deeply questionable. Is it only an empirical truth about available causal mechanisms that makes the learning of intellectual skills, or the acquisition of character traits, a matter of social practices of teaching, learning, and upbringing? The very concept of the capacities and traits we are talking about would seem to involve testing and feedback – seeing how other French speakers react to your speeches, how your calculations and proofs, your attempts at historical narrative, or your moral conduct, are received and reacted to by others. I do not know how to settle in any final way the question whether it makes sense to suppose these abilities could be acquired merely pharmacologically or by neural stimulation. But the present point is only that Fichte regards education or upbringing through human interaction as not merely a technical causal requisite but a transcendentally necessary condition for rational agency. This may be a controversial claim, but it is not an obviously mistaken one.

Fichte's view is that the summons is the basis for free interaction (communication) between rational beings in which their highest aim is simultaneously their own education and the education of one another. The relation of the I to the material not-I (the physical world) is one in which we aim at *subordination* of material things to rational human ends. Material things limit our freedom, and we seek to overcome the limitation. But our relation of the I to other rational beings is one that does not merely limit but also liberates us. It aims at co-ordination.

> The social drive aims at *interaction*, *reciprocal* influence, *mutual* give and take, *mutual* passivity and activity. It does not aim at mere causality, at the sort of mere activity to which the other person would have to be related merely passively. It strives to discover free, rational beings outside ourselves and to enter into community with them. It does not strive for *subordination* characteristic of the physical world, but rather for *coordination*. (EPW, 158; SW, VI: 308)

The Summons as the Ground of Individuality

"A human being," Fichte argues, "becomes a human being only among human beings … so that it follows that if there are to be human beings at all, there must be more than one … Thus the concept of a human being is not the concept of an individual, but rather the concept of a species" (*FNR*, 38; *SW*, III: 39). The summons is equally the foundation of human *individuality*. The mere concept of a self-positing I or of a rational being, even when put in opposition to the concept of an object (a material world of objects) does not yet yield the concept of an *individual* I.

In the context of the *Foundations of Natural Right*, human individuality is seen as constituted through the reciprocal summons that constitutes the relation of right. Each rational being "distinguishes itself, through opposition" from the other (*FNR*, 40; *SW*, III: 41). "The concept of individuality is a reciprocal concept (*Wechselbegriff*) … Thus this concept is never mine; rather it is … mine and his, his and mine; it is a shared concept within which two consciousnesses are unified into one" (*FNR*, 45; *SW*, III: 47–8). More generally, individuality depends on free self-making through specific free choices. But these depend on my having been summoned (brought up) to be rational, and therefore on my interaction with others:

> Properly speaking, who am I? I.e., what kind of individual am I? … I am what I freely make myself to be, and this is who I am because this is what I make of myself … Under the present presupposition, however … the root of my individuality is not determined through my freedom but through my connection with another rational being. (*SE*, 211; *SW*, IV: 222–3)

Fichte's deduction of the summons is simultaneously a transcendental argument for "other minds" and a contribution to practical philosophy, since it provides us with an account of the conditions for the possibility of practical reason. Its bold originality anticipates much that is later taken up in modern continental philosophy, in a wide variety of philosophical projects aiming at the critique of the Cartesian subject, the phenomenology of "the other," the dialogical conception of reason and the ethics of domination-free communication. All these projects can be traced back to Fichte, and also illuminated by the further study of his deduction of the summons.

CHAPTER 5

Fichte's Kabbalistic Realism: Summons as ẓimẓum

Paul Franks

The deduction of the concept of right in Fichte's *Foundations of Natural Right* is one of the most ambitious transcendental arguments ever attempted. If successful, Fichte's argument would establish not only the existence of the sensible world and of other minds but also the fundamental, normative principle of natural right. My thesis is that the major innovation in this argument – the *Aufforderung* or summons – is supposed to satisfy the desideratum that I call *Kabbalistic Realism*, which requires an adequate realism to account for the possibility of being addressed in the second person by something other than oneself, and that it seeks to satisfy this desideratum by instantiating the logic of the kabbalistic concept of *ẓimẓum*.[1]

If it seems surprising that Fichte's thought should be illuminated by kabbalah, this is for three reasons. First, the significant role of Jewish and Christian kabbalah in the history of European philosophy – especially in the seventeenth and eighteenth centuries and in particular in German Idealism – is not widely known. Second, to the extent that this role is known, it is all too often regarded as a historical curiosity with no major impact on the interpretation and contemporary renovation of German Idealism. Third, Fichte is notorious for his role in the development of virulent anti-Semitism, including his opposition to Jewish civil rights. This may be thought – quite wrongly – to preclude the deployment of kabbalistic resources in his philosophy and especially in his account of reciprocal recognition. But the interconnectedness of German Idealism is more thoroughgoing than hitherto suspected.

[1] I will not address the necessity of the desideratum for the possibility of consciousness.

The ideas in this chapter have been brewing for some time and have been discussed with many people. I am grateful to audiences in Chicago, Dublin, Tel Aviv, and Toronto, and to Ariel Zylberman, Gabriel Citron, James Conant, David Finkelstein, Eli Friedlander, Gabriel Gottlieb, Shai Lavi, Michael Morgan, Hindy Najman, Brian O'Connor, Benjamin Pollock, and Robert Stern.

What's the Problem?

Frederick Beiser has proposed a clear account of the problem addressed by the argument of the First Division of *Natural Right*:

> Fichte intends his argument [in the first section of *Foundations of Natural Right*] to be first and foremost a refutation of "egoism," the doctrine that I am the only mind in existence. But he also casts it in an even stronger role by making it his refutation of empirical idealism, the view that everything exists only in my own mind. The argument has indeed such implications: if I have to ascribe equal and independent reality to the minds of others, then I can no longer assume that everything exists only in my own mind.[2]

He situates this refutation within a general account of German Idealism as a "struggle against subjectivism."

By "subjectivism," Beiser means "the doctrine that the subject has an immediate knowledge only of its own ideas, so that it has no knowledge beyond its circle of consciousness."[3] This is surely what Kant calls empirical or material idealism, and it is easily recognizable as a Cartesian assumption shared by many early modern philosophers, who must then explain how it is possible to justify belief in a world beyond my mind, or in minds other than my own.

I could not agree more with Beiser's contention that a standard interpretation of German Idealism, and of Fichte's idealism in particular, as a variety of subjectivism or empirical idealism, is profoundly wrongheaded. I also agree that it would be much more accurate to see both the species and the particular as alternatives to subjectivism. However, in my view, Beiser concedes too much to the standard interpretation – and to a certain approach to philosophy in general – by treating subjectivism as a coherent position held by an opponent whom Fichte sets out to *refute* on his or her *own terms*. Instead, Fichte's strategy, I believe, is to develop a coherent train of philosophical thought that starts from a first principle and that proceeds in a way that entirely *preempts* subjectivism, while attending to the source of the temptation to subjectivism.

There are certainly numerous passages in which Fichte sounds like a subjectivist, as when he says that there is no escape from the circle of consciousness or representations.[4] But, as Fichte explains most clearly in his attempt to unravel the misunderstandings that had led to the accusation

[2] Beiser 2002: 341.
[3] Beiser 2002: 1.
[4] See, e.g., *EPW*, 97; *SW*, I: 11.

of atheism, he distinguishes between the use of words from the empirical or ordinary standpoint and the use of words from the transcendental standpoint.[5] Like Kant's predecessor distinction,[6] this entails that there are two uses or meanings of, for example, "representation."[7] When used from Fichte's version of the transcendental standpoint, "representation" does not mean "mental item with content." Instead, it means "mode of the positing activity of the I." To say that there is no escape from the circle of representations in this transcendental sense is not to say that there is no escape from subjectivism. It is to say that we have no cognitive access to any reality independent of the positing of the absolute I, which is *the essentially first-person activity of reason as such*, and not the activity of any particular individual as opposed to another.[8] One of Fichte's principal goals is, of course, to show that something may be regarded, from one point of view, as a mode of the positing activity of the absolute I and, at the same time but from another point of view, as independent of any particular individual I. Whether he succeeds in showing this – or whether it is correct to characterize the absolute as the I at all – is, to be sure, contested by Schelling and Hegel, and ultimately Fichte himself changes his mind on this score, which is why, in the Berlin versions of the *Wissenschaftslehre*, he stops speaking of "the I." But there can be no doubt that, even at the earlier stage of the Jena *Wissenschaftslehre*, Fichte does not intend to be a subjectivist.

Against Beiser's interpretation of the problem addressed by Fichte's deduction of the concept of right, Gabriel Gottlieb has made an important further point: namely, that "Fichte himself even acknowledges that an indulgence in questions about representational activity inevitably leads to external world skepticism … [Consequently,] Fichte does not think that we should attempt to explain representational activity alone, by which he means from a theoretical standpoint, 'within the seclusion of thought'."[9] I would add that, in this respect, *Natural Right* is a breakthrough work, making possible the second presentation of the Jena *Wissenschaftslehre*, in which a principal innovation, as Fichte explicitly states, is the overcoming of the distinction between theoretical and

5 See, e.g., *IW*, 156–76; *SW*, V: 375–96.

6 See *CPR*: A 373 on "unavoidable ambiguity."

7 In "From a Private Letter," Fichte notes that he uses all words ending in "*-ung*" to refer to vital activity and not to refer to the product of that activity (*IW*, 161; *SW*, V: 382). Although it is not the example he discusses, this must apply to "*Vorstellung*" or "representation."

8 Idealism, formulated in this way, is essentially a version of the rationalist principle of sufficient reason, along with a view that reasons are fundamentally first-personal. On this fundamental first-personal character, see Franks (forthcoming a).

9 Gottlieb 2015: 222.

practical philosophy.[10] Whereas Fichte had organized the first presentation into theoretical and practical parts, proceeding to show their ultimate unity, he assumes from the outset of the second presentation that the distinction between theory and practice – or representing and willing – is derivative from a primordial unity. This is, of course, the point of the first theorem of *Natural Right*.[11]

What, then, is the problem to which Fichte's argument is responding? Gottlieb ascribes to me the view that it is Agrippan skepticism.[12] This is almost correct. I would prefer to say that the problem is *nihilism*, which becomes a threat because of the character of the optimal *solution* to Agrippan skepticism.

The problem of nihilism is best understood, as I have argued elsewhere, through examination of Jacobi's account of Spinozism. Here, once again, I must contend with Beiser's important body of work. For an interpretation of what Jacobi calls nihilism runs through several of Beiser's books. Indeed, this interpretation is intimately connected to Beiser's conception of subjectivism and of its role in German Idealism.

In his first book, *The Fate of Reason*, Beiser writes:

> The most important point to note about Jacobi's use of the term ["nihilism"] is that he uses it to designate a specifically epistemological position. The term is virtually synonymous with, although slightly broader than, another term of Jacobi's: "egoism" (*Egoismus*). According to the early Jacobi, the egoist is a radical idealist who denies the existence of all reality independent of his own sensations. He is indeed a solipsist, but a solipsist who disputes the permanent reality of his own self as much as the external world and other minds. In his later writings, however, Jacobi tends to replace the term "egoist" with "nihilist." Like the egoist, the nihilist is

[10] See *WLnm*: 85–6; *GA*, I, IV: 17: "In the present lectures, however, the hitherto familiar division between theoretical and practical philosophy is not to be found. Instead, these lectures present philosophy *as a whole*, in the exposition of which theoretical and practical philosophy are united. This presentation follows a much more natural path, beginning with the practical sphere, or, whenever it would contribute to the clarity of the exposition to do so, inserting the practical into the theoretical, in order to explain the latter in terms of the former: a liberty for which the author was not yet sufficiently self-confident at the time that he published his *Wissenschaftslehre*."

[11] Beiser 2002: 259: "In Fichte's view the chief error of all previous epistemology, and especially that of the subjectivist tradition, is its purely contemplative or speculative paradigm of knowledge, according to which knowledge is possible apart from, and prior to, activity. For Fichte, however, knowledge is only the result of activity, and ultimately the will itself." However, this formulation appears to leave the distinction between theory or representation and practice or willing intact, while rendering theory asymmetrically dependent on practice. I take Fichte to make the more radical claim that, at its deepest level, positing is neither theoretical nor practical, although it contains the seeds of both, and that, on this deepest level, exhibited in the summons, the seed of practice precedes the seed of theory in the order of explanation, although neither can exist alone.

[12] Gottlieb 2015: 222, n.28.

> someone who denies the existence of everything independent of the immediate contents of his own consciousness, whether external objects, other minds, God, or even his own self. All that exists for the nihilist is therefore his own momentary conscious states, his fleeting impressions or representations; but these representations represent, it is necessary to add, nothing.[13]

On this interpretation, the nihilist is a subjectivist or empirical idealist who proceeds to question or reject, not only belief in the external world and other minds, but also belief in the existence of the I that Descartes took as given by means of the *cogito*. Nihilism, so understood, is an epistemological position, but it is one with ethical consequences, since one can be ethically obligated only to someone in whose existence one justifiably believes.[14]

Now, I do not wish to deny that subjectivism in Beiser's sense constitutes one strand of Jacobi's thinking about the problem of nihilism. Jacobi explicitly connects nihilism to what he had earlier called egoism, and egoism in Jacobi's early writings does indeed appear to be a radicalized version of subjectivism.[15] But there is another strand of Jacobi's thinking about nihilism, which becomes clearer when one considers the connection between his struggle with nihilism, which he first thematizes explicitly in his open letter to Fichte of 1799, and his earlier account of the specter of Spinozism. Far from regarding Spinoza as a subjectivist, Jacobi says that he is indebted to Spinoza's exemplification of realism.[16]

Agrippan skepticism is best understood as a response to the philosophical dogmatist's claim to have discovered the best way of life for a human being, within which knowledge claims are embedded.[17] Since there is a plurality of dogmatists making such claims, he or she may legitimately be challenged to exhibit the ground of his or her philosophy. The discussion may terminate – either immediately or after a while – with what is effectively a shrug of the shoulders. This amounts to a mere hypothesis or arbitrary presupposition, which is hardly adequate. Alternatively, the dogmatist may prove capable of providing answers to successive why-questions, but the answers may be such that each invites another why-question, with no prospect of the regress ever ending. This amounts to an infinite regress,

[13] Beiser 1987: 82.

[14] Beiser 1987: 82–3.

[15] See Franks 2005: 154–62 for discussion of Jacobi's subjectivist misinterpretation of Kant. See also Franks 2008.

[16] For Jacobi on Spinoza's realism, see, for example, *Concerning the Doctrine of Spinoza in Letters to Herr Moses Mendelssohn* (1785), paras. XXVII, XXIX (Jacobi 1994a: 223). Jacobi credits Spinoza with "the seminal ideas" for his realistic deduction of causality in a footnote added to *David Hume on Faith or Idealism and Realism: A Dialogue* in 1815 (Jacobi 1994b: 297, n. 25).

[17] Called after the Agrippan modes. See Sextus Empiricus 2000: 164–7.

which is also inadequate. A third alternative is that, at a certain point in the discussion, the dogmatist repeats an answer given in response to an earlier why-question. If the answer did not satisfy the demand for justification, it is hardly likely to do so now, and if the earlier token of the answer depends on the later token of the very same answer, then the dogmatist's justification appears to form a vicious circle. Properly understood, however, the challenge faced by the dogmatist is to escape what has come to be known as the Agrippan trilemma: to give a justification that is neither arbitrary, nor infinitely regressive, nor viciously circular.

As I have reconstructed it elsewhere, the master argument that Jacobi finds in Spinoza's *Ethics* is an attempt to escape from the trilemma.[18] Jacobi's contention is that Spinoza's solution is the *optimal* response to the Agrippan challenge, given the assumption on which the challenge itself is based. This contention, I have argued, is remarkably influential and marks one of the main themes of German Idealism, distinguishing it from, among other things, Kantianism. Reinhold, Maimon, Fichte, Schelling, and Hegel[19] all agree that the systematic structure of grounding advocated by Spinoza, as interpreted by Jacobi, is indeed the optimal response to Agrippan skepticism and is therefore the required structure of any adequate philosophical system.

The structure in question is what I call Holistic Monism. On this view, an adequate philosophical system must be (1) monistic in the sense that it has a unique, absolute, and infinite first principle; and (2) holistic in the sense that this first principle constitutes the unity of the totality of finite items, is immanent within that totality, and is in no sense transcendent of it. This characterization is of course, deliberately schematic, leaving open the characters of the first principle and of the finite items, as well as the proper philosophical idiom for expressing those characters and their relationship. In any version, however, there will be a sense in which the first principle is at once both "One and All."

The argument for Holistic Monism has been reconstructed elsewhere. Here, what is important is what Jacobi takes to be the consequence of Holistic Monism, however it is construed. Jacobi assumes that a genuine individual (*Individuum*) must have both an internal or intrinsic character

[18] See Franks 2005: 99–104.

[19] This requires some qualification. For example, after developing his own pioneering version of a Holistic Monist system incorporating Kantian elements, and after then endorsing Fichte's version instead, Reinhold abandons the project and becomes one of its foremost critics. From 1804, Schelling endorses the traditional kabbalistic idea that the absolute must be thought *both* as transcending the totality of the finite *and* as immanent within it.

and extrinsic relations to others. But, he argues, neither the finite items nor the first principle of a Holistic Monist system can be an individual.[20] Each finite item has no internal character, being determined as the item that it is solely by its extrinsic relations, while the first principle has only an internal character, lacking any relation to anything other than itself. Although Jacobi does not use the term "nihilism" until his 1799 open letter to Fichte during the atheism controversy, he focuses on Spinoza's incidental remark that "determination is negation" in his Spinoza book of 1785, adding remarks about "annihilation" ("*Vernichtung*") in the 1789 edition of his book, remarks that he republished in his 1799 letter. The problem of nihilism, then, as I understand it, is the problem of accommodating individuality, and it arises for Jacobi and the German Idealists, in the first instance,[21] because Holistic Monism seems both to be required and at the same time to exclude the very possibility of individuality.

Now, one of the instances of individuality with which Jacobi is principally concerned is the individuality of the epistemic and ethical agent. That is why his conversation with Lessing turns to the question of fatalism and the freedom of the will. Similarly, Fichte is concerned with the individuality of the epistemic and ethical agent.[22] In response to the threat of nihilism, Fichte's objective in the first Division of *Natural Right* is to show that his version of Holistic Monism, which construes the first principle as the absolute I, can indeed accommodate the individuality of the epistemic and ethical agent, and must do so in order to provide a grounding for the natural rights of human beings. Fichte explicitly states that the strategy of the deduction of the concept of right is to show "that the rational being cannot posit itself as a rational being with self-consciousness without positing itself as an *individual* (*Individuum*), as one among several rational beings that it assumes to exist outside itself, just as it takes itself to exist." In the *Wissenschaftslehre nova methodo*, which was to have been published

[20] Jacobi 1994a: 190, n. 3: "an absolute individual is just as impossible as an individual Absolute. *Determinatio est negatio.*"

[21] I say "in the first instance" because there are other ways, independent of Holistic Monism, in which nihilism is problematic. For example, although Jacobi himself recommends a sort of historically embedded faith as an alternative to inferentialist philosophy and hence as a preemption of nihilism, historical reflection itself can generate nihilism, as the development of historicism in the nineteenth and twentieth centuries shows.

[22] Gottlieb 2015: 218–19 says that the problem to which Fichte is responding in his deduction is "ethical skepticism." I can agree with this insofar as, in *Natural Right* in particular, as well as in *The System of Ethics*, Fichte's focus is on the agency involved in being the sort of agent who has rights and can make claims on that basis. However, I would want to set this against the more general background of nihilism as a threat to both epistemic and ethical agency. I believe that this is congenial to Gottlieb's approach, since he objects to Beiser's reading on the grounds that it does not do justice to Fichte's overcoming of the distinction between theory and practice.

in a more polished version as *The New Presentation of the Wissenschaftslehre*, Fichte undertakes to go further and to show that Holistic Monism as such *requires* individuality.[23]

Kabbalistic Realism as Desideratum

Fichte's debt to Jacobi is not exhausted by his responsiveness to the problem of nihilism. It also includes his commitment to a desideratum articulated by Jacobi, a criterion for an adequate solution of the problem. For reasons that will become clear, I call this desideratum *kabbalistic*.

In a letter to Jacobi dated August 30, 1795, Fichte expressed his sense of the proximity between their positions:

> [Your novel,] *Allwill* allows transcendental idealists to hope for peace and even for a sort of alliance [with realists], so long as idealists are content to protect their own boundaries and to make these quite clear. I believe that I have already met this condition. If I were to go even further, and were I, from within the supposedly hostile territory, to guarantee the security of realism's domain, then by rights I should be able to count upon – not merely an alliance of a sort – but upon an alliance in every respect. (*EPW*, 412: *GA*, III, 2: 393)[24]

He insists that the accusation that he is a "practical egoist" is a misunderstanding based on the conflation of the absolute I of which he spoke in *The Foundations of the Entire Wissenschaftslehre* with the individual I, and he promises a clarification in what would become the *Foundations of Natural Right*:

> Instead, *the individual must be deduced from the absolute I*, and the *Wissenschaftslehre* will immediately proceed to such a deduction in conjunction with its treatment of natural rights ... (*The conditions which make individuality possible are called "rights"*).

Clearly, Fichte understands – even prior to Jacobi's open letter of 1799 – that what is at stake is the threat of annihilation to the individual, which Jacobi will call nihilism.[25]

Fichte expresses his hope, not only for peace but for an "alliance in every respect" between Idealists and Realists, grounded in Idealism's

[23] See Fichte, *Foundations of Transcendental Philosophy*, sec. 13, titled, "The Intelligible Pure Will. The Feeling of 'Ought.' The Individual in the Realm of Rational Beings" (*WLnm*, 72).

[24] Fichte may be responding to the fourth (1792) edition of Jacobi's novel *Eduard Allwill's Collection of Letters*, and perhaps to the appended letter "to Erhard O**" (Jacobi 1994c: 484–96).

[25] For Fichte's awareness of the background problematic of Agrippan skepticism, see *Concerning the Concept of the Wissenschaftslehre* (*EPW*, 94–135; *SW*, I: 29–81).

capacity "to guarantee the security of realism's domain." This is not to be understood, I suggest, merely as the domain of relations between my mind and objects independent of my mind, a class that includes other minds. Rather, it is to be understood as the domain of *relations between the first person and the second person, between myself as an agent capable of being addressed and addressing others in the second person, and other agents capable of being addressed and of addressing me*. Another, so characterized, is more than a mere obstacle or factual limitation confronting my agency; he or she is also a *normative* limitation on my agency. For, as we shall see, this is how Jacobi characterizes the realism about individuality that would satisfy him.

Jacobi contends that, insofar as every demonstration – every maximally water-tight chain of inference – has premises on whose truth the soundness of the argument depends, and that, since the attempt to find an unconditioned premise that escapes the Agrippan trilemma leads to nihilism, the only alternative is to think of every sound demonstration as resting on premises based on a *revelation* in which one either has or does not have *faith*:

> Through faith we know that we have a body, and that there are other bodies and other thinking beings outside us. A veritable and wondrous revelation! For in fact we only sense our body, as constituted in this way or that; but in thus feeling it, we become aware not only of its alterations, but of something else as well, totally different from it, which is neither mere sensation nor thought; we become aware of *other actual things*, and of that with the very same certainty with which we become aware of ourselves, for without the *You*, the *I* is impossible.[26]

Jacobi notes immediately after this passage that, contrary to Mendelssohn's suspicion, the revelation and faith of which he speaks are not specifically Christian: "The religion of the Christians teaches another faith." He would later insist that one important source for his conception of faith is the natural belief or everyday resistance to skepticism thematized by Hume, who was not exactly known for his Christian religiosity. Similarly, the revelation of which Jacobi speaks is presumably not the revelation of prophecy or scripture, but rather the revelation of the world through sense perception. Still, there can be no doubt that Jacobi is investing these terms with at least a flavor drawn from his Pietist background.

[26] Jacobi 1994a: 231. I have decided, with some trepidation, to replace di Giovanni's accurate but archaic "Thou" with "You."

As I noted above, Jacobi influentially contends that Holistic Monism is the optimal response to Agrippan skepticism, *given the assumption on which this skepticism rests.* The assumption in question is what I call *inferentialism*: the view that the proper form of justification for a belief is inferential, consisting in a demonstration in which the belief is soundly inferred from at least one premise. In Jacobi's view, Agrippan skepticism constitutes a challenge only if one accepts inferentialism. His conception of faith is meant, not as a rejection of reason and justification, but rather as a rejection of the inferentialist conception of reason and justification.

The faith that Jacobi advocates is faith in the You, without revelation from whom the I would be impossible. One might take Jacobi's talk of "the You" and "the I" as a merely literary embellishment of the relationship between a Cartesian mind and the world given to it through sense perception. But I take it to be more: to be the expression of a desideratum for an adequately realistic alternative to nihilism. On this reading, a view that assures me of the reality of external objects, given to me in sense perception and resisting my will while sometimes yielding to it, is not enough. A genuine realism must assure me of the reality of at least one other agent, who is capable of addressing me in the second person. Such an other is not merely an object. He or she is, like me, an agent.

In the *Foundations of the Entire Wissenschaftslehre* (1794–5), Fichte uses similar language: "No You, no I; no I, no You" (*SK*, 172–3; *SW*, 189). Fichte is surely alluding to Jacobi and, once again, one might take the use of first and second person pronouns to be merely literary embellishment, especially since Fichte says nothing whatsoever in his 1794–5 work about other minds. Alternatively, one might take Fichte to be issuing a promissory note to satisfy Jacobi's desideratum *eventually* – a note redeemed, as we shall see, in *Natural Right.*

What, though, does this have to do with kabbalah? In his conversation with Lessing, Jacobi reports having expressed his own view to Lessing in the following terms:

> I took the occasion to speak in favour of the Kibbel, or the kabbalah in the *strict* sense – that is, *taking as starting point the view* that it is impossible, in and for itself, to derive the infinite from a given finite, or to define the transition from the one to the other, or their proportion, through any formula whatever. Hence, if anyone wants to say anything on the subject, one must speak on the basis of revelation. Lessing insisted on having everything "*addressed to him in natural terms*," and I, that there cannot be any natural

> philosophy of the supernatural, yet the two (the natural and the supernatural) obviously exist.[27]

I take this to be the very same view that Jacobi expresses later in the book – in the passage cited above – in terms of faith. Here, however, revelation is characterized as "the Kibbel, or the kabbalah in the *strict* sense." It was well known among Christian students of kabbalah that the word "kabbalah" had the same root as the Hebrew verb meaning "to receive."[28] I suggest that this explains what Jacobi means by "revelation." His point is not that, since the relationship between the infinite and the finite cannot be understood by means of any rational proportion or formula, it must be understood on the basis of prophecy or scripture. It is rather that the relationship between the finite and the infinite that must be understood on the basis of *the fact of second person address*. When I am addressed as You by another, this exemplifies the relation between the infinite and the finite.

In Section 5, I will return to this exemplification. For now, I want to draw attention to the remarkably prominent role played by kabbalah in Jacobi's seminal conversation with Lessing. As we have seen, Jacobi presents his alternative to nihilism, which is the inevitable result of inferentialist rationalism, as "kabbalah in the *strict* sense." But Jacobi also portrays both of the other options, between which Lessing vacillates, in kabbalistic terms as well.

The first view to which Lessing is attracted is, of course, Spinozism, which Jacobi understands as kabbalah *rendered immanent*:

> The spirit that inspired Spinoza himself ... is certainly nothing other than the ancient *a nihilo nihil fit* that Spinoza made an issue of, but with more abstract concepts than the philosophers of the kabbalah or others before him. In keeping with these more abstract concepts he established that with each and every coming-to-be in the infinite, no matter how one dresses it up in images, with each and every change in the infinite, *something* is posited *out of nothing*. He therefore rejected any *transition* from the infinite to the finite. In general, he rejected all *causae transitoriae, secundariae* or *remotae*, and in place of an emanating *ein-soph* he only posited an *immanent*

27 Jacobi 1994a: 195–6.

28 For an early statement, see, e.g., Reuchlin 1517: fol. B6r: "Mose kibel. i. Moyses audiuit et accepit legem de Sinai. Vnde Kabala dicitur ab auditu acceptio." For a statement of which the German Idealists are more likely to have been directly aware, see Brucker 1762: 2.916: "Vocatur haec philosophia Cabbalistica, quod nomen a voce Hebraea, Kibbel, *accipere* vel *recipere.*" The significance of the name, "kabbalah," is usually explicated with respect to the oral method of transmission, as in Reuchlin's explanation, but the thought articulated in this chapter is that it is equally or perhaps even preferably to be explicated with respect to the character of the content transmitted.

> one, an indwelling cause of the universe eternally unalterable *within itself*, One and the same with all its consequences.[29]

This interpretation of Spinoza's philosophy may seem bizarre today, but the idea that Spinoza was indebted to kabbalah had been a tradition for almost a century prior to Jacobi's conversation with Lessing in 1780.[30] The publication in 1677–84 of *Kabbala Denudata*[31] – a multi-volume library of translated kabbalistic texts and commentaries – had made these ideas familiar to European philosophers and had led a number of people to speculate that Spinoza, whose works were published at the same time and whose Jewish origin was a source of great curiosity, could be understood as a kabbalist. Since the twelfth or thirteenth century, kabbalists had used the term "*ein sof*" – "infinite" – to express the inexpressible: God as God is in Godself, independent of any relation to us, transcending any concept or linguistic utterance. At the same time, they emphasized that God also reveals Godself to us and interacts with us under another aspect, or rather under a complex system of aspects known as the *sephirot*. According to Jacobi and Lessing, Spinoza appropriates and transforms the kabbalistic conception of the infinite God, rendering it entirely immanent – and presumably intelligible – instead of transcendent: "The *philosophy* of the kabbalah, or so much of it as is available to research, and *in accordance with the best commentators, von Helmont the younger and Wachter*, is, *as philosophy*, nothing but undeveloped or newly confused Spinozism."[32] In Salomon Maimon's formulation, based on first-hand knowledge, "the kabbalah is nothing but expanded Spinozism."[33] Conversely, Spinozism is conceptually clarified kabbalah, shorn of ambition to transcend the bounds of reason. The result is a philosophy that characterizes the infinite and unconditioned principle of reality as *hen kai pan*: one and all, that is, both unique and at the same time entirely immanent within the whole of the finite. More precisely, it is what I characterized above as Holistic Monism.

The God of Spinozism – the immanent *ein sof* – is impersonal. Sometimes, however, as Jacobi reports, Lessing felt attracted to a personal,

[29] Jacobi 1994a: 187–8.
[30] See Franks forthcoming b.
[31] Knorr von Rosenroth 1677–84.
[32] Jacobi 1994a: 233–4. Franciscus Mercurius Van Helmont was the greatest promoter of Christian kabbalah in the seventeenth century, one of the principal motivators of *Kabbala Denudata*, while Johann Georg Wachter, in Wachter 1699, was the first to argue that there were significant affinities between Spinoza's views and those in *Kabbala Denudata*.
[33] Maimon 1792: 141.

but still immanent divinity: "Whenever Lessing wanted to represent a personal Divinity, he thought of it as the soul of the All; and he thought the Whole after the analogy of an organic body." Such a philosophy is no less committed than Spinozism to the principle that *a nihilo nihil fit*, and no less resistant to the idea of any transition from the infinite to the finite or vice versa. It draws upon the Neoplatonic notion of the world soul, which is Plotinus' third hypostasis, but eliminates the first – the transcendent One. Whether Lessing retains the second hypostasis of intellect – which has an important role in Spinoza's philosophy – is unclear. Now, the idea of the world soul had also been incorporated into kabbalah, especially within the highly Neoplatonic versions of Lurianic kabbalah developed in Italy under the influence of Israel Sarug. One of these versions was well known to European philosophers because of its translation in *Kabbala Denudata*: the *Puerta del Cielo* of Abraham Herrera, which specifies a three-level world-soul in terms of the kabbalistic structures of four principal worlds or dimensions, each of which has its own structure of ten *sefirot*: the rational soul is identified with the lowest *sefirah* of *malkhut* (kingdom, dominion) in the world of *atẓilut* (emanation), which governs the worlds of *beriyah* (creation) and *yetẓirah* (formation), respectively the sensible and nutritive souls, and this tripartite soul is embodied in the material world of *asiyah* (action).[34] If Lessing's first, Spinozistic version of the philosophy of the *hen kai pan* is an immanentization of the *ein sof*, then his second version eliminates the *ein sof* while retaining the immanent animation of the world by means of the *sefirot*, configured as soul.[35]

In short, Lessing vacillates between two positions and he characterizes both in kabbalistic terms. Meanwhile, Jacobi, who sees these two positions as equally grounded in the principle that *a nihilo nihil fit* and as equally leading to nihilism, proposes an alternative, which he also couches in kabbalistic terms, which indeed he presents as more in accordance than the other two positions with the idea of kabbalah as reception.

In Jacobi's Spinoza book, then, the philosophers who would come to be known as German Idealists were confronted with a choice between an initial triad of options, each characterized kabbalistically, and the systems

[34] For the correlation, with explicit reference to Plotinus, see Herrera 2002: Part VIII, ch. 14; Aboab 1655: Part VI, ch. 14; *Porta Coelis*, Part VI, ch. 14, in *Kabbala Denudata*, I.2, 132. For an earlier kabbalistic reference to the "soul of the world," see Fano 1648: 2a. Both Herrera and Fano were students of Israel Sarug, who promulgated a version of Lurianic kabbalah incorporating Neoplatonic elements in Italy, the Balkans, and Europe in the late sixteenth and early seventeenth centuries.

[35] For an attempt to work out a version of this option within the framework of Kant's dynamic account of matter as well as Holistic Monism, see Schelling 1798.

that they would later develop would be variations on these options – which is, of course, not to deny the innovative character of their ideas. For example, Reinhold's and Fichte's early systems may be seen as attempts to maintain the basic structure of Spinozism in a way that is compatible with individual agency, Schelling's philosophy of nature may be seen as an attempt to develop Lessing's retrieval of the Neoplatonic-kabbalistic idea of the world soul, and, in the case with which I am occupied here, Fichte's *Natural Right* and, more generally, his second Jena presentation of the *Wissenschaftslehre* may be seen as an attempt to reconcile an idealist version of Spinozism with Jacobi's Kabbalistic Realism, as I will now explain.

Vicious and Virtuous Circles

I have argued that Fichte's deduction of the concept of right is supposed to show how a Holistic Monist system, which takes the absolute I as its first principle, is compatible with the individuality of the agent required as a bearer of natural rights. In the First Theorem, he undertakes to show that a self-conscious or self-positing I must ascribe to itself two activities: a theoretical or representational activity of world-intuiting in which the I takes itself to be determined by something other than itself, and a practical or efficacious activity of end-setting, in which the I takes itself to be freely self-determining in a way that is directed at the determination of objects; and it ascribes these two activities to itself in such a way that the two activities "stand in constant, necessary, reciprocal interaction" (*FNR*, 22; *SW*, III: 21). This sets the scene for the introduction of the concept of the summons in the Second Theorem.

It is a feature of Fichte's method, both in *Foundations of the Entire Wissenschaftslehre* and in *Natural Right*, that the deduction of an *a priori* concept, a task assigned by Kant to the analytic part of a critical work, proceeds by means of the generation and resolution of antinomies and other rationally problematic or Agrippan trilemma situations that would seem to call for a skeptical suspension of judgment, a task assigned by Kant to the dialectic part of a critical work.[36] The particular problem in response to which the summons is introduced is a vicious circle arising directly from the First Theorem:

> Any act of comprehension is conditioned by a positing of the rational being's own efficacy; and all efficacy is conditioned by some prior act of

[36] Philonenko 1980.

> comprehension of the rational being. Therefore, every possible moment of consciousness is conditioned by a prior moment of consciousness, and so the explanation of the possibility of consciousness already presupposes consciousness as real. Consciousness can be explained only circularly; thus it cannot be explained at all, and so it appears to be impossible. (*FNR*, 29; *SW*, III: 30)

Note the role of chronology in this vicious circle. Each act of representation presupposes a *prior* act of self-determination to achieve an end. For sense perception ("world-intuition") is not merely passive reception. An indefinitely large amount of sensible information is available at any given moment. Only if an agent has already set him or herself an end or undertakes a project is he or she in a position to perceive certain sensible features of the world as salient. Conversely, ends cannot be framed and projects cannot be undertaken without prior information about the world. To frame an end is not merely to make a wish. Indeed, wishes too make sense only against the background of prior information. And prior information must surely come from sense perception. So there can be no self-determination to frame an end without *prior* sense-perception.

Now, this might be thought to generate, not a vicious circle, but an infinite regress, since each representational moment presupposes a prior volitional moment and each volitional moment presupposes a prior representational moment, and so on ad infinitum. Fichte formulates the problem in this way as well (*FNR*, 32; *SW*, III: 33). However, he may assume that, in light of the discontinuity between consciousness and merely natural existence, there cannot be a regress and there must be a first moment. In any event, his underlying concern is with the *explanation* of consciousness, and chronology is of interest only insofar as it sheds light on the order of explanation.

This is why Fichte can endorse Holistic Monism, which conceives the philosophical system as a virtuous circle in which the first principle grounds all other principles but cannot be thought without them, and can at the same time regard some circles as vicious.[37] While the first principle and every other component of the system are mutually conditioning, there is an irreversible order of explanation or grounding, which *must* start with the first principle. In vicious circles, such as the one encountered in the Second Theorem, there appears to be no determinate and irreversible order of explanation, which Fichte finds unacceptable. The quest for a first moment of consciousness is one way of conducting a quest for the

[37] For a helpful survey of issues concerning Fichte and circularity, see Breazeale 2013a.

proper order of explanation and, in his lectures, Fichte reformulates both the circle and its resolution via the summons in a non-chronological way (*WLnm*, Sec. 16).

In *Natural Right*, the solution is to find a moment that is at once representational and volitional, theoretical and practical, that could serve as the first moment of consciousness. Fichte's brilliant proposal is that this moment can only be thought as the subject's "*being-determined to be self-determining*, i.e., as a summons to the subject, calling upon it to resolve to exercise its efficacy" (*FNR*, 31; *SW*, III: 33).[38]

Suppose a parent, Pete, is feeding a small child, Sue. At an early stage in their relationship, feeding may appear to be mainly a business of physical manipulation, although one hopes that even then the insertion of bottle teat into infant mouth is accompanied by the gentle communication of loving care. Gradually, however, feeding comes to involve the idea that, if Sue shows no interest, then Pete must give Sue *a reason* for eating or drinking. Pete may make "yummy" noises suggesting that the food or drink is delicious, or he may make a game out of the transportation of food into mouth on spoon. At some point, Sue – clever girl! – recognizes what Pete is up to. In recognizing his summons to act for a reason, she discovers herself as a free and individual agent, who has a choice: either to do what Pete wants, or not. She is free, but she cannot escape her own freedom. If she now ignores Pete, that too is a free choice.

Insofar as Sue perceives Pete's playful attempt to make the ingestion of semolina seem like a good idea, she is engaged in representation. But this is not the sort of merely theoretical representation that is independent of the will. Insofar as Sue perceives Pete's act as a summons – as an attempt to solicit her free self-determination to act – her will is necessarily engaged. Whatever she does or does not do will count as a response.

This is the logic of any summons. But here Fichte is concerned with what I will call an *original* summons, a summons that lies at the origin of consciousness. The summons contains *in nuce* the structure of Holistic Monism: the first principle is the inescapable and absolute will to responsiveness, in which the circle of individual representation and volition is grounded, and by which it is conditioned. There is a virtuous circle with an irreversible order of explanation.

[38] Compare Baier 1985: 89–90: "My first concept of myself is as the referent of 'you,' spoken by someone whom I will address as 'you.' If never addressed, if excluded from the circle of speakers, a child becomes autistic, incapable of using any pronouns or indeed any words at all. The second person, the pronoun of mutual address and recognition, introduces us to the first and third, and to that relationship between first person ascriptions and others which Strawson has emphasized."

Violence, Communicative Action, and Normativity

The summons, I claim, obeys the logic of what kabbalists call *ẓimẓum* or the self-limiting contraction of God. I will now explain what that logic is.

The idea of *ẓimẓum* has biblical and midrashic roots, although it takes its classic forms in the early modern kabbalah of the sixteenth and seventeenth centuries – especially in what is known, after Isaac Luria (1534–72), as Lurianic kabbalah.[39]

In these classic forms, *ẓimẓum* figures primarily as a precondition of the possibility of creation. However, in earlier biblical and midrashic traditions, *ẓimẓum* features primarily as a condition of the possibility of revelation. I do not take this merely to signal a shift. Instead, I take it to show that, in early modern kabbalah, creation is proto-revelation: not only a precondition of the possibility of revelation but also a proto-communicative act.

Biblical texts do not use the word *ẓimẓum* or any cognate. But they speak pertinently of the potentially annihilating force of the divine presence and of the consequent danger of confronting this presence directly. In the Sinai periscope, Moses is warned (Exodus 19:12–13) – and then warned again (Exodus 19:22–23), surprising him and underlining God's concern – not to let the people near the mountain where God is about to be revealed, "lest many of them perish." Later, the divine presence settles in the sanctuary, so that it can accompany the people throughout their wanderings. At the inauguration of the sanctuary, a fire breaks forth from God, consuming offerings but also suggesting a destructive and dangerous force (Leviticus 9:24). Taking insufficient heed, two of Aaron's sons bring their own fire, although they were not commanded to do so, and the divine fire consumes them (Leviticus 10:1–2). In Deuteronomy 4:24, God is said to be a consuming fire. In late ancient and early medieval midrash, the contraction (*ẓimẓum*) of the divine presence (*shekhinah*) in the sanctuary is characterized as a careful balancing between God's desire to reveal Godself to the people on the one hand, and the destructive danger of divinity to mortals on the other. The location of revelation is necessarily and by the same token the location of the threat of annihilation.[40]

[39] For helpful surveys, see Idel 1992 and Schulte 2014. For a classic account of *ẓimẓum*, see Scholem 1978: 129–35.

[40] See, e.g., Midrash Shemot Rabbah 34.1, which elaborates on God's moderation of force in revelation in order not to overwhelm the recipient, as well as God's contraction within the sanctuary.

Medieval kabbalists, combining biblical and midrashic with philosophical traditions, spoke of God as *ein sof* or infinite.[41] The problem of the possibility of revelation – how could God reveal Godself to humans without consuming them – became the question: how could the infinite reveal itself to the finite without annihilating it? The crucial step to Lurianic *ẓimẓum* was now possible. The problem of the possibility of creation became the question: how could the infinite make room for the finite to come into being?

With this briefly sketched background in place, we may approach one of the classic Lurianic formulations of *ẓimẓum*, which became known to European philosophers in the seventeenth century through the translations compiled in *Kabbala Denudata*:

> You should know that before the emanations were emanated and the creations created, a most supreme, simple light filled the whole of existence. There was no vacant place, no aspect of empty space or void, but everything was filled by that simple, infinite light. It had no aspect of beginning or end, but was all one pure, completely uniform light, and this is what is called the light of the infinite.
>
> When it arose in His pure will to create worlds and to emit emanations, to bring out the perfection of His actions, His names and His attributes – for this was the reason that the worlds were created … then the infinite contracted itself at its midpoint, in the exact center of its light …
>
> After the contraction that we described above, the void, vacuum and empty space remained in the exact middle of the light of the infinite, as mentioned above. As a result, a place was already there for what would be emanated, created, formed, and made.[42]

The first emanation to be emanated within the space constituted by divine contraction is *Adam Kadmon*, the primordial human, who is at once the image of God and the ideal of humanity which, however, is not stable in its own right. From successive contractions and emanations – or withdrawals and expansions – there proceeds a succession of "worlds" or dimensions of time and reality, eventuating in the material world which we inhabit, where our task is to do what we can to constitute the perfected image of God or ideal of humanity.

According to Jacobi's report, Lessing was particularly fascinated by the idea of *ẓimẓum*. Not only did he think, in accordance with an already venerable tradition, that Spinoza was a kabbalist, but he also thought

[41] See Valabregue-Perry 2012.
[42] Vital 1999: 12–15.

that Leibniz was committed to Spinozism, and tried to recall a passage in which Leibniz says that God is in an incessant state of contraction and expansion.[43] Lessing found the idea of *ẓimẓum* to be an inexhaustible source of humor. "He said, with half a smile, that perhaps he was himself the supreme Being, and he was now in the state of extreme contraction. I beseeched him for my existence."[44] But Lessing also took the idea seriously enough to incorporate it into his conception of the world-soul, which he thought could animate the whole world and at the same time constitute an organism – which requires an environment with which to interact – only if it could "withdraw within itself from time to time; unite death and resurrection within itself with life."[45] Thus the idea of *ẓimẓum*, well known to Lessing and Jacobi because of *Kabbala Denudata*, became well known to a younger generation including Fichte, Schelling, and Hegel. While Lessing connected the idea primarily to one of the three options – the Kabbalistic Naturalism that portrays God as the world-soul – Fichte connects it to another: the Kabbalistic Realism that demands the reality of another who can address me in the second person.

I will now itemize six features of *ẓimẓum*, after which I will show that Fichte's summons also exhibits these features. 1) In order to make room for another, the infinite must be limited and – despite initial appearances – this is not impossible, because the infinite can limit itself without compromising its infinity. 2) This self-limitation consists in a renunciation or restraint of a force that would otherwise be annihilating in its effects. 3) This self-limitation is also a communicative act, as well as 4) the solicitation by the infinite of its own image as addressee. 5) In self-limitation, a norm – the primordial human – is inaugurated or revealed. 6) Self-limitation initiates an activity whose end is reciprocal recognition: the finite is to recognize the infinite – as merciful, as gracious, as king, and so on – in the second person, whereby the finite will ultimately recognize itself as the image of the infinite, and the infinite will ultimately recognize itself as infinite in a way that essentially involves the finite.

1) Jacobi formulated the problem to which the three options – Spinozism or "expanded kabbalah," Kabbalistic World-Soul Naturalism, and Kabbalistic Realism – are proposed solutions as the problem of the relation between the finite and the infinite. The underlying assumption is that

[43] Jacobi 1994a: 191.
[44] Jacobi 1994a: 195, 196.
[45] Jacobi 1994a: 196.

the only possible escape from the Agrippan trilemma is the absolute that is infinite. Fichte does not speak in terms of the finite and the infinite in *Natural Right*, but he uses this terminology earlier in *Foundations of the Entire Wissenschaftslehre*, and his solution is presupposed in *Natural Right*:

> Both [finite and infinite] are to be one and the same; this signifies, in brief: *no infinity, no bounding; no bounding, no infinity; infinity and bounding are united in one and the same synthetic component.* – If the I's activity did not extend into the infinite, it could not itself set limits to this activity; it could posit no bounds thereto, though this it is obliged to do. The activity of the I consists in unbounded self-assertion: to this there occurs a resistance. If it yielded to this obstacle, then the activity lying beyond the bounds of resistance would be utterly abolished and destroyed; to that extent the self would not posit at all. But for all that, it must also posit beyond this line. It must limit itself, that is, it must posit itself to that extent as not positing itself; it must set the indeterminate, unbounded, infinite limit ... within this sphere; and if it is to do this, it must be infinite. – Moreover, if the I did not bound itself, it would not be infinite. (*SK*, 192; *SW*, I: 214)

In short, the solution exhibits the logic of *ẓimẓum*: the absolute and infinite I can coexist with the finite, and Fichte's Holistic Monist system can thereby avoid nihilism – insofar as the absolute I is self-limiting, which does not compromise its infinity and is in fact the only way in which the absolute I can be *intelligible as infinite.*

One of the major disputes among kabbalists concerns the question whether *ẓimẓum* is to be understood as a timeless determination of the activity of the *ein sof* or whether it is to be understood as a primordial event pre-conditioning creation. Put in another way: is the mythic characterization of *ẓimẓum* in Lurianic writings to be understood as an allegorical representation of a timeless truth, or is it to be understood in terms of some mythic conception of temporality? In *Foundations of the Entire Wissenschaftslehre*, the self-finitization of the infinite is timeless. In *Natural Right*, however, it becomes the primordial event at the genesis of consciousness.

2) In the summons situation, the summoner has an end for the realization of which he or she desires the summonee's action as a means. One way to achieve the summoner's end might be to use the summonee's action *solely* as a means, by treating the summonee as a material object for physical manipulation. However, if the summoner instead issues a summons to the summonee, he or she foregoes the use of physical force and instead

attempts to solicit the summonee's self-determined action as a means for the realization of the end. Thus the summoner's self-limiting act is at the self-restraint of an annihilating force that would treat the other as a not being an individual agent:

> Unless I act upon him in conformity with the concept of him as a rational being, I cannot demonstrate to him that he – just as surely as he himself possesses reason – must necessarily have regarded me as a rational being. For every expression of force can originate from a natural power operating in accordance with mechanical laws; only the moderation of force by means of concepts is the unmistakable and exclusive criterion of reason and freedom. (FNR, 43; *SW*, III: 45)

3) Regarded negatively, the summons is a self-restraint of infinite force. Regarded positively it is a communicative act. The summoner communicates to the summonee both what the desired action is and some reason why the summonee should self-determine to perform the action. This communication need not be linguistic and cannot be linguistic in the case of a summons in which self-consciousness originates.

4) In the summons, the summoner solicits his or her own image. Here, of course, lies a major difference between kabbalistic accounts and Fichte's. For kabbalistic accounts are primarily concerned with the solicitation by God of what is not God – of the human. In contrast, Fichte deals with the solicitation by one human being of another. Each of the human parties to a Fichtean summons exhibits its own self-finitization of the infinite, and there is no question of the kabbalistic *ein sof*, which is infinite in a way that transcends any self-finitization and relation to another.[46] Notwithstanding these differences, however, there is more affinity than one might initially realize. First, the kabbalists regard the essentially human aspect of the soul, which is solicited through divine *ẓimẓum*, as a "portion of God from above,"[47] since the human is created "in the image of God" – which is to say, as a participant in the being of the primordial human or *Adam Kadmon*. Second, although the primary kabbalistic concern is with the divine–human relation, a derivative concern is with interhuman relations, which given the preceding point, exhibit or should exhibit the same structure. *Ẓimẓum* is explained by analogy to education,

[46] True, Fichte alludes to God as summoning the first humans (*FNR*, 40; *SW*, III: 39). But this is plainly incompatible with his impersonal conception of God as the living principle of the moral world-order.

[47] See, e.g., Alshekh 1595; Horowitz 1612: Hakdamah; Zalman 1797: ch. 2; Menasseh ben Israel 1651: ch. 9, objects to this formulation.

in which the teacher must speak on a level accessible to the student and, conversely, education through the self-restraint of the teacher that solicits and enables the free development of the student is encouraged.[48] Fichte, for his part, says that, "The summons to free self-activity is what we call upbringing (*Erziehung*)" (*FNR*, 38; *SW*, III: 39).

5) That the original summons inaugurates a norm is, of course, one of Fichte's main claims in *Natural Right*. I will not enter here into the question of the relation between the norm inaugurated and the principle of right.[49] What concerns me is simply that a norm is inaugurated at all. This may not be obvious. From one viewpoint, the summonee may choose whether to act as the summonee desires or not, or whether to ignore the summons. From another, the summonee has no choice at all: whatever he or she does, including ignoring the summons, counts as an action responsive to the summons. Where is the normativity?

The answer, I believe, lies in the summoner's foregoing of force and mere instrumentalization, as discussed above. Once the summoner foregoes force and recognizes the summonee as an individual agent, it is a violation of that recognition to return to the use of force. It is a violation of the summonee's *body*, now recognized as the embodiment of individual agency, irreducible to a mere material object. This is why Fichte says that "original right" includes, not only freedom to exercise agency in the world but also "the right to the continued existence of the absolute freedom and inviolability of the body (i.e., there should be absolutely nothing that exercises an immediate effect on the body)" (*FNR*, 108; *SW*, III: 119). By foregoing force and instead issuing a summons, the summoner has invited the summonee into a realm of communicative action, in which there are not only material objects but also embodied individual agents, not only physical events but also free actions. This is at the same time a realm of norms, and the primordial norm is the inviolability of the bodies of both parties.[50]

6) In an original summons, the summoner may of course have any number of ends, while the summonee initially has no end at all and frames one only in response to the summons. Yet we may say that the summons as such has its own end, independent of any particular end of the

48 For educational illustration, see Schneerson 1820, *Sha'ar ha-Yihud*, ch. 12. For educational application, see Shapira 1932: Discourse 1, ch. 2–3 and Discourse 2, ch. 3.

49 Nance 2015.

50 I owe this important point to Bernstein 2007.

summoner: namely, the reciprocal recognition of the two parties. This is also what the Lurianic texts mean when they say that the creation of the worlds is "to bring out the perfection of His actions, His names and His attributes." Vital says earlier: "Calling Him Lord means that He has servants and that He is a lord over them. But if He had not created them it would not have been possible to call Him by the name Lord."[51] Efraim Panzieri, student of Vital and editor of another version of Luria's expositions, writes in his introduction: "The master, may his memory be for the life of the world to come, said that creatures necessarily possess three aspects: that each should recognize and receive from what is superior; also that each should recognize itself; and further that each should communicate to what is inferior."[52]

That the first and third types of recognition are second-personal is not always made explicit in kabbalistic texts. But I would argue that it is not made explicit because it is presupposed. The central concept of Jewish practice is not impersonal law, but commandment (*mizvah*), in recognition of whose essentially second-person character the performer utters a rabbinically ordained blessing (*berakhah*) addressing God in turn in the second person singular: "Blessed are You who have sanctified us with Your commandments."[53]

We have already seen that Jacobi's "kabbalah in the *strict* sense" focuses on I–You reception, which I take to involve second-person address. One way to put the point of Fichte's conception of the summons is that, in Annette Baier's words, "Persons essentially are *second* persons, who grow up with other persons."[54] For I can come to recognize myself as myself only through my recognition of someone else's second person recognition of me. As Fichte realizes, this has special importance for the foundations of natural right. In earlier work, he had tried to develop an account of right on the basis of the concept of the morally permissible. But, as Fred Neuhouser has shown, Fichte had broken through to the insight that, "The question 'Do I have a right?' does not mean 'May I?' but rather 'May someone prevent me?'"[55] This point may be connected to Stephen Darwall's distinction between the agent-neutral reason one may give another for removing her foot from on top of yours, which might consist in showing her that the world would be a better place if she removed it,

[51] Vital 1999: 4. Cf. *Kabbala Denudata*, I.2, 32–3.
[52] Panzieri 1995: 1.
[53] Rosenzweig's letter to speakers at the Lehrhaus: November 1924 (Rosenzweig 1979).
[54] Baier 1985: 84.
[55] *GA* II, 3: 396 and 399: cited by Neuhouser 1994: 172.

and the agent-relative, essentially second-person reason one may give by addressing her as the person causing gratuitous pain to another person.[56] If I have a natural right to do something, then you may not prevent me and, if you do, I may address you in a demand that you stop violating my right and hence my status as an individual agent. A demand for respect of one's rights is a kind of summons, and the original summons deduced by Fichte in the Second Theorem contains a necessary condition for the possibility both of having rights that can be violated and of making demands that express second-person reasons for others to act or to refrain from acting.

Conclusion: Anti-Semitism and Nihilism

What emerges from the preceding analysis is that Fichte combines, in an insightful and innovative way, features of all three options discussed in the conversation with Lessing reported by Jacobi. Like the Spinozist, he rejects any transition from the infinite to the finite, and espouses Holistic Monism as the optimal response to Agrippan skepticism, hence as dictating the virtuously circular structure of the system, in which the absolute and infinite first principle is both One and All: the unique ground of unity, which is immanent within the totality of the finite. Like Jacobi, he seeks to validate a Kabbalistic Realism that can accommodate, not merely a space in which I coexist with external objects which are obstacles to my will, but a normative and intersubjective space in which I coexist with other individuals who can address me and whom I can address in the second person, for example in the demand that individual rights not be violated. Like the kabbalistic naturalist, he draws on the idea, central to Lurianic kabbalah, of the creative and revelatory self-finitization of the infinite, incorporating it into a worldview that dispenses with the transcendent *ein sof*.

I do not claim that Fichte had any first-hand familiarity with kabbalistic texts, not even with *Kabbala Denudata* or Brucker's exposition. What is necessary for my argument is only Fichte's familiarity with the options and conceptual resources informed by kabbalah that are discussed in Jacobi's report of his conversation with Lessing and elsewhere in his Spinoza book.

Still, Fichte is notorious for his virulent anti-Judaism and for his contribution to the anti-Semitism that developed in Germany in the late

[56] Darwall 2005. Darwall rejects Fichte's attempt to demarcate right from morality, but that deserves discussion elsewhere.

nineteenth century and that came to a head with the Nazi destruction of European Jewry. He opposed recognition of the civil rights of Jews on the grounds that they already had civil rights in a global state that was engaged in a world war against Germans and others. The only way for Jews to be citizens would be "to chop off all their heads and replace them with new ones in which there would not be one single Jewish idea" (*SW*, VI: 150 n.). He also anticipated the "German Christians" of the Nazi period by trying to purify Christianity of all of its Jewish elements, which left him only with the apparently anti-Jewish Gospel of John (*SW*, VI: 150 n.). Could such a person draw on kabbalistic ideas and themes?

There is no conflict here, although there is some irony. The history of Christian kabbalah – and the history of Christianity more generally – contains numerous precedents for the appropriation of elements of Judaism alongside the idea that, precisely since they are worthy of appropriation, these elements are not in fact Jewish at all. If Fichte was aware that he was deploying kabbalistic ideas that had attracted Lessing and Jacobi, he may not have thought of them as "Jewish ideas."

As we know all too well, the German state was eventually mobilized, in a horrific betrayal, for the annihilation of its Jewish citizens and of European Jewry in general. Civil rights were violated, then human rights, and finally life itself. Yet there had been a largely unacknowledged conversation involving Jewish ideas and texts at the heart of German philosophy, even at the very foundation of natural right. Despite everything, there still is.

CHAPTER 6

Fichte's Developmental View of Self-Consciousness

Gabriel Gottlieb

One of the more influential arguments in the history of German Idealism is Fichte's argument in the *Foundations of Natural Right* that self-consciousness requires mutual recognition (*gegenseitige Anerkennung*). Broadly conceived, self-consciousness, for Fichte, is a self-reflexive form of mindedness in which there is the awareness of some representational content that, as a result of the I's self-reverting intuitive activity, is immediately taken as one's own representation.[1] Self-consciousness, however, is not achieved simply through a single subject's free self-activity, but requires two subjects freely engaging with each other through a reciprocal interaction. On Fichte's view, this free engagement between subjects cannot take just any form; it is essential that it involves what Fichte calls the "summons (*Aufforderung*) to engage in free self-activity" (*FNR*, 38; *SW*, III: 39), an act in which one subject calls upon another subject to exercise its efficacy by actively determining itself. In a "corollary" to the deduction of the summons, Fichte identifies the summons with "upbringing" (*Erziehung*) (*FNR*, 38; *SW*, III: 39). This important point appears to be in tension with his account of the I as an activity that absolutely posits itself. Furthermore, Fichte's descriptions of the self-positing I appear to characterize I-hood as originating all at once: "the I posits originally its own being absolutely" (*SK*, 99; *SW*, I: 98;

Many thanks to Mike Nance, James Clarke, Owen Ware, Tim Brownlee, Evan Strevell, G. Anthony Bruno, and James Dow for reading and carefully commenting on earlier drafts of this chapter. Special thanks to Kristen Renzi for her incisive philosophical and editorial comments. A number of the ideas here stem from my dissertation work and I am grateful for Jay Bernstein's feedback and support. A draft of this chapter was presented at The New York German Idealism Workshop at the New School, and I am thankful for the feedback I received there from the participants.

[1] It is important not to confuse the activity of the I with self-consciousness proper. For example, Fichte remarks that the I's self-reverting activity "produces no consciousness, not even self-consciousness … The described act of the I merely serves to put the I into a position in which self-consciousness – and, along with this, all other consciousness – becomes possible" (*IW*, 42–3; *SW*, I 459).

translation modified). Fichte also asserts in his *Wissenschaftslehre nova methodo*, "In a *single stroke*, I exist and the world exists for me" (*WLnm*, 103; *K*, 22–3; my emphasis). Even Fichte's deduction of the summons suggests that the subject posits itself and the object at once: "*the subject's* efficacy is synthetically unified with the *object* in one and the same moment" (*FNR*, 31; *SW*, III: 32). However, Fichte's additional claim in *Natural Right* that self-consciousness results from a summons, or upbringing, suggests there is a developmental dimension to his theory of self-consciousness. On the one hand, the I posits itself absolutely and all at once as a self-conscious being, while, on the other hand, the I gradually develops into its self-consciousness by virtue of being summoned to self-activity. Now, if the I posits itself all at once and the summons constitutes a kind of development or upbringing, then it remains unclear why a summons to self-activity is required. Resolving this apparent tension should shed light on the role and nature of the summons in Fichte's theory of self-consciousness.

I will argue that this tension can be resolved since there is a reasonable way to reconcile Fichte's views about upbringing with his views about the self-positing I. A reconciliation is possible when one appreciates that Fichte has in mind two conceptions of the I: a pure I and an individual I. Furthermore, each conception of the I has its own status. The pure I has a fictional or ideal status, while the individual I has an empirical status. One might then wonder, of the two I's, which one is subject to upbringing. By distinguishing the status of the pure I from the individual I, one can see more clearly that it is only the individual, empirical I that is subject to development, or upbringing.[2]

Fichte's concept of individuality in *Natural Right* is not entirely straightforward, yet it is at the heart of his views about development. On my view, in *Natural Right* Fichte makes a distinction between two conceptions of the individual. On the one hand, there is the *individual human being* that is brought up to be responsive to reasons in the form of the summons, and on the other hand, there is the *political individual* that, as a rational human being, is free to voluntarily commit itself to consistently engaging in relations of reciprocal recognition in society.[3] It is important to note that Fichte's two conceptions of the individual are

[2] Bernstein 2007 and Nance 2015 consider Fichte's theory of recognition and self-positing in developmental terms. For a recent interpretation of Hegel's theory of self-consciousness from the standpoint of its development, see Dahlstrom 2013.

[3] Fichte's use of the terms "human being" and "individual" is for the most part consistent, although on some occasions he could have been more careful. See note 17 below.

not exactly metaphysically distinct, but rather two *potential* shades of a person's standing as an individual I. In extraordinary circumstances, one might not choose to enter political society and, thus, resign oneself to only a single shade of individuality as a human being.[4]

Relevant to Fichte's distinction between individual human beings and political individuals is an overlooked, yet parallel distinction operating in his theory of recognition. Central to my account of Fichte's developmental view of self-consciousness is the disambiguation of two types of recognition: elementary recognition and political recognition. The summons as a form of upbringing requires elementary forms of recognition in a child's development that are aimed at developing and fine tuning the child's ability 1) to exercise, in a norm-governed fashion, its capacity to self-consciously ascribe its actions as its own in response to the reasons (or the summons) of another; and, 2) to eventually take responsibility for those actions and reasons as a practical agent in a community of free rational beings. These elementary forms of recognition are neither essentially political in nature nor rights bestowing acts of recognition; they are, rather, forms of recognition aimed at promoting the development of the child's capacity to freely determine itself to an ever greater degree while learning to take the freedom of others as a constitutive end of its action. Political recognition, in contrast, is the recognition of another subject as a right-bearing individual to whom the self-limitation of one's own external freedom is due for the sake of the other's external freedom. The summons, as the paradigm of free intersubjective engagement, correlates, first, with elementary recognition when upbringing is the goal of the engagement; and, second, with political recognition when respect for external freedom and rights are the end. A careful reader of Fichte's deduction of the summons and the concept of right might not take note of his remarks about what I am calling elementary recognition, as they are most evident in the fourth section of the "Outline of Family Right" titled "On the Reciprocal Relation of Right between Parents and Children," a little-studied section of *Natural Right*. Before turning to Fichte's views about parents and children, I will first address his views about the pure I and the individual I.

The Pure I and the Individual I

In the *Wissenschaftslehre*, Fichte places a principle or postulate about self-consciousness, or I-hood, at the foundation of philosophy and on its

[4] For his remarks about removing oneself "from all human community" see *FNR*, 12; *SW*, III: 11.

basis he deduces normative principles that govern rational life. The "First Theorem" of *Natural Right* offers such a principle: "*Activity that reverts into itself in general* (I-hood, subjectivity) *is the mark of a rational being*" (*FNR*, 18; *SW*, III: 17). Fichte proceeds to deduce as a necessary condition of I-hood the concept of right. The concept of right states that a rational being must limit its own external freedom through its inner freedom to permit others to exercise their external freedom (*FNR*, 10: *SW*, III: 9). In the opening of the "First Theorem" Fichte characterizes the self-conscious activity of a rational being as involving "an activity that *reverts into itself and determines itself*" (*FNR*, 18; *SW*, III: 17). The I, he says, is "nothing other than an acting upon itself" (*FNR*, 3; *SW*, III: 1). In contrast to Descartes's conception of the I as a thinking thing, Fichte claims that this "acting upon itself" does not involve a commitment to viewing the I as a substance or object upon which one reflects. Considering self-consciousness as the achievement of an act of reflection upon oneself invites thinking of the I as a substance or object, a position Fichte explicitly rejects, since such a view of the I issues in an infinite regress.[5] Fichte's description of the I as self-reverting ultimately captures the self-directed and self-referential nature of self-consciousness. Perhaps Fichte's most distinctive characterization of the I, however, is his claim that its very constitution as an I is the result of its own self-positing, or self-reverting activity,[6] what he calls a *Tathandlung*:

> Thus, the positing of the I through itself is the pure activity of the I. The I *posits itself*, and it *is* by virtue of its mere positing through itself. Inversely, the I *is*, and it *posits* its being (*Seyn*) in virtue of merely being. It is at once the agent and the product of the action; the active and what the activity brings about. Action (*Handlung*) and deed (*Tat*) are one and the same, and thus *I am* is an expression of an a*ct* (*Tathandlung*). (*SK*, 97: *SW*, I: 96; translation modified)

The main claim here is that the activity of the I should be considered a self-constituting activity in which, by dint of its own self-reverting activity, the I achieves its standing as an I.[7] Elsewhere, Fichte discusses the original activity of the I in even more striking terms: "I posit myself and a world at the same time – in a single stroke" (*WLnm*, 103; *GA*, IV, 2: 27).

[5] Fichte is clear about this point in the "Preface" where he writes in a footnote: "In order not to suggest the idea of a substratum that contains within itself this power of acting, I do not even want to call the I an *acting something* (*ein Handelndes*)" (*FNR*, 3; *SW*, III, 1). See Henrich 1982 and Neuhouser 1990 for a discussion of Fichte's reasoning.

[6] For the identification of self-positing with self-reverting see *Wlnm*, 97; *K*, 18.

[7] See also Neuhouser 1990. For a creative exploration of this idea see Nozick 1981.

It is on the basis of such passages one appears justified in concluding that the I posits itself once and for all as a full-fledged I.

Just how one should understand Fichte's analysis of the I as a self-constituting activity or *Tathandlung* is a matter of much consternation and debate. A long tradition of commentators has assumed that Fichte endorses a realist picture of the pure I. On the realist picture, Fichte is committed to considering the pure I as a metaphysical "ego" that brings itself into existence just in the manner described by the *Wissenschaftslehre*.[8] The realist picture, however, is difficult to square with the transcendental nature of the *Wissenschaftslehre* as an explanatory account of experience. Additionally, it fits poorly with Fichte's insistence that "idealism only postulates a series of original actions. It does not affirm that such a series *actually* exists" (*WLnm*, 102; *K*, 22; my emphasis). Finally, the realist picture cannot make much sense of Fichte's assertion that the "original construction" of the pure I is a "fiction" (*Fiktion*), rather than "a narrative of some true event occurred at some particular time" (*CC*, 98; *SW*, II: 398).

In contrast to the realist picture, Daniel Breazeale and Benjamin Crowe offer a fictionalist reading of the I that takes seriously Fichte's scattered remarks about the I's fictional status. The pure I as a *Tathandlung*, on the fictionalist reading, is a "necessity of thinking" that must be posited to explain the possibility of experience (*WLnm*, 103; *GA*, IV, 2: 27); yet, as such a condition, it does "not possess the sort of actuality that experience does" (*WLnm*, 103; *K*, 23).[9] As Crowe shows, Fichte considers the pure I to possess a type of reality, even if that reality is distinct from the reality of objects experienced in space and time. Fichte writes, for instance: "These actions do possess reality for the person who raises himself to the philosophical level; that is, they possess the reality of necessary thinking" (*WLnm*, 104; *K*, 23). As fictional, the I is not a mere fabrication or illusion, but an explanatory philosophical fiction the philosopher must posit to make sense of the objectivity of experience.[10]

The fictionalist reading is particularly helpful when considering whether or not the I (and with it the world or not-I) is posited all at once, or "at the same time" as Fichte seems to suggest. If the I and the world are posited all at once, then the I would be posited in time, albeit all at

[8] Bertrand Russell writes, for instance: "[Fichte] holds that the Ego is the only ultimate reality, and that it exists because it posits itself; the non-Ego, which has subordinate reality, also exists only because the Ego posits it." Russell goes on to conclude, "The Ego as a metaphysical concept easily became confused with the empirical Fichte" (Russell 1945: 717).

[9] See Crowe 2008 for a discussion of Fichte's use of the terms "actuality" and "reality."

[10] Crowe 2008: 278.

one moment in time – but the actions of the I as a *Tathandlung* are not *in time*. "These actions," Fichte clarifies, "do not possess the sort of actuality that experience does; nor can one say that they occur within time, for only appearances have temporal reality" (*WLnm*, 103; *K*, 23). The pure I then is a logical posit: "it must be thought of as something that is necessarily thinkable, as something ideal" (*WLnm*, 104; *K*, 23). To say that the I and the world are posited at once or at the same time is to speak figuratively, since otherwise Fichte would have committed an obvious category mistake.

Returning to the tension between the I as posited all at once and the I as developmental, it should be clear at this point that Fichte is not committed to thinking of the pure I as part of his developmental story, since for a thing to develop in the requisite sense would entail that it is subject to the passage of time. The pure I is not "actual" as it is not a feature of the empirical world of appearances; yet, as Fichte acknowledges, "the I we encounter within experience is the person" (*WLnm*, 104; *K*, 23).[11] Since the individual or person is subject to the passage of time, Fichte's developmental view of self-consciousness pertains to only this aspect of the I. The pure I, then, does not develop, though the empirical I of the individual does gradually develop.

What, then, is the relationship between the two? If the pure I is fictional or ideal and the individual I is actual, to what extent is the individual person an instantiation of the pure I? While answering this question is certainly no easy task, a simple, if incomplete, response can be given: the individual I is always an imperfect instantiation of the pure, idealized conception of the I, yet it is the only *actually* existing I, and as such, the I that develops through an empirical process of upbringing. Upbringing is the first stage in a human subject's striving for harmony between its pure and empirical conditions – its divided situation.[12]

Human Beings, Individuality, and the Interrelationist Tradition

Before examining Fichte's developmental view and the place of recognition in it, I want to take a closer look at how Fichte understands

[11] See Crowe 2008 for a discussion of actuality in Fichte.

[12] Breazeale puts this point well: "An *embodied* subject, a *social* self, and a *moral* agent: this, not the 'absolute I,' is the only actual I. An endless *striving* for unity, but a constant *struggle* with duality: this is the sum and substance of Fichte's conclusion in his Jena system concerning the human condition" (Breazeale, 2013b: 123). See also Breazeale, 2013c.

individuality in *Natural Right*, since the outcome or achievement of the developmental process is that the subject is in some sense an individual self-conscious agent that, as an embodied person, empirically instantiates to some imperfect degree the pure I.

Fichte's theory of the self-conscious individual falls within what John Haugeland calls the interrelationist tradition. In Haugeland's words, the interrelationist tradition accepts "as a premise that the mental, or at any rate the cognitive, has some essential feature, such as intentionality or normativity, and then argue[s] that this feature is impossible except through participation in some supra-individual network of relations," where a supra-individual network is a set of relations that extends beyond a single subject or individual.[13] Fichte employs this pattern of reasoning in *Natural Right* and elsewhere with respect to individual self-consciousness. Consider, for instance, the following remark from Fichte's lectures on the *Wissenschaftslehre nova methodo* where he expands upon the conception of the summons presented in *Natural Right*:

> Consciousness begins with consciousness of a summons, though this too can be thought of only in order to explain consciousness. In short, in the course of the development of consciousness it appears that what conditions our will is something that lies within us. At the point where consciousness of our individuality commences, however, what conditions the will appears to lie outside of us in another rational being. In this way, individual reason generates itself from reason in the larger sense. (*WLnm*, 370; *GA*, IV, 2: 190)[14]

There are, then, two conditions on the I: 1) an *external condition* in which another subject initiates consciousness of one's self-activity through the summons; and 2) an *internal condition* according to which the subject becomes aware of its determinability (its capacity to act in any number of ways) and transitions into self-consciousness by determining itself to act.[15] Now, when a subject achieves "consciousness of a summons" it becomes conscious of its free activity through its consciousness of another rational being's expectation of it. The summons is, on Fichte's view, communicated discursively as a concept, or reason to act, that contains three contents essential to the development of self-consciousness. The first content of the

[13] Haugeland 1998a: 207.

[14] I've substituted Breazeale's suggested English translation for the Greek term χατεξοχην, which appears in the Halle manuscript (*WLnm, 370*; *GA*, IV, 2: 190). See also, *WLnm*, 355; *K*, 179.

[15] Fichte speaks of the interaction between subjects as one in which a subject initiates (*anfangen*) the consciousness of another in his letters to Reinhold (*EPW*, 408; *GA*, III, 2: 386) and Jacobi (*EPW*, 411; *GA*, III, 2: 392), though he does not use the term "summons" there.

summons is that a rational being distinct from oneself possesses a concept that one is in fact a practical being that has the capacity to respond to reasons. The second content of the summons is an expectation that one will act in a certain way expressed by the summons, thereby exhibiting one's reasons responsiveness. The third content of the summons is that one is a free agent capable of determining oneself in accordance with the summons by taking it up as a component of one's reason to act (*WLnm*, 357; *K*, 181). Consciousness of the summoner's awareness and expectation of itself is an initial moment of consciousness that is ultimately completed by transitioning from awareness that it is determinable to actually determining itself in a specific way. With the requirement of the external condition and the summons' contents about others, Fichte's account of the initiation of consciousness refers to a supra-individual network of relations.

In *Natural Right*, Fichte also claims the human being and the political individual must be understood in terms of this supra-individual network. The concept of the human being, Fichte explains, "is not the concept of a one (*Einzelnen*) – for a singular (*Einzelnen*) human being is unthinkable – but rather the concept of a species" (*FNR*, 38; *SW*, III: 39).[16] Fichte continues, "All individuals (*Individuen*) must be brought up to be human beings, otherwise they would not be human beings" (*FNR*, 38; *SW*, III: 39).[17] Fichte's point here is to acknowledge that the concept of human being is a species-concept. There are two dimensions to his use of "human being" as a species-concept. First, the most obvious dimension is that human beings come in groups of two or more: "*if there are to be human beings at all, there must be more than one*" (*FNR*, 37; *SW*, III: 39). Second, human beings constitute something akin to a natural-kind: "nature completed all of her works; only from the human being did she withdraw her hand, and precisely by doing so, she gave him over to himself" (*FNR*, 74; *SW*, III: 80). Fichte, thus, acknowledges the human being as a product of nature, one that has natural mechanical drives (*FNR*, 76; *SW*, III: 81), though unlike animals which Fichte conceives as determinate and complete by nature, the human being is left "utterly incomplete" by nature (*FNR*, 76; *SW*, III: 82), thereby requiring an engagement with other human beings through a summons to become

[16] The English word "individual" is a reasonable translation of *Einzelnen* and *Individuum*, both of which are used by Fichte in his deduction of right. I've altered Baur's translation by not translating *Einzelnen* as "individual," but instead as "one" or "singular," to avoid any confusion.

[17] Here I think Fichte's formulation is a bit sloppy, since one cannot be an individual in Fichte's technical sense prior to being a human being. He might have avoided this confusion by stating "all children must be brought up to be human beings."

a full-fledged human being (*FNR*, 38: *SW*, III: 39). Based on the incomplete nature of the human being, Fichte asserts that "Formability, as such, is the character of humanity" (*FNR*, 74; *SW*, III: 80). However, formability is ultimately an internal formation, one that is responsive to concepts, or reasons and knowledge. This is clear from how Fichte describes the character of humanity elsewhere in *Natural Right*: "Only free, reciprocal interaction by means of concepts and in accordance with concepts, only the giving and receiving of knowledge, is the distinctive character of humanity, by virtue of which alone each person undeniably confirms himself as a human being" (*FNR*, 38). To be a human being, then, is to be a particular "incomplete" product of nature, a member of the human species, that is capable of determining itself in accordance with reasons and knowledge. With respect to the supra-individual network, Fichte's concept of human being requires that any potential human being engage with other human beings in order for it to realize its reasons responsiveness capacity and complete what nature has left indeterminate. Given this view, Fichte's conception of the human being is a biological notion inflected with a normative and social aspect, since being a human being involves responding to the reasons of others.

One might take these remarks to suggest that Fichte believes individual self-consciousness is interrelational in a weak sense, as one's relation to another appears only to *initiate* individual self-consciousness and not to *constitute* it. In *Natural Right*, however, one finds a stronger, constitutive sense of individuality. Here the interaction between subjects is said to constitute individuality, rather than simply initiate it. This constitutive point is found in Fichte's claim that "the concept of individuality is a *reciprocal concept*" (*FNR*, 45; *SW*, III: 47). As Fichte clarifies:

> As has been demonstrated, the concept of individuality is a *reciprocal* concept, i.e. a concept that can be thought only in relation to another thought, and one that (with respect to its form) is conditioned by another – indeed by an *identical* – thought. This concept can exist in a rational being only if it is posited as *completed* by another rational being. Thus this concept is never *mine*; rather, it is – in accordance with my own admission and the admission of the other – *mine and his, his and mine*; it is a shared concept within which two consciousnesses are unified into one. (*FNR*, 45; *SW*, III: 47–8)

Since the concept of individuality is a shared concept, one that is not simply shareable and public, a condition that presumably holds for all concepts if Wittgenstein's private language argument is correct, but a concept "*completed* by another rational being," individuality is constituted by virtue of two subjects coming together in a certain normative practice. On Fichte's view, the normative practice consists in comporting oneself in accordance with the concept of right. The attitudes, thoughts, and comportment of the two subjects constitute the very concept of individuality and the normative standing of a subject as an individual. If such a view seems magical – it's not.

Consider the game of tag, and in particular how the concept "tag-player" is constituted or completed by another. In the game of tag there is someone who is designated as "it." If this person tags you, then you are "it." They transfer the status of "it" to you by tagging you. This is the main rule of the game – the "tag–you're it" rule. The object of the game is relative to one's standing in the game. If one is not "it," the object is to avoid being tagged. If one is "it," then the object is to tag someone else, thereby making them "it." The basic rule of the game, the "tag–you're it" rule, regulates the actions of the players in the game. Notice that being a tag-player involves at least two people having a particular attitude toward each other, one realized in thought *and* action. It is not sufficient for me to consider myself a tag-player in order to achieve that status, nor is it enough for another person to consider me a tag-player. The two of us must entertain the thought and engage in the relevant actions for the concept tag-player to be constituted or completed and for it to be applicable to each, thereby constituting us as tag-players. In this sense, the concept "tag-player" is a shared and reciprocal concept.

Notice, further, that the "tag–you're it" rule has two dimensions. First, the rule is a *constitutive regulation*, a rule or principle that regulates actions and determines legal and illegal actions.[18] It would be illegal, for instance, to spontaneously consider yourself "it" and tag another person "it" without being legally tagged. Determining that the "tag–you're it" rule is a constitutive regulation does not exhaust the constitutive role the rule plays in the game. Second, the rule is also a *constitutive standard* of the game. Constitutive standards operate to determine what the phenomena in the game are by constituting their status. A secondary constitutive regulation in tag might include a rule specifying the perimeter of the legal playing field, but this rule would not count as a constitutive standard. What essentially distinguishes constitutive standards from constitutive regulations is that constitutive standards determine the normative standing of a player or piece in the game. In the case of tag, the constitutive standards constitute the standing of the players as tag-players.

[18] I follow Haugeland's use of constitutive regulation and constitutive standard in 1998b.

With this in mind, we can move from the game of tag to the game of life. My use of tag is meant to illustrate how a particular standard operates to constitute a normative standing and my suggestion is that there is a parallel between the "tag–you're it" rule and the concept of right in that both operate as constitutive regulations *and* constitutive standards, the former in the game of tag and the latter in the game of life. Acting on the basis of the concept of right involves limiting one's own external actions in order to make room for others to exercise their own agency. In other words, a constitutive end of one's action as an individual agent is that one formulates the action with the other person's external freedom as a consideration, even if the formulation of the action and consideration of the other's freedom is, in some sense, implicit. With respect to the standing of an agent as a political individual, and not only as a human being, the recognition of rights, either implicitly or explicitly as a consistent and continual practical commitment, is a necessary condition of that status.[19] If a subject does not act in such a way, it fails to follow the constitutive standard of individuality.

Individuality, however, does not need to be an "all-or-nothing" standing, unlike the concept of tag-player.[20] Fichte's developmental view of self-consciousness can handle the idea of a subject emerging into its standing as an individual human being, where at certain moments in its development the child realizes features of its responsiveness to the summons, yet in others fails to take or even appreciate the summons as a reason for consideration. This status of individuality that potentially results from relations of elementary recognition presupposes development as a human being, and the status of human being should be considered distinct from a second conception of individuality, political individuality. Once the child reaches its development as full-fledged human being it can posit itself as a political individual by committing itself to a community of right.[21] At this point, the subject attains its political status as an individual by virtue of its practical commitment and involvement in the community of right.

19 In a letter to Reinhold, Fichte is clear that rights are conditional for individuality: "There can be no individual (*Individuum*) unless there are at least two of them. *The conditions which make individuality possible* are called *'rights'*. It is absolutely impossible for me to attribute a right to myself without attributing it to a being outside of myself, because it is absolutely impossible for me to posit myself as an individual without positing a being outside of myself as an individual" (*EPW*, 409; *GA*, III, 2: 387). See also his letter to Jacobi (*EPW*, 411; *GA*, III, 2: 392).

20 See Nance's 2015 analysis of the modal dilemma and problems with a strong constitutive view of individuality.

21 I do not take up directly the issue of voluntarism. See Darwall 2005, Ware 2010, Nance 2015, and Nomer 2013.

If the subject willfully leaves such a condition, then it will cease to be an individual in the political sense, though not in the human sense. Removing oneself from a community of free beings entails that the law of right is no longer binding on oneself and others who remain outside the community, as these subjects cease to be individuals in the relevant sense. However, as a human being, the moral law is still binding on these subjects:

> I am absolved from adhering to the law requiring me to treat him as a free being, and the question of how I will treat him depends solely upon my free choice, or I have a right of coercion against him. These claims mean, and can mean, nothing other than: this person cannot, *through the law of right alone*, prevent my coercion of him (although he may well do so through other laws, by physical strength, or by appealing to the moral law). (FNR, 83; SW, III: 90)

The moral law constrains any possible treatment of other human beings, those creatures possessing the mark of humanity, yet the law of right holds only for individuals who have subjected themselves to its regulations. What the law of right does, with respect to one's status, is raise the human being to the standing of a political individual, in which case norms, regardless of whether one's will is good (i.e. certain non-moral norms), hold. Willfully leaving the political community, perhaps under some extraordinary circumstance, and ceasing to be constitutively a political individual bears on one's practical self-consciousness and practical self-identity since one is no longer positioned to act politically and conceive of oneself as a member of the political community, even if awareness of oneself as a reason responsive human being is still possible.

Elementary Recognition and the Developmental View

The model of self-consciousness Fichte presents in *Natural Right* entails a developmental thesis: the nature of upbringing or education (*Erziehung*) is that of a summons between two subjects which over time initiates individual self-consciousness, where individual consciousness includes consciousness of oneself as a reason responsive human being and, eventually, as a political individual. The first, perhaps obvious, point to note about the developmental thesis is that upbringing, or the rearing of children, requires an interactive engagement. Second, the interactive engagement is constituted, at least in part, by a summons in which a subject attempts to influence another subject by calling, requesting, or demanding it to act appropriately in response to a conceptually structured rational influence, one whose content presupposes the subject influenced is in some sense rational, or reasons responsive: "the influence is supposed to be exercised upon a rational being *as a rational being*" (*FNR*, 70; translation modified). Third, the interaction between subjects takes place over an extended period of time, and so is not a one-time occurrence in the child's rearing in which, upon being summoned, it immediately posits itself as a full-blooded self-conscious rational being. This third point deserves some elaboration.

First it is worth noting that the interaction and summoning involved in upbringing, in contrast to political recognition, constitutes a unique form of recognition: elementary recognition. Fichte endorses elementary recognition in §56 of "On the Reciprocal Relation of Right between Parents and Children." Since the child is not yet free, on Fichte's view, it "is not at all a possible subject of rights or duties" (*FNR*, 311; *SW*, III: 359). However, the child develops a sense of freedom, and "as the child grows in understanding, [the child's parents] ought to give him increasingly more freedom, anyway – *not in consequence of the child's rights, but in consequence of an important rule of upbringing*" (*FNR*, 316; *SW*, III: 365; my emphasis). Below I will account for what Fichte has in mind by this "important rule of upbringing" but first notice that an extended sphere of freedom is granted to the child not because the child is a right-bearing individual, but for the purpose of further developing its sense or consciousness of freedom as a human being. The child can eventually become a right-bearing political individual by willing to live in a community of political individuals constituted and regulated by right.

The second point worth recognizing is Fichte's choice to characterize the summons with the term *Erziehung*. *Erziehung* can be translated as "education" (as in Kroeger's translation) or "upbringing" (as in Baur's translation).[22] Another, perhaps, more limited option is "rearing." The verb "*erziehen*" means to educate, bring up, or rear a child by forming the mental dispositions and character of the child so that it is in unison with the norms and practices of society.[23] It is useful to examine "*Erziehung*" and the verb form "*erziehen*" morphologically, with the caveat that too much philosophical weight should not be placed on such an analysis. The root word is the verb "*ziehen*," which can mean to move something by force, to pull, drag, or tug. The prefix "er-" sometimes alters the meanings of words by signifying an

[22] For Kroeger's translation, see Fichte 1869: 61.

[23] See, the entry for *Erziehung* in Ritter 1971–84 and the entry in the "Digitale Wörterbuch der Deutschen Sprache:" http://www.dwds.de/?qu=Erziehung (accessed: June 11, 2015).

achievement or the completion of a process (e.g. "*stechen*" means "to stab," yet "*erstechen*" means to stab to death). With this in mind, we can begin to identify "*erziehen*" as a process that eventually comes to completion – it is a certain kind of achievement. Fichte, in fact, claims as much: "education is a means to an end; and the means falls away once the end has been achieved. The end of education was to make the child's forces useful for furthering the end of reason in some field and in some manner" (*SE*, 323; *SW*, IV: 342). Understanding *Erziehung* as an achievement that is the result of a *process* that unfolds over time supports the suggestion that the summons occurs not in only one discrete moment, but over a period of time and on a number of occasions throughout the child's rearing.

In *Natural Right*, Fichte does not situate the summons and the achievement of self-consciousness in the context of a subject's *Bildung* as Hegel does in the *Phenomenology of Spirit*.[24] The robust notion of *Bildung* one finds in Hegel and Gadamer, for instance, possesses a broader normative scope than that of Fichte's conception of *Erziehung* in *Natural Right*. When the language of *Bildung* does appear in *Natural Right*, it is largely subordinated to *Erziehung*, a form of development that eventually comes to an end. By way of example, one end of *Erziehung* is achieved once the "child's capacities are developed (*entwickelt*) and cultivated (*gebildet*) so as to be useful for all sorts of ends" (*FNR*, 310; *SW*, III: 359). In contrast, *Bildung*, as Gadamer nicely illustrates, evokes "the ancient mystical tradition according to which man carries in his soul the image of God, after whom he is fashioned, and which man must cultivate in himself."[25] However, in the German Enlightenment tradition and in the works of Goethe, Herder, and the German Idealists, the internal image (*Bild*) is not exactly God, but rather the secular notion of humanity. To raise oneself to humanity is to raise oneself out of one's "natural being to the spiritual" by making or forming oneself according to the pre-given "language, customs, and institutions of [one's] people" in such a way that those norms are not alien, but one's very own.[26] The relevant point, for my purpose, is that *Bildung* as an ongoing developmental initiation in and reconciliation with the cultural and normative frameworks of a historical

[24] See the entry for *Bildung* in Ritter 1971–84: "the concept of *Bildung* is first joined with the problem of subjectivity and spiritual actuality (*geistigen Wirklischkeit*) in German Idealism" (925). While this connection is nascent in *Natural Right*, where *Erziehung* is the predominant concept in this respect, it is clearer in Fichte's *The Vocation of Man*. See *VM*, 11–14; *SW*, II: 179–83.

[25] Gadamer 1989: 11.

[26] Gadamer 1989: 14.

culture's very form of life extends considerably beyond the relatively austere normative framework Fichte considers essential to *Erziehung*, particularly when he conceptualizes it as a summons to self-activity in *Natural Right*. Furthermore, it is not obvious that there is a discrete end to *Bildung*, as conceived by Hegel and Gadamer, whereas there is such an end on Fichte's view of *Erziehung*.[27]

What then, at least in *Natural Right*, is the normative scope of *Erziehung*? Fichte does comment explicitly on the normative scope of upbringing in §44 when he identifies two ends or goals of *Erziehung*. Addressing these goals will additionally bring to light the "important rule" of upbringing that distinguishes elementary recognition from political recognition. The first goal of *Erziehung* I just noted: the development and cultivation of a child's capacities to realize various or "all sorts of ends" (*FNR*, 310; *SW*, III: 359). The second goal of *Erziehung* is to direct the child's mind (*Sinn*) "towards morality" by promoting moral deliberation and the willing of moral ends (*FNR*, 310; *SW*, III: 359). These two goals of upbringing are similar to the extent that each aims to cultivate in the child a capacity to exercise its ability to freely form the concept of an action's end. The first goal is certainly broader since any end of action would seem to fall within its domain, although this cannot be entirely correct. Fichte actually restricts the legitimate ends of action to "all sorts of ends," excluding ends that work against the "child's preservation and health" or any end of action that would work against the development of its capacity to will ends in the first place (*FNR*, 310; *SW*, III: 359). Although Fichte does not make it explicit in §44, the concept of right, for reasons similar to maintaining the child's "preservation and health," restricts the "sorts of ends" the child might legitimately will, since willing an end that violates the strictures of the concept of right will result in conditions in which the child's very will is limited in its capacity to be exercised. In other words, the sorts of ends the child, as a result of its upbringing, may legitimately will are the ends of actions that stand in accordance with the concept of right and are responsive to the summons of others. Thus, a goal of upbringing is to cultivate in the child reason responsive capacities that are used to will actions that take respect for another person's external freedom as a constitutive end of the action.

[27] Gadamer writes: "Bildung has no goals outside itself. (The word and thing Bildungziel – the goal of cultivation – is to be regarded with the suspicion appropriate to such a secondary kind of Bildung. Bildung as such cannot be a goal …). In having no goals outside itself, the concept of Bildung transcends that of the mere cultivation of given talents" (Gadamer 1989: 11).

Before turning to the second goal of upbringing, it is worth pausing for a moment to return to the idea of elementary recognition as distinct from political recognition. I suggested at the outset that the dividing line between each form of recognition is the constitutive end of each act of recognition. The end of the former is conditioned by what Fichte calls a "rule of upbringing," whereas the end of the latter is respect for another's external freedom and rights. Fichte never actually states what this rule of upbringing consists in, so one is left to piece it together. My suggestion is that the rule he has in mind is, at least in part, the first goal of upbringing – to develop and cultivate the child's capacity to formulate reason responsive ends of action, which entails respect for the external freedom of others.

The second goal of *Erziehung* is clearly restricted even more than the first since its aim is to cultivate not simply the capacity to formulate and will an end of action, within certain limits, but to will, in particular, moral ends. Fichte, in fact, identifies this second goal of *Erziehung* as "the child's *higher upbringing*" (*FNR*, 310; *SW*, III: 359). By implication, the first goal of *Erziehung* constitutes the child's *lower upbringing* and is, it appears, a necessary condition of the child's higher upbringing as well as a prior developmental stage. Fichte opens §44 with the largely ungrounded claim: "it is the universal moral duty of every morally good human being to spread morality beyond himself and to promote it everywhere" (*FNR*, 310; *SW*, III: 358). From this it would follow that it is the moral duty of each parent, insofar as each is a "morally good human being," to promote the child's lower upbringing by instilling in their child respect for the external freedom and rights of others, since this is a necessary and developmental condition of instilling morality. It should be clear, at this point, that the normative scope of lower upbringing extends to external freedom, but not internal freedom, which falls under the normative scope of higher upbringing. To illustrate: a child acts in accordance with right when she freely chooses to not steal her friend's toy, although her action may fall short of achieving moral worth if her will issued from something other than her moral duty or autonomy. It seems clear that if the first goal of upbringing constitutes in part the "rule of upbringing," the second goal of moral development makes up a second dimension of the rule, if not a second rule of upbringing.

The normative scope of *Erziehung* in the form of lower upbringing is limited to the austere normative framework of right, the exercise of external freedom, and reasons responsiveness. This entails that certain interactions between parents and children involved in elementary recognition are constrained by the summons and the concept of right. In order for those interactions to satisfy the conditions of the summons, the interactions of the parent must not interfere with the child's external freedom. As the child develops the ability to reciprocate, first, perhaps, through imitation and eventually freely and intentionally, the child exhibits its gradually developing individuality.[28] Certainly, there are many moments when the parent must jettison acting on the basis of the concept of right and the summons either because the concept is inapplicable (the child's will has yet to properly take shape), or because doing so is necessary for the child's preservation, health, or general well-being. Considering these points, we can, for the moment, imagine that the upbringing of any child falls within a continuum that extends between two poles: the coercion pole and the freedom pole. Depending on the point in the child's development, the force exercised by coercion is necessary to raise the child, while at other points allowing the child to exercise its own agency is at times necessary, because it is required for the realization of its self-efficacy. In many instances in the child's development, the parent oscillates between these two poles, exercising limited amounts of force in one moment, only to immediately oscillate to allowing the child to determine its own actions in another moment. Fichte makes just this point: "Some uses of freedom would be detrimental to the child's preservation, which the parents also desire. Thus the parents will … restrict the child's freedom so that the child's exercise of his freedom does not endanger his preservation" (*FNR*, 309; *SW*, III: 358).

During the process of upbringing, the parents self-limit their actions in *accordance with right*, but not *from right*. Here the import of distinguishing between the elementary recognition of human beings (in accordance with right) and the political recognition of political individuals (from or for the sake of right) becomes clear. When parents self-limit with respect to their children it is not out of respect for the child's right itself, since the child, lacking freedom, is not a right-bearing individual. The parents self-limit out of respect for the child's upbringing and in accordance with the rule of upbringing. This is what Fichte has in mind when he suggests, "As the child grows in understanding, [the parents] ought to give him increasingly more freedom, anyway – not in consequence of the child's rights, but in consequence of an important rule of upbringing" (*FNR*, 316; *SW*, III: 365). By giving the child an increasing sphere of freedom, the

[28] See Fichte's remarks about children and imitation in *SE*, 320; *SW*, IV: 339.

parents are engaging in elementary recognition. From the standpoint of right, upbringing eventually comes to a close when the parent and other individuals can engage in non-coercive relations with the child by acting solely by virtue of the summons, a point in the child's development Fichte believes is best identified by the parents, although the state might legally mark the end of upbringing or liberate a child from its parents (*FNR*, 316; *SW*, III: 365).[29] Upbringing, then, clearly extends beyond the achievement of self-consciousness in ways that may not obviously appear to contribute to the child's consciousness of itself as an agent; however, these later moments in the child's upbringing do contribute to the child's fine tuning of its theoretical and practical understanding of the concept of right – its understanding of its practical agency.

Nature, Reason, and Development

In his discussion of the relations between parents and children, Fichte begins to outline a naturalistic foundation to the summons. First, he notes that the relationship between parent and child does not hinge originally on relations of right, but on relations established by nature and morality (*FNR*, 305; *SW* III; 353). In particular, the mother has an "organic bond" with the child established by the fact that her body, in Fichte's words, nourishes and preserves the fetus. Once born, the infant is an "incomplete animal" that must be further shaped by reason, rather than mere mechanical necessity. After birth, the organic bond persists as the mother's milk provides the child nourishment. Fichte characterizes the organic bond between the mother and child as a law of nature since the child and mother interact in a law-like manner in which they reciprocally depend on each other. The child has a natural drive for food or nourishment and the mother needs the child to relieve her of her milk: such a reciprocal drive–need relationship when found in the workings of nature Fichte conceives of as an "organic bond" (*FNR*, 306; *SW*, III: 354–5). Plants and animal relations also exhibit a similar reciprocal drive–need relation, or organic bond, yet the difference between plants and animals and intelligent beings is the role consciousness of the drive plays in the drive's expression in the case of intelligent beings. With plants and animals, the

[29] Marriage could serve as another marker of the end of upbringing, but this marker still places either the parents or the state in the position to judge that the child's upbringing is ready to come to an end, since parents or the state would determine that the child is ready to marry (*FNR*, 316; *SW*, III: 365).

drive–need relationship is merely a mechanical instinct or reflex, and thus, not an expression of freedom. Consciousness enters as a "third thing" in the case of intelligent beings who attend to their feeling or awareness of the natural drive. The natural drive becomes a feeling when there is a consciousness of it, and once there is a consciousness of the natural drive, the subject can endorse the drive as one to act upon or deny. As Fichte remarks, "since reason is also at work here, this drive can be resisted if the human being sinks to doing what is unnatural" (*FNR*, 307; *SW*, III: 356). Animals would seem to illustrate Fichte's well-known account of the dogmatist theory of experience, since they are incapable of denying the contents of consciousness or denying their natural drive.[30] With consciousness of the natural drive the activity of the drive comes under the influence of freedom, particularly with respect to the drive's end or satisfaction. The subject is capable of offering reasons for satisfying the drive or is capable of appreciating, to some extent, its motivations for realizing the drive.

In the mother, Fichte argues, the natural drive to satisfy the needs of her child takes the form of *sympathy*, "a feeling of the needs of another, just as she feels her own" (*FNR*, 307; *SW*, III: 355). Her sympathy aims at the preservation of the child's physical being. We can infer that this also includes sympathy for the child's psychological being, since a well-formed or healthy psychology promotes in the child a care of its own physical being. The natural drive or feeling of sympathy is characterized in mechanistic terms, but unlike the mechanisms found in plants and animals it is "a mechanism of both nature and reason, together in unity" (*FNR*, 307; *SW*, III: 356). What makes it a mechanism containing a natural dimension is the organic bond at the heart of the mother's sympathy, yet the mechanism contains a rational dimension, the mechanism is, in other words, subject to reason, since it can be consciously or rationally denied, unlike the natural mechanisms involved in digestion. While Fichte's understanding of the mother's sympathy for her child is naturalistically grounded in the mother and child's organic bond, he conceives of the father's sympathy, or "special love for his child" to arise "*originally*" from the father's love or "tenderness for the mother," from his desire to realize her "every wish and end" as his own (*FNR*, 308: *SW*, III: 357). There is no doubt that many will find much to take issue with in Fichte's account of

[30] Fichte writes, for instance: "Dogmatism is supposed to explain representations, and it tries to make a particular representation comprehensible on the basis of an efficacious action of the thing itself. The dogmatist, however, is not permitted to deny the testimony of immediate consciousness regarding representations" (*IW*, 20; *SW*, I: 435).

parental love, whether or not one is a mother or father. What is of interest, however, is Fichte's naturalistic approach to theorizing this parental love and its relevance for understanding his conception of upbringing and the child's development.

Fichte's remarks on parental love and in particular the mother's sympathy for her child's physical preservation offer a way of grounding, from a naturalistic standpoint, his understanding of the recognitive relations of upbringing or summoning. Parental sympathy grounds the intersubjective relations involved in upbringing: "The parents … will summon him to engage in free activity: and so reason and freedom will gradually manifest themselves in the child. According to the necessary concepts of human existence, freedom is part of well-being: the parents desire the well-being of their child, and so they will grant him his freedom" (*FNR*, 309; *SW*, III: 309). Fichte makes a similar point in *The System of Ethics*:

> Since human beings are only too inclined to transfer the concept of reason and freedom to everything outside them, the father and mother could also be expected to transfer to their child this concept of reason and freedom and to treat the child in accordance with this presupposition, and in this case it could not fail to happen that traces (*Spuren*) of reason would, when summoned by this mutual interaction, manifest themselves in the child. (SE, 317; SW, IV: 335)

In both passages, Fichte emphasizes the gradual development of reason in which traces of reason manifest themselves by virtue of the family's intersubjective engagement. As these traces of reason emerge, the parent readjusts its orientation toward the child by granting it more freedom by relying less on force and more on the summons.

Conclusion

In *Natural Right*, Fichte presents a developmental view of self-consciousness in which the self-activity of the individual agent is initiated over time and not all at once, as his conception of the pure I would seem to suggest. The outcome of *Erziehung* is a subject, whose standing as an individual, is initiated and constituted by virtue of its relations with other rational individual agents. My argument hangs on a distinction between two types of recognition, elementary recognition, which recognizes individual human beings as reason responsive agents, and political recognition, which recognizes individuals as political right-bearing individuals. Elementary recognition is involved primarily in lower upbringing, as it is engaged in for the sake of developing the child's capacity to will the kinds of ends that are compatible with living in a community of free rational political individuals. This developmental process relies on parental love and sympathy as well as a form of elementary recognition that tracks the child's developing ability to respond to the summons and will ends compatible with the freedom of others. As the child develops, the parent provides the child with more room to exercise its freedom, and eventually, to achieve political individuality. While Fichte's remarks are at times merely suggestive, it is clear that Fichte understood individual self-consciousness to result from a process of elementary and political recognition.

CHAPTER 7

The Body as Site of Action and Intersubjectivity in Fichte's Foundations of Natural Right

John Russon

Fichte's *Foundations of Natural Right according to the Principles of the Theory of Scientific Knowledge (Wissenschaftslehre)* of 1796–7 is a profound reflection on the nature of freedom that has as its chief focus the demonstration of the sorts of political institutions that are necessary for free beings to exist as such. One of the most original and exciting dimensions of this demonstration is Fichte's analysis of the necessary finitude of the free being. Freedom can only be realized in and as finite agents operating in the natural world, and the body is the unique reality that is the site for this mediation of the finite and the infinite, of nature and freedom. Furthermore, Fichte demonstrates that our free action is inherently a matter of integrating ourselves with the free agency of others, with the result that freedom is necessarily an intersubjective realization. As the site for the worldly enactment of our finite freedom, the body is thus also the site of our inescapable intersubjectivity. Explicating these various dimensions of Fichte's analysis will ultimately reveal that the human body only assumes its distinctive and definitive form when it exists as language. In other words, what is distinctive of the human body as the embodiment of freedom is that it exists as the enactment of the gesture by which free agents recognize (or deny) the freedom of others.

"I" as First Principle of Knowledge and Action

Our experience is situated at the intersection of theoretical and practical experience: we experience ourselves as subject to appearances – the world presents itself to us – and we experience ourselves as engaged in the transformation of that same world through action; correspondingly, we find ourselves simultaneously subjected to the norms of objectivity and morality. Both of these sides of our experience – presentation and action – are indefinitely ongoing, that is, they are not particular, optional practices that are circumscribed by some broader domain of our experience that would set limits to them.[1] On the contrary, their continuous happening is the very substance and fabric of our experience, the conditions without which there would not be experience. It is, however, common for us to identify ourselves, both psychologically and theoretically, as something prior to and independent of experience that "has" the power to "represent" and the power to will as if those powers were properties of a detachable, substantial "self," a separately existing "mind" construed as an agent who "does" the representing and willing. Imagining things this way in turn encourages imagining theoretical experience and practical experience as if they existed separately from each other. Fichte's analysis of the "I" challenges this familiar interpretation of experience, demonstrating both the inseparability of theoretical and practical experience, and, concomitantly, the non-"substantial" nature of the "I" (*FNR*, 22; *SW*, III: 21).[2]

Fichte's distinctive project is to parse out the different, constitutive dimensions of our familiar experience, taking experience up not just as an immediate, empirical whole but in terms of its logical and ontological "layering."[3] As he writes in the "First Introduction" to his philosophical system, the *Wissenschaftslehre* or "*Theory of Scientific Knowledge*" of 1797:

> Only the whole occurs in consciousness, and this totality is in fact experience. Idealism seeks a closer acquaintance with this whole, and so must analyze it, and this not by a blind groping, but according to a definite rule of composition, so that it may see the whole take form before its eyes. It can do this because it can abstract. (*SK*, 27–8; *SW*, I: 448)[4]

Engaging in such a philosophical reflection shows the empirical "I" – the "I" interpreted as the independently existing subject behind our perceiving and acting – not to be primitive, but to be rooted in more

[1] Fichte writes: "Thus willing and representing stand in constant, necessary reciprocal interaction, and neither is possible if the other is not present at the same time" (*FNR*, 22; *SW*, III: 21).

[2] See *FNR*, 22; *SW*, III: 22: "Intuiting and willing neither precede nor follow the I, but rather are themselves the I." In its challenge to the substantial conception of the "I," Fichte's philosophy also offers rich resources for engagement with the Buddhist notion of *anatta* or "no self." Compare Breazeale 1999: Fichte's project is "a merciless and uncompromising exposé of the vanity of the 'absolutely self-positing I' " (p. 106).

[3] I use the term "layering" to allude to the continuity between Fichte's philosophy and Husserl's phenomenology. See Costello 2013. On the idea that, in our ongoing experience, we have always already accomplished the syntheses Fichte's argument progressively generates, see, for example, *SK*, 255–6; *SW*, I: 290–1.

[4] See also the "First Introduction": "A finite rational being has nothing beyond experience; it is this that comprises the entire staple of his thought. The philosopher is necessarily in the same position; it seems, therefore, incomprehensible how he could raise himself above experience. But he is able to abstract; that is, he can separate what is conjoined in experience through the freedom of thought" (*SK*, 8; *SW*, I: 425).

fundamental processes, the understanding of which gives the lie to the familiar self-interpretation that characterizes our "natural attitude."[5] As we work step-by-step through Fichte's dynamic exposition of the constitutive (and conflicting) dimensions of self-experience we will witness how it is the very nature of the "I" to reveal about itself that it exists only in and as the simultaneously practical and theoretical relation of finite self to finite other.

Referring to "I-hood" as "rationality," Fichte writes in the *Foundations of Natural Right* that, "the character of rationality consists in the fact that that which acts and that which is acted upon are one and the same" (*FNR*, 3; *SW*, III: 1). Consequently, "there is nothing in a rational being except the result of its acting upon itself" (*FNR*, 3; *SW*, III: 1), with the result that:

> What the rational being intuits, it intuits within itself; but there is nothing in the rational being to be intuited except its own acting: and the I itself is nothing other than an acting upon itself. (*FNR* 3; *SW*, III: 1)

This claim is both a phenomenological claim and a truth by definition. The "I" is, first, a reality that each of us does find, and that can only be found, within experience. To grasp what Fichte points to with his reflection on the "I," one must, as he indicates, abstract from one's own "I" and reflect on what it is to be an "I" in principle (*FNR*, 3; *SW*, III: 1). In thus reflecting on this experience, we can recognize that it is the very meaning of "self-consciousness" that we become self-conscious beings only in and as the act of being self-conscious. In this sense, then, the "I" by its very nature is exclusively a self-relation and it does not exist as anything other than this act of self-relation. As Fichte writes in the First Introduction to the *Theory of Scientific Knowledge* of 1797:

> The intellect, for idealism, is an *act* (*ein Thun*), and absolutely nothing more; we should not even call it an *active* something (*ein Thätiges*), for this expression refers to something subsistent in which activity inheres. (*SK*, 21; *SW*, I: 440)[6]

5 This is Husserl's name for this form of experiential self-interpretation. See Husserl 1982: 5. Like Husserl's notion of the "bracketting" (*Einklammerung*) of our presumptions about reality, Fichte's philosophical method demands that "the speculative philosopher achieve distance (*entfernen*) from this conviction for a time" (*FNR*, 27; *SW*, III: 27; translation modified).

6 Fichte makes the same point in *FNR*, 3; *SW*, III: 1 n. a: "I do not even want to call the I an *acting something* (*ein Handelndes*)." Compare *FNR*, 23; *SW*, III: 22: "As soon as we hear of the I as active, we do not hesitate to imagine a substratum that is supposed to contain this activity as a bare capacity. This is not the I, but rather a product of our own imagination, which we construct in response to the demand to think the I."

Similarly, in the *Foundations of Natural Right*, he writes:

> The I is not something *that has capacities*, it is not a capacity at all, but rather is *active*; it is what it does, and when it does nothing, it is nothing. (*FNR*, 23; *SW*, III: 22)

Holding on to the experiential reality of the "I" thus requires that we acknowledge, as Fichte says, that the "I" is not a substratum but is "its *own deed and product simultaneously*" (*FNR*, 23; *SW*, III: 22; emphasis in original).

This claim parallels the argument of Fichte's earlier *Foundations of the Entire Theory of Scientific Knowledge* (*Wissenschaftslehre*) of 1794/95.[7] In any experience, Fichte there argues, it is necessary that the experiencer be tacitly aware *that* she is experiencing; otherwise, there would precisely be no *noticing*. Alongside any of my explicit recognitions of objects is my implicit recognition that these are precisely *my* recognitions.[8] In that sense all of my experience is at root an experiencing of my act of experiencing, and thus, as Fichte argues, the "First, Absolutely Unconditioned Principle" of all experience is that "the I posits itself" (*SK*, 93; *SW*, I: 91). To be an "I" is precisely to experience oneself as exclusively self-related, in the sense that one necessarily finds oneself "inside" one's own experience. Inasmuch as this self-relation is definitive, it further follows that the "I" can be something that only exists in and as its act. Such a being that is the activity of self-defining, self-enactment – of self-determination – is precisely a *free* being, a being that in principle is beyond determination by another, and that experiences itself as the source of its own situation.

Now, to be free, one must not be determined by something alien, but, at the same time, freedom only is if it actually does something – otherwise it would not be anything at all.[9] Hence the "First Theorem" of the *Foundations of Natural Right*: "A finite rational being cannot posit itself

[7] This work, *Foundations of the Entire Theory of Scientific Knowledge (Wissenschaftslehre)*, though included in the English translation entitled *Science of Knowledge* should not simply be equated with the *Wissenschaftslehre*. "*Wissenschaftlehre*" is not the title of a separate book but is the name Fichte gives to his whole system of philosophy. On the nature of the *Wissenschaftslehre* as a philosophical system, see Breazeale (2014). On the relationship between this argument in the *Foundations of the Entire Theory of Scientific Knowledge (Wissenschaftslehre)* and the corresponding argument in the *Foundations of Natural Right*, see Wood (Forthcoming).

[8] This is concisely rendered in the 1797 *Attempt at a New Presentation of the Theory of Scientific Knowledge* (*Wissenschaftlehre*): "I can be conscious of any object only on the condition that I am also conscious of myself, that is, of the conscious subject" (*IW*, 112; *SW*, I: 527).

[9] Compare *Foundations of the Entire Theory of Scientific Knowledge (Wissenschaftslehre)*, 4th discourse: "The self's striving, the not-self's striving, and the equilibrium between them, must be posited" (*SK*, 253; *SW*, I: 287). Though Fichte explicitly distinguishes "striving" from "efficacy," the point is analogous.

without ascribing a free efficacy (*Wirksamkeit*) to itself" (*FNR*, 18: *SW*, III: 17). The "I" only exists as efficacy: I am only inasmuch as I effect a change. To effect a change, however, I must have an impact on another, and thus I must be in relation to another. Fichte writes:

> The activity we are seeking can be posited by the rational being in opposition to the world, which would then limit the activity … such an activity is the sole condition of the possibility of self-consciousness. (*FNR*, 19; *SW*, III: 18)

The freedom that constitutes the rational being, then, can only be if it is a relation to another.[10] This condition has two important consequences.

The first consequence is that the "I" exists only in and as a body acting in relation to other bodies. This is the central theme of the "Fourth Theorem" of the *Foundations of Natural Right*: "The rational being cannot posit itself as an individual that has efficacy without ascribing to itself, and thereby determining, a material body" (*FNR*, 53; *SW*, III: 56). Freedom, our infinite self-relation, can only be enacted as the freedom *of* a finite, determinate body. And, indeed, it is the freedom "of" this body in the sense that it is exactly *as* this body that I am free: the body is "mine" to the extent that it is the immediate expression of my will.

> Since the body thus described is nothing other than the sphere of the person's free actions, the concept of such a sphere is exhausted by the concept of the body, and *vice versa*. The person cannot be an absolutely free cause (i.e., a cause that has efficacy immediately through the will) except in the body … Conversely, no determination can occur in the body, except as a result of the person's efficacy. (*FNR*, 56; *SW*, III: 59)

My body is not some alien thing with which I somehow come into contact; on the contrary, it is my immediate realization. Indeed, we can immediately notice phenomenologically the difference between my body and other bodies in that, whereas I act instrumentally *upon* other bodies, I act instrumentally *with* or *by means of* my body.[11] If I act upon those other

[10] See Breazeale 2013d: 207: "an I that is not 'for itself' is not really an I at all, and … only a limited I can posit itself for itself and be conscious of its own efficacy. Hence the concept of the 'pure I' refers to nothing *real*, but simply to the *abstract structure* of I-hood as such." Compare also to Fichte: "Here the meaning of the principle, *the self posits itself absolutely*, first becomes wholly clear. There is no reference at all therein to the self given in actual consciousness; for the latter is never absolute, its state being invariably based, either mediately or immediately, upon something outside the self. We are speaking, rather, of an idea of the self which must necessarily underlie its infinite practical demand, though it is inaccessible to our consciousness, and so can never appear immediately therein (though it may, of course, mediately, in philosophical reflection)" (*SK*, 244; *SW*, I: 277).

[11] For an excellent account of Fichte's argument here, see Bernstein 2010: 67.

bodies, I will do so through the intermediary of my own body, but in the case of moving my own body, there is no such intermediary: whereas my will mediately affects other bodies, my will immediately informs my body:

> A material body (*Körper*) such as the one described, whose permanence and identity we tie to the permanence and identity of our own personality – a body we posit as a closed, articulated whole, and within which we posit ourselves as a cause that acts immediately through our will – is what we call *our human body* (*Leib*). (FNR, 58; SW, III: 61)[12]

My body is "mine," not in the sense of a possession, but in the sense of being the very realization of my agency: within my experience, my body is the reality I *live* intimately (*Leib*) – indeed, it is the very form of my living – and not an alien thing (*Körper*) to which I might stand in a relation of possession.[13] The first consequence of the necessary other-relatedness that defines free efficacy, then, is that the "I" necessarily exists as an acting body in bodily interaction with other bodies.[14]

The second consequence is that, in its immediate condition, the experience of freedom involves a contradiction: the pure self-relation can only be if it is a relation to another. This seeming contradiction again has its parallel in Fichte's discussion of the nature of the "I" in the *Foundations of the Entire Theory of Scientific Knowledge.*

We saw above that the first condition of experience is that it must be a matter of the "I" positing itself. If that self-positing were all that happens in experience, though, there would be no experience, because the experience would not be "of" anything. If there is to be experience, there must be something experienced and, qua something experienced, it must be experienced *as* something other than the experiencing. Thus, Fichte argues, the second principle of experience is that the "I" must oppose itself to a not-"I," that is, it must find itself in relation to an other which it precisely experiences *as* not a consequence of its own positing.[15] Just as there is freedom only in the context of the having of an effect upon a determinate other, so is there experience only in the context of a presenting

[12] Nuzzo notes: "The body is the first and foremost agent (not just the medium) of human concrete interpersonal activity and freedom." We will see in Section III the significance of the remark with which she follows up this comment: "The body is the material principle of individuality but is also, at the same time, that which makes visible the intrinsically public and intersubjective dimension of human individuality" (Nuzzo 2006: 71).

[13] The distinction between *Leib* and *Körper* is richly explored in twentieth century phenomenological literature. For a discussion of this theme, see Carman 1999.

[14] See especially *FNR*, 104–6; *SW*, III: 114–17 on the necessity that a free body affect other bodies.

[15] See Fichte's Second Principle in *SK*, 102; *SW*, I: 101.

of a determinate other.[16] In both "representing" (knowing) and in "willing" (action), it is only in and as a finite relation-to-other than an infinite relation-to-self is possible.

The problem, for both awareness and action, is that experience seems to rest on a contradiction: it must be exclusively a relation-to-self *and* a relation-to-other.[17] The problem in each case is that embracing one of these necessary sides seems to make the other side impossible. In the case of knowledge, the problem is that having the pure self-relation necessary to experience would seem to make the relation to other, and hence knowledge, impossible: since I must always experience myself in and through my experience of my object, it would seem that the other can never be truly other – can never truly put a "check" (*Anstoß*) on my self-absorption – for its very otherness seems to be my ascription, and thus, in place of an exposure to an alien, knowledge is only ever a closed circle of solipsistic self-assurance.[18] In the case of action, actual other-determination would make freedom impossible: if the other were truly able to determine the form of my experience, I would be the effect of a deterministic cause, not a free agent. In either case, then, it seems as if the conditions of the possibility of experience are in fact the conditions of its impossibility.[19]

Of course, though, we do experience, and so, Fichte argues, we must understand how the specific nature of this relation to an other is such that the seeming contradiction does not entail the elimination of experience.[20] The solution to this problem in the domain of "presentation" (that self-determining appears to make knowledge impossible) is, roughly, that there can be experience only on condition that we experience a world of nature that is open to our efforts of understanding: there will be an experience of being "checked" by presentation precisely in the experience

[16] And, inasmuch as presentation depends on freedom, the possibility of presentation depends on the reality of the situation of having an effect on another.

[17] See Fichte's "First Introduction": "Now *the presentation of* the independence of the self, and that of a thing, can assuredly coexist, but not *the independence of* both" (*SK*, 14; *SW*, I: 432; my emphasis).

[18] This issue is discussed clearly in Zöller 1998: 50–3.

[19] Breazeale offers a parallel description of this situation: "The very *concept* of a human being thus harbors within itself a real *tension*, if not an outright *contradiction*: on the one hand, reason must never allow itself to be cancelled by sensibility; but on the other, without finite limits a human being is not an 'I' at all … The only way to 'resolve' this contradiction is to recognize that the distinctive task … of such an 'ontological centaur' … is to strive constantly and endlessly to overcome its self-division by means of concrete action in the world" (Breazeale 2013d: 204).

[20] For the basic statement of the tension, the necessity of its resolution and the relationship of this to Fichte's method, see *SK*, 120–4, 218–21; *SW*, I: 123–8, 246–50. For an excellent discussion of Fichte's overall position here, particularly in relationship to the theme of the "check" (*Anstoß*), see Breazeale 1999.

of oneself *as* sensibly intuiting a causally independent nature that one is compelled to understand by using one's free rationality to grasp its causality.[21] Experience of oneself as an "I," in other words, is only possible in experience that is "empirically real," in Kant's language.[22] And yet, this self-determining not-self within the domain of cognition remains only problematically established in that, while I am experientially compelled to treat my presentations *as* presenting a thing-in-itself, I am intellectually (philosophically) compelled to understand that such a thing-in-itself is only something necessarily posited by me to explain experience (which is experience as "transcendentally ideal," in Kant's language); and, indeed, its putative absoluteness is outstripped precisely by my free ability to posit a moral world to which I hold the actual world answerable in my practical action.[23] Rather than explore this solution to the constitutive tensions of "presentation," though, what I want to focus on in Section 2 is how it is the experience of another self-consciousness that is pivotal to the solution to the parallel problem of action (that being determined by another amounts to the annihilation of my freedom).[24] We shall see that it is precisely the *nature* of the other's "determining" – which is its own acting *as* a

[21] Effectively, we experience ourselves as determined to be self-determining. See *Foundations of the Entire Theory of Scientific Knowledge* (*Wissenschaftslehre*): "In the very respect in which the self is determined, it must be self-determining, and must likewise be determined in the very respect in which it determines itself" (*SK*, 125; *SW*, I: 129). Compare *FNR*, 31; *SW*, III: 33.

[22] For experience as "empirically real" and "transcendentally ideal," see Kant's "Transcendental Aesthetic" (*CPR*, A 27–8/B 44, A35–5/B 52), and especially the "Fourth Paralogism" from the A edition (*CPR*, A 366–80).

[23] For the development of the theoretical meaning of the "not-self" from "check" to the "thing-in-itself" and the Kantian antinomies, see the "Deduction of Presentation," *Foundations of the Entire Theory of Scientific Knowledge* (*SK*, 203–18; *SW*, I: 227–46). For the contextualization of theoretical experience by moral experience, consider the following "This boundless [moral] striving, carried to infinity, is the *condition of the possibility of any object whatsoever*" (*SK*, 231; *SW*, I: 261–2); and "reason cannot even be theoretical, if it is not practical … there can be no intelligence in man, if he does not possess a practical capacity; the possibility of all presentation is founded on the latter" (*SK*, 233; *SW*, I: 264). See also: "The thing-in-itself is something for the self, and consequently in the self, though it ought *not* to be *in the self*; it is thus a contradiction, though as the object of a necessary idea it must be set at the foundation of all our philosophizing, and has always lain at the root of all philosophy and all acts of the finite mind, save only that no one has been clearly aware of it, or of the contradiction contained therein. This relation of the thing-in-itself to the self forms the basis for the entire mechanism of the human and all finite minds" (*SK*, 249, *SW*, I: 283). For a discussion of the theme of the "thing in itself" in the context of debates in post-Kantian idealism, see Martin 1997: Chapter 3 and Breazeale 1999, who offers an insightful discussion of how this notion relates to Fichte's analysis of "feeling" (*Gefühl*). See also Fichte in *Foundations of Natural Right*: "Philosophy must deduce our belief in the existence of an external world … [T]his belief has been shown to be a condition of this self-consciousness" (*FNR*, 24; *SW*, III: 24).

[24] On the idea that the "summons" (*Aufforderung*) of the other person is a form of the "check" (*Anstoß*) defined in the *Foundations of the Entire Theory of Scientific Knowledge (Wissenschaftslehre)*, see Breazeale 1999: 102.

free being – that will allow the interaction of self and other to be a mutual performance of free self-consciousness.

The Summons as Medium of Freedom

As we saw above, in our discussion of the "First, Absolutely Unconditioned Principle," to experience an object, I have to experience myself as an experiencer, which means I have to experience myself as free. We have seen further, though, that experiencing myself as free means experiencing myself as having efficacy. I experience myself as efficacious, however, only if, (a) I exist in and as the positing of a specific end,[25] and (b) I experience the object as defined in terms of that positing, where that means that object must itself (i) *be* something fixed in its own right, but also (ii) be something open to alteration by me (*FNR*, 28; *SW*, III: 30). But in order to experience the object as thus having a fixed character of its own (so as to be that upon which I act), I must experience it as *already* something, that is, I must already have recognized it as something prior to the moment of my transformation of it. But, to have experienced it already as an object, I would already have had to experience myself as free in that same prior moment, for my free self-experience is the condition of my recognition of any object. Fichte writes:

> The rational being cannot posit … an object without simultaneously … ascribing an efficacy to itself. But it cannot ascribe an efficacy to itself without having posited an object upon which such efficacy is supposed to be exercised … And so the explanation of the possibility of consciousness already presupposes consciousness as real. (*FNR*, 29–30; *SW*, III: 30–1)

The possibility of the free positing is thus infinitely deferred backwards, that is, on these terms it is impossible. But consciousness is, obviously, actually occurrent – it is happening. Therefore, there must be something more than the simple "either/or" of the priority of either the subject or the object: specifically, there must be an experience in which *simultaneously*, "in one and the same moment," I experience myself as free (i.e., self-determining) and as determined:

> [The impossibility] can be canceled only if it is assumed that *the subject's efficacy* is synthetically unified with the *object* in one and the same moment, that the subject's efficacy is itself the object that is perceived and

[25] *FNR*, 20; *SW*, III: 19.

> comprehended, and that the object is nothing other than the subject's efficacy. (*FNR*, 31; *SW*, III: 32)

Only the experience of a particular kind of object makes this possible. This is the experience of a summons (*eine Aufforderung*):

> Both [the natures of subject and object] are completely unified if we think of the subject's being-determined as *its being determined to be self-determining*, i.e. as a summons to the subject, calling upon it to resolve to exercise its efficacy. (*FNR*, 31; *SW*, I: 32–3)

In the experience of being *addressed as* free, one experiences an object (the address) that anticipates one will be free – that requires one will be free in order to recognize that anticipation. Thus, a call to be free is an object, the experience of which is the same as the experience of oneself as free.

The experience of the summons itself can only be realized as a relation of two free subjects. A summons to "be self-determining" can only be perceived *as* such by a free being:

> The rational being's activity is by no means to be determined and necessitated by the summons in the way that – under the concept of causality – an effect is determined and necessitated by its cause; rather, the rational being is to determine itself in consequence of the summons. (*FNR*, 35; *SW*, III: 36)

Equally, such a summoning can only be performed by a free being, and thus, to perceive a summons as summons is only possible as the recognition of the summoner as a free being:

> The purposiveness of the summons is conditional on the understanding and freedom of the being to whom it is addressed. Therefore, the cause of the summons must itself necessarily possess the concept of reason and freedom … it must also be a free, and thus a rational, being, and must be posited as such. (*FNR*, 35; *SW*, III: 37)

In this sense, then, the summons to be free is in fact the summons to recognize the other as free. In short, one can experience oneself as free only as the experience of responding to a summons, which is itself the experience of the imperative to recognize the other as free. Hence the "Second Theorem": "The finite rational being cannot ascribe to itself a free agency in the sensible world without also ascribing such efficacy to others, and thus without also presupposing the existence of other finite rational beings outside itself" (*FNR*, 29; *SW*, III: 30). Thus individual freedom can be realized only in and as the mutual recognition of free subjects. As Fichte writes in summary:

> Only free, reciprocal interaction by means of concepts and in accordance with concepts, only the giving and receiving of knowledge, is the distinctive

> character of humanity, by virtue of which alone each person undeniably confirms himself as a human being. (*FNR*, 38; *SW*, III: 40)

And thus, "if there are to be human beings at all, there must be more than one" (*FNR*, 37; *SW*, III, 39). To understand more fully the sense of this intersubjectivity that is constitutive of free existence, let us reflect concretely on the experience of freedom.

Basically, the question is, "Where" or "In what circumstances do we experience ourselves as free?" We tend to think immediately of our freedom as universally and equally present in all of our practices, all of our experiences. It is a very different thing, however, to struggle for breath in the water, and to forage for food, or again to work for a master, and to read a novel. Each of these situations is an engagement with a kind of other, an engagement in which, on the one hand, one brings one's interests to bear on the object and, on the other hand, that object addresses one in a particular way. What it is about one that is brought out in the exchange, however, is different in the different cases. In the case of not-drowning, it is something like one's strength and endurance in preserving one's organism against the indifference of the inorganic that is realized, whereas in the case of foraging for food, it is something like one's ability to carry out a self-designed, instrumental project that is on display. Reading a novel, on the other hand, engages one as a language user, and as one who can deliberately inhabit a world of imagination. Many beings can keep from drowning or forage for food, but only a very distinctive kind of being can read a novel. The important thing to notice is that the former behaviors do not address the "I" *as such*, and it is indeed not only "I"s who can enact such behaviors; in the examples I have given, it is only in this last activity – reading – that it is the definitive nature of the object to address specifically the distinctive capacities of the "rational being."[26]

We experience ourselves as free, and we generally imagine our freedom to be equally definitive of all our activities, but, as the above examples make clear, not all environmentally transformative behavior is *ipso facto* an expression of pure self-determination. In each case, a change is indeed being effected, but the "why" of the change in the examples of drowning and foraging is not just the "I" but is also the imperatives of nature – the constraints of the inorganic, the impulsions of instinct, and so on – that determine why the behavior takes the form it does. Though we are indeed

[26] This theme is explored in rich detail throughout Dewey 1916: Chapters 1–4 and especially 10–14, 26–7, 29–30, and 49.

free beings and, as such, our distinctive nature is surely manifest in all that we do, it is not the case that all of our activities automatically realize our distinctive humanity. We realize our distinctly free nature – our nature as "rational beings – in those actions in which the nature of "I" as such *is* the why.

We concluded Section 1 with the question of how to resolve the tension that the agent must be both self-determining and other-determined. In the behavioral situations we have just sketched out, we have reflected on how the subject was addressed by the object – how the object "determined" the subject. We can now see that situations in which we are addressed *as* an "I" will precisely be situations in which our object "determines" us *as* self-determining.

The water in which I could drown cannot address me as a free being because it is not itself a reality capable of *recognizing* freedom; indeed, inorganic nature is precisely defined by its constitutive indifference to all of the concerns that animate the world of life and, *a fortiori*, the world of cognition and self-conscious rationality. It is in fact a familiar, tragic reality of life, that nature, both inorganic and organic, brings death upon human individuals in a way that does not differentiate between them on grounds of morality or merit. Even our animal companions, who are so much more responsive to us and to each other than is water, are not themselves open to those same dimensions of morality and merit, and there are fundamental limits to our ability to engage with them. What it in fact takes to recognize a free self-consciousness – a "rational being" – is precisely another "rational being." It is to such experiences that Fichte directs our attention with his discussion of the "summons," in order to clarify the conditions in which the tension between self-determination and other determination is resolved, and the conditions for the enactment of freedom are met.

The situation in which another free self-consciousness seeks from me the recognition of her as a free self-consciousness is a situation in which the other with whom I am in relation (a) proves, by recognizing me, her own freedom, and hence her capacity to recognize me, and (b) makes her otherness – the challenge to my self-determinedness – into the very affirmation of my self-determination. By her self-determination, the self-determining other is precisely empowered to affirm my self-determination from the very location from which it is threatened.

It is the other self-consciousness who makes it possible for one to be free. It is exactly their *mutual* recognition that performatively realizes for both their freedom. We both become free in our recognition of our mutual equality. "I-hood," in short, is not an individual possession, but is an intersubjective accomplishment. Recall that, in addition to drowning, foraging, and reading, I noted one other possible behavioral situation above, namely, working for a master. What Fichte's discussion reveals overall is that we are free in principle, but that that freedom requires real conditions to be met in order to be realized. Various ontological conditions must be met – such as, for example, we must be bodies, there must be a world, and so on – but there are also practices that must be enacted if we are to realize our free "I-hood."[27] Specifically, being free requires that we recognize each other as equals, and this is the meaning of the "Third Theorem": "The finite rational being cannot assume the existence of other finite rational beings outside it without positing itself as standing with those beings in a particular relation, called a relation of right (*Rechtsverhältniß*)" (*FNR*, 39; *SW*, III: 41). This, unfortunately, is not something that we always do. Even in a world of members of the natural species "human," it is not a given that the conditions will be met for allowing the realization of the freedom that is distinctive of that humanity, for we can relate to each other in ways that deny the other's freedom, as happens, for example, in relations of slavery (in Hegel's famous development of this point) or alienated labor (in Marx's development). Our freedom is realized only when our existence takes the behavioral form of our mutual recognition of our equality as free beings. We noted above something about the distinctive nature of the body of the free being. Let us now return to that theme in light of this notion of the mutual recognition in which freedom in realized.

Expressing Mutual Recognition

Fichte's initial account of efficacy led us to realize the necessarily finite and determinate character of any free agent. Though our nature is to be infinitely self-determining, each of us is nonetheless necessarily a particular "I," engaged in determinate practices of knowing and acting from within the circumscribed parameters of our individual existence within a world of others. Our freedom is indeed enacted in common, but we are not, for that reason, melded into a single being; on the contrary, establishing our freedom is precisely affirming the ineradicability of the distinction between my "here" and your "there" (*FNR*, 53–4, 112; *SW*, III: 57, 123–4). We are thus separate, and yet we act upon each other in our

[27] Compare *FNR*, 79; *SW*, III: 85.

summoning of and responding to each other. In Section 2, we sorted out the way in which the opposition between other-determination and self-determination is overcome in recognition. In parallel to that, let us now consider the implications of that for the notion of "acting upon" another "I," that is, let us now consider what the character of our (inter)action must be such that we can performatively enact our shared freedom.

It is incumbent upon us to recognize each other but, though this is by definition a matter of freedom responding to freedom, it can only be enacted as the matter of bodies interacting with bodies: just as the freedom of the individual is only enacted in bodily efficacy, so is the free recognition between individuals only realized through its bodily enactment. Indeed, because freedom is enacted bodily, and bodies, as participants in the natural world, are causally implicated with other bodies, the bodily enactment of our freedom cannot fail to be an action already involved with other bodies. Inasmuch as my body is in the natural world, it is vulnerable to the impact of other bodies, and hence to agency enacted through your body. Hence the "Fifth Theorem": "The person cannot ascribe a body to himself without positing it as standing under the influence of a person outside him, and without thereby further determining it" (*FNR*, 58; *SW*, III: 61). For this reason, the interaction between bodies is not just the quantitative relations of natural causality: it is also the qualitative engagement of one freedom with another.[28]

Pre-figuring the works of Hegel and Marx, Fichte here demonstrates transcendentally and phenomenologically the necessarily dialectical relations of quality and quantity that are integral to the very existence of freedom. Each free being, *qua* free, is ontologically irreducible to the other and thus each of us presents to the other a qualitatively different kind of reality – truly, an "other." The recognition of such otherness, though, *qua* recognition, will be enacted in a shared medium, hence the differentiation between us can only be within the same: it will be the recognition of the quantitative difference that identifies you as that portion ("there") of the common world in which I am this portion ("here"). Freedom demands, then, that, on the one hand, a relation of qualities must be enacted as a relation of quantities and that, on the other hand, the relation of quantities must be experienced as the relation of qualities.

The qualitative recognition of one freedom by another immediately appears in and as the quantitative differentiation of two bodies, but the

[28] See *FNR*, 103; *SW*, III: 103 on the necessary translation of qualitative freedom into quantitative relations.

need to translate qualitative recognition into quantitative relations has implications that necessarily extend beyond the limits of individual bodies. Indeed, whereas we initially distinguished the "mine" of agency from the "mine" of possession, we will now see that, nonetheless, it is precisely necessary to the enactment of the "mine" of agency that it be translated into the "mine" of ownership: in short, freedom requires property.

As we saw in Section 1, it is the nature of my freedom that it *inhabits* "my" body in an irreducible and non-transferable way such that, in order to be free, that body *must* be mine in a necessarily exclusive sense – the *metaphysically* exclusive sense of being my very realization, as opposed to the simply empirical exclusivity of "owning property." Further, though, the freedom I enact *through* that body is itself enacted *on* other bodies: to be free, I must inhabit my body as a site of free efficacy, an efficacy that is only enacted through laying claim to some other body as its object. But whereas my body is the one and only body that I inhabit in a metaphysically exclusive manner, all other bodies are possible objects of my freedom.[29] Simply on its own terms, then, freedom lays claim to all other bodies as possible objects of its freedom:

> It is within the sphere of the given and under the condition that something is given that one is free to leave the given as it is or to make it into something else – that is, as it ought to be in accordance with his concept of an end. The person is free to relate the manifold elements of the given reciprocally to one another, to determine them by means of one another, to adapt them to one another, and to arrange them into a whole that is purposive for him. If one of these pieces is missing, the person is not free and not dependent solely on his own will. (*FNR*, 104–5; *SW*, III: 115)

But this logical need to claim all bodily reality as the domain for the possibility of enacting my free agency is no more true of my freedom than of any other's, and thus those other bodies to which I lay claim are necessarily the bodies to which other free beings lay claim as well. In enacting my freedom, I necessarily act in and upon bodies that could equally be a site for the enactment of another's freedom: the entire bodily domain, including both my exclusive body and the other bodies that are my objects, is necessarily the site for the mutual overlapping of my freedom and that of everyone else. For this reason, there is nowhere in the natural world that is not in principle and by definition the site of a conflict of wills, and hence nowhere that is not a site for the enactment of recognition, and hence a relation of right.

[29] On the metaphysical uniqueness of the "here" of my body, see Merleau-Ponty 2012: 102–3. For discussion, see Russon 2007.

It is for this reason that freedom depends upon property rights, that is, upon establishing what, within the world, we will accept to be the legitimate domain for the enactment of each other's freedom.[30] To be me cannot be separated from having what is mine, and this "mine" must be (quantitatively) carved out as an actual possession within a domain that could have been "yours" (or, indeed, anyone's – this latter fact points to essential dimensions of the necessary development of law and society).[31] And, in determining what is "mine" and what is "yours," we also determine the parameters for transgression – for bodily actions that violate the non-immediate bodily world – the property – of the other.

What it is important to remember, though, is that property relations, though quantitative matters of body, have as their *substance* the qualitative reality of mutual recognition. Setting the limits that determine property is a matter, first, of declaring to each other the specificities to which we lay claim: "All relations of right between particular persons are conditioned by their reciprocal declaration of what they will to possess exclusively, and all relations of right become possible only through such declaration" (*FNR*, 115; *SW*, III: 127). It further requires, second, that we agree to each other's claims, and thus, "All property is grounded in the unification of several wills into one" (*FNR*, 117; *SW*, III: 129). Therefore, in sum, "All property is grounded in reciprocal *recognition*, and such recognition is conditioned by *mutual declaration*" (*FNR* 117; *SW*, III: 130; emphasis in original). Through our bodily actions (of, for example, setting up fences and either stepping across or not stepping across the fences set by others), we are *expressing* our recognition or lack thereof of the other's freedom.[32]

Property rights exist in and as recognition: the establishment of property is the way that we *say together* "this is mine" and "this is yours." Property thus exists in and as an act of communication. The issue of property arose, however, in the context of recognizing that as free beings we must exist as bodies acting on each other. What the analysis of property reveals to us is that the *only* way that free beings can interact *as* such is in and through bodily interaction that takes the form of communication: the action of one body upon another is an action of a free being upon another, not insofar as that action is a quantitative matter of natural causality, but only

[30] See *FNR*, 106, 112–17, 121–2; *SW*, III: 116–17, 123–30, 134–6.

[31] On the necessarily quantitative character of right, see *FNR*, 109; *SW*, III: 120. On the implications for right of the fact that property could be "anyone's," see *FNR*, 115–18; *SW*, III: 127–31.

[32] On fences and ditches as ways of "drawing the line" that sets the determinate limit to our freedom, see *FNR*, 55, 121; *SW*, III: 58, 133. The detailed working out of these issues is the core of the whole of Part II of the *Foundations of Natural Right*, "Applied Natural Right."

insofar as it is a matter of the recognition of freedom by freedom, and, in that sense, all bodily interaction between free beings must be a matter of expression, a matter, that is of the "summons."

Consider an example: my hand can strike a blow to your body, and the material character of my hand will have a material effect on your body according to the laws of physical nature. But what does that blow *mean*? Was I assaulting you? Did I hit you accidentally? Was I boisterously demonstrating affection? These questions cannot be answered by looking at the physical bodies in interaction, but can be determined only by appeal to my free self-consciousness – my intention. This is the significance of Fichte's point that the unity of the movements of the human body can *only* be grasped as an expression of freedom, that is, there is no way to understand the articulate movement of a human body without appeal to the self-determining perspective that that body realizes (*FNR*, 74; *SW*, III: 79). This fact that my actions can only be understood as a reflection of my perspective is equally true on your side. Are you angry when I hit you? Are you patiently tolerant? Are you amused? These are determinations of your freedom, and can be found out only by appeal to your freedom. My intention, expressed in and as a bodily blow, is a sort of offer to you, but it is up to you to determine for yourself how you will take up that offer. Thus, strictly speaking, I cannot "act upon" you: what I can do is summon you, exhort you, appeal to you, but it is in every case up to you to take up that call for yourself and through your response, determine its significance for you:

> This influence on the subject is supposed to be such that only a rational being outside the subject can be posited as its cause. This rational being's end would have been to exercise some influence on the subject. But, as we have shown, there can be no influence on the subject at all, unless the subject, through his own freedom, accepts the impression that has been made upon him and internally imitates it ... Therefore, the subject himself must bring to completion the attainment of the external being's end. (FNR, 62; SW, III: 66)[33]

My hand has an impact on your body, but my intention is what you respond to. The interaction of our bodies works according to the laws of natural causality, but the interaction of our freedom happens according to the call and response of meaningful dialogue.

[33] In the free being – the being that can freely give or withhold its attention – there is thus a difference between hearing and listening, between seeing and looking, between feeling and touching, and so on; compare Fichte's discussion of the distinction between higher and lower functions in human sense organs (*FNR*, 60–2; *SW*, III: 64–6).

It is only as bodies that we can be free beings, and it is only as bodies that we can engage with each other. The bodily interaction that defines the interaction of free beings as such, however, is not defined by the parameters of natural causality (though it surely must answer to those laws and work within them). The bodily interaction of free beings is the call and response of mutual solicitation.[34] In the relations between free beings acting as such, the body functions as the medium of the communication of our intentions, of our freedom: it functions precisely as language. This, ultimately, is the import of Fichte's discussion (*FNR*, 74; *SW*, III: 80) of the necessary "formability" of the human body: the ability to "articulate" herself requires that the subject – the individual – must be able to make her body express herself, so the relevant articulations – the "joints" – of the human body are not the naturally given articulations of the animal organism, but are articulations of *her*. The free being, that is, must relate to her own body as her sign. In this sense, then, communication is the very *nature* of the human body: communication is not something one might or might not do; on the contrary, one *is* engaged in communication with others simply by virtue of being a human body (*Leib*) and thus the question is not whether one is communicating with others, but how. In short, the kind of action that is definitive of the free being is precisely expression, and it is only in and as taking up our bodies as language that we perform the mutual recognition that is the enactment of our freedom.

In the context of free beings recognizing each other as such, the bodies of those free beings must exist for those free beings as language: the very body of the free being must exist for other free beings *as a summons*, as a call to be recognized as an expression of freedom. Anticipating Levinas's phenomenology of "the face," Fichte thus concludes his analysis of the body with the claim that the human body is a "sacred" form for the human being, and we can see now why this is so.[35] The free being enacts itself in the experience of responding to the "summons" of another, which is expressed in and as the body of another, and this means that the free being must be the one for whom the body of another is immediately experienced *as* a request for recognition. Just by its presence, the human body calls for recognition, and the entire domain of freedom is contained

[34] Compare Nuzzo: "For Fichte, the human body is the expression of the person's intersubjective determination and destination (*Bestimmung*)" (Nuzzo 2006: 79); and "All our bodily actions, on the other hand, directly translate freedom into existence and are identical with freedom's actuality" (Nuzzo 2006: 86–7). For a parallel development of this idea in relationship to Hegel's philosophy, see Russon 2014.

[35] *FNR*, 79; *SW*, III: 85–6.

within the parameters of how we take up this, our constitutive, intersubjective condition.

Conclusion: The Human Body

In his writings on animal motion, Aristotle noted that the joint is the necessary articulation of the body if there is to be movement: only jointed bodies offer the material conditions of which self-movement can be the soul.[36] We can similarly ask, "What are the necessary bodily conditions for free self-consciousness – 'the rational being'?" What Fichte's analysis shows is that it is the body as language that is the material condition for the possibility of freedom. A body cannot be language on its own, however, but can only exist as such in a context of the mutual recognition of it as such: language is the body held in common between two individuals as the shared medium for the communication of their freedom. It is a body held in common as a shared system of articulation that is the necessary condition of free self-consciousness.[37]

[36] Aristotle 1981: III.10.433b12–26.
[37] Compare Bernstein 2010: 64 on the notion of the body as a "reciprocal concept."

CHAPTER 8

Fichte's Transcendental Deduction of Private Property

Wayne Martin

Private property is a central organizing principle in the modern world, and a powerful force in shaping human relations. But is private property itself legitimate? If so, what is the basis of its legitimacy, and what are its proper limits? What forms of private property should be supported and sustained by the power of the state? And by what norms should contemporary practices regarding private property be assessed? In what follows, I argue that Fichte made an important contribution in grappling with these difficult and important issues. Fichte addresses a question that had been overlooked by other prominent theorists of property and he provides an answer that directly engages those who are skeptical about the very institution. His overall strategy opens up a critical perspective on positive arrangements regarding private property that is of continuing relevance today.

Property is a major theme in the ethical and political writings of Johann Gottlieb Fichte, particularly in his *Foundations of Natural Right* of 1796–7. The most extensive discussion of private property in *Natural Right* comes in §§18–19, where Fichte lays out the details of the property contract. But in what follows, I shall largely set aside these details.[1] Instead, I propose to focus on the treatment of private property in §11 of *Natural Right*. I focus on §11 because it is there, I argue, that Fichte provides what is best understood as a *transcendental deduction of private property*. Or more exactly: he does not actually provide it in §11 in its entirety, but his deduction culminates there, in the passage where he writes: "Here lies the ground of all property rights" (*FNR*, 106; *SW*, III: 116).[2]

[1] For excellent discussions of the property contract see Merle 2001 and James 2011: esp. Ch. 1.
[2] Translation modified.

Earlier versions of this chapter were presented at Jilin University (Changchun, China), the New York German Idealism Workshop, the University of Oxford Post-Kantian Philosophy Seminar, and the Essex German Idealism Reading Group. I am grateful for the helpful feedback from participants at these events, to James Rodwell for assistance in the preparation of the manuscript, and to the editor of this volume for extensive comments on an earlier draft.

Before turning to the particulars of Fichte's treatment of property, a clarification about terminology is in order. Fichte uses the word *Eigenthum* in his discussion of the issues that concern us here. I will follow the Baur/Neuhouser edition, which generally translates this term as "private property." But we need to exercise care with this translation. There is in German a word for private property (*Privateigentum*), which was already in usage (albeit not in widespread usage) as Fichte was writing.[3] One might accordingly translate *Eigenthum* simply as property – although "*Eigen-*" might of itself be taken to suggest something individual. This niggling philological concern corresponds to a larger philosophical concern. In our world, "private property" refers to something rather specific and complex. In particular it is contrasted to public property and communal property, as well as to certain parts of the world that we think no one should own. We will need to be careful about assuming that the (private) property that Fichte "deduces" is the same as the form of private property that figures in modern societies. I return to this point at the end.

A Fichtean Critique of Locke

Philosophical discussions of private property generally begin with Locke. Fichte himself hardly mentions Locke at all; when he does, the doctrines he associates with "the Lockean system" are generally epistemological.[4] Nonetheless, I think that Fichte should have discussed Locke's position in social and political philosophy, so I propose to do so on his behalf.

At least in broad outline, Locke's position on private property is familiar. Start from the state of nature situation, understood as any situation

[3] Kant uses *Privateigenthum* in *The Metaphysics of Morals*, for example, but only in rather specialized contexts. For example, he uses the term in making the point that the sovereign should not be allowed to own private property or estates (4: 323–4). Elsewhere he typically uses the term *Eigenthum*. Data from Google's NGram Viewer suggests that the word *Privateigenthum* (and its orthographical variants) came in to broad usage only after 1850, with prevalence in Google's source corpus tripling between 1800 and 1900. Source: https://books.google.com/ngrams (consulted: November 29, 2014); search parameter: <Privateigenthum+Privateigentum; Language: German>.

[4] In the Jena corpus, Fichte makes reference to "the Lockean system" in his review of Aenesidemus and again in the *Grundriß* (*EPW*, 67, 290; *SW*, I: 12, 389); in both cases the discussion is confined to the theory of representations. Similar references are scattered throughout the corpus. Fichte in several passages treats Locke as the exemplar of the philosophical position that treats all knowledge as a posteriori. See, for example *GA*, II, 11: 346. In his late book on *The Characteristics of the Present Age*, he at one point rather casually describes Locke's philosophy as "*das allerschlechteste philosophischen System*" – the very worst philosophical system (*SW*, VII: 103). I have found no clear evidence indicating that Fichte had *direct* knowledge of Locke's writings, or *any* knowledge of Locke's theory of property. I do not myself see any particular reason to suppose that the "old dispute" to which Fichte refers (*FNR*, 106; *SW*, III: 116–17) has anything specifically to do with Locke, but this is a matter on which further scholarship is required.

absent positive law and established state authorities. Locke holds that property, both communal and private, already exists in the state of nature as a matter of natural right. Natural man's original private property comprises both his own person and his own labor; he can acquire additional property by mixing his labor with unclaimed materials from "the commons." There are then Locke's two famous provisos: enough and as good must be left for others, and one must not let these acquisitions spoil. Finally (to leap ahead to the end of Locke's story) the primary function of the state is to protect private property.[5]

On two important points, Fichte's position aligns with Locke's. Like Locke, Fichte treats private property as a matter of natural right. He also thinks that a primary function of the state is to protect that right. But these points of agreement should not blind us to very fundamental disagreements. I will not undertake a comparison here; instead, my plan is to attempt, on Fichte's behalf, a Fichtean refutation of Locke's defense of private property.

There are three problems with Locke's argument, when viewed from Fichte's perspective. The first has to do the theological premises in Locke's proof. Fichte's first real result in philosophy was the principle that religious revelation must be subjected to critique. Unlike some of his contemporary hardline deists, Fichte held that there is nothing wrong with revealed religion *per se*; indeed he provides a carefully qualified argument for its necessity. But the validity of a purported revelation must always be assessed. That task cannot and should not be undertaken by theoretical reason (here is where Dawkins and the New Atheists tend to go wrong), so we must do so by assessing its practical content – what it tells us about right and wrong.[6]

From Fichte's perspective, Locke gets things exactly the wrong way round. We need a *secular* assessment of the principle of private property in order to critically assess the Biblical narrative. But Locke has run things in the other direction, justifying the ethical critique by appeal to revealed religion.[7] An important giveaway for our purposes pertains to the two

[5] The canonical primary source is the fifth chapter of *The Second Treatise on Government* (1690/1988). For a detailed reconstruction of Locke's position, see Waldron 1988: Ch. 6.

[6] For a summary of these points see *ACR*, 131–2; *SW*, V: 159–60.

[7] I am aware that there are secular readings of Locke's position, and that Locke himself sought a kind of "overlapping consensus" in political philosophy. Locke was a politician, and an apologist; he wanted to bring everybody on board with his position. So he included both religious and secular arguments. But on this matter I side with Waldron's claim that the *Second Treatise* is "not fit to be taught as secular doctrine," although I would not go as far as MacIntyre's *bon mot*: "not fit, constitutionally, to be taught in the public schools of the United States of America." For both remarks, see Waldron 2002: 82 and 44, respectively.

provisos – "enough and as good" and "no spoilage." Locke's justification for them has everything to do with idea of *the commons*. Prior to having my labor mixed in, what was the status of all those acorns and berries? Locke's answer: they were part of the commons. And what is the commons? It is that portion of the earth that is owned in common by all men. And what is the basis for that claim? Locke's answer is saturated with theology: the earth and all therein was a gift from God to man for the support and comfort of their being (*Second Treatise*, §26); "Nothing was made by God for man to spoil or destroy" (*Second Treatise*, §31). So we have revealed premises at the foundation. And those revealed premises then warrant the provisos. My co-owners of the commons would have cause for complaint if I violated the provisos; I would have violated their natural communal ownership rights.

The deeper problem with Locke's argument is already in view. Has he really provided a justification of private property at all? Fichte's answer should be *No*! What he has done is to provide an account of the legitimate *transfer* of pre-existing property rights. First of all, as we have just seen, he starts out with the claim that the un-appropriated portion of the natural world is owned in common. And indeed, before that, he implicitly assumes that God owned the earth and so was able to give it away as a gift. (To give a gift is to transfer property rights from one owner to another.) He also starts out from the assumption that we stand in an owning relationship to our own persons and labor. In the *Second Treatise* Locke says exactly nothing in defense of this proposition, which is far from obvious and theologically contentious.[8] (One of the traditional theological arguments against suicide starts from the thought that our lives belong to God.) He then goes on to provide us with a theory about how we can validly *extend* that original ownership stake to other things. So Locke does not *establish* the validity of property at all; he *assumes* it.

My third Fichtean objection is really just the second objection, reframed in a post-Kantian idiom. Put the point this way: Locke has failed to answer the *quid juris* about private property. Are we even entitled to apply this concept at all? Does it have objective validity? Locke assumes that this is one of those concepts that it is legitimate to use, but he fails to ask about its credentials. If we really want a vindication of private property, we need to start by establishing the validity of the category; for that

[8] For a modern attempt to reconstruct a defense of Locke's position on this last point, see Tully 1980: 105–8.

we need a transcendental deduction – not just a theory of fair transfer that takes the underlying concept of ownership for granted.

Some might complain that this way of putting the challenge is misleading. After all (it might be objected) in the case of private property our concern is not with the validity *of the concept*; the contested issue is only about the validity *of the institution*. There is no serious question about our license to use the concept "private property"; private property is undoubtedly real. The question is whether it is justifiable. In this key respect, it is unlike causality, so a transcendental deduction is not required. One justifies the concept in the same way that one justifies any empirical concept.

To see the mistake in this objection, the first point to recognize is that the concept of private property is not a straightforwardly descriptive empirical concept. It has inescapably normative content. To say of some piece of the world that it is private property is to claim that there is a range of rights and obligations that implicate it. (As a first and rough approximation: the owner has the right to use it, sell it, destroy it, etc.; others have an obligation not to do so without consent from the owner.) So private property only exists at all insofar as there are indeed such rights and obligations. But the skeptic about private property either doubts or denies that there are any such rights and obligations. He thereby doubts or denies that there really is any private property – rather than just a bunch of people illegitimately asserting ownership. In short, private property is *not* undoubtedly real, and this in turn constrains our options for legitimating the concept. If the very existence of genuine-article private property is open to doubt then one cannot establish the validity of the concept of private property simply by pointing to some. Once we are exercised by the *quid juris*, and appreciate that no empirical answer will suffice, we seem to be faced with no other option: we need a deduction. So how (if at all) does Fichte provide one?

One final note before moving on: I have been framing all this in terms of a refutation of Locke, but my main concern is not to show that Locke is wrong. Perhaps Locke and his many supporters have resources for answering all three Fichtean objections. My point is to establish certain Fichtean constraints on any successful vindication of private property. From my imagined exchange with Locke, we bring two constraints into view: (i) a satisfying vindication of private property must be secular; (ii) a satisfying vindication of private property must establish the objective validity of the concept of property rights.

"Here Lies the Ground of All Property Rights"

In looking for Fichte's deduction of private property, it makes sense to begin from the textual signpost to which I have already referred – the dramatic point in §11 where Fichte writes, "Here lies the ground of all property rights." Now the indexical expression in this pronouncement has a certain degree of ambiguity. Where exactly is *here*? The immediate context is a long parenthetical remark, which follows a series of rather extravagant claims about the importance of *stability*:

> [I]t is necessary that *everything remain as it was once known* by the free being and posited in his concept (regardless of whether it is now specifically modified by him or not). (FNR, 105; SW, III: 115; emphasis original)

In the following paragraph he adds:

> The person has the right to demand that in the entire region of the world known to him *everything should remain as he has known it*, because in exercising his efficacy he orients himself in accordance with his knowledge of the world and as soon as a change occurs in the world he immediately becomes disoriented by the course of the world's causality, or he sees results completely different from the ones he intended. (FNR, 105–6; SW, III: 116; emphasis added)

It is immediately following this last claim that the parenthetical begins: "*Here lies the ground …*"

These remarks have led some commentators to argue that Fichte's defense of private property turns specifically on its role in ensuring stability as a condition on the possibility of orientation in action. Hence, for example, Bruce Merrill finds the basis of Fichte's defense of private property in "our right to a stable 'orientation' … The *demand for stability* engenders a legitimate property claim." Michael Vater makes a similar claim: "The basic assumption these rights claims make is that I require that empirical reality (I and the world) *stay structurally the same*, and that practically *things stay as I have put them*. The latter claim is the basis of property."[9]

I hope in due course to be able to make some sense of these extravagant claims, but if we take them at face value, and as bearing the whole weight of Fichte's deduction, then his position looks decidedly unpromising. If we are going to provide a proper deduction of property rights, then we need to have something to say to the skeptic, who either doubts

[9] Merrill 2006: 109 and Vater 2006: 201.

or denies their validity. My preferred skeptic would be a variant of someone like Abbie Hoffman, who insists that things *should not* stay as they are, because our current situation is desperately in need of changing. Fichte is right to recognize that this change will be disorienting for some. The skeptic's answer: "*So be it.*" Secondly, the skeptic will go on to add, there is no reason to have any confidence that the changes that need to be made will be wrought by the owners of private property. Indeed, the skeptic will suspect, private property owners probably hold no small part of the blame for the current dismal state of affairs. Nor, finally, should we be persuaded by Fichte's point about the conditions under which it is possible to act so as to change the world. It is simply not true that action requires a situation in which everything remains the same and others leave a piece of the world alone for me to act in. We very often undertake action in a dynamic setting in which other actors are engaged. So if we read Fichte's "*here*" narrowly, such that private property is justified by its need to ensure an extreme form of stability ("the entire region of the world shall remain as he has known it") then Fichte's deductive strategy is a loser.

Fichte's indexical signpost has a further significance, which, if anything, makes matters even harder. The deduction of private property comes in the context of Fichte's presentation of what he calls "the deduction of original right" (*FNR*, §§9–11). Fichte explicitly presents this portion of his doctrine as "an abstraction [of] free speculation," and even as "a mere fiction," albeit one that is "necessary for the sake of science of right" (*FNR*, 101; *SW*, III: 112). Fichte's explanation of these claims is far less clear than one might have hoped. At the outset of §9 he reiterates a thesis that he claims to have established earlier in the book, namely, that subjectivity is essentially intersubjective (the I requires an Other), and that all talk about rights finds its meaning in the context of reflection on the conditions of possible community.[10] But even while insisting on this point, and proposing his "principle of any judgement of right" in intersubjective terms (*FNR*, 102; *SW*, III: 102), Fichte immediately qualifies the thesis. While any *real* rights can only be discussed in an intersubjective context, there is nonetheless a need to adopt a speculative standpoint in which we consider "the conditions of personality" while "abstract[ing] from the limitations imposed by the rights of others" (*FNR*, 101; *SW*, III: 112). The so-called

[10] "We can talk about rights only under the condition that a person is thought of as person, i.e., as an individual, [and] accordingly as related to other individuals, among whom at least a possible community, even if not an actual one, is imagined" (*FNR*, 101; *SW*, III, 111; translation altered).

doctrine of original right is then formulated in the context of such an abstraction.[11]

For our purposes, this matters. Because it is in the context of this discussion of original right that Fichte first introduces property rights, it follows that "the ground of all property rights" must be identifiable, at least in principle, in abstraction "from the limitations imposed by the rights of others" (*FNR*, 101; *SW*, III: 111). This in effect provides a third constraint on any reconstruction of Fichte's basic deductive strategy: although real property rights always implicate the existence of others, the ground of the validity of property rights should be reconstructable in abstraction from the limitations imposed by others. It should be clear, for example, that nothing like the Lockean provisos can play a role in such an account.

One further lead from the existing scholarship will be helpful in plotting our way forward. In his contribution to a collaborative commentary on the *Natural Right*, Rolf-Peter Horstmann took responsibility for the section of the text that presents Fichte's theory of original rights. Horstmann does not say much about the deduction of property rights, but what he does say is worth noting and pursuing:

> [To enjoy] this exclusive relationship to something simply is, according to Fichte, to consider that thing as one's property. Property in this way becomes for Fichte a necessary condition for identifying and acknowledging myself and others as free persons.[12]

Horstmann immediately goes on to describe this as Fichte's *unzureichend explizierten Grundgedanken* ("insufficiently explicit fundamental thought"). Fichte's intriguing idea seems to be that private property is justified because it plays an essential role in a person's identification and recognition of free beings – including the recognition *of oneself* as a free being. Otherwise put, private property is a necessary condition on self-knowledge, or self-consciousness, or self-positing.[13] It is this idea that I propose to explore in the balance of my remarks.

[11] This is not the place to consider the warrant for Fichte's characteristic strategy of adopting an explicitly counterfactual approach. For a discussion of this methodology, see Breazeale 2002 and Crowe 2008.

[12] Horstmann 2001: 122.

[13] The claim here is that property is a *necessary* condition on self-positing. It is not sufficient. Among the other necessary conditions on self-positing, Fichte certainly also includes the encounter with an Other. On the interpretation I defend in what follows, Fichte deduces these two conditions independently. The necessity of the Other is established in *FNR* §3; the necessity of property is defended in §11, without relying on claims about Others. It is from §12 onward that Fichte seriously turns his attention to consider these two individually necessary conditions in mutual interaction.

Fichtean Work and the Self-Positing Gambit

In the passage that Horstmann describes as expressing Fichte's "insufficiently explicit fundamental thought," there is an important concept that we have not yet discussed. One feature of that passage, as we have seen, is the obsession about constancy and stasis. But the second key concept in that passage is *efficacy*:

> Here is the ground of all property rights. The part of the sensible world that is known to me and subjected to my ends – even if only in thought – is originally my property ... No one can affect that part of the sensible world *without restricting the freedom of my efficacy*. (*FNR*, 106; *SW*, III: 116; emphasis altered)

So what exactly is efficacy, and what role does it play in Fichte's deduction? I find it useful to address that question initially by stepping outside the *Natural Right*, and looking instead to his *System of Ethics* (1798). The passage that concerns me is one where Fichte is explicating the notion of obligation. He writes:

> "I *ought* to do something" means: I ought to produce the thing in question outside of me; or even if I could never complete what I ought to do, inasmuch as an infinite goal is undoubtedly posited for me thereby, a goal I could never realize and which therefore never *is* but only *ought* to be: in that case I at least always ought to act efficaciously in a manner that advances me along the path toward my goal. In the latter case I certainly ought actually to produce a good many things that lie along this path. (*SE*, 68; *SW*, IV: 66)

This passage from Fichte's ethics conveys a number of important themes from his practical philosophy. Notice the quiet invocation of the thought that our ethical obligations may well be unending – the doctrine that Hegel denounces as "bad infinity." Note also the idea that the basic demands of ethics are that we *produce* something, make a change in the world, indeed that we produce "a good many things." It is clear from this passage that an ethics of good intentions will not satisfy Fichte. Nor could an Aristotelian contemplative life (or a life in prayer) suffice for fulfilling our ethical obligations. It should also be clear that, for Fichte, one cannot act morally simply by avoiding some set of proscribed activities.

But what matters for our purposes here is the appearance of this idea of "acting efficaciously." "Acting efficaciously" is not an entirely happy translation, in my view. For one thing, the German just has one word (*wirken*) rather than two ("act efficaciously"). But "act efficaciously" also sounds like something rather abstract. The German is far more concrete: "*so soll ich immer so wirken.*" The verb *wirken* is cognate with the English word "work." So for Fichte, we might say, the basic demand of ethics is: *I ought to work.* Indeed, in a particularly extreme version of the protestant work ethic, the demand is: *I ought to work infinitely.*

Fichtean work – *efficacy* – does have a mental dimension. It begins with a deontic judgment: a representation of how things ought to be. The basic structure of practical reason is then to make a change in the world ("make modifications") so as to bring the world into correspondence with that normatively inflected representation.[14] Significantly, then, not all sweat-producing labor amounts to work. A prisoner on a chain gang may indeed be sweating, and making modifications to the world; the prisoner's representations may be playing a role in the production of those modifications. But he is not working (acting efficaciously) in Fichte's sense, for his exertion is not guided by *his representation* of how the world *ought* to be changed. Instead, the modifications are determined by someone else's deontic judgment. Fully alienated labor is not work in Fichte's transcendental sense of the term.

This Fichtean conception of work also figures in Fichte's very first theorem in *Natural Right*: "A finite rational being cannot posit itself without ascribing a free efficacy to itself" (*FNR*, 18; *SW*, III: 17). So not only is Fichtean work a moral obligation; it also figures in the founding proposition of his political position, and as a condition on the possibility of self-positing. This last thought will not surprise Fichte veterans, of course, who are accustomed to the idea that *everything* is purportedly a condition on self-positing! But there is in fact something quite surprising here. Fichte's claim will be that work, and indeed private property, are conditions on the possibility of self-consciousness!

In trying to make sense of this provocative thesis, we need to keep in mind the full title of Fichte's book: *Foundation of Natural Right According to the Principles of the Wissenschaftslehre.* So what are the principles of the *Wissenschaftslehre* that are operative here? In fact there are several, but for present purposes I propose to focus on the most important one: the principle of self-positing. And what is the principle of self-positing? I will not hazard a direct answer to that question here (I offer a partial model in the next section), but as a start it will be helpful to remind ourselves of the variation and progression in Fichte's formal presentation of his principle

[14] I have discussed Fichte's account of *Wirksamkeit* in Martin 2015.

over the course of the Jena period.[15] "I = I";[16] "The I posits itself absolutely and unconditionally";[17] "The I posits itself absolutely as positing itself";[18] "The I posits itself as self-positing."[19]

At the time of the writing of the *Natural Right*, it is this last formulation that was ascendant in the Fichte's thinking: the I posits itself *as self-positing*.[20] Günter Zöller has helpfully described the relevant structure of self-positing subjectivity as "autopredicative."[21] The I's act of self-positing is not blank; it does not just produce the I through the act of what Fichte calls "self-reverting activity." It also *makes a claim* about the I that results from that activity. The I posits itself as existing *in a particular way* – as self-positing, as rational, as *free*. It is worth noting that this autopredicative structure of self-positing is clearly on view in the *Natural Right* from the very beginning. Immediately after introducing his first theorem, Fichte goes on to elaborate: "If a rational being is to posit itself *as such*, then it must ..." (*FNR*, 18; *SW*, III: 17; emphasis altered). In that "as such" we have the marker of the autopredicative structure.

This autopredicative structure has some important consequences as regards the distinctive normative shape of self-positing subjectivity. In particular, Fichtean self-positing is like *a move in a game that one can win or lose*. In self-positing, the I makes a claim about itself that it must go on to *vindicate*. And that claim is essentially *threatened*. In short, self-positing is *a gambit*. Allow me to pursue this very abstract thought with the help of an example that will bring the relevant phenomenon (and Fichte's larger deductive strategy) into view.

[15] This is a matter that Dieter Henrich long ago documented in detail in an influential paper. See Henrich, 1966/1983.

[16] *SK*, 96; *SW*, I: 95.

[17] *SK*, 99; *SW*, I: 98. I have followed Lachterman's translation of this important but difficult-to-translate sentence. Fichte's original reads: "*Das Ich setzt ursprünglich schlechthin sein eigenes Seyn.*" A more literal translation might be: "The I originally and absolutely posits its own being." For a simplified version of this formula see *SK*, 243; *SW*, I, 276: "*Das Ich setzt sich selbst schlechthin.*"

[18] This is Henrich's rather free paraphrase of a passage from Chapter One of the aborted 1797 *Wissenschaftslehre*: "*Die Anschauung, von welcher hier die Rede ist, ist ein sich Setzen als setzend (irgend ein Objectives, welches auch ich selbst, als blosses Object, seyn kann), keineswegs aber etwa ein blosses Setzen*" (*IW*, 113; *SW*, I: 528).

[19] *WLnm* 119; *GA*, IV, 2: 32: "*[M]an setzt sich als sich setzend.*" In a note added to an 1802 reprint, Fichte proposed yet another formulation: "The I is the necessary identity of subject and object, a subject-object, and is so absolutely, without further mediation" (*SK*, 99; *SW*, I: 98). For an earlier use of a variant of this formula, see *SW*, II: 448.

[20] Although it achieves increased prominence in the later Jena formulations of the *Wissenschaftslehre*, the inclusion of the "as" (what Henrich refers to as "the particle of representation") appears already in one important passage in the 1794–5 *Wissenschaftslehre*. See *SK*, 243; *SW*, I: 276: "If it is to be a self, the I must also posit itself *as self-posited*" (emphasis added).

[21] Zöller 1998: 53.

A Tale of Two Emperors

In December 1804, in Notre Dame Cathedral, Napoleon was crowned as Emperor of France. The coronation was a very elaborately staged event, famously represented in David's 20x32 foot painting in the Louvre. David's colossal painting actually shows us not the crowning of Napoleon himself, but Napoleon's crowning of Josephine as Empress. But there is a related work at the Louvre, a sketch made by David on the day inside the cathedral, in which we see Napoleon's own coronation. In the large and famous painting, David shows us about 100 separate figures, but in the sketch we see only two: Napoleon himself and Pope Pius VII, who had traveled to Paris for the coronation. Unlike the painting, David's sketch shows us the crucial moment: instead of submitting to the Pope to be crowned, Napoleon takes the crown and crowns *himself* as emperor.

Napoleon's act of self-coronation is important for all kinds of reasons: politically, historically, theatrically, theologically. But, I also think it has a certain affinity with Fichte's philosophical position.[22] Pius does not posit Napoleon as emperor; *Napoleon posits himself as emperor*. Notice that even in this way of putting it we can see what in Zöller's terms we can describe as the "autopredicative" structure of Napoleonic self-positing. Napoleon posits himself *as emperor*. Through a self-reverting activity, he both brings into existence something that had not existed before, and he makes a claim about what he has thereby produced. Finally, notice that Napoleon's act of self-positing exhibits what I am calling *gambit normativity*. It is a move in a game that can be won or lost; it involves making a claim that one must vindicate; it is essentially fraught with risk. In all these respects it is a close analog to what Fichte means by an act of self-positing.

To see what is at stake here, it helps to contrast Napoleon's imperial self-positing to a second case. Puyi (1906–67) is known as "the Last Emperor of China." He became emperor when he was not quite three years old. His initial reign only lasted four years, until China became a Republic in 1912, following the Xinhai Revolution. But in the early 1930s, Puyi attempted to

[22] That is *not* to say that Fichte admired Napoleon, or agreed with his political or military actions. For an example of Fichte's personal views of Napoleon, see, e.g., *SW*, VII: 512. Hans Kohn reports on a 1805 letter of Friedrich Schlegel which describes Napoleon as "a certain Fichtean in Paris" (Kohn 1949: 329). At the time of this writing, the Mainz edition of Friedrich Schegel's correspondence has not yet covered the letters of 1805, and I have been unable to locate a published version of this letter. I am grateful to Jean-Christophe Merle and Gabe Gottlieb for drawing these references to my attention.

restore the imperial order, collaborating with the Japanese in order to do so. He fled from Beijing to Manchuria, a self-declared emperor in exile, where he remained until the military defeat of Japan in 1945. Whereas Napoleon's act of imperial self-positing was a success (at least for a time), Puyi's was a dismal failure. Both undertook the gambit; Puyi clearly lost the game. It became immediately apparent that he lacked imperial authority. His "palace" at Changchun was effectively his prison. His Japanese minders *called* him emperor; he had a uniform and the imperial seals. But he himself quickly saw the lie in all this, and spent most of his time withdrawn in his private quarters.

In drawing some philosophical lessons from these two cases, it is worth thinking for a moment about how one might go about figuring out whether an act of imperial self-positing has been successful or not. Suppose that you now posit yourself as Emperor of your hometown or university. You have the seals, and the robes, and trappings of office. We stage an elaborate coronation. How do you then find out whether you are really emperor (like Napoleon) or a puppet of an emperor (like Puyi)? No stack of formal documents will suffice to tell you the answer; Puyi had those but they were little more than theatrical props. Asking the people around you will not suffice either. (When Puyi was a boy, the eunuchs in the Forbidden City continued to *tell* him that he was emperor, although the empire had long been overthrown. The same kinds of lies were repeated in Changchun in the 30s.) So testimony cannot be the answer, nor the formalities of deference by those around you. So how do you find out? How do you reassure yourself, satisfy yourself that you really are the emperor that you have posited yourself to be? How do you recognize yourself as such?

The only answer, I submit, is efficacy: *Wirksamkeit.* It turns out that even emperors have to work. If you want to find out if your act of imperial self-positing has been successful, then you have to try to exercise some imperial power. Order that all lectures be delivered in pajamas. Create a tax on cliché. Whatever. Form a representation of how you judge that things ought to be, and then order that your world conforms to that representation. You will then quickly get a data point as to where you stand on the spectrum that reaches from Napoleon to Puyi.

What is the lesson here? Imperial self-positing is a gambit, a move in a high-risk game. The act of self-positing may begin at a particular moment (11 Frimaire, Year XIII in the case of Napoleon), but it is an act that projects ahead into a future time when the positing must be fulfilled. And crucially: in order to carry out that fulfillment, a self-positing emperor needs an empire. Without an empire, there can be no emperor, and the act of self-positing is a failure. And what is the basic transcendental structure of that empire? It is what Fichte calls a "sphere of free efficacy" – a portion of the public world in which the emperor has an exclusive authority to transform his representations of how things ought to be into changes in material reality (*FNR*, 110; *SW*, III: 121). He can recognize himself as emperor only insofar as he can recognize the fruits of his imperial work in his empire.

We need to exercise care here. Imperial self-positing is not the same as the Fichtean self-positing that lies at the center of the *Wissenschaftslehre*. The most important difference is that imperial self-positing is itself a dated intentional act by an individual who is already self-conscious. I do not think that we can say any of those things about Fichtean self-positing. It is not dated; it is not an action; it is not undertaken by a being that is already and independently self-conscious. But I find the imperial case helpful in demystifying some of Fichte's claims about self-positing. It is a self-reverting activity. It brings into existence something that simply does not exist independently of that activity. And it is autopredicative with gambit normativity. Of course the autopredicative content is different. The Fichtean I does not posit itself as an emperor, it posits itself as self-positing. It posits itself as free.

So how does a Fichtean I go about vindicating that claim? In order to fulfill an act of imperial self-positing, an emperor needs an empire; in order to fulfill the act of self-positing, the Fichtean I needs property. Property, on this account, is first and foremost a piece of the world on which the I can *work*. And it is only by working that I can recognize myself as free.

The Deductive Strategy

We are now in a position to return to Fichte's argument in the *Natural Right*. In reconstructing his deduction, it will be important to interpret the "*here*" of §11 broadly. The deduction is not itself contained within §11 of the *Natural Right*; indeed it is not wholly contained within the *Natural Right* at all. But the deduction of private property – that is, the proof of the validity of the concept, the answer to the *quid juris* – does culminate in §11, and it is completed prior to the treatment of conflicts (in §12) and the analysis of the property contract (in Part II of the text). The deduction itself comprises four main concepts, and four main steps: self-positing, freedom, work, private property.

The first step in the deduction is largely taken over from Fichte's other Jena writings. In particular, Fichte here takes for granted the central claims of the Jena *Wissenschaftslehre*, namely that part of the essential structure of subjectivity involves an autopredicative, self-relating activity. It is in positing itself, and positing itself as self-positing, that the subject is constituted as a subject. Self-positing is not itself a dated intentional action; it is better understood as a structure that is itself implicit in every manifestation of subjectivity – notably in the characteristic exercise of subjectivity in judgment and intentional action. Both in judging and in acting, the subject (person, judge, agent) is implicitly self-aware, and implicitly claims for itself a status and authority: the authority to judge/act. To make a self-referential claim on such an authority *is*, for Fichte, what it is to be a subject; in this sense self-positing is itself a form of self-constitution.

The second step in the deduction, freedom, is also taken over from the earlier writings, but is further developed in the *Natural Right*. The very idea of self-constituting self-positing is already a trope for a kind of radical self-authoring or self-authorizing. Like Napoleon, the I makes itself into what it is. This abstract formula of radical autonomy has a more concrete reality in judgment and action. To be a judge is to *make up one's own mind* – to determine one's own representations in light of the relevant evidence. (If I am not self-determining in this sense then I might *transmit* a judgment made by someone else, but I am not genuinely the *author* of the judgment; I am not the judge.) Similarly, in order for some movement of my body to constitute an action of mine, it must be genuinely attributable *to me* as agent; I must be the originator of the action, not simply a conduit of causal determination.

In the *Natural Right*, Fichte emphasizes a further claim about freedom that was itself already implicit in the earlier formulations of the position. Freedom, for Fichte, is "not … something that exists in the present moment … but … something that ought to exist in the future" (*FNR*, 32; *SW*, III: 33).[23] Fichtean freedom is a task to be accomplished – or rather, indefinitely to be pursued and approximated but never fully accomplished – rather than something that can ever properly be said already to exist. This itself is a claim that may seem to contradict the claims that we have been making. If self-positing is indeed implicit in every judgment and action, and if self-positing requires a form of freedom, then surely freedom must be really present in every instance of judging or acting.

[23] For anticipations of this thought in the earliest Jena writings, see *SK*, 118–19; *SW*, I: 121; *EPW*, 149; *SW*, VI: 297–8.

How can Fichte *also* claim that freedom always and ever remains a task to be accomplished? The answer lies in what I have been calling gambit normativity. What is present in the characteristic exercises of subjectivity is not freedom as an accomplishment, but freedom as a claimed status. I set up myself (*sich selbst setze*) as a free judge and agent; I claim this status for myself. But such a claim is a kind of bet or promissory note – a gambit that I must go on to vindicate.

The vindication of this claim to freedom requires efficacy, *Wirksamkeit* – work. The full defense of this claim requires Fichte to bring in a host of further claims from the *Wissenschaftslehre*, which are themselves presented *in staccato* in the opening paragraphs of the *Natural Right*: the I's act of self-positing can never be immediate, but always takes place in a confrontation with something not-I, which itself resists the I's act of self-determination. In the struggle between self-determination and determination-by-other, this not-self takes the form of the sensible world. In order to realize its freedom (or better: in pursuit of a progressive but never completed realization of its freedom), the I must determine the sensible world in accordance with its representation of how it ought to be – that is, the I must work.

It is in order to carry out this project, Fichte claims, that the subject requires property. Property is a sphere of efficacy, a portion of the sensible world upon which the I can work, transforming it as necessary from how it is to how the I judges that it ought to be. Only in effecting such a change can the I progressively realize, and recognize, its freedom. Notice that property is legitimated on this account not in the first instance as a strategy for managing scarcity of resources, nor for serving the material needs of the body. The institution of property has applications to these important matters, to be sure, but it is deduced in the service of a spiritual need rather than a material one. Private property, on Fichte's account, is a prerequisite of real freedom, and indeed a condition on the fulfillment of self-consciousness.

There are undoubtedly lots of problems with this deductive strategy, but at this point it is worth pausing to notice some of its advantages. Fichte's account has a first advantage over Locke's in that, if successful, it provides a deduction of the very concept of property – not just a theory of appropriation that takes the objective validity of the category of property for granted. Secondly, Fichte's account is genuinely secular, insofar as it demonstrates objective validity by showing that property is a condition on the possibility of self-positing subjectivity. No premises of the argument rely on revealed religion. Finally, on this account, Fichte's deduction of property meets the textual constraint we established above. Although the property contract implicates the relationships between one property-owning subject and another, and although the real existence of any property rights (and indeed any subjects) requires relationships with and recognition by others, the transcendental deduction of property – that is, the proof of the validity of the category – does not implicate others at all. It therefore makes sense for Fichte to include it in the context of his "Deduction of Original Right," which explicitly abstracts from the limitations imposed by others.

Two Outstanding Problems

With this outline of Fichte's deduction in hand, we can return to two of the difficulties that we left unresolved above. Consider first the question about the sense of Fichte's term *Eigenthum*. What we need to appreciate in the first instance is that the concept of property that is deduced in §11 is a high-level abstraction – a pure a priori concept. In Kantian terminology, what is validated in Fichte's deduction is an *unschematized category*. That is, his argument shows (at most) our right to apply the concept of *Eigenthum*; it does not of itself provide a rule or schema for doing so.[24] What Fichte has shown – if indeed his deduction is successful – is that a self-positing subject requires a "sphere of efficacy" where she can get to work, making changes in accord with her judgment, and recognizing her own free agency in the changes she has wrought in accord with her determination of how the world ought to be. This is a highly abstract specification of a particular form of determining interaction between I and not-I. It does not tell us what empirical form that interaction will take, how extensive such a sphere should be, or what positive legal arrangements need to be in place in order to sustain it.

Of course any actual realization of this abstract structure will have to be fully concrete. For all we can tell from the deduction, it might be an allotment to garden, or tools and raw materials for manufacturing, or a brush and canvas with which to paint. The schematization is not fully determined by the a priori concept. On the other hand, some forms of private ownership familiar in the contemporary world might *not* count as property in Fichte's sense. If what I own is preferred stock in a corporation

[24] The situation is in this respect analogous to the result at the end of Kant's transcendental deduction of the categories: we know that we are justified in applying the concept of cause and effect, but we do not yet have the means for actually doing so in any particular case.

in which I have no scope for action, or patent rights upon which I passively collect royalties, then I am simply a consumer of what I own; no sphere of work is involved and hence no property in Fichte's sense of the word. Accordingly, we certainly need to take care when translating Fichte's *Eigenthum* as "private property." Taking a lead from the etymology, we might rather think of *Eigenthum* as a "domain of ownness" – an "*own-dom*" on analogy with a *king-dom* (*Königtum*). The exact form that such an own-dom must take awaits a full schematization of the pure a priori category.

To get a sense for the range of possibilities, it may help to think of a rather extreme example. Think of a goal scored by a football player. The pitch on which he plays is owned by the community; the ball and net belong to the opposing club. None of this is his private property in the contemporary positive sense of the term. Nonetheless, the player is able to modify the sensible world in accordance with his judgment as to how it ought to be: *this* ball in the back of *that* net. Having effected the change in the world, he is recognized (both by himself and by others) as the agent of that modification. At first glance, it may seem that we have here an empirical counter-example to Fichte's transcendental claim: it is a case of attributable action (work, in Fichte's sense) absent private property.

But the matter merits further reflection. The property with which the player interacts is not his private property in our ordinary sense of the word. But it is significant that we nonetheless talk about the player's *possession* of the ball. Indeed more than this, the rules of football themselves sustain a robust distinction between *rightful and wrongful* possession. The footballer had *fair possession* of the ball in the moments leading up to his goal – the ball was, in this sense, part of his *Eigen-thum* (his "own-domain"), even though it was not his private property in a positive legal sense. So speaking transcendentally, we could say that there was indeed a form of private property (rightful possession and control by an individual) at work in the situation. And this in turn is internally connected to the fact that the player was able to make the change he intended in the world, and to be recognized as the genuine agent of that change.

What the example shows, I submit, is that Fichte's deduction of *Eigenthum* leaves open the possibility that the property which satisfies the transcendental condition might in principle be public or common property in our ordinary legal sense of the term. But not just any form of common property will do. A fully collective enterprise like a commune would not suffice, if there was nothing in the common property over which the individual had effective and recognized control. Fichtean work presupposes effective exclusive control over at least some among the means and objects of production. Common property can therefore satisfy the transcendental conditions on *Eigenthum* only insofar as our interaction with it is so structured (whether by explicit regulation or mutually recognized authoritative practice) such that there is a genuine phenomenon of individual fair possession sufficiently robust to sustain both an opportunity for individual work (in Fichte's sense) and the recognition and attribution of its products.

In light of how much is left open by Fichte's deduction, however, it might be complained that the deduction accomplishes nothing of substance. What is to be gained from a deduction of private property (in Fichte's sense) that does not tell us whether private property (in our sense) is legitimate? In the face of such an objection, I would offer two replies on Fichte's behalf. First, it is important not to measure the success of the deduction by the wrong standard. We have grown so accustomed and habitualized to the application of the concept of private property that we do not pause to recognize how puzzling it is. Why, after all, should I be allocated exclusive use-rights over a piece of the world unless my use of it is the best possible use? To recognize my property right over even this scrap of paper is to recognize my right to make sub-optimal use of it. The application of such a normative framework requires a validation, even if that validation does not itself answer all the hard questions about property rights. On the reconstruction I have proposed, it is this skeptical question that Fichte can rightly claim to have answered by the end of §11. Secondly, although the deduction of private property does not provide us with a set of rules for delimiting the institution, it does establish an important criterion which constrains us in seeking to develop such rules. In particular, it teaches us that any justifiable regime of property rights must be so constructed as to guarantee such rights to everyone.

Let's return, finally, to Fichte's extravagant claims about private property and stasis: the demand that things remain the same. Are we now in a position to make sense of these puzzling remarks? It is important, first of all, to keep these remarks in context. The two paragraphs concerning the need for stability are themselves interpolated within a larger deductive strategy, where they play a subordinate role. *Natural Right* §11 is itself divided into brief numbered sections, which themselves provide an analysis of the constituent elements of Fichtean work or efficacy. These comprise (I) a determination of how a portion of the sensible world ought to be formed or re-formed; (II) a systematically ordered relationship between the motions of a disciplined body and changes in the world that is sufficiently regular for the results of the person's bodily movements to be predictable in their effects on the environment; (III) the stasis condition; (IV) the continued existence of the person/agent so as to be able to perceive the physical results of his work. (The fifth numbered subsection mainly provides a summary.) Seen in this context, the third and fourth components are best understood in tandem. Their primary concern is not so much with the conditions under which the person can work, but the conditions under which the person can witness the results of her labors. The third condition (the stasis condition) specifies that the changes made to the world must be allowed to endure; the fourth condition specifies that the person who wrought those changes must endure so as to witness them. The need for these conditions can be seen as deriving from the terms of the original gambit. The self-positing subject must not only freely change the world; she must also be able to satisfy herself that she has done so.

Even understood in these terms, Fichte's explicit claims about stasis in §11 (III) will likely strike us as too strong. Even to the sympathetic reader, it will be hard to fathom the thought that "everything should remain as he knows it." Surely the conditions of Fichtean work would be satisfied if at least *something* remains as the person has determined it should be. Here it may help to keep in mind that this whole section of the text (§§9–11) is put forward as a deliberately exaggerated fiction, specifying the demands that the subject could legitimately make if, counterfactually, there were no other persons whose equally legitimate claims limit those of the first. Starting already from §12, and continuing both in Part II of the *Natural Right* and in *The Closed Commercial State*, Fichte sets out to apply his now-validated conception of property rights to the real-world context in which the rights of one are balanced and limited by the rights of others. Many of the details of Fichte's proposed social and legal arrangements have struck readers (both his own contemporaries and our own) as problematic or even bizarre. But at least one idea deserves to be taken seriously. A just and legitimate socio-political order must be so arranged as to provide all persons with access to the means and objects of production in a manner and degree such that they have an opportunity to fulfill the claim to freedom that is itself a fundamental component of their existence as subjects.

CHAPTER 9

Fichte on Personal Freedom and the Freedom of Others

David James

Right and Recognition

Fichte's deduction of the concept of right (*Recht*) in the first main division of the *Foundations of Natural Right* (§§1–4) helped make recognition into a central concept of social and political philosophy, albeit indirectly through its influence on Hegel's account of recognition.[1] This deduction consists in an attempt to explain the possibility of self-consciousness, which in this particular context means consciousness of oneself as a free, rational agent capable of realizing one's ends by effecting changes in the world. In the first main division of the *Foundations of Natural Right*, Fichte sets out an argument which aims to show that self-consciousness requires an object that *qua* object is independent of the subject but *qua* object of *self*-consciousness is not purely external to the subject and non-identical with it. Rather, the object reflects what the subject itself essentially is, that is to say, self-determining. What we have is, in effect, a practical form of the identity of subject and object which is presupposed by any conscious experience, but which, as the condition of any experience whatsoever, can itself never become a direct object of experience.

In the course of this deduction of the concept of right, Fichte comes to identify the object in question with a "summons" (or "request," "demand," "invitation" as the German word *Aufforderung* can also be translated) by means of which the subject is determined to be self-determining (*FNR*, 31; *SW*, III: 33). For this summons to reflect what the subject essentially is, it must demand only an act of free choice on the part of the person to whom it is addressed. The summons does not, therefore, exercise a purely causal influence on this person. Thus, on the one hand, the summons presupposes the capacity to act freely in accordance with ends on the part of the person to whom it is addressed, while, on the other hand,

[1] See Siep 1979a, Williams 1992, and Wood 1990: 77ff.

it presupposes an understanding of what it means to act in such a way on the part of the person who summons another person to engage in free activity. Consequently, not only the person to whom the summons is addressed, but also the person who summons another human being to act freely must be assumed to be free and rational.

Fichte then proceeds to determine the precise nature of the relation between finite rational beings that this recognition of the freedom and rationality of others entails. The relation is held to be one in which the freedom of each person is limited by the freedom of other persons in such a way that each person is left free to act within the limits granted to him or to her by others. This form of mutual limitation requires that each person is both a subject that summons others by means of an act of self-limitation and the object of a summons in the sense that others limit their activity in relation to him or her. This is because it is only by summoning others that each person demonstrates that he or she is a free and rational being to which a summons can be directed, while conversely it is only by being the object of such a summons that consciousness of oneself as a free and rational being becomes possible. Fichte accordingly defines the concept of right itself as "the concept of the necessary relation of free beings to one another" (*FNR*, 9; *SW*, III: 8).

Although Fichte's attempt to deduce the concept of right as a necessary condition of self-consciousness may be regarded as wildly ambitious if it is meant to demonstrate that practical self-consciousness as such is not possible in the absence of the type of relation between human beings described above, the central role that this deduction accords to the recognition of others as free and rational beings allows it to be viewed in terms of "an ideal socialization process for individuals in a culture in which values such as individual freedom and autonomy hold an important place."[2] Recognition and right as its legal guarantee are here regarded as necessary only in the weaker sense of constituting conditions of how individuals can come to think of themselves in a certain way. The legal form of recognition associated with the concept of right is not then an absolutely necessary condition of self-consciousness, because this type of account of Fichte's deduction of the concept of right does not show that this recognition represents the *only* way in which such a self-conception is possible, nor that individuals ought to develop this self-conception as opposed to other possible ones. In this way, the

[2] Wood 1990: 83.

claim to strict necessity made by Fichte himself when he attempts to deduce the concept of right as a condition of self-consciousness must be dispensed with.

Fichte's claims concerning the necessity of recognition have nevertheless led some interpreters to view his position in decidedly moral terms, as when the summons is said to have "ethical significance" and it is asserted that its "telos is an acknowledgement of the claim of the other, a summons to responsible freedom."[3] Typically, reference is made to Kant's notion of rational beings as the possessors of a moral status, or "normative standing as such," which demands that they treat each other in certain ways and not in other ways.[4] Fichte's deduction of the concept of right is consequently said to "commit him to the idea that reciprocally recognizing agents presuppose the principle of right as a dignity-defining law that is normative for them as one free and rational person among others, that is, as a Kantian categorical imperative."[5] Fichte's deduction of the concept of right is said to presuppose, moreover, the idea of moral autonomy, in that it involves a demand made in relation to others that presupposes "the will's capacity to be a law to itself independently of object-dependent desire,"[6] and thus the capacity of rational agents "to conform to the principle of right just because they recognize its validity."[7] In other words, the concept of right which Fichte attempts to deduce as a condition of self-consciousness together with the recognition which this principle demands are held to entail the existence of an unconditional obligation to respect the freedom of others purely in virtue of their moral status or "normative standing as such." This moral status is associated with the "dignity" which an agent must recognize in others and respond to, but which an agent does not confer on others through an act of will,[8] and this dignity is itself to be explained in terms of a rational agent's capacity to act autonomously in accordance with principles of pure practical reason.

[3] Williams 1992: 59.

[4] Darwall 2005: 101.

[5] Darwall 2005: 93. In a similar vein, it is claimed that the concept of a summons and the concept of recognition "concretize Kant's moral philosophy – the consciousness of freedom, the categorical imperative, kingdom of ends – and transform it into a social philosophy" (Williams 1992: 50). The relation of right is therefore said to be "a morally necessary one, i.e., the idea of a rational-moral community, not unlike Kant's kingdom of ends. In his concept of community (*Gemeinschaft*), Fichte reflects the concept of a universal law made by freedom that places restrictions upon the freedom of all, a freely imposed self-restraint" (Williams 1992: 54–5).

[6] Darwall 2005: 101.

[7] Darwall 2005: 92.

[8] See Darwall 2005: 111.

I shall argue, however, that Fichte's separation of right from morality shows that for him there is an essential connection between the notion of right and a specifically non-moral form of respect for the freedom of others, but not necessarily respect for their moral dignity as well. Although this connection between the notion of right and a certain attitude towards others allows us to speak of a "standing" which each person enjoys in relation to others, it does not entail the adoption of a distinctively moral or ethical standpoint. The way in which the moral import that some interpreters of Fichte's account of recognition and right find in the first main division of the *Foundations of Natural Right* conflicts with his own strict separation of right from morality is evident from the following passage:

> In the domain of natural right, the good will has no role to play. Right must be enforceable, even if there is not a single human being with a good will; the very aim of the science of right is to sketch out just such an order of things. In this domain, physical force – and it alone – gives right its sanction. (*FNR*, 50; *SW*, III: 54)

This strict separation of right from morality leads Fichte to base his theory of right on the methodological assumption of a "universal egoism" (*FNR*, 134; *SW*, III: 152), that is to say, on the idea that human beings are motivated solely by self-interest, even if this is not in fact universally the case. Since Fichte's approach to the question of the essential nature of right is here announced to be a matter of method only, it does not commit him to the anthropological claim that human beings typically act from motives of self-interest alone, nor to the claim that right and morality are not only conceptually independent of each other but also practically independent of each other, in the sense that right does not ultimately need to be supplemented by morality in order to become truly effective.[9] This method only requires proceeding on the assumption that human beings always do act from motives of self-interest and that they do not, therefore, *directly* concern themselves with the freedom or moral dignity of others.

Fichte's separation of right from morality may appear to be at odds with his description of the summons, for as well as implying recognition of the freedom and rationality of others, the act of summoning others is described by him as one whereby the other person "has, in *his* choice, in the sphere of his freedom, taken my free choice into consideration, has purposively and intentionally left a sphere open for me" (*FNR*, 44; *SW*,

[9] For an attempt to show how for Fichte right can be considered to be practically dependent on morality or ethics despite his separation of right from morality, see James 2011: 131ff.

III: 46). This claim gives the impression that the person who summons another person acts with the *intention* of enabling another person to act freely and thereby demonstrates an interest in this other person's freedom. A distinction needs to be drawn, however, between (1) respecting the freedom of others and intentionally acting in a way that demonstrates such respect because doing so represents a condition of one's own freedom – essentially, if I do not respect the freedom of others they will have no reason to respect mine – and (2) respecting the freedom of others in the sense of concerning oneself directly with their freedom. In the second case, the freedom of others is conceived to be not only something that one has an obligation to respect in the sense of not violating it, but also something that ought to be adopted as one of one's own fundamental ends.

I shall argue that what Fichte says in the *Foundations of Natural Right* implies only (1), given the methodological assumption of a universal egoism with which he operates. Right is only necessary given this assumption and legal recognition would not, therefore, be a constitutive feature of a genuine moral community.[10] The fact that what Fichte has to say does not also imply (2) lends his account of the concept of right a critical dimension which is overlooked by interpreters who appeal to its alleged moral foundations. The "ideal socialization" interpretation of Fichte's deduction of the concept of right admittedly suggests that individuals who had already achieved the relevant self-conception among themselves, and seek to educate or socialize other individuals in such a way as to enable them to develop a conception of themselves as self-determining agents, would be motivated by a direct concern with the freedom of others and would have made this freedom into one of their own fundamental ends. Yet even here one could cite, in accordance with Fichte's methodological assumption of a universal egoism, such reasons as the wish to produce individuals who are not a constant threat to social order because they have not developed the capacities and dispositions that would enable them to coexist peaceably with others.

Another reason for observing the distinction between respecting the freedom of others and intentionally acting in a way that demonstrates such respect because doing so represents a condition of one's own freedom, on the one hand, and respecting the freedom of others on the grounds of a direct interest in their freedom, on the other, is as follows.

10 The idea of the abolition of the state appears throughout Fichte's writings. It is, in fact, more a matter of the state's self-abolition in the sense that the state is what provides the means of bringing about its own disappearance as a coercive legal and political institution. See James 2015.

By observing this distinction Fichte's position can be shown to be an essentially consistent one, whereas he has been accused of inconsistency on account of the way in which he accords recognition a central role in his deduction of the concept of right but at the same time separates right from morality. It is said, for example, that despite making recognition into a transcendental condition of right, Fichte "does not develop his theory of rights concretely out of intersubjective recognition. Moreover, individual acts of recognition do not play any role in securing right in Fichte's theory of the state, and Fichte allows that recognition may be bypassed altogether."[11]

Fichte's theory of right as set out in the third main division of the *Foundations of Natural Right* has in fact been viewed as a reversion to the type of position concerning right and the basis of political authority typically associated with Hobbes.[12] In what follows, I shall show that although Fichte does indeed adopt a position that can in certain respects be compared to some things that Hobbes has to say, he is not being inconsistent despite the essential role played by recognition in his theory of right. Rather, even those aspects of Fichte's theory of right that have something in common with Hobbes's views on right and the basis of political authority presuppose recognition of the freedom and rationality of others. This does not mean, however, that Fichte is committed to viewing recognition at the level of right as being anything more than a matter of respecting the freedom of others because doing so represents a condition of one's own freedom, as would be the case if he took it also to involve a direct interest in the freedom of others. Nor is the form of autonomy that Fichte acknowledges to be a necessary condition of right – that is, the capacity to limit one's actions in relation to others by imposing general principles of action upon oneself – to be viewed as desire-independent in the sense of consisting in an act of subjecting oneself to unconditionally valid principles of pure practical reason. For Fichte, this second form of autonomy obtains only when one makes the moral law into one's principle of action, and he clearly does not think that this is what happens in the case of right. Attempts to assimilate these distinct forms of autonomy ignore the critical aspect of Fichte's approach of basing his theory of right on the assumption of a universal egoism by uncritically investing the legal sphere of right with moral notions that imply a direct interest in the freedom of others which may, in fact, be

[11] Williams 1992: 64.
[12] Schottky 1995: 184ff. and 198ff.

completely absent, and whose absence is masked by the introduction of moral notions of recognition and obligation.

The Conditional Nature of Right

One of the main considerations motivating Fichte's separation of right from morality has to do with the conditional nature of right and the unconditional nature of morality. Fichte's treatment of right as something conditional must be held by moralized readings of the first main division of the *Foundations of Natural Right* to conflict with his attempt to demonstrate how the mutual recognition and respect entailed by the idea of a summons are necessary conditions of self-consciousness. This is because the necessity of these conditions implies that the obligations which right imposes upon individuals cannot be regarded as obligations that are voluntarily assumed by them; rather, these obligations are ones that are necessarily generated by the moral status enjoyed by others.[13] In stressing the conditional nature of right, Fichte can be seen to adopt a position that is similar to the amoral one adopted by Hobbes in his account of right and the basis of political authority, in that the obligations that we have towards others are explained in terms of legal and political structures to which self-interested rational agents can be expected to consent. Thus the conditional nature of right represents an issue which can be used to assess the validity of both moralized readings of the first main division of the *Foundations of Natural Right* and the claim that Fichte reverts to a recognizably Hobbesian account of right, despite his earlier appeal to the notion of recognition.

According to Fichte, if an individual wants to coexist peaceably with others, and to possess a sphere free from external interference in which to exercise his or her capacity for self-determination under reliable, stable conditions of agency, he or she must will the rule of right. This rule expresses the principle that must govern a condition of right and it reads as follows: "limit your freedom through the concept of the freedom of all other persons with whom you come in contact" (*FNR*, 10; *SW*, III: 10). The act of willing this rule amounts in effect to limiting one's activity in such a way that others can also be free, though only because logical consistency requires willing the necessary means to any end that one sets oneself. The end in question here is that of securing for oneself a sphere

[13] See Darwall 2005: 108ff.

of activity free from the actual or possible interference of others. This end concerns only the sphere in which the person "exclusively makes choices," thereby determining him- or herself as an individual distinct from others in virtue of the different choices that he or she makes (*FNR*, 53; *SW*, III: 56).

Willing this personal freedom – that is, the freedom to set any ends whatsoever independently of others and to distinguish oneself from others by acting in accordance with such ends – does not imply a direct interest in the freedom of others. Rather, one could conceivably respect their personal freedom simply because doing so represents a necessary condition of securing one's own personal freedom. Yet an individual does not think or act inconsistently if he or she renounces the means to an end at the same time as he or she renounces the end itself, which in this case is the end of coexisting peaceably with others with the aim of securing personal freedom. Thus someone can consistently refuse to live peacably in community with others by refusing to subject him- or herself to the law of right, but only if he or she at the same time renounces the end of securing a sphere of action free from interference by others, that is to say, a sphere of action whose recognition by others is legally secured. Consequently, although Fichte claims in the corollary to his deduction of the concept of right that "we are both *bound* and *obligated* to each other by our very existence," the consistency in question relates only to the rules of thinking in general that he describes in the same paragraph as "scientifically presented in general *logic*" (*FNR*, 45; *SW*, III: 48). This consistency does not therefore imply such distinctively moral considerations as recognition of the dignity of others in the sense of holding their freedom to be something which ought to form one of our own ends, irrespective of what we happen to desire to do.

Although it may be doubted that in a modern society an agent could completely renounce the end of coexisting peaceably with others, in the sense of willing not to be part of a legal community in which his or her personal freedom is secured on the condition that he or she recognizes the personal freedom of others, Fichte can be seen to be making a valid point about what legitimizes legal constraints in such a way that individuals are obliged to obey them even in the absence of any overriding desire to do so. This point is that they have freely subjected themselves to these constraints. The view that legal constraint is legitimate only in virtue of the fact that an individual has consented to it broadly corresponds to Hobbes's claim that "where no Covenant hath preceded, there hath no Right been transferred, and every man has right to every thing; and consequently, no action can be Unjust. But when a Covenant is made, then to break it is *Unjust*."[14] Like Hobbes, Fichte argues that the consent which produces an obligation to act in accordance with the law of right consists in partly giving up a right that was originally one's own to others. This is the right of a person "to extend his freedom as far as he wills and can, and – if he so desires – the right to take possession of the entire sensible world" (*FNR*, 111; *SW*, III: 122). I shall have more to say about this particular right.

Given the conditional nature of right, Fichte argues that it would be inconsistent to rely on the good will of others when it comes to their adoption of principles of reason that instruct individuals to enter into agreements with others so as to secure for themselves a sphere of freedom. In effect, he is concerned with the problem of the contingent nature of relations of mutual recognition in the absence of other necessary conditions. Ultimately, what is required is the establishment of a coercive state. Consequently, individuals can be expected to consent to the establishment of such an institution in so far as they adopt the end of securing a sphere of personal freedom and also think and act consistently in relation to the realization of this end. Here Fichte is in broad agreement with Hobbes's statement that, "Covenants, without the Sword, are but Words, and of no strength to secure a man at all."[15]

Fichte's treatment of right as something conditional implies that the obligations which right imposes on individuals are voluntarily assumed ones. Although the idea of a summons as a necessary condition of self-consciousness suggests otherwise, this condition cannot be invoked with the aim of showing that right is not something voluntary and thereby conditional without raising a significant problem of its own. This is because to claim that right is not conditional in the relevant sense would be to assume that the act whereby one person summons another person in the appropriate way is not only a necessary condition but also a sufficient condition of mutual recognition. This particular problem arises equally if we view Fichte's deduction of the concept of right as a transcendental deduction, as he does, or if it is more modestly viewed as the description of some kind of socialization process.

In the first case, to maintain that the form of recognition implied by the idea of a summons is both a necessary and sufficient condition of the consciousness of oneself as a being with the capacity to engage in acts of rational self-determination would be to confuse two issues which Fichte

[14] Hobbes 1996: 100.

[15] Hobbes 1996: 117.

himself treats separately in his deduction of the concept of right and his application of this concept respectively: the transcendental issue of the conditions of self-consciousness as such and the issue of how these conditions can be met in the case of individual human beings standing in spatio-temporal relations to each other. Even if recognition is assumed to be a necessary condition of the relevant form of self-consciousness, it is not also a sufficient one when other factors, such as self-interest, are taken into consideration and the issue of how relations of mutual recognition can be effectively maintained and guaranteed is introduced. Since the idea of mutual recognition as a condition of self-consciousness presupposes that human beings are capable of limiting their own activity in relation to each other and freely forming the end to do so, the transcendental account of the necessity of recognition will, moreover, need to be supplemented by a genetic one, given that these capacities are not ones that human beings self-evidently possess in the absence of some kind of educational or socialization process. While the "ideal socialization" interpretation of Fichte's deduction of the concept of right directly confronts this issue, there is no guarantee that a person who has attained the relevant form of self-consciousness by means of a process of education or socialization will continue to limit his or her activity in relation to others in the appropriate way. In short, we can conceive of such a person as attaining the relevant form of practical self-consciousness without there being anything to prevent him or her from subsequently violating the conditions of ongoing mutual recognition in relation to some, or even all, other persons with whom he or she comes (or is likely to come) into contact.

This shows that although mutual recognition and the relation of right which is its formal expression constitute the basis of all further determinations of right, their status as conditions of self-consciousness does not by itself guarantee the existence of relations of mutual recognition. Rather, right remains conditional in virtue of being dependent on the ends that individuals set themselves, including the end of coexisting peaceably with others in a condition in which a sphere of personal freedom is legally guaranteed to each of them. Fichte's acknowledgment of this point and the necessity of further conditions of right can be detected in the following passage from the *Foundations of Natural Right*:

> It has indeed been shown that, if a rational being is to come to self-consciousness – and hence if it is to become a rational being – then another rational being must necessarily exercise an influence upon it as upon a being capable of reason. These are reciprocal propositions: no influence as upon a rational being, no rational being. But that, even after self-consciousness

> has been posited, rational beings must continue to influence the subject of self-consciousness in a rational manner, is not thereby posited, and cannot be derived without using the very consistency that is to be proven as the ground of the proof. (*FNR*, 81; *SW*, III: 87)

I take the missing proof mentioned in the last sentence to be a proof of the fact that it would be consistent to will to limit one's activity in relation to others independently of the desire to secure for oneself a sphere of personal freedom. This shows how the claim that in this passage acting rationally means limiting one's freedom in relation to others as a response to an absolute obligation that rational agents have in virtue of the moral dignity possessed by others would beg the question. As we have seen, Fichte denies that from the standpoint of right there would be any inconsistency involved in not limiting one's activity in relation to others so long as one also renounced the end of securing for oneself a sphere of personal freedom. Indeed, the conditional nature of the obligation to limit one's activity in relation to others means that the failure of others to limit their activity in relation to oneself would be sufficient to remove one's own obligation to do so in the absence of an independent power with the authority and means to punish any transgressions of right.

This is not to say that in asserting the conditional nature of right Fichte rejects his earlier account of recognition. In connection with the question of the precise nature of this recognition, Fichte's views on the conditional nature of right again invite comparisons with certain things that Hobbes has to say. The necessity of recognition nevertheless reveals a fundamental difference between Fichte's views on the freedom and related capacities that we must attribute to others with whom we stand in relations of right and Hobbes's views on them. This difference shows, moreover, that although Fichte thinks that a form of recognition which requires attributing to others the capacity for rational self-determination is necessary at the level of right, this demand in no way implies such moral notions as the dignity of others, let alone a direct interest in the freedom of others in the sense of making the freedom of others into one of one's own fundamental ends, as opposed to its being something that is recognized for purely instrumental reasons. The demand in question does, however, imply the notion of some kind of "standing," in the sense of a status that must be accorded to others in virtue of our recognition of their freedom and rationality. Yet the limitations of this recognition of the standing of others will be shown to reveal the critical dimension of Fichte's theory of right that moralized readings of it fail to detect.

Right and Freedom

The way in which Fichte associates the concept of right with a mutual limitation of freedom echoes what Hobbes has to say concerning the right of nature and the partial renunciation of this right which marks the transition from the state of nature, in which individuals enjoy natural freedom without security, to a condition in which individuals enjoy security and a limited form of freedom. Hobbes describes the right of nature, or that "which Writers commonly call *Jus Naturale*," as follows: "the Liberty each man hath, to use his own power, as he will himselfe, for the preservation of his own Nature; that is to say, of his own Life; and consequently, of doing any thing, which in his own Judgement, and Reason, hee shall conceive to be the aptest means thereunto."[16] This view of the right of nature brings to mind Fichte's previously mentioned "infinite" right of the person to extend his freedom as far as he wills and can do so, although he does not identify this right simply with a right to do whatever one judges to be necessary to preserve one's life as Hobbes does.

Fichte's position differs from Hobbes's in that he treats freedom, rather than self-preservation, as primary, so that preserving one's own nature for him ultimately means preserving the conditions of free, rational agency. This is shown by his claim that it is not a matter of willing to continue to exist simply for the sake of existence as such; rather, it is a matter of willing to continue to exist for the sake of a determinate state of existence (*FNR*, 107; *SW*, III: 118). In other words, individuals will to continue to exist only for the sake of other ends. These ends may vary and right cannot prescribe what they are, because doing so would represent a violation of the personal freedom which it is meant to guarantee. The realization of such ends, whether they have to do with mere enjoyment or a "higher" end, will require the exercise of some degree of rational agency, though the pursuit of some ends requires more in the way of such agency than others do. Nevertheless, Fichte's understanding of right as a relation consisting in the mutual limitation of the right to extend one's freedom as far as one desires and has the power to do so is compatible with what Hobbes has to say concerning the act of renouncing the right to everything that human beings enjoy in the state of nature, even if there is the major difference that for Fichte the end in accordance with which this act is undertaken is that of securing a sphere of personal freedom in which

[16] Hobbes 1996: 91.

the conditions of effective rational agency are secured, rather than that of mere self-preservation.

Although each individual has the right to everything in a condition of natural freedom, he or she may partly renounce this right by agreeing not to hinder another individual in his or her exercise of this same right. One individual does not thereby grant another individual a right that he or she previously lacked. On the contrary, the individual who partially surrenders this right must be thought to have originally had, like everyone else, a right to all things, a right that is of a purely negative kind in the sense that it has to do only with the absence of any obligation to limit one's freedom in relation to others. This is enough to distinguish the right in question from those rights that generate legal obligations in relation to others, and which for Fichte are possible only "within a commonwealth and under positive laws" (*FNR*, 132; *SW*, III: 148).[17] Thus the individual who partially renounces his or her natural or original right to everything by limiting it for the benefit of another individual, as Hobbes puts it, "onely standeth out of his way, that he may enjoy his own originall Right, without hindrance from him."[18] In short, one individual agrees no longer to impede another individual's enjoyment of the right to everything by means of the act of partially limiting his or her enjoyment of this same right. This act of "standing aside" formally corresponds to the summons whereby for Fichte one person signals to another person that he or she is willing to limit his or her freedom and thereby grant the other person a sphere of freedom.

At the same time, Hobbes implies that the act of partially renouncing the right to everything that one originally enjoys must be of a reciprocal kind when he claims that all voluntary acts must be explained in terms of some good that an individual hopes to attain.[19] Presumably, the individual who partially renounces his or her original right to everything expects to get something in return which provides him or her with a good enough reason for engaging in the act of partially renouncing the right in question, and the other individual's act of partially renouncing this original right in his or her favor would provide such a reason. Thus the right to all things that each individual originally enjoys turns out to be subject to a process of mutual limitation, in which each individual partially gives up the right to everything without renouncing the right to certain other things. Indeed, it is only in order to secure these things that one consents

17 For more on this point see James 2011: 24ff.
18 Hobbes 1996: 92.
19 See Hobbes 1996: 93.

to the partial renunciation of this right, so that this desire explains why one willingly performs the act of "standing aside." In short, I agree to limit my natural freedom and corresponding right to everything if you agree to limit your natural freedom and corresponding right to everything. If this act of mutual limitation were to take place between each individual and every other individual, we would end up with the kind of situation described by Fichte in the following passage:

> If a million human beings exist alongside one another, each individual may very well will for himself as much freedom as possible. But if the will of all were to be united into one concept as in one will, this will would divide the sum of possible freedom into equal parts, with the aim that all would be free together, and that therefore the freedom of each would be limited by the freedom of all the others. (*FNR*, 98; *SW*, III: 106)

Hobbes's claim that an individual "onely standeth out of his way" when partially renouncing the right of nature is of further significance in at least two other respects in relation to the first main division of Fichte's *Foundations of Natural Right*.

First of all, despite its figurative nature, the notion of standing aside not only gives us some idea of what an actual summons might involve but also makes clear that the human body will have a central role to play in the act of summoning another person as the means whereby one is able to signal to others through words produced by the organs of speech or through gestures that one is willing to limit one's freedom if they agree to do the same. Given that the concept of right concerns the thought of finite rational beings exercising an influence upon each other, Fichte attempts to deduce the conditions of the possibility of interpersonal relations in the second main division of the *Foundations of Natural Right* (§§5–7), so as to demonstrate that the concept of right can be applied, and among these conditions he includes the human body and human speech. Yet, as we shall see, Fichte's account of the role of embodied agency differs from Hobbes's account of what must be presupposed in order to explain the act of standing aside, because he accords to human beings a capacity for self-limitation that Hobbes does not explicitly grant them and is arguably not in the position to do so. Secondly, the notion of standing aside can be related to the idea of status or standing that informs moralized readings of Fichte's account of the role of recognition in the first main division of the *Foundations of Natural Right*. This notion can therefore serve to reveal certain assumptions underlying such readings.

Hobbes's views on freedom imply a particular conception of the act of standing aside which serves to differentiate this act from Fichte's account of the summons. In *Leviathan*, Hobbes states that, "LIBERTY, or FREEDOME, signifieth (properly) the absence of Opposition; (by Opposition, I mean externall Impediments of motion;) and may be applyed no lesse to Irrationall, and Inanimate creatures, than to Rationall."[20] As this definition makes clear, the fact that freedom consists only in the absence of external impediments to motion implies that it is something that all material objects, and not only human bodies, can be said to enjoy under certain conditions. In this respect, human beings are, to use one of Hobbes's favorite images for illustrating his conception of freedom, like flowing water which is free to the extent that it may move freely within certain bounds.[21] Hobbes also employs the example of someone who, like water in a channel, is free to move in one direction but not in another, in the form of a traveler who is prevented by hedges and walls from trampling on the vines and crops adjacent to the road he is walking along.[22] To view freedom in terms of the unimpeded motion of bodies in space renders the act of standing aside rather mysterious, however, since this act requires more than freely following a natural course within certain bounds, namely, an act of self-limitation. We may assume, moreover, that unlike flowing water the traveler mentioned above can choose to move in one direction rather than another one within the bounds set to his movements by the hedges and walls. He could, for instance, stand aside for another person as when one moves aside to let someone pass if there is not sufficient room available. How, then, would Hobbes explain such acts of standing aside?

The answer to this question relates to Hobbes's view that all human action is determined by the passions natural to humankind, which include fear, greed, and the desire for glory. These passions drive human beings, causing them to act (or not to act) in certain ways, provided there is no opposing passion. The passions are nevertheless susceptible to the influence of deliberation, because the latter can have a role to play in determining the strength of one passion relative to another one. What ultimately distinguishes human behavior from that of flowing water is, then, deliberation, which Hobbes defines as "simply weighing up the advantages and

[20] Hobbes 1996: 145.
[21] See Hobbes 1996: 146 and Hobbes 1997: 111.
[22] See Hobbes 1997: 111.

disadvantages of the action we are addressing (as on a pair of scales), where the weightier consideration necessarily goes into effect by its own natural inclination."[23] Consequently, identifying both the passion that determines an action and the grounds of this passion, that is to say, its external cause and the series of deliberations that explain its greater strength relative to other passions, will be sufficient when it comes to explaining the act of standing aside whereby an individual agrees to limit his or her right of nature in relation to others. Hobbes's explanation of the act of standing aside in terms of which passion happens to be the strongest one in a given situation means that it would surely not be rational simply to rely on the good will of others. In doing so, one would put oneself at the mercy of whatever happened to be the strongest passion driving a person at a given point in time, even if insight into human nature might provide some means of reliably predicting what will turn out to be the strongest passion in particular circumstances.

The type of explanation of the possibility of an act of standing aside which may signal to others a willingness to limit one's right of nature in relation to them available to Hobbes must be thought to be inadequate when it comes to explaining Fichte's claim that right, which has its basis in mutual recognition, involves an act of *self*-limitation. This is because this act implies the existence of a capacity to exercise self-constraint even in the face of desires that would otherwise determine one's actions according

[23] Hobbes 1997: 152. This definition is offered in connection with the idea that a legislator who assigns a penalty which fails to outweigh the greed that motivates a crime would be proceeding in a way that is contrary to the purpose of punishment, and it assumes, therefore, that human beings can deliberate concerning whether or not acting on a passion would be prudent in a given situation. Thus a human being is presupposed to be capable of foresight and able to engage in the following type of prudential reasoning based on past experience: "he that foresees what wil become of a Criminal, re-cons what he has seen follow on the like Crime before; having this order of thoughts, The Crime, the Officer, the Prison, the Judge, and the Gallowes" (Hobbes 1996: 22). It is the passions, nevertheless, that ultimately determine a human being's actions, for although the force of the passions may be moderated by prudential considerations, these considerations will themselves be determined by certain passions, such as fear. In this way, Hobbes's voluntarism turns out to be reducible to the following conception of the will: "In *Deliberation*, the last Appetite, or Aversion, immediately adhaering to the action, or to the omission thereof, is that wee call the WILL; the Act, (not the faculty,) of *Willing*" (Hobbes 1996: 44). One acts voluntarily for Hobbes, then, even when one acts from practical necessity, as when one throws one's goods overboard to prevent a boat that one is on from sinking (Hobbes 1996: 146). Here we must assume that a person neither wants to throw his or her goods overboard nor to drown. However, the desire for self-preservation proves stronger in the end and when throwing his or her goods overboard he or she acts voluntarily in the sense of acting on the basis of a desire that he or she has, namely, the desire to preserve his or her own life, and also because he or she could have acted on the basis of the other desire, namely, to retain possession of his or her goods. When providing this example Hobbes does not mention, however, that he or she could have acted on the basis of this other desire only *if* it had turned out to be strongest one in this particular situation.

to the degree of power that they happened to possess relative to other desires. In this respect, it would be less irrational to rely on the good will of others, even if Fichte maintains that some kind of independent guarantee of recognition is still needed, given the assumption of a universal egoism and the conditional nature of right. For reasons that I have already provided, this act of self-limitation nevertheless does not imply an act that is completely desire-independent; rather, it can be explained in terms of the fundamental desire to secure a sphere of personal freedom in which to exercise the capacity for rational self-determination under conditions of stable agency. Achieving this end requires recognizing that others also have the capacity to limit their own activity in accordance with the same end, even though they may have a strong desire not to do so. For only on the basis of this understanding of others as not being driven to act by whatever happens to be the strongest desire at any given point in time would it be rational to renounce voluntarily the infinite right to everything which one originally enjoys, that is to say, before the establishment of a condition in which one enjoys certain legally guaranteed rights which at the same time impose on us obligations with respect to how we treat others and how far we seek to extend the sphere of our personal freedom.

The capacity to stand aside in the sense of limiting one's right to everything in relation to others does not, however, entail a direct interest in the freedom of others, even if it does require having certain beliefs about them, especially about their capacity for self-directed action. Rather, although the realization of the end of securing for oneself a sphere of personal freedom requires assuming that others share the same capacities and fundamental ends as oneself – and in this sense recognition and respect must be demonstrated in relation to them – this form of recognition does not by itself explain why one must regard *their* freedom as an unconditional good which imposes an absolute obligation upon oneself and generates a completely desire-independent reason for respecting their freedom. Fichte's account of recognition in the first main division of the *Foundations of the Natural Right* and the subsequent parts of this work are therefore consistent both with each other and with the method adopted in this work which assumes the existence of a universal egoism.

This is not to say that Fichte thinks of the standpoint demanded by the method that he employs in the *Foundations of Natural Right* as the only one in terms of which we can conceive of forms of human association. Indeed, the fact that he bases his theory of right on the methodological assumption of a universal egoism implies the very opposite, given the negative account of egoism found in his ethical theory developed in *The*

System of Ethics from 1798, in which we do find references to the notion of human dignity (*Würde*) explained in terms of rationality and autonomy,[24] along with statements that imply a direct interest in the freedom of others and an unconditional obligation to promote it, such as the following one: "Everyone ... with whom we are in any way acquainted becomes assigned to our care simply by virtue of this acquaintance; he becomes our neighbor and a part of our rational world (*Vernunftwelt*), just as the objects of our experience belong to our sensible world (*Sinnenwelt*). We cannot abandon him unless we lack conscience" (*SE*, 223; *SW*, IV: 235).

Fichte's theory of right can in this respect be thought to possess a critical dimension in that it enables us to view right as something essentially limited when seen from another, higher standpoint. This in turn suggests that any notion of moral standing viewed in purely legal terms must be thought to be subject to certain inherent limitations. In order to pursue this point, I shall introduce the counterpart to the notion of standing aside which I have shown links Fichte's views on recognition with Hobbes's account of what it means to renounce, if not fully so, one's natural or original right to all things. This counterpart to the notion of standing aside is the notion of standing one's ground in cases when sufficient respect is not shown to one by others, which can here be taken to mean a failure on the part of others to recognize one's capacity for rational self-determination by not limiting their activity so as to grant one a sphere of personal freedom. Thus right implies not only acts of self-limitation but also acts of self-assertion. Historical struggles to achieve recognition in this respect testify both to the conditional nature of right and to the necessity of standing one's ground rather than standing aside in certain circumstances.

Yet even if acts of self-assertion are justified under such conditions, with the need to engage in them reflecting the contingent nature of recognition, these acts of self-assertion may primarily or even exclusively be a matter of *my* freedom or that of a particular oppressed group to which I belong. Such acts do not, therefore, entail an interest in the freedom of others as such. Within a purely legal framework of rights self-assertion is, moreover, compatible not only with the absence of any direct interest in the freedom of others but also with the closing down of the possibility of a richer relation to others which consists in a condition of mutual concern and social recognition. This is because others may be viewed simply as

[24] See *SE*, 135; *SW*, IV: 142; *SE*, 245; *SW*, IV: 256; *SE*, 316; *SW*, IV: 334; *SE*, 333; *SW*, IV: 352; *SE*, 341; *SW*, IV: 362.

limits to one's own acts of self-assertion, limits that one may seek to push back as far as is legally permissible so as to give up as little as possible of one's original "infinite" right to everything, while at the same time enjoying the benefits of social order and peace.

In this connection, Fichte's theory of right itself becomes problematic in so far as he wants to accord right an instrumental function in relation to morality, as shown by his claim that although humanity "separates itself from citizenship in order to elevate itself with absolute freedom to the level of morality … it can do so only if human beings have first existed within the state" (*FNR*, 178–9; *SW*, III: 206). This attempt to locate the state within some kind of moral teleology sits uncomfortably with the way in which Fichte bases right, and thus the state, on the methodological assumption of a universal egoism. This is because the type of disposition which he associates with right may turn out to be self-perpetuating in the sense of reinforcing and even creating in individuals a desire only to assert themselves, rather than also developing in them a direct interest in the freedom of others and thus an openness to the more social conception of freedom that Fichte wants to associate with the standpoint of ethics or morality. After all, Fichte's methodological assumption of a universal egoism makes sense only if experience teaches us that there is at least some evidence of a tendency, if not a universal one, for human beings to concern themselves directly only with their own freedom.

CHAPTER 10

Freedom, Coercion, and the Relation of Right

Michael Nance

From Hegel's *Differenzschrift* and "Natural Law" essay up to the present day, Fichte's critics have alleged that his 1796/97 *Foundations of Natural Right* is an internally inconsistent work.[1] These critics argue that there is a deep tension in *Natural Right* between Fichte's initial analysis of the relation of right as a relation of free reciprocal recognition, and his heavy reliance in later sections of the work on coercive law as the primary means to protect individual rights. The tension is as follows. On the one hand, Fichte's argument in §§1–4 of *Natural Right* is supposed to establish that, as a condition of the possibility of self-consciousness of our free agency, we must conceive ourselves as standing in relations of reciprocal recognition with other free, rational agents outside of us, who "summon" us to exercise our agency.[2] In these early sections of *Natural Right*, Fichte characterizes this relation as one of outwardly expressed, free, reciprocal self-limitation: to recognize the other as a bearer of rights, I must limit my actions in the external world so that I leave this other a sphere of freedom in which only she decides what to do. The other, in turn, limits her activity so that I also have a sphere of freedom. Fichte emphasizes that these acts of self-limitation must be freely undertaken by the two agents who reciprocally recognize each other (*FNR*, 10, 38, 48; *SW*, III: 9, 40, 52). Otherwise the relation would not be one between "*free beings, qua free beings*" (*FNR*, 79; *SW*: III, 85).

Yet in later sections of *Natural Right*, individuals within the Fichtean state are portrayed, not as freely recognizing the rights of others, but

[1] See Hegel 1999, Siep 1979a: esp. 34–6, Williams 2002, and Williams 2006.

[2] I discuss this argument in Nance 2015.

Special thanks to Gabriel Gottlieb for encouragement and detailed comments on several drafts. I also wish to thank audiences at UMBC and the New School for Social Research, and the following individuals: Fred Neuhouser, Jean-Christoph Merle, James Clarke, Whitney Schwab, Jim Thomas, Jessica Pfeifer, and Steve Yalowitz. For research assistance, I thank Ryan Sullivan and Elise Bonin. For funding and research support, I thank the Dresher Center for the Humanities and the CAHSS Dean's Office at UMBC.

rather as egoists who respect the rights of others only because the legal system, backed by coercive threats, forces them to do so. In these later arguments, it seems that Fichte's understanding of the relation of right, and the conception of rightful freedom that lies at the basis of that relation, has undergone a fundamental shift. Whereas Fichte's initial account of a community of free beings standing in the relation of right emphasized *free* self-limitation, now Fichte claims that we cannot trust others freely to regulate their own activity so as to leave room for our sphere of freedom. Instead, the state must set up a system of coercive laws to insure that each person will be *forced* to respect the freedom of others. The critics of *Natural Right* that I discuss in this chapter hold that, although his initial account of recognition is a genuine innovation, Fichte's subsequent reliance on state coercion shows that he fails consistently to follow through on the implications of his account of recognition for his theory of the rightful state. Because Hegel was the first to pose it, I call this the "Hegelian objection." By choosing that title for the objection, I do not mean to imply that it is Hegel's only, or even primary, objection to *Natural Right*. It does, however, seem to be the objection that has gotten the most traction among contemporary Hegelians, and it raises important issues about the internal coherence of *Natural Right*, which is why I focus on it.

Some commentators have responded to this alleged inconsistency in *Natural Right* by arguing that Fichte never intends to rule out coercive enforcement of relations of right at any point in the text.[3] But I agree with the Hegelians that Fichte *does* regard coercion as inconsistent with rightful freedom in §§3–4 of *Natural Right*. I attempt to construct an alternative reply to the Hegelian objection by arguing for three inter-related claims. First, against the Hegelians, I argue that uncoerced reciprocal recognition *does* play a role in Fichte's account of the state. For Fichte conceives of individuals' entry into the "civil contract," the basis of legitimate state authority, as an instance of precisely the kind of uncoerced reciprocal recognition Fichte describes in *Natural Right* §§3–4. Thus, on the interpretation I advocate, the Fichtean state is founded, quite literally, on the free, reciprocal recognition of rights. Second, after the civil contract has been agreed upon and the rightful state is up and running, Fichte's reliance on state coercion to enforce relations of right within the state does not contradict his earlier account of the relation of right. For the underlying conception of freedom within Fichte's theory of the state differs from his conception of freedom in the context of his initial discussion of the

[3] Clarke 2009: 370–1; James 2011: 13–15 and 114–15.

relation of right. Third, I suggest that, with a few caveats, Fichte has good reasons for relying on different views of freedom in different contexts in *Natural Right.* The Hegelian charge of inconsistency therefore proves unwarranted.

I proceed as follows. Section (1) explains the Hegelian objection in more detail. In section (2), I characterize four key features of Fichte's conception of the relation of right as a relation of free reciprocal recognition: the relation of right is a relation of (i) *self-limitation* and (ii) *reciprocity* that must be (iii) *socially expressed*, and the reciprocal acts of self-limitation that constitute the relation must be (iv) *freely performed.* In section (3), I distinguish three different roles in *Natural Right* for relations of right, understood in terms of the four features described in section (2). These three roles constitute three species of the genus, "relation of right." Here I argue that there are two kinds of rightful freedom in play in *Natural Right,* only one of which rules out coercion. In section (4), I use the results of sections (2) and (3) to respond to the Hegelians by arguing for my three main claims.

The Hegelian Objection

The Hegelian objection holds that there is a mismatch in *Foundations of Natural Right* between Fichte's initial deduction of the relation of right as one of free reciprocal recognition and Fichte's subsequent focus on coercive law as the primary social institution tasked with instituting rightful relations. Consider the following passage from Hegel's "Natural Law" essay:

> The former pure self-consciousness, pure unity, or the empty law of ethics (*Sittengesetz*) – the universal freedom of all – is opposed to the real consciousness, i.e. to the subject, the rational being, and individual freedom – which Fichte, in a more popular manner, expresses as the presupposition that "loyalty and faith are lost." On this presupposition, a system is established which aims to unite both the concept and the subject of ethical life, despite their separation (although because of the latter, their union is only formal and external); the resultant relation is called *coercion.* Since this externality of oneness is thereby totally fixed and posited as something absolute which has being in itself, the inner dimension (*Innerlichkeit*), the reconstruction of the lost loyalty and faith, the oneness of universal and individual freedom, and ethical life [in general] are rendered impossible.[4]

[4] Hegel 1999: 132. See also the discussion of Clarke 2011: 211–15 and Williams 2002: 59–62.

In this passage, Hegel analyzes Fichte's *Natural Right* in terms of three stages. First, there is an initial moment of "loyalty and faith,"[5] which involves the "oneness of universal and individual freedom." In this first moment, individuals are taken to be internally motivated to respect or recognize others. Individual consciousness does not yet view the demands of right – the demands of "universal" freedom – as foreign to its individual freedom. We might take Hegel to be referring to Fichte's initial account of rightful recognition in *Natural Right* §§3–4. At this stage of Fichte's argument, the demands of individual freedom are not viewed as opposed to the requirements of universal freedom, since recognition of the freedom of the other is the *condition* of my own freedom. But in a second moment, after individuals violate each other's rights, these original relations of "loyalty and faith" are lost. The subjects of right, who are now distrustful of each other, come to view the requirements of right as an external constraint that diminishes their freedom to pursue their interests. Since individuals no longer freely choose to recognize others' rights, Fichte's theory now requires some other means to generate compliance with norms of right. The third moment Hegel identifies is the attempt by Fichte to use state coercion to reunify universal and individual freedom. Hegel's point is this: if we take the laws of the rightful state to express principles of universal freedom (principles that allow for the recognition of the equal freedom of everyone), then in Fichte's account, coercion is supposed to force individuals' recalcitrant private wills to conform to those laws of freedom, thereby bringing the exercise of individual freedom in line with universal freedom. However, Hegel claims that the reconstruction of the "inner dimension" of loyalty and faith by means of coercion is impossible.[6] The social unity created through coercion remains merely "external" because, on Hegel's reading of Fichte, individuals do not freely adopt laws of universal freedom, as in Fichte's initial portrayal of rights relations in *Natural Right* §4. Rather, these norms are imposed upon them from outside by the threat of force. Therefore, if we construe Fichte's project in *Natural Right* as aiming to institute political relations of free reciprocal recognition as those relations are understood in *Natural Right* §§3–4, then the work is a failure. The Fichtean state settles for second-best, a merely external approximation of genuine mutual recognition and ethical life.

[5] The phrase, lost "loyalty and faith" (*Treu und Glaube*), is a direct allusion to *Natural Right*, although Baur translates the phrase differently as lost "honesty and trust." See *FNR*, 124–5; *SW*, III: 139–40.

[6] Fichte admits as much at *FNR*, 125; *SW*, III: 139.

Hegel's line of argument continues to appeal to more recent commentators on *Natural Right.* Robert Williams offers the most prominent recent statement of this objection.[7] Relying in part on Ludwig Siep's influential reconstruction and critique of Fichte's position in *Anerkennung als Prinzip der praktischen Philosophie*, Williams advances the thesis that there is a "contradiction in Fichte's argument concerning recognition as the foundation of right."[8] According to Williams, Fichte initially argues that "reciprocal recognition grounds right and community, and community is both the condition and expression of freedom's actuality in the world."[9] However, according to Williams:

> In the latter half of the work ... Fichte introduces the problem of a loss of trust and confidence that appears to shatter not only his account of intersubjectivity, but also to undermine his claim that right is grounded in mutual recognition. Further, Fichte contends that trust and confidence, once lost, cannot be restored. This impossibility leads him to replace the community based on recognition of freedom with a concept of community as an instrument of coercion.[10]

These passages nicely summarize the Hegelian objection. We can infer from these quotes that, on Williams's reading, Fichte contradicts himself by initially claiming that free reciprocal recognition is the ground of right, but then later making the incompatible claim that state coercion is the ground of right.[11]

Siep frames his version of the Hegelian objection somewhat differently. For Siep, Fichte derives a novel concept of right as reciprocal recognition, but fails to deploy that concept to analyze relations of right within the state. In Siep's words, Fichte has not "consistently developed (*konsequent entwickelt*) in his theory of the state the original conception of recognition that lies at the ground of his deduction of the concept of right."[12] Siep offers several reasons in support of this claim. First, according to Siep, "Fichte ... does not show that and how different recognition-relations lie at the basis of particular institutions, or are made possible by them."[13] This step is taken only by Hegel, which is part of the reason that, for Siep,

7 I focus on Williams 2002. See also Williams 2006.

8 Williams 2002: 47.

9 Ibid.

10 Ibid.

11 See also Williams 2002: 54: "The outlines of Fichte's proposed 'solution' to the problem of security are becoming clear: coercion by an external third party displaces mutual recognition and trust."

12 Siep 1979a: 36.

13 Ibid. 34.

Hegel is the first true recognition theorist.[14] Second, on Siep's interpretation, the goal of the Fichtean state – "mutual security" – "can be reached through institutions, which directly make superfluous the kind of recognition through which individual self-consciousness can first arise: voluntary (*freiwillig*) self-limitation, which has the freedom of the other as its end."[15] Consequently, Siep concludes that recognition "as the end of individuals' actions" is "dispensable" in the Fichtean *Rechtsstaat*.[16] Free recognition of others' rights is not necessary for rights to be respected if the state uses its coercive power to guarantee that rights will be respected, irrespective of the wills of individual citizens.

The Relation of Right in *Natural Right* §4

The Hegelian objection, in all of its versions, rests on a particular understanding of Fichte's initial analysis of the relation of right as a relation of reciprocal recognition in the "First main division" of *Natural Right*. To evaluate the objection therefore requires us to get clear about Fichte's initial understanding of the relation of right in *Natural Right* §§3–4, which is my goal in this section. It is important for my account to distinguish between the genus "relation of right" and the various species of such relations that Fichte discusses in *Natural Right*.[17] This distinction is especially important because I take Fichte to discuss *both* the genus "relation of right" *and* one species of that genus, the "summoning" relation, in *Natural Right* §§3–4. In this section, I focus on defining the genus "relation of right." Fichte derives the structure of that relation in *Natural Right* §§1–4. I proceed by identifying four distinct features of Fichte's generic account of the relation of right, explaining each feature as I go. The four features I discuss are: self-limitation, reciprocity, expression, and freedom.

Self-Limitation

Fichte consistently characterizes the relation of right in terms of the self-limitation of the subjects who relate to each other. The core Fichtean imperative of right is nicely captured in this sentence, from the "Introduction" to *Natural Right*: "limit your freedom through the concept

[14] Ibid. 34–5.
[15] Ibid. 36.
[16] Ibid. 35.
[17] For the suggestion that there are multiple instances of relations of right in *Natural Right*, see the textual evidence in section (3) below as well as *FNR*, 79; *SW*, III: 85.

of the freedom of all other persons with whom you come in contact" (*FNR*, 10; *SW*, III: 10). This is simply the Fichtean "law of right," stated as an imperative. What the law of right requires is not merely that each person's sphere of rightful freedom should not be violated, which could conceivably be achieved without any human volition at all, but that individuals must "purposively and intentionally" will the limitation of their own agency (*FNR*, 44; *SW*, III: 46).[18]

Reciprocity

According to Fichte, not only must each person recognize the rights of others by limiting her own sphere of freedom, but each person must also recognize the other as *recognizing her*.[19] In other words, the relation of right in the full Fichtean sense requires both acceptance of the acknowledgment offered and reciprocation of the same kind of acknowledgment on the part of the recognized. For Fichte, the reciprocity of the relation of right is extremely important, for at least two reasons. First, it explains the sociality of agency. As Fichte writes regarding the concept of "individuality," "this concept is never *mine*; rather, it is … *mine and his, his and mine*; it is a shared concept within which two consciousnesses are unified into one" (*FNR*, 45; *SW*, III: 47–8). If reciprocal recognition is a condition of the possibility of self-conscious practical agency, as Fichte argues in §§1–4, then it follows that our practical agency is partially constituted by the recognitive relations in which we stand to other agents. Second, the reciprocity of the relation of right explains the fragility of that relation, and the merely hypothetical force of the law of right. Since the relation of right requires uptake and reciprocation on the part of the other, each person's duties of right are binding only on the condition that others reciprocate.[20] Fichte later introduces coercive law into *Natural Right* as a way to guarantee that others will in fact reciprocate.[21]

Expression

In §4, Fichte claims that the relation of right requires, "*not* that I merely refrain from acting contrary to the concept of C as a rational being, but

[18] See also *FNR*, 125–6; *SW*, III: 140.
[19] See *FNR*, 42; 68–9, 111; *SW*, III: 44, 73, 123.
[20] For discussion, see Ware 2010.
[21] On Fichte's engagement with Hobbes in this context, see Schottky 1995: 184–204.

rather that I actually act in conformity with it, that I actually enter into reciprocal interaction with C."[22] According to Fichte here, the relation of right requires that individuals *express* through their actions that they recognize the other as a rational being. Epistemic considerations motivate this aspect of Fichte's view.[23] If to have a right is to be recognized as entitled to a sphere of freedom, but no one expresses that he or she has so recognized you, then you will not know if you have any rights, nor will you know the boundaries of any rights you might have. That is why Fichte's theory requires that recognition must be outwardly expressed.

Putting together the last two points, we see that, as a reciprocal, expressive relation to an other, the Fichtean relation of right has a distinctly *second-personal* character: for me to recognize you, I have to address you in a way that expresses my recognition; and for you to reciprocally recognize me, you must address me in a way that shows that you have understood and responded to my recognition by recognizing me.[24]

Freedom

We have already seen that Fichte's account of the relation of right involves self-limitation. Fichte further holds in §4 that the acts of self-limitation that constitute the relation of right must be freely undertaken. Hence, I turn to an analysis of Fichte's conception(s) of rightful freedom.

Within a relation of recognition as free reciprocal self-limitation, each of the two persons in the relation can be conceived as playing two conceptually distinct roles. Freedom is implicated in both of these roles, but in different ways. Each party to the relation is both 1) the possessor of a sphere of personal freedom that is partially made possible by the other's self-limitation, and 2) a freely self-limiting agent with respect to the other's sphere of freedom.

In the following quote, Fichte analyzes the relation of right by referring to both of these aspects of freedom: "just as I demand my freedom for all the future, so too I also demand that the other be limited, and – since he is to be free – limited by himself for all the future" (*FNR*, 48; *SW*, III: 52). The individual demands his own sphere of freedom; but he also demands that the other should freely limit his agency, as opposed to having limitations forced upon him, "since he is [also] to be free." Thus, each person's

[22] *FNR*, 42–3; *SW*, III: 45.

[23] See *FNR*, 42–3; *SW*, III: 44–5.

[24] Cf. Darwall 2005.

possession of a personal sphere of freedom requires the other's free self-limitation, if both persons are to relate to each other as free beings. In a similar passage, Fichte discusses the second aspect, the freedom involved in self-limitation, in more depth. Fichte writes that individuals must "have made it a law for themselves" to leave the other a sphere for her free activity:

> But since these beings [those who limit themselves in the relation of right] are posited as free, such a limit could not lie outside freedom, for freedom would thereby be nullified rather than limited *as freedom*; rather, all would have to posit this limit for themselves through freedom itself, i.e. all would have to have made it a law for themselves not to disturb the freedom of those with whom they stand in mutual interaction. (*FNR*, 10; *SW*, III: 9)

The difficult interpretative issue in passages such as these is determining what precisely "freedom" means in the context of individuals' "free" self-limitation. The Hegelian objectors understand "freedom" to rule out the use of coercive force to get the individual to limit her agency, whereas Clarke and James hold that free self-limitation here is meant to be compatible with coercion.[25]

How, then, should we understand Fichtean rightful freedom? Given that rights, for Fichte, are inherently relational, I assume that rightful freedom also must be relational: rightful freedom is a matter of the practical relations one agent stands in to another. I want to suggest that there are *two* relational conceptions of freedom at play in *Natural Right*, only one of which is necessarily incompatible with coercion. First, Fichte sometimes discusses freedom in terms of the absence of interference.[26] Second, Fichte sometimes analyzes freedom in terms of the absence of the *power* to interfere *arbitrarily* with a right-holder.[27] Using some resources from more recent philosophy, we can formulate these two conceptions of freedom more precisely:

1. *Non-Interference:* According to Isaiah Berlin, freedom consists in the absence of interference, where "interference" includes especially, but not only, coercion.[28]

[25] See note 3 above.
[26] See, e.g., *FNR*, 85; *SW*, III: 92.
[27] See, e.g., *FNR*, 95–6; *SW*, III: 103–4.
[28] Berlin 1998: 194–203.

2. *Non-Domination:* According to Phillip Pettit, freedom is the absence of domination, where A dominates B iff A possesses the power arbitrarily to interfere with B's free choice.[29]

As is evident from its definition, coercion *necessarily* undermines freedom as non-interference (1). Accordingly, if Fichte holds (1), then his use of coercion to enforce relations of right is inconsistent. However, on a conception of freedom as non-domination (2) coercion *can* reduce or nullify freedom, but it does not *necessarily* do so. On Pettit's account, coercion does not dominate the coerced if the coercion has been freely instituted by the coerced. Pettit offers a useful example that illustrates the point:

> Suppose you worry about drinking too much in the evenings and give me the key to the alcohol cabinet, making me promise to hand it back to you at twenty-four hours' notice and only at such notice. If I thwart your wishes on a given evening by refusing to return the key, I do not thereby impose my will on your choice, because what I do is subject to your control.[30]

This example does not directly deal with coercion, but the basic conceptual point extends to the case of coercion: if the coercion that is exercised against me has been instituted or authorized by me, then it does not force me to follow someone else's will. Instead, the coercion becomes an expression of my own will, since I am coerced only on terms that I myself have freely set. If both non-interference and non-domination conceptions of freedom are in play in *Natural Right*, then we would expect freedom to rule out coercion in some cases but not in others, depending on which conception of freedom is at issue. And, as I show in the next section, that is in fact what we find in the text.

The Relation of Right: Three Contexts

Although Fichte is not as clear about this as one might wish, I take him to hold that in actual human social life, there are a variety of intersubjective relations that qualify as relations of right. Fichte's initial transcendental deduction of the relation of right specifies four generic structural features of a kind of relation that can be instantiated in various particular forms.[31]

[29] Pettit 2012: 81. See also Neuhouser 2013: 197–204. Neuhouser offers an alternative account of domination in terms of obedience.

[30] Pettit 2012: 80.

[31] See Franks 2005: 324 for a similar view.

Only one of these forms, the "summons," is, for Fichte, necessary for *any* kind of self-conscious practical agency.[32] But it is possible to read Fichte as holding that agency exists on a continuum, and that richer and more on-going forms of reciprocal recognition condition richer and more stable forms of practical agency.[33] I present evidence for this interpretation in this section by highlighting three distinct species of rights-relations in *Natural Right*. The three species of rights-relations are: 1. The "summons," which Fichte describes as a process of "upbringing" or "education" (*Erziehung*) that takes place in the course of child development; 2. The act of entering into the social contract with others to form or join a rightful state; and 3. Subsequent on-going interactions between citizens of a rightful state. I argue that Fichte conceives of each of these social interactions as an instance of a rights-relation with the four structural features outlined in section (2) above.

The Summons

After deriving the necessity of reciprocal recognition for the possibility of self-conscious practical agency, Fichte immediately describes one crucial role that recognition relations play in human life, which he refers to as the "summons": "The summons to engage in free self-activity is what we call upbringing (*Erziehung*)" (*FNR*, 38: *SW*, III: 40). I take the "summoning" relation to be the minimal form of recognition necessary for any form of self-conscious free agency.[34] If human beings are not brought up in a community of rational agents who summon them to consciousness of their own agency, they will not be agents at all. As described by Fichte, the summoning relation has all four features of the relation of right: it is an outwardly expressed relation of freely bestowed, reciprocal self-limitation. The summoner expresses a demand upon the summoned while limiting her agency to leave room for the summoned agent to respond, and in a successful case of summoning, the summoned agent responds by reciprocally recognizing the summoner's sphere of freedom (*FNR* §4).

[32] Fichte alludes to this point at *FNR*, 79; *SW*, III: 85, where he distinguishes between "necessary" and "voluntarily chosen" relations of right.

[33] I argue for these claims in Nance 2015: 622–4.

[34] See Nance 2015: 623, and Gottlieb's discussion of "elementary" recognition in his contribution to this volume. I agree with Gottlieb that it is crucial to distinguish "elementary" recognition as described in Fichte's account of the summons from "political" recognition. I further distinguish two kinds of political recognition.

Fichte writes that the summoner leaves the summoned agent a sphere of freedom within which to respond to the summons. Consider the following passage:

> Within this sphere ... the subject has chosen from among the possibilities contained in the sphere: the subject constitutes its own freedom and independence out of these possibilities ... But within this sphere, only the subject could have chosen, and *not the other*; for, according to our presupposition, the other being has left this sphere undetermined. (*FNR*, 40; *SW*, III: 42)

The question I want to address is what form of freedom Fichte has in mind in this passage. Presumably the summoning relation is one of asymmetrical power – paradigmatically, the summoner is a parental figure, and the one summoned is a child. As Fichte conceives such a relation, it is likely the case that the summoner possesses the power arbitrarily to interfere with the actions of the one summoned, ruling out non-domination as a plausible interpretation of the freedom of the summoned.[35] Thus Fichte's claim that "the other being has left this sphere undetermined" is best read in terms of non-interference: the summoner chooses not to interfere with the freedom of the summoned, even though she could do so.[36]

The Civil Contract as Reciprocal Recognition

Throughout his political writings in the 1790s, Fichte holds a demanding actual-consent criterion for the legitimacy of political authority.[37] It is not sufficient, for Fichte, that a state be configured such that rational agents *could* agree to it.[38] Rather, Fichte holds that individuals must actually and explicitly choose to subject themselves to a state's authority.

[35] Note that whether the parent's authority over the child counts as domination depends on the legal background structure. A regime of family law could force the parent's interference to track the interests of the child, in which case parental interference would not count as dominating. That is why I add the qualifier: *as Fichte conceives such a relation*, since Fichte does not have in mind such a legal background structure and thus regards parental authority as more or less arbitrary. I return to this point in my conclusion below.

[36] It follows from this analysis that not all parent–child interactions are summoning relations – in cases in which the parent coerces the child by threatening her with consequences, the child is not being summoned, for the child is not free from interference. See *FNR*, 32–3; *SW*, III: 33–4 and *SE*, 319–320; *SW*, IV: 337–338 for more discussion.

[37] See Schottky 1995: 240.

[38] Compare Kant's discussion of the "original contract" as a merely hypothetical "idea of reason" in "On the common saying: That may be correct in theory, but it is of no use in practice" (8: 297–9).

Fichte describes this choice in contractualist terms: each citizen enters into a multi-stage "civil contract" with each other citizen (*FNR* §17). On my interpretation of *Natural Right*, agreeing to subject oneself to state authority through entering into the civil contract just is to recognize and be recognized by others as entitled to a sphere of equal freedom. To make my case for this claim, I will show that the Fichtean civil contract has all four features of the relation of right. If I can make it plausible, this interpretation would have several interesting consequences. First, the kind of relation Fichte derives in §§1–4 of *Natural Right* would turn out to have a central place, not only in Fichte's account of human development (the summons), but also in Fichte's theory of the basis of state authority. Second, for better or for worse, Fichte's actual-consent account of legitimacy would turn out to be centrally important to *Natural Right*.[39] I now turn to a discussion of the civil contract in terms of the four features of the relation of right.

First, the act of joining a state via the civil contract is an act of self-limitation in a straightforward sense, for in subjecting herself to the laws of a state, a person chooses to take on the constraints embodied in those laws. For their consent to be genuine, Fichte holds that individuals must be highly informed regarding the particularities of the civil contract and civil legislation, which is to say that they must know exactly what limitations they are taking on:

> I ought to be able to see for myself that all possible future judgments of right … can turn out only as I myself would have to pronounce upon them in accordance with the law of right. Therefore, *norms* concerning these future judgments of right must be submitted for my inspection … Such norms are called *positive laws*. (*FNR*, 95; *SW*, III: 103)

The civil contract specifies the precise limits to individual freedom that each citizen accepts in entering the civil state so that each other person is able to enjoy an equal sphere of free activity.[40]

[39] Actual-consent views of political obligation and legitimate authority have well-known problems, and in presenting my interpretation of *Natural Right*, I am not *endorsing* Fichte's actual-consent theory of legitimacy. But it is important for understanding Fichte's political philosophy to see that he holds a strong-voluntarist account of legitimate authority, and that this view plays a central role in *Natural Right*. For a reading of the Fichtean civil contract in less demanding, "metaphorical" terms, see James 2011: 127–8. James explicitly aims to move Fichte toward Kantian hypothetical contractualism. My interpretation suggests that James underestimates the centrality of Fichte's voluntarist account of legitimacy in *Natural Right*.

[40] This includes specifying precisely what property each person will control in the civil state. Fichte's broad conception of "property" includes such matters as one's occupation. See, e.g., *FNR*, 183–7; *SW*, III: 210–14. See also James 2011: Chapter 1.

Second, Fichte is quite clear that the act of consenting to become a member of the state is fully reciprocal between the citizen who consents to join the state and each other citizen. In describing the first part of the civil contract, which he calls the "citizens' property contract," Fichte writes:

> Think of an individual at the moment of making such a contract; he is the first of the parties required for a contract. Now, in one general concept, bring together all those individuals with whom this first individual must, one by one, enter into a contract. The group of individuals constitutes all the rest – but *only as individuals* ... What I am saying is that all of these individuals constitute the second party in the contract. Each individual has said to all of them: I will to possess this, and I demand of you that you give up your claim to have any right to it. And all of them have responded: we shall relinquish our claims on the condition that you relinquish your claims to everything else. (*FNR*, 169; *SW*, III: 195)

In this passage, Fichte nicely captures the second-personality and reciprocity involved in the civil contract. Each person entering into the contract says to each other person that she wills to possess a certain sphere of freedom (her property), and each other person responds by recognizing the first person's sphere of freedom.

Third, although the passage I just quoted is couched in hypothetical language, Fichte immediately proceeds to state that every member of the Fichtean state "has at one time *actually* expressed himself in the manner described, whether through words or actions, by dedicating himself publicly and openly to a particular occupation" (*FNR*, 170; *SW*, III: 196).[41] Thus Fichte regards the choice to enter into the civil contract as one that must be actually expressed to others "through words or actions." There are two primary motivations for the expressive requirement in the Fichtean civil contract. First, because duties of right are conditional on the reciprocation of others, each person must somehow find a way to express that she is committed to norms of right. But because individuals do not have access to others' inner dispositions, the only way that the parties are able to express their commitment to the law of right to each other is by reciprocally submitting to a set of coercively backed laws that fully determine each person's rights and guarantee "with mechanical necessity" that no one's rights can be violated in the future (*FNR*, 127; *SW*, III: 142). Submission to state coercion is thus the crucial means by which citizens are able to demonstrate to others that they are genuinely committed to recognizing their rights. Second, if everyone else is supposed to recognize

[41] See also *FNR*, 96; *SW*, III: 104.

my property rights in the civil contract, and I am supposed to reciprocally recognize their rights, then each person must express to everyone else precisely what aspects of the shared social world she wills to have as her property.[42]

Lastly, I turn to the fourth feature of the relation of right: freedom. Although there is textual evidence on both sides of the issue, a good case can be made that, for Fichte, one must be able to choose freely whether or not to contract with others to submit to the authority of a state. The primary basis for this claim is Fichte's strongly voluntarist account of legitimate political authority. Fichte recognizes that his deduction of the relation of right establishes only a hypothetical imperative of right, and that consequently there is no categorical duty of right to establish membership in a rightful community: "the postulate that a community among free beings as such ought to have an enduring existence appears here as arbitrary, as a postulate that each could adopt simply by his own free choice; but if one adopts this postulate, one thereby necessarily makes oneself subject to [the law of right]" (*FNR*, 81; *SW*, III: 87–8).[43] Fichte's actual-consent view of legitimate political authority is a consequence of this conceptual point, for given that there is no duty of right to join the civil state, the matter is ultimately left up to each individual's personal choice.

Given these commitments, it seems that Fichte's position should be that there is no right to coerce people to enter into the civil contract. And indeed, in the main text of *Natural Right*, there are a number of passages that support the view that the choice to join a state must be a free choice. As Fichte describes his view in §7, each person must "have resolved with complete freedom … to exist in community with free beings."[44] Fichte repeats the point in §8: "above all else, *I must subject myself with complete freedom*" (*FNR*, 94; *SW*, III: 102). Now, it seems that coercing someone to become a citizen of a state would violate the requirement of "complete freedom."[45] This is clearly the case if we construe "complete freedom" here in terms of non-interference. And even if we read "complete freedom" as non-domination, in the context of a stateless individual's entry into a civil

[42] Fichte makes this point in various ways at *FNR*, 114–17; *SW*, III: 126–30. "Property" here includes one's occupation, as indicated in the first quote in this paragraph.

[43] See Fichte's entire discussion at *FNR*, 80–1; *SW*, III: 86–8, as well as *FNR*, 94; *SW*, III: 102; and *FNR*, 15; *SW*, III: 14 for elaboration of this theme. For discussion, see Ware 2010, Estes 2006, and Nance 2015. By contrast, Kant holds that there is a duty of right to exit the state of nature and enter into a civil condition (*MM*, 6: 307–8). See also Varden 2008.

[44] *FNR*, 81; *SW*, III: 88.

[45] See also Fichte's remarks at *FNR*, 162; *SW*, III: 184.

contract, the authorization condition necessary on a republican account for the legitimacy of coercion has not been met, for the stateless person has by hypothesis not authorized any state or any citizen of a state to exercise coercion against her. Thus, on either non-domination or non-interference readings, the use of coercion to force someone to join a specific state would seem to be contrary to right.

Yet in §1 of the second appendix on "the right of nations (*Völkerrecht*) and cosmopolitan right (*Weltbürgerrecht*)," Fichte writes:

> According to what was said above, every individual has the right to force any other individual he encounters either to enter into a state with him or to stay out of the sphere of his efficacy. If one of them already lives in a state and the other does not, then the first will coerce the other to join him in his state ... someone who does not live in a state can rightfully be coerced by the first state that encounters him either to subject himself to it, or to stay away from it. (*FNR*, 320; *SW*, III: 369)

It is hard to reconcile this passage with Fichte's strongly voluntarist view of legitimate political authority, for the passage appears to endorse the claim that a citizen of a state may coerce an unaffiliated individual to join her state.[46] What has become of the supposed "complete freedom" with which individuals choose to submit to political authority?

In his contribution to this volume, Jean-Christoph Merle writes that for Fichte, "*all* human beings have the unique human right to enter into a social contract," which is the condition for them having any further rights.[47] This is a consequence of Fichte's strong voluntarism: rights exist only within a civil state that has actually been authorized by its citizens. A stateless individual therefore has no determinate rights. But Fichte still wants to have an account of cosmopolitan right, understood as a theory of the rights of individuals in the international domain. Given strong voluntarism, if individuals are to have determinate rights in the international domain, they must first be citizens of states, for determinate rights exist only within states. Fichte then conceives of states as standing in rightful relations to each other. Individual cosmopolitan rights are mediated by

[46] A further textual difficulty concerns Fichte's confusing discussion of the "right of coercion" in *FNR* §8. He seems to suggest that there is a right to unlimited coercion in the state of nature, but then later suggests that such a right can never be applicable. At some points Fichte distinguishes between coercing everyone to join some state or other, and coercing people to join a *specific* state, where the former is rightful but the later is not (e.g., *FNR*, 145; *SW*, III: 164). I am skeptical that this distinction can bear much weight. Overall, it is difficult to find a consistent reading of these passages. See *FNR*, 90, 114, 132, 166–7; *SW*, III: 97, 126, 148, 193.

[47] Merle, Chapter 12, p. 252.

these rightful relations between states. This line of thought leaves Fichte with a conundrum: given his commitments, if he is going to have an account of cosmopolitan right, then he needs it to be the case that every individual person belongs to some state. That seems impossible to achieve without authorizing states, or citizens of states, to exercise coercion against stateless individuals. But such coercion undermines the very foundation of Fichte's theory of legitimate political authority by making the choice to join a state a matter of force, not freedom.

To resolve this tension, *Natural Right* clearly requires a more robust and developed account of the rights of stateless individuals, and of the conditions under which the human right to join a civil contract can be respected. I cannot resolve this complex issue here. But I think the textual evidence I have presented shows that Fichte regards the act of entry into the civil contract as a rightful relation, which means that this relation must be one between "free beings as such." By allowing states to force stateless individuals to enter into the civil contract, Fichte does not consistently follow through on this commitment in his theory of cosmopolitan right.[48] But an analysis of the civil contract as a rightful relation is clearly a core part of Fichte's account of legitimate state authority in *Natural Right.* Thus I take it that Fichte regards the civil contract relation as a species of rightful relation, his remarks in the appendix on cosmopolitan right notwithstanding.

Rightful Relations Among Citizens

So far, I have focused on two species of rights-relations in *Natural Right*: the summoning relation and the civil contract. Both of these relations exhibit all four features of the relation of right. And I have suggested that neither of these two relations can be instituted via coercion, for in these contexts the use or threat of force undermines the freedom required for a rightful relation to exist. In this section I turn to a third species of rightful relation: the case of relations among citizens within the Fichtean state. Now, Fichte clearly holds that the state must use coercive threats to institute and enforce relations of right after individuals enter the civil contract (see, e.g., *FNR*, 171; *SW*, III: 197). But he just as clearly holds that everyday relations among citizens are relations of right, and thus are supposed to be relations of free reciprocal self-limitation (e.g., *FNR*, 191; *SW*,

[48] Fichte is actually clearer that it is not rightful to force someone to enter into a social contract in *Contribution to the Rectification of the Public's Judgment of the French Revolution* (*SW*, VI: 240, 250).

III: 219). At this point, the Hegelian objectors pose the question: why is coercion suddenly compatible with rightful freedom, when it was not in the case of the summons?[49] They hold that this shift in Fichte's view is blatantly inconsistent. But we are now in a position to address the Hegelian worry, in two steps.

The first step is to establish that Fichte's conception of rightful freedom within the state is republican. Fichte goes to great lengths to structure the rightful state in such a way that no citizen is subject to the arbitrary power of any other citizen.[50] Consider the following passage:

> (a) the free being *can* … interfere with the freedom of other rational beings … (c) if within a community of rational beings such interference *never* occurs and *never* can occur, the only possible explanation for this is that the free beings have freely made this way of acting into a *law* for themselves. (*FNR*, 85; *SW*, III: 92)

Note the modality of Fichte's analysis of non-interference in this passage. Fichte says that in a community of free rational beings, not only does interference with rightful freedom not actually occur, but more demandingly, such interference "*never* can" occur. I take his point to be that even if no one actually interferes with anyone's freedom, if arbitrary interference with another's freedom is *possible*, then the state is not yet rightful. In other words, Fichte advocates a republican conception of rightful freedom within the state. This reading is confirmed by a number of other passages, one of which I discuss below.

The second step in answering the Hegelian objection is to show that the Fichtean state meets the authorization condition that is necessary for coercion to be consistent with republican freedom. As I pointed out in section 2.4 above, coercion does not violate republican freedom if the use of coercion has been authorized by the one coerced. Fichte relies on precisely this point in explaining how individuals can subject themselves to coercive laws without being dominated:

> When I subject myself to the law, a law that has been inspected and approved by me (which inspection is – as has been proved – the exclusive condition of the possibility of my being rightfully subjected to it), I am not subjecting myself to the changeable, arbitrary will of a human being, but rather to a will that is immutable and fixed. In fact, since the law is exactly

[49] The Hegelian objectors do not recognize that Fichte intends the civil contract to be a relation of right, which is why I leave it out here.

[50] This, I take it, is the ultimate point of Fichte's doctrine of the "ephorate": to guarantee that state authority is not exercised arbitrarily. See *FNR*, 151–6; *SW*, III: 171–8.

> as I myself would have to prescribe it, in accordance with the rule of right, I am subjecting myself to my own immutable will ... Although I am subjected, I remain always subjected only to *my* will. I actually did exercise my right to be my own judge this one time, and I exercised it as applying to my entire life and to all possible cases. (*FNR*, 95–6; *SW*, III: 103–4)

Just as in Rousseau's account of the general will, Fichte here argues that, because individual citizens authorize the laws of the state, their obedience to those laws constitutes obedience to their own will. Again, Fichte's emphasis on individuals' actual consent to enter into the civil contract takes on central importance. The fact that I freely choose to subject myself to the coercive enforcement of the system of laws makes this subjection into a case of obedience to myself. Coercive enforcement of laws within the Fichtean state is therefore consistent with the rightful freedom of the citizens subject to the laws.

In fact, not only is there no contradiction between Fichte's account of republican freedom and his reliance on coercion but there is also a close conceptual connection between Fichte's republicanism and his account of the coercive state. In the above passage, Fichte contrasts subjection to the "immutable and fixed" will of the law with subjection to the "changeable, arbitrary will of a human being." This contrast points toward a non-Hobbesian, republican rationale for Fichte's reliance on methodological egoism and coercive law in his theory of the state. Fichte sometimes poses the problem of legitimate political authority in Hobbesian terms as consisting in an assurance problem between rationally self-interested agents.[51] Just as in Hobbes's *Leviathan*, in these parts of *Natural Right* Fichte gives the impression that the role of the state is to use coercion to incentivize pro-social behavior. But at other moments, such as the above quote from §8, Fichte suggests that the reason for the state to use coercion to enforce rights is because otherwise citizens would be dependent upon the arbitrary will of other private citizens for the enjoyment of their rights, and would therefore be unfree. Now, a useful procedure for guaranteeing that one's theory of the legitimate state does not force citizens to rely on the good will of others is to adopt the methodological assumption that *no one* has a good will toward anyone else.[52] If individual rights can still exist even in a society devoid of good will, then each individual can rest secure in the knowledge that her status as an equal rights-bearer does not depend

[51] See, e.g., Fichte's remarks at *FNR*, 90–1; *SW*, III: 98–9.

[52] For some objections to this strategy, see Pettit's discussion of the "deviant-centered strategy" of institutional design in Pettit 1996: 72–8.

on the good will of anyone else.[53] Each individual is guaranteed a sphere of rightful, non-dominated freedom, backed by the state's standing threat of force against would-be rights-violators. Each depends on the will of the state for protection of her rights, but given Fichte's stringent legitimacy conditions, each also knows that the will of the state is guaranteed not to be arbitrary like an ordinary human will.[54] Thus citizens can subject themselves to the laws, but remain as free as before.

The result is that there are two conceptually independent strands of argument in *Natural Right* for the necessity of state coercion as the means for protecting individual rights. One line of argument is republican, while the other is Hobbesian. Fichte sometimes runs these two strands of argument together, but I believe they are distinct. Even if the Hobbesian assurance problem did not arise, there would still be a rationale in *Natural Right* for introducing coercive backing of rights. For namely: even if I trust that others will in fact have a good will toward me and respect my sphere of freedom, I am nonetheless dominated if others have the *power* to interfere within my sphere on an arbitrary basis. Others need not exercise this power for me to be unfree; I am dominated just in virtue of the *possibility* of others' arbitrary interference.[55]

Critical Assessment and Conclusion

We are now in a position to return to the Hegelian objection. According to Siep's version of the objection, the goal of the Fichtean state – "mutual security" – "can be reached through institutions, which directly make superfluous the kind of recognition through which individual self-consciousness can first arise: voluntary (*freiwillig*) self-limitation, which has the freedom of the other as its end."[56] But we can see now that this characterization of Fichte's position is not correct. For on Fichte's view, the civil contract, which is the basis of legitimate state authority, is itself an instance of the same "kind of recognition through which individual self-consciousness can first arise." Fichte's theory of the state does not make such recognition superfluous; on the contrary, his theory of legitimate state authority rests on precisely the same kind of relation that he describes in his doctrine of the summons. I argued for this point by showing that

[53] Compare Kant's famous remark that "The problem of establishing a state … is *soluble* even for a nation of devils" (*TPP*, 8: 366).

[54] Again, the "ephorate" plays a special role in guarding against arbitrary rule.

[55] See Pettit's discussion of "invigilation" in Pettit 2012: 81.

[56] Ibid. 36.

the summons and the civil contract are two species of the genus, "relation of right."

In Williams's version of the objection, Fichte grounds his theory of the state on coercive law, thereby contradicting his initial deduction of free reciprocal recognition as the ground of rightful community. But again, Williams fails to recognize that Fichte in fact grounds the state on free reciprocal recognition in the civil contract, and that the legitimacy of state coercion itself rests on the civil contract. Furthermore, Williams and Hegel do not recognize that state coercion does not violate republican freedom if 1) it has been explicitly and freely authorized by all citizens, and 2) citizens regard state coercion as the condition of their own non-dominated freedom. Under these circumstances, coercion no longer appears to the citizens as an "external" relation; instead, state coercion in support of individual rights expresses all citizens' reciprocal recognition of the rights of each.

Still, it may seem that I have conceded too much to the Hegelian objection by admitting that the summons and, perhaps, the civil contract presuppose a conception of freedom as non-interference, while the Fichtean state rests on a republican conception of freedom. Now, I think that the differences between these contexts adequately explain why Fichte regards differing conceptions of freedom as appropriate.[57] So unlike the Hegelians, I do not find this shift to be evidence of an obvious inconsistency in Fichte's view. But I also think it is compatible with Fichte's basic position to modify his theory of rightful freedom so that it is republican throughout the various rights-relations discussed in *Natural Right*. Such a modified version of Fichte's theory of right would hold that the summoning relation, the civil contract, and relations among citizens within the Fichtean state *all* must be non-dominated relations of socially expressed reciprocal recognition. Here is a brief outline of how one might arrive at such a theory. First, Fichte's account of the summons would need to be complemented by an account of family law that would force parents' choices to track the interests of their children. Forcing parents' interference to track the interests of their children would prevent these patterns of interference from being dominating.[58] Second, Fichte's account of the

[57] I should note, however, that Fichte must view the civil contract as non-dominated if the choice to enter that contract is supposed to legitimize state coercion. If I enter into a coercive relationship because I am dominated by another agent, then my entry into that relationship does not amount to a free endorsement. There is clearly some incoherence in Fichte's account of the choice to enter the civil contract, but I think a coherent view can be salvaged.

[58] For discussion of the issue of children's rights and republican freedom, see Ferejohn 2001: 77–97, esp. 82.

civil contract and cosmopolitan right would be complemented with an account of the rights of stateless persons vis-à-vis states. The aim of such an account would be to ensure that the choice to enter into the civil contract would respect the rightful, non-dominated independence of stateless individuals, which is a precondition for their authorization of state coercion to play a legitimizing role. Fichte's account of rightful freedom within the state is already explicitly republican, so no modifications of that account are necessary. By supplementing Fichte's accounts of the summons and the civil contract along the lines I have suggested, we can arrive at the outline of a consistently republican Fichtean view that clearly avoids the Hegelian charge of inconsistency.

CHAPTER 11

Fichte's Organic Unification: Recognition and the Self-overcoming of Social Contract Theory

Dean Moyar

The theory of *mutual recognition* inaugurated by Fichte in the *Foundations of Natural Right* seems to offer an alternative to the standard grounding of liberalism in the voluntary consent of the individual. Yet there is a prominent thread of voluntarism running throughout the text and in "Part II, or Applied Natural Right" Fichte presents his own version of the social contract. The account is thus marked by a tension between a conception of freedom as interdependence (mutual recognition) and the idea that freedom is grounded in the voluntary act of the bare individual (social contract). While many commentators have noticed the main tension, relatively little attention has been focused on the move by which Fichte resolves the tension, namely the move in §17 to a "unification contract" through which individuals as parts are absorbed into the community as an organic whole. This move to the organic is surprising, at least in part because Hegel took it upon himself to criticize Fichte's political philosophy for an individualism that is supposed to contrast unfavorably with Hegel's own organicism. But as in many aspects of his philosophy, this is a case of Hegel critically appropriating a Fichtean concept and in the severity of his critique obscuring the novelty and complexity of Fichte's original view. Rather than treat Fichte's organicism primarily as a precursor to Hegel, in this essay I foreground Fichte's relationship to the social contract tradition. My thesis is that Fichte's theory of intersubjectivity draws out tensions internal to social contract theory, and that in the end his move to the organic pushes beyond the bounds of contract theory, showing how contractualism overcomes itself.

I would like to thank the audience at the New York German Idealism Workshop meeting on this volume for helpful questions and comments. I would also like to thank Gabe Gottlieb for critical comments on several earlier versions.

Two Types of Social Contract Theory

One of the main difficulties in assessing Fichte's relation to social contract theory is that so many different versions of the social contract have been proposed. There are clearly some affinities between Fichte's overall theory and the theories of Hobbes, Locke, and Rousseau, to name just the three most prominent exemplars.[1] But those three authors are quite different, both in their starting premises and in the conclusions that they draw from the idea that political authority is grounded in a social contract. In this section I will make a distinction between the *atomistic contractualism* of Hobbes and Locke, on the one hand, and the *holistic contractualism* of Rousseau (who would be followed by Kant and Rawls). My purpose with this rough distinction (which will ignore many important differences) is to fix these two strands of the tradition in order to show which elements of Fichte's position move him from one strand to the other and eventually push him beyond the ideas that gave contractualism its intuitive appeal.

To understand the importance and novelty of organic unification it is essential not to jump the gun on Fichte's divergence from the contractualist paradigm. In this section I therefore critically review accounts of how Fichte's intersubjectivity and transcendental method already serve to divide him from the contractualist tradition. While I do think there is something to these claims, I also think that Fichte held his contractualism to be consistent with his theory of mutual recognition, and it is that fact that we need to understand first before we can see how the logic of intersubjectivity drew him beyond contractualism.

The following elements are integral to the model of social contract theory that I am calling *atomistic contractualism*. The name derives from the basic claim that the individual person in the contractual situation is a self-enclosed entity, an original source of authority:

- The *state of nature* defines both the *equal status* of the individuals prior to entry into political community and the conditions of scarcity and competition that drive individuals to form a contract.
- Individuals are *motivated* by fear of injury and death, and by the self-interest of acquiring and securing property.
- The *source of obligation* is the individual's own *act of consent* to the terms of the social contract.

[1] See Siep 1992 for an excellent discussion of Fichte's relation to the tradition.

- The public authority's main purpose is the *protection of individual property* and the maintenance of public order.
- By the terms of the contract, the public authority is *limited* in how much it can encroach upon the rights of the individuals, especially upon their property rights.

This picture clearly has great intuitive appeal, deriving mainly from the following four points:

- The motivational sources (fear and self-interest) are clear and uncontroversial.
- The source of authority is familiar from ordinary contracts in which each holding up his end of the bargain is conditional on the other doing so as well.
- There are pre-contract claims that are fixed, non-negotiable points of reference to guarantee individual liberty.
- The social contract can be dissolved if its terms are not upheld, and this gives teeth to the conditional nature of the agreement.

While neither of these lists is exhaustive, I hope that they capture the basic ideas and appeal of the original contractualist framework.

With these elements now in place, we can see why one might think that Fichte's opening moves in the *Foundations of Natural Right* are in tension with atomistic contractualism. First of all, Fichte sets up his derivation as aiming to secure the conditions of *individuality*, which he thinks of as a *contrastive* concept that requires determinately distinct human beings. This alone implies that he is not taking individuals in a state of nature as self-contained units on the basis of which a contract could be reached. Atomistic contractualism assumes that the individuals are free agents, but Fichte's first major move in the *Natural Right* is to argue that one can only be free as the result of a summons to freedom by another individual. This summons is fraught with implications for political theory given that it precedes the category of right and that it is a relationship of education, or nurture, rather than a relationship based on self-interest and fear.

Matters are complicated by the fact that Fichte's next main move, to *mutual recognition*, is not a straightforward extension of the *Aufforderung* argument (a point I will emphasize in Section 2). But one can argue that the recognition argument, too, puts Fichte at odds with the contractualist tradition. Wayne Martin writes, "For the contractarian presupposes what Fichte holds must be established by deduction: namely that the very category of political obligation (of *Recht*) has a legitimate employment."[2] This is just what the recognition argument aims to establish, and it does so through Fichte's method of deducing the conditions of self-consciousness. Martin argues that the category of right is not deduced in a contractualist manner and that we should therefore separate the contractualist argument of the second half of *Natural Right* from the arguments of the first half.

Yet Fichte does in fact share many elements with atomistic contractualism. Most conspicuous among these elements is Fichte's claim that the bindingness of right comes from the voluntary act of the individual. He repeats this claim several times, and even mentions it *within* his argument for mutual recognition (more on this below). Second, Fichte's much discussed separation of morality and right is consonant with atomistic contractualism. Fichte insists that right is a separate category that presupposes no moral motivation, and that in fact assumes a universal egoism, so right is based on a theory of self-interest. Closely connected with this point is Fichte's embrace of force as the only motivating element within right. His thesis that "faith and trust" cannot be assumed within right also puts him in a camp with Hobbes on the issue of the mutual antagonism that leads to political community.

What should we make of these conflicting strands in Fichte's account? One route is that taken by Robert Williams in his Hegelian criticism of Fichte. Williams takes a stand against Fichte's contractualism because he holds it to be a betrayal of the ethical potential of the summons and recognition arguments. Williams argues that Fichte's "ontological grounding" in recognition is betrayed by the subsequent contractualism because recognition is ontological not only in the sense of a requirement for *being* a subject but also in the sense that recognition underwrites a deep sense of community: "Community in this ontological sense reflects a union of individuals that is deeper than contracts which are conditional, contingent unions of wills."[3] Against Fichte's avowal of separating morality and right, Williams insists that the recognition relation is an ethical relation, and therefore that the subsequent phases of the argument, premised as they are on universal egoism, are a betrayal of the insight of recognition.

My alternative interpretive route is to see Fichte's seemingly contradictory tendencies as his way of supporting a version of contractualism that

[2] Martin 2006: 7. See also Baur 2006 for an argument that Fichte's summons argument puts him at odds with social contract theory.

[3] Williams 2006: 30.

alters the standard atomistic account. I read Fichte as the most daring representative of the tradition of holistic contractualism inaugurated by Rousseau. There are several ways in which this alternative strand of contractualism is holistic.

- The *first* dimension is methodological: we cannot think of the starting point, the state of nature or circumstances of justice, as a fixed base on which the subsequent normative claims can be built. In this sense, the holism is opposed to the *foundationalist* aspect of atomistic contractualism. Whereas the atomist takes the human condition as a foundational starting point, the holist typically posits the goals of the account and then develops an account of how our social condition must be transformed in order to fit the posited political norms.
- A *second*, related dimension of holism concerns the agents themselves. The *identities* of the agents in the social condition are bound up with the community – the whole is a condition of the identity of the individuals. The *punctual act of consent* can no longer be the model of the subjectivity that grounds the state. Once an individual joins society her subjectivity will be thicker, and can be the basis for thicker sorts of norms. This is also an issue of motivation, for while the pre-social individual is characterized only by fear and self-interest, the individual within society is a moral being with a developed sense of justice.
- *Third* and finally there is the question of how to conceive the specific claims, especially the property claims, prior to entry into the contract. Here of course Locke and Hobbes will be opposed, and it is the Lockean pre-social property claims that stand out as atomistic. In the holistic program, pre-social property rights will be provisional at best, for the claim is that only in the political state can property be rightful, lawful. The whole, the political community, is in the position to conclusively secure an individual's property rights, but also to say what the limits are of those rights are.

Taken together, these three dimensions of holism are a major shift from atomistic contractualism, for they complicate the conceptions of the voluntary individual and the way in which that individual authority is transmitted to social institutions. The pressing question for holistic contractualism is how far it can depart from the atomistic model without losing the intuitive elements that make contractualism attractive in the first place.

Free Choice and Hypothetical Reasoning in the Recognition Argument

In this section, I examine the main elements of Fichte's argument for the concept of right based on mutual recognition, the argument that Martin and Williams hold to be in tension with Fichte's contractualism. While there are in Fichte's recognition argument traces of the pressures that will eventually lead him to move to holistic contractualism, I will emphasize the ways in which recognition is consonant with atomistic contractualism. This should not be completely surprising, since the social contract is, after all, also a way of binding individuals to shared norms. Yet the direct I–thou intersubjectivity of the *Aufforderung* and recognition arguments seem to promise something different. I will argue later that there is indeed an intersubjective element that breaks open the contractualist paradigm when Fichte introduces the unification contract. To understand how Fichte's political philosophy is a *self*-overcoming of contractualism, though, we first have to understand how he aims to unite his intersubjective insights with the atomism and voluntarism of the tradition.

Fichte's argument for an *Aufforderung* or summons to freedom in §3 is based on the idea of the efficacy of a finite being who can only posit ends in a determinate way if there is an object to resist the activity. Fichte sets up the summons with the idea that any object encountered in the world would negate the subject's efficacy unless that object were in fact the activity of another subject. Following the principles of the Jena *Wissenschaftslehre*, Fichte's deduction here is based on the conditions of the possibility of self-consciousness. His argument is that a doubling of finite consciousness must be thought in order for the activity of an individual subject to be thought. The summoning is an act in which one subject calls another to freedom, leaving the subject who is summoned free to act in a manner of her choosing. That subject is determined, but determined *to be self-determining*. Fichte thus proposes to ground a self-limitation not through fear or self-interest, but rather through the basic demand to secure the conditions of free individuality. Fichte's thesis is about *how one becomes a human being*, and he thus seems to build into the heart of his theory the priority of the community over the individual, or the whole over its parts.

In the mutual recognition argument for the concept of right Fichte continues to stress the uniquely second-personal conditions of individual freedom. Each individual needs a discrete sphere of efficacy, but my sphere can only be determined by another, whose status can in turn only be secured through my recognition of his freedom. The fundamental premise is: "*I can expect a particular rational being to recognize me as a rational being, only if I myself treat him as one*" (*FNR*, 42; *SW*, III: 14). This recognition is not mediated by a third party, and is not a recognition in my conscience, but is a recognition between particular individuals in a "common consciousness." He writes of the concept of individuality, "This concept can exist in a rational being only if it is posited as *completed* by another rational being. Thus this concept is never *mine*; rather, it is – in accordance with my own admission and the admission of the other – *mine and his, his and mine*; it is a shared concept within which two consciousnesses are unified into one" (*FNR*, 45; *SW*, III: 47–8). The result of mutual recognition appears to be a condition of full mutuality in which our obligation to each other constitutes our identity: "we are both *bound* and *obligated* to each other by our very existence" (*FNR*, 45; *SW*, III: 48).

Fichte's claim of *constitutive intersubjectivity* is seriously complicated by his claim that one is bound to a rightful relation only through a *voluntary* act. This voluntarism comes out clearly when Fichte makes a point of distinguishing the *Aufforderung* argument from the *Anerkennung* argument, stressing the necessity of the former and the voluntary character of the latter. After writing of the need for mutual influence for the genesis of self-consciousness, he writes: "But that, even after self-consciousness has been posited, rational beings must continue to influence the subject of self-consciousness in a rational manner, is not thereby posited, and cannot be derived without using the very consistency that is to be proven as the ground of the proof" (*FNR*, 81; *SW*, III: 87). For the genesis of self-consciousness one needs other people, but there is no original obligation of right, and no demand of rationality (considered apart from the rationality of the moral law) that requires us to be in the relation of right with others.[4] The consistency that Fichte refers to in this passage is the very same "law of thought" that plays a large part in the recognition argument. The voluntary character of the recognition relation stems from Fichte's claim that I have to will to act *consistently* with regard to the other for the argument of right to go through. I must treat another as a rational being "only to the extent that I proceed rationally, i.e. with theoretical

[4] Fichte writes: "I live in community specifically with them as a result of my free decision, not through any obligation. Applied to the civil contract, this means it is originally up to the free and arbitrary choice of every individual to determine whether he wants to live in this particular state or not" (*FNR*, 15; *SW*, III: 14).

consistency" (*FNR*, 44; *SW*, III: 47). The other "is required by virtue of theoretical consistency – to recognize me *categorically*" once the other has voluntarily accepted the law of consistency by choosing to interact with me (*FNR*, 44; *SW*, III: 47).

A key element of Fichte's recognition argument is that the two agents must engage in "reciprocal interaction" while acting in the sensible world (*FNR*, 43; *SW*, III: 45). The point I wish to stress is that Fichte utilizes within the recognition argument an example of actual interaction that represents a typical move of the atomistic contractualist. The imagined scene is that of the other agent robbing me of my freedom and my judging the other by a law that we share. Fichte introduces this as a digression, but it should be seen as a component of the recognition argument itself. Once we appreciate this point, we can see how close the recognition argument is to standard contractualist accounts. Imagining a kind of punishment I am entitled to exercise, Fichte writes:

> I judge him by reference to a concept that he himself – according to my claim – must possess. (Hence the *positive element* in the concept of right, whereby we believe that we impose on the other an obligation not to resist our way of treating him, but even to approve of it. The source of this obligation is certainly not the moral law; rather, it is the law of thought; and what emerges here is the syllogism's practical validity.) (*FNR*, 47; *SW*, III: 50)

In so far as you are consistent you must concur in my judgment that you deserve punishment. The consistency of the laws of thought once again applies to actions – you have willed the violation of freedom and you therefore must also have willed the judgment that your own activity should be curtailed in equal measure according to the law. If you will the end of community, you will the freedom of each and the punishment of anyone who breaks the law. That you could be the lawbreaker and therefore be subject to punishment must be acknowledged by you in so far as you are bound by the law of thought.

Fichte's invocation of theoretical rationality in relation to the practical makes most sense if we think of the norm of consistency as a norm of *instrumental rationality*.[5] Fichte's use of the instrumental principle becomes clear if we think of the relation of *condition to conditioned* as a relation of *means to end*. He has shown that activity and individuality is possible only *on the condition of* another leaving a space of freedom open for me, and in

[5] Ware 2010 also takes this consistency to represent instrumental rationality.

that sense the other's recognition is a *means* to my end of free activity. It would be irrational of me not to recognize the other in turn, since in doing so I would be thwarting the means to my own end. Utilizing the *modus ponens* schema, we can think of Fichte's argument as follows:

1. If I will free action, I must will your recognition of my free agency.
2. I will free action.
3. Therefore, I must will that you recognize me as a free agent.

But this inference by itself is incomplete, and must be paired with a second in order to complete the argument.

1. If I will that you recognize me as a free agent, I must recognize you as a free agent.
2. I will that you recognize me as free agent.
3. Therefore, I must recognize you as a free agent.

In Fichte's terms, I would be *inconsistent* if I aimed at an action, acknowledged that another's recognition of me was a necessary means to that action, and yet did not do my part in recognizing the other, for my granting that other's freedom is a condition of his recognizing mine. Since I need the other to treat me as a free being, and he can do so only if I treat him as a free being, I *must* treat him as a free being. Thinking of the laws of thought in terms of instrumental rationality makes it easier to understand Fichte's claim that "consistency here depends on the freedom of the will" (*FNR*, 80; *SW*, III: 86) and it is impossible "to provide an absolute reason why the rational being should be consistent and why it, in consequence of this, should adopt the law that has been established. But perhaps it is possible to offer a hypothetical reason" (*FNR*, 80; *SW*, III: 86). Fichte's idea is that *if* you will community, *then* there is a reason for you to be bound by right. You must *make* consistency and community *into your end* through an act of choice. In this way the demands of community and consistency are mutually reinforcing, for consistency is a kind of means to the end of community, and community is the realization of the choice of consistency. His point is that if you do not choose to be consistent, you *cannot* choose to live with other people because you would not have committed yourself to treating them as free beings.

Fichte's recognition argument is surprisingly in line with atomistic contractualism, yet we can see within this means–end structure the root of the move towards holistic contractualism. Fichtean right is atomistic in so far as the end of community is posited from the perspective of an independent, already formed individual. The individual may need others to become a fully formed agent, but his *choice* to enter into community is independent of that story about his origins. At the point I decide to enter into (or remain in) relations with others, I view the others as means to the end of my own preservation, security, property, and so on. The question, then, is in what way exactly I must will the freedom of the others in order to claim from others respect for my freedom. The basic contractualist answer is that I must will the same conditions for others that I will for myself: the same laws, the same protective powers treating us equally, the same judicial procedure for all, and so on. But Fichte's framework makes the issue of the *extent* of the individual's activity and ownership claims unavoidable. The definition of right, "*I must limit my freedom through the concept of the possibility of his freedom*," includes nothing about how much I or the other must realize the capacities for activity and ownership (*FNR*, 49; *SW*, III: 52). But the formulation in terms of an indeterminate possibility is misleading. When I will the realization of an end, willing the *possibility* of the same end being *realized* by others amounts to willing that the conditions for the realization of that freedom by others obtain. The principle of reciprocity in recognition thus implies that any rightful exercise of my freedom entails that I will *the same freedom* for others. If I will the security of my job, I must will that security for all others as well. In this situation, it is not hard to imagine that I will for myself the political norms that would allow me to realize my capacities. If that is the case, then I am committed to willing the realization of the capacities of everyone else as well. It is not a very big step from here to *holistic contractualism*, and as we shall see, Fichte takes the holism even further in claiming a holistic character for the social agency instituted with the unification contract.

The Property and Protection Contracts

Before turning to Fichte's actual discussion of the three contracts, a brief look at one crucial dimension of his theory of property rights will help set the stage for the move from atomistic to holistic contractualism. Fichte says some puzzling things about the nature of an "original right" that make most sense if we read him as setting up a holistic contractualism. The issue is how it is possible to think about an individual's rights prior to thinking about the individual within a commonwealth. Fichte claims both that one can think of such rights prior to the social contract proper, and that this concept of original rights possesses "no real meaning" (*FNR*, 101; *SW*, III: 112). He writes:

> There is no condition in which original rights exist; and no original rights of human beings. The human being has actual rights only in community with others, just as – according to the higher principles noted above – the human being can be thought of only in community with others. An original right, therefore, is a mere *fiction*, but one that must necessarily be created for the sake of a science of right. (*FNR*, 102; *SW*, III: 112)

Fichte's theory of original rights and its exact relation to property rights and coercion is too complex to go into here. The point I want to stress is that this use of a necessary fiction is a paradigmatic example of how holistic contractualism works.[6] The theory relies on principles that define the rights of individuals provisionally, but with the attendant claim that those principles only receive their full meaning in the system of social practices instituted by the contract. Notice in the above passage that Fichte links his claim of "actual rights" to the idea of the *Aufforderung*, the intersubjectivity that *precedes* the argument for recognition. This gives a hint that Fichte's theory of actual rights in society will have the more thoroughgoing intersubjective character that the recognition argument lacked.

Fichte's preliminary account of the nature of a contract confirms that it is an extension of, rather than a departure from, the recognition argument. He discusses the contract as a relation of right between two people, thus essentially recapitulating the recognition argument with the help of the additional claims about property and coercion that he has developed in the intervening sections. He does emphasize that property should be understood in a broad sense as "a person's right to free action in the sensible world in general," but for the most part the property contract proceeds along standard atomistic contractualist lines (*FNR*, 168; *SW*, III: 195). The contract is negative in the sense that it just guarantees that each of us will *refrain* from doing anything to the property of the other. Each of us is bound to limit ourselves in relation to the property of others, leaving the others free to use their property for their own purposes, as was the case in the original recognition argument.

The first important move beyond the property contract is the shift from the merely negative guarantee (I refrain from taking your property) to the positive guarantee that I will *protect* your property. This move to the *protection contract* changes the nature of the conditional argument.

6 See Breazeale 2002.

Instead of, "I won't touch your stuff if you don't touch mine," it is now "I promise to actually protect your stuff on the condition that you actually protect mine." Fichte writes, "each individual would promise to all the other individuals (who are still regarded as individuals) that he will use his own power to help them protect the property that is recognized as theirs, on the condition that they, for their part, will likewise help to defend his property against violation" (*FNR*, 171; *SW*, III: 197). In this contract, "the person's will, which had been merely negative in relation to the other's property, now becomes a positive will" (*FNR*, 171; *SW*, III: 198). Each protects the property of the other on the condition that the other protects him. If you protect my property I will protect yours. I have the end of protecting my own property, and I promise to protect your property as the means to protecting my own.

The protection contract seems to be a conditional contract with the same structure of conditional mutuality as recognition and the property contract. But Fichte holds that it is fundamentally different. In the protection contract, the condition – that you *actually* protect my property – cannot be continuously met, for it goes beyond the mere *promise* of protection to *actual acts* of protection. There is an insoluble problem with such a hypothetical contract based on a condition of *actual* performance. My promise to protect your property is conditioned on you protecting my property, but this condition has to be met at every moment for my duty to you to be in effect at every moment. Even your past protection of my property is not enough to satisfy the condition, since it would still leave me relying on your continued good will from that prior moment until now. Fichte writes:

> In the sphere of right, there is no way to bind human beings together other than through the insight: whatever you do to the other, whether good or bad, you do not to him, but to yourself. In the case at hand, this means that I would have to be able to see that, in protecting the other, I protect only myself; I do so either actually in the present, or else – if in the future I should need protection – his protection of me follows with absolute necessity from my having protected him. The former is impossible; for insofar as I do the protecting, I neither need, nor receive, protection; the latter is equally impossible; for the decisions of the other's free will cannot be foreseen with absolute certainty. (*FNR*, 172–3; *SW*, III: 199)

Recall that the laws of thought that underwrite the rationality of right depend on conditionals, where only the implications of adopting certain ends can be demanded by reason (you must will the means if you will the end). With the protection contract Fichte is claiming that each individual must *actually will* the protection of others' property, must adopt the protection *as his end*. But *that* one has adopted an end can only be established by an internal act of the good will, which would be inappropriate for the domain of right, or by the actual performance of the protective act at every moment. Yet the latter route could not even work in principle, for if I am always able to protect others then I am never in need of protection for myself and I therefore cannot receive my end of the bargain. As Fichte makes clear in the passage above, only if I can see my protection of you as simultaneously a protection of myself – only if my protection of you is a means to my own protection – would we be bound together through right.

The lesson of the protection contract is that atomistic contractualism gets in the way of its own fulfillment. The conditional, instrumental reasoning at the heart of contractualism entails that the purpose of security will always remain elusive because each person's adopting of the end of another's security depends on a condition – that very same adoption – that cannot be reliably met. The issue can also be formulated in terms of obligation. I am obligated to protect your property on the condition that you protect mine, but unless you are already protecting my property then I have no obligation, and you would not be protecting my property if you were yourself in need of protection. What is needed is an agreement that would not be conditional in this way. But a non-conditional agreement might not share enough characteristics with an ordinary contract to qualify as contractualist, and it may compromise the overall contractualism of a political theory if such a non-conditional agreement is one of the theory's essential elements.

The Unification Contract

The protection contract is not a feasible contract, yet it contains a demand that is enacted and is enforceable once the *unification contract* has been sealed. Fichte's unification contract is puzzling for several reasons. For one, while it does not *at first* depart very much from the standard atomistic contractualist line (that the social contract has as its main objective protecting property by means of an overwhelming common force), the result of the argument is an organicism that dramatically alters the atomist's premises. Another puzzle is just how the argument is supposed to function at the motivational level. To motivate the unification contract Fichte does not depart dramatically from the egoism that guides much of his account, yet in the organic whole Fichte thinks of individuals as having duties to others and as being involved in a quasi-moral educational process. My claim is that this organic unification argument does indeed represent Fichte's shift from the atomist to the holistic contractualism, but also that the theory that emerges is unstable, and that its very instability highlights the tensions internal to social contract theory that result in its self-overcoming.

Fichte sets up the unification contract by asking with whom the individual negotiates in entering into the contract: is it one specific other person, as would seem to be required by the basic structure of recognition? Or can it somehow be a contract with all others for mutual protection? His surprising answer to this question is that the very indeterminacy of the concept of the counterpart in negotiation changes the nature of the contract. He writes:

> The second party demands protection; – for which particular individual, then, does this party demand protection? For no particular individual at all, and yet for all of them; that is, for every individual whose rights are violated; now every one of them may or may not be such an individual. Therefore, the concept of who is to be protected is in *oscillation* [*im Schweben*]; it is an indeterminate concept: and this is precisely how we get the concept of a whole that is not merely *imagined*, i.e. not merely produced by our thought, as was the case above (I), but rather the concept of a *real* [*reellen*] whole, one that is unified by virtue of the subject matter itself; it is not the concept of a bare "all," but of an "all-ness" or totality [*nicht bloss Aller, sondern einer Allheit*]. (*FNR*, 175; *SW*, III: 202)

The basic difference is between a whole that is composed by adding the independently existing parts and a whole that comes about in such a way as to make clear the dependence of the parts of the whole. The contrast in the passage is with the whole developed in the *property contract* (*FNR*, 169; *SW*, III: 195). In that contracting situation, the individual contracts with every other individual one by one, and the sum total of those individual contracts adds up to a contract with the whole. In the current case, the other party to the contract could be anyone, so (Fichte argues) a whole–part relation arises with the character of an organism, in which the parts (the individuals) depend on each other through the concept of the whole (the common power).

Since we do not know in advance who will need protection, we each have a stake in making sure that we all are protected. At the outset of the argument Fichte emphasizes the sense in which this contract does tap into the self-interest or egoism that he has stressed at many points in the *Natural Right*. He writes, "No one ever knows who will actually be transgressed against; it can happen to anyone. Thus each individual can believe that this whole protective arrangement has been established solely for his benefit, and so will gladly make his own small contribution to it" (*FNR*, 175–6; *SW*, III: 202). The entry into the whole seems to be a straightforward instrumental willing of one's own self-preservation. Fichte stresses that each part "wills its own self-preservation" in willing the preservation of the whole (*FNR*, 176; *SW*, III: 203). It would seem that one could still maintain an instrumental relation to the state, seeing the whole simply as a means to the end of one's own self-preservation.

Yet there is a shift in the turn towards the organic, for the very idea of an organic whole is supposed to rule out the kind of atomistic self-interest that characterizes strategic entry into a contract. The argument from fear of transgression does not simply involve the *self-centered* fear of my own death. Rather, the argument also involves the *de-centering* move to a shared knowledge that we all equally bear this risk. This is why Fichte writes, "this uncertainty as to which individual will first be transgressed against ... is the real bond that unites the different individuals" (*FNR*, 176; *SW*, III: 203). The idea is that the uncertainty over who will need protection produces a kind of solidarity, the wholeness or commonality that had previously been lacking in the contract. If the fear was a fear of each other – which would be more in line with the idea that "faith and trust is lost" – then we could hardly expect a "real bond" to arise from this uncertainty.

Fichte writes that "the individual becomes a part of an organized whole, and thus melts into one with the whole" (*FNR*, 177; *SW*, III: 204). This melting into one with the whole is striking given that Fichte's account started from the conditions of individuality. Fichte emphasizes that individuals retain a real claim to the property that is not required by the state, so in that sense we do preserve our claims as discrete individuals. But the dependence on the whole does fundamentally alter the nature of individuality, bestowing on us both a particular place and a more stable set of desires. Fichte writes:

> Similarly, it is only within the unity of the state that the human being attains a particular place in the scheme of things, a fixed position within nature; and each person maintains *this particular* place in relation to others and in relation to nature only by existing in *this particular* unity. Apart from the state, human beings would experience only passing gratification, but never the least concern for the future. (*FNR*, 181; *SW*, III: 208)

In a sense this just spells out the summons argument, for the particular–whole relation is quite like the individual–community relation laid out at the beginning. The reference to "passing gratification" makes clear the educative or transformative dimension of the membership in the state.

One of the key issues in this transformation concerns the conditionality at the heart of contractualist views, and indeed of his own recognition argument. After unification I do not need to actually be protected before I am bound to protect others, for in the whole there is a power that will protect each individual. By entering the contract I can expect the common power to protect me, so I am now bound to hold up my end by contributing to this whole (through taxation and whatever else is required of me). Viewing the whole as a living system, the question of actual performance is no longer pressing since we now assume a proper functioning of the whole and a proper functioning of the parts. Fichte writes:

> This contract is its own guarantee: it contains within itself the sufficient ground of its fulfillment, just as every organic being has within itself the complete ground of its existence. For any person, either this contract does not exist at all, or, if it does, then it binds him completely. Anyone who does not fulfill this contract is not a part of it, and anyone who is a part of it necessarily fulfills it entirely. If someone exists apart from this contract, then he stands outside every rightful relation whatsoever and is rightfully excluded altogether from any reciprocity with other beings of his kind in the sensible world. (*FNR*, 180; *SW*, III: 207)

This passage might seem to affirm the conditionality that we have been considering throughout: if you will to coexist with other beings, you must will to stand in rightful relations with them. But it actually takes the argument further, for it asks the contractor to negate his independence in a more radical way than any of the previous moves. The contract "binds him completely" and the agent "necessarily fulfills it entirely" because there is no perspective outside of the whole from which he would make claims that would release him from his obligations.

Fichte's Holistic Contractualism

Let us return now to the three dimensions of holistic contractualism to see how Fichte's theory lines up. The first dimension is *methodological*, and hinges on the idea of not seeing the opening moves as fixed justificatory points that are supposed to provide a foundation for the rest. Fichte does sometimes encourage such a foundationalist reading of his idealism when arguing for the first principle of free activity, yet even at the basic level his idealism is holistic in that he holds that the first principle must prove itself in the execution of the system based upon it. For our purposes, the issue is what happens to the initial claims of individuality, summons, and recognition. I suggested in section 1 that it is a mistake to take these ideas as abstract ideals against which the execution of the theory could be measured. This is the mistake Williams makes when he takes recognition as the basic form of ethical community and then criticizes the development of right (especially coercion) on the basis of its failure to meet that standard. Rather, Fichte's opening moves are best thought of as unsaturated formal structures that are only actual in their development in the dialectical process. Focusing our attention on the unification contract brings to light the way in which the integrative dimension of the opening moves, which had gone missing for much of the intervening text, remains in place and comes to fruition only after the more formal aspects of right have been worked out. Fichte's frequent claim that he is going beyond merely "formulaic philosophy" is born out in the way he raises oppositions to the formal criteria in order to better work out their application, their actuality, in a social system (*FNR*, 7; *SW*, III: 6).

The second sense of holism has to do with the subject's *identity* as a party to the contract. Fichte is willing to go pretty far with the idea of the individual who has "melted into the whole," as when he writes of "the place that has been determined for it [the citizen] by the whole" (*FNR*, 182; *SW*, III: 209). In the part–whole relationship the particularity is determined by the whole: the whole subordinates the individual parts for the sake of the overall end of mutual protection. This identity shift is also evident in a shift in Fichte's view on the split between morality and right. Whereas the domain of right was supposed to be independent of morality, there is a proto-moral dimension to the unification contract. He writes, "Humanity was divided into several independent members; the natural institution of the state already cancels this independence provisionally and molds individual groups into a whole, until morality re-creates the entire species as one" (*FNR*, 176; *SW*, III: 203). The reference to nature here is meant to highlight the sense in which the theory of right is part of a system of nature, relying only on the natural incentives rather than on moral motives. Striking in this respect is the reference to the duties that come with the unification contract. While he had earlier written of the permissive character of right in contrast to the commanding character of duty, that separation seems to recede in importance given that he now endorses a strong conception of civic duty.[7]

[7] He writes: "*For all individuals have promised to protect all other individuals. And a cry for help is an announcement that there is danger that cannot, at present, be remedied by the representative of the protective power (the state).* Therefore, a person's cry for help transfers back upon every individual not

On the third dimension of holism, the unification contract clearly represents a move to holistic consideration of property rights. The shift to the organic in effect enables Fichte to provide a theory of social justice by subordinating individual property rights to the right of all individuals to be able to exercise their capacities.[8] This comes out most clearly in his discussion of the right of each person to live off of his labor and the redistribution of property that must take place to help those unable to make a living. He writes:

> As soon as someone suffers from need, that portion of others' property that would be required to spare him from such need no longer belongs to those others; rather, it rightfully belongs to the one in need. The civil contract must provide for such a repartitioning of property. This contribution of property to persons in need is just as much a condition of all civil justice as is a contribution to the protective body of the state, since such assistance to the needy is itself a part of providing the necessary protection. (*FNR*, 186; *SW*, III: 213)

One indication that Fichte is taking contractualism in a new direction is that he states that he is going further than Rousseau in eliminating the validity of *any* pre-social claims. Against Rousseau's claim that individuals "give up everything" in the civil contract, Fichte writes, "According to our theory, no individual can bring anything with him to the civil contract, for prior to this contract he *has* nothing. … Therefore, this contract – far from starting with *giving* – ought to begin with *receiving*" (*FNR*, 177; *SW*, III: 204–5). In this statement, Fichte affirms once more that the earlier original rights were merely fictional. They were not meant to be real claims to property that are valid in the pre-social state of nature. Fichte here dramatically affirms the holistic character of the contractualism by stating that what is to be protected is actually only established once the social system is up and running. We should wonder, though, whether a contract that is all receiving and no giving retains enough of the sense of an ordinary contract to retain the intuitive appeal of the original model. Without a conception of a right, even a provisional right, prior to entry into the contract, we seem to lose one of the main intuitive bases of thinking of political authority as a contract.

only the right, but also the civic duty, to offer immediate protection. If a person can be shown to have heard but not heeded someone's cry for help, he is punishable, for he has acted contrary to the civil contract; and the laws must take this into account. Such assistance in an emergency is not just a *duty of conscience or a Christian duty*; it is an *absolute civic duty*" (*FNR*, 219–20; *SW*, III: 252).

[8] My account here supports the reading of property by James 2011, who argues that we should not read Fichte as exclusively concerned with property rights in the liberal sense, but should see him as offering a broader defense of property as realization of one's capacities.

The Self-overcoming of Social Contract Theory

While atomistic contractualism is based on the idea of *withholding* – in particular withholding my consent if the community encroaches on my goods – holistic contractualism is centered on the idea of *identifying* my interests with the interests of the community and its members. Instead of thinking of what I can exclude from the use of others, I think of how my pursuit of my own good is compatible with and helps to secure the good of all. The atomistic contractualist, and indeed the reader of some individualistic passages of the *Natural Right*, will find quite jarring the post-unification contract claims for the civic duty to aid others and the forfeit of property when someone is in need. It was not clear at the beginning that such measures could be implied by the basic recognition of right, that is, in the voluntary decision to live in community with others. The atomistic contractualist might object that there is a bait and switch here. You supposedly enter the contract as a means to the end of your own well-being, but the final result of the contract is that you become a means to the well-being of the whole (in the service of the well-being of others). You wanted to secure your own good, but you end up committed to securing the good of the whole. The holist can respond that if you have really taken the unification contract seriously you will have "melted into the whole" in the sense that you will now have the proper motivations, both civic and moral, so you will no longer view the sacrifice for others as an imposition. But the atomist will say that he entered the contract as a self-interested person, plain and simple, and it is not okay to change the terms of the contract on the condition that those new terms will make you into someone who accepts them.

These remarks are intended to highlight the distance between atomistic and holistic contractualism. We can now see that the turn towards holism undermines all four points of contractualism's intuitive appeal that I laid out in section 1. The complex motivational shift in Fichte's account shows how holistic contractualism moves away from self-interest and towards morality, compromising the clarity of the original motivational picture. We have seen that the unification contract is designed to overcome the conditionality of an ordinary contract, replacing the conditional dependence on the will of another with a (nearly) unconditional dependence on the whole. I have already addressed the third point in noting that Fichte holds the pre-contract property claims to be non-existent and original right to be fictional. Whatever one makes of this structure, it clearly does not have the intuitive basis of an ordinary contract. On the fourth and final point, of exiting the contract, Fichte's theory offers different complications. He has an elaborate system involving an "ephorate" to dissolve the government if it has violated the trust of the people. But as we have just seen, he really offers the individual no exit from the unification contract short of abandoning all human contact.

None of this is to say that the move to holism is wrong. The intuitive appeal of contractualism might simply be the result of *confusing* the political relationship with an ordinary contractual relationship. What Fichte's theory brings out is that it is very hard to be a holist and remain a contractualist, for the two pull against each other, especially in the all-important domain of property claims. Fichte holds that the property rights should be thought of in general as a subject's capacity for the free exercise of her faculties in the sensible world. To guarantee those rights in social institutions means guaranteeing the realization of those capacities, and no contract that would fail to guarantee that realization can be deemed reasonable. But for that contract to work, each of us would need to take responsibility for the realization of the capacities of all. Once the unification has taken place that sense of responsibility would seem to follow. The trouble is: how do we motivate the move to unification without presupposing the motivations that we will have once we are already in that organic condition? Fichte's argument depends on the indeterminacy of who will need protection, but the binding force of that indeterminacy seems to require more than the egoistic concern for our own safety. The indeterminacy can help make sense of the civic duty to assist others in need (we may need such assistance ourselves), but it is not clear that it can ground the sense of citizenship and the willingness to sacrifice for others that the unification contract entails. In a well-ordered state with virtuous citizens such a sacrifice is perfectly intelligible, but it is unlikely that such a citizen would think to invoke a contract situation to explain her motivations. The social contract is much more often invoked when we feel oppressed, when we say we did *not* consent to something, than when we explain why we are committed to each other and to the state. The kind of contract that "contains within itself the sufficient ground of its fulfillment" would seem to require a non-contractual devotion to the state, an ethical disposition that involves a shared conception of the good.

The development of the contractualist model in a holistic direction tends to erase the context of the contract's original application. To think of the conditions under which we can all exercise our capacities for free activity, we have to think of the social world in which those capacities are developed and realized. If the content of the social order is determined as rational, part of that rationality will consist in producing the individuals who live within it and are motivated by the demands of justice. But then they cannot be the same agents who consent to the contract from a position outside of the social order. Social contract theory is supposed to generate reasons that are operative in a cooperative setting, but once we think through that cooperative setting the reasons take on a status independent of the contractualist framework. At that point the idea of an individual who wills to opt out of the community is no longer a useful fiction, but rather a harmful fantasy that undermines the very political obligation it was originally designed to create. On an organic model, individuals can still fail to identify with the social order, but that failure is interpreted as a sign of the deficiency, or even pathology, of that order itself. It is a kind of alienation not best conceived as a broken contract, but rather as a symptom of a society's failure to provide the context for the realization of the free capacities of each, and of all.

CHAPTER 12

Fichte and Human Rights

Jean-Christophe Merle

Fichte puts human rights (*Menschenrechte*) at the core of his first political writing, *Contribution to the Rectification of the Public's Judgment of the French Revolution* (1793), like other essayists supportive of the French Revolution did before him, including Mary Wollstonecraft in *A Vindication of the Rights of Men* (1790) and Thomas Paine in *Rights of Man* (1791). As in the case of those writings, Fichte, in the *Contribution*, explicitly poses the question, "Does a people have the right to modify its constitution?" (*SW*, VI: 80). The basis on which he answers this question is his concept of human rights. In fact, he draws the following lesson from the French Revolution:

> Thus, all events happening in the world seem to me to be instructive descriptions that the great teacher of humankind makes in order for the world to learn in them what it needs to know. It is not so that humankind would learn *from* them – in the whole world history we will never find anything that we have not put into history in the first place; but, humankind develops in an easier way what lies in itself through judging actual events happening in the world. In that way, the French Revolution seems to me to be a rich painting about a great text: human rights (*Menschenrechte*) and human value (*Menschenwert*). (*SW*, VI: 39)

Whereas the word "human right" (*Menschenrecht*) occurs multiple times throughout the *Contribution*, in later writings, Fichte almost never uses it. However, human rights still remain at the core of his later thinking, and the disappearance of the word "human rights" corresponds to a radical revision of his concept of human rights. Although Fichte could not know Jeremy Bentham's *A Critical Examination of the Declaration of Rights* (1796, unpublished until 1816), which has been so influential on the current way of conceiving human rights, the revision of Fichte's concept of human rights between the *Contribution* and the *Foundations of Natural Rights* (1796–7) remarkably addresses the core of Bentham's criticism of human rights. Although it shares some major elements with Kant's

Doctrine of Right (1797), the *Foundations of Natural Rights* develops a concept of human rights that is both more original and more elaborate than Kant's.

Human Rights in the *Contribution* (1793)

The *Contribution* does not really inquire into the concept of human right. Instead, it argues on the basis of a few human rights in favor of several political – revolutionary – claims. Yet, one can distinguish *two elements* of Fichte's concept of right and, although they do not seem original at first sight, one can observe that Fichte understands them in a distinctive way.

The *first* conceptual element is the *innate* origin of human rights, which Fichte understands as natural rights, as the French *Declaration of Human and Civil Rights* (1789) does (the *Preamble* mentions them as "the natural, inalienable, and sacred rights of man"). Yet, more precisely, the origin of the human rights considered as natural rights is moral conscience (*Gewissen*) in the Kantian sense:

> Let us draw a circle in order to make concrete the extent and the relationship of these different domains. This entire circle is the domain of conscience (*Gewissen*).[1] Let us draw within its circumference a much smaller circle. This comprises the visible world – that part of the domain of conscience under which natural right, the law of perfect duty, regulates. Let us draw within this second circle a third smaller circle. Within its circumference, under conscience and natural right, contract right regulates. Within this third circle, a fourth smaller circle is drawn, giving the space in which, under the aforementioned judges, the specific civil contract exercises its rule. (*SW*, VI: 132)

Fichte's location of human rights in conscience in the Kantian sense follows the mainstream of Kantian legal scholars (Hufeland and Schmalz) who did not shift their views until the publication of Kant's *Doctrine of Right* (1797), whereas Fichte changed his view prior to Kant's *Doctrine of Right*, and more precisely already in his book review "Zur Rezension der Naturrechte für das Niethammersche Journal" in April–August 1795 (*GA*, II, 3: 395–406). According to Hufeland (1790) and Schmalz (1792), natural rights cover the realm of what is allowed to human beings, that is, both what Kant's categorical imperative does not prohibit and what it commands. In the *Contribution*, this has at least *three consequences*. In fact, unlike in Ernst Tugendhat's essay on human rights the role of such

[1] By *Gewissen* Fichte understands conscience in the sense of moral consciousness.

an origin is not, in Fichte's *Contribution*, to provide an addressee towards which human rights are actionable (*einklagbar*).[2]

The *first consequence* is that the domain of human rights is defined merely through excluding any right of positive and contractual origin. *One the one hand*, this potentially leads to a huge domain of human rights, since it may comprise any moral right, whereas, in the common understanding, human rights were always considered as being only a small part of all rights, and, more precisely, as being a group of rights that enjoy priority over all other rights, because they protect fundamental human interests. *On the other hand*, Fichte's view on the domain of human rights excludes from the domain of human rights some rights that Fichte himself considers as being human rights, although they are partly of contractual origin. Here is an example:

> This race after a possession (*Besitze*), which can be futile, these conflicts and hostilities, which necessarily develop, do not please us, human beings proclaimed, as they became citizens – and they said this rightly. Henceforth, each takes what is nearest him and thus saves himself and others from this procedure. He takes what was in his father's cottage and around his grandfather's cottage; each of us does sacrifice his right to appropriate this settled possession, if he wants his part of his right to appropriate the belongings of any other deceased fellow citizen. You do not have, according to this, the civil right of inheritance for free. In receiving it, you have, however, relinquished an alienable human right (*veräusserliches Menschenrecht*), the right to inherit from any deceased person, if you can. (*SW*, VI: 127)

Property rights as human rights (Article 2 of the French *Declaration*) are conceived of by Kant as the right to inherit from one's parents; such a right is partly of contractual origin. The human right to take possession of the possession of any person who has just died was a human right of non-contractual origin. However, in Fichte's view, it has been fully replaced by the human right of contractual origin to inherit from one's parents. Thus, in this example, Fichte himself does not comply with his own definition of the domain of human rights. This should lead to the conclusion that the fact that human rights are not merely positive rights, but always entail the character of moral rights, does not imply that they are innate. On the contrary, human rights need to specify more general moral principles. Thus, human rights cannot be associated with the general "circle" of conscience.

[2] Tugendhat 1993: 17th Lecture. In Tugendhat, this addressee is conscience as the source of self-obligation.

The way in which Fichte handles the right to inherit from one's parents is also problematic with respect to a *second* conceptual element of human rights as conceived both by Fichte and by the common understanding of human rights. Fichte rightly considers human rights as *inalienable*. Yet, in the example above, Fichte asserts that the right to take ownership of the possession of any person who has just died is at the same time a human right *and* an alienable right. The correct view is that the right to take ownership of the possession of any person who has just died is alienable, and that this practice should be prohibited in any rule of law, for such an alleged right certainly never qualified as a human right under any circumstances. Only the right of property, mentioned in all declarations of human rights from the beginning, is a human right, because it is relatively abstract and it puts aside the issue of the acquisition and transfer of property, that is, of the specificities of property law.

But let us go back to the consequences of the *first conceptual element*, the innate origin of human rights. The *second consequence* of this element is that human rights exist before the social contract and that they do not owe their validity to the social contract, whereas the social contract must recognize them:

> Whoever promises me by means of a contract not to violate any of my inalienable human rights promises me nothing: first of all, he was not allowed to violate them prior to the contract. (*SW*, VI: 110)

The *third consequence* is that human rights are derived from duty. There is something right in this view. In fact, in the current common understanding of human rights, they are not the kind of claim one can arbitrarily or at will invoke toward others. Human rights also apply against the will of the bearer herself. The human right not to be enslaved includes the prohibition of voluntary enslavement. The human right not to be tortured or maimed cannot be waived by the bearer's consent to torture or mutilation. However, by making the realm of human rights "the part of the domain of conscience under which natural right, the law of perfect duty, regulates" (*SW*, VI: 132), Fichte clearly does not distinguish morality from right. In fact, there is a perfect duty to keeps one's promise, though Fichte insists that there is a human right to break contracts that one has freely accepted, because there is an "inalienable human right to modify one's choice (*Willkür*)" (*SW*, VI: 166), and there is no mention that lying violates any human right. Furthermore, by identifying the realm of human rights with perfect duties, Fichte contradicts some of his examples of human rights like the "inalienable human right … to infinitely progress in this culture [of freedom]" (*SW*, VI: 106) that obviously refers to imperfect duties in the Kantian sense.[3]

The more consistent way to formulate what Fichte presumably has in mind is to distinguish between two dimensions of human rights that are present in Fichte's writings as well as those already in Wollstonecraft's and Paine's writings. Human rights are both a set of rights that one vindicates *and* an ideal, not only of a future situation of the rule of law but also of non-coerced, virtuous behavior between fellow human beings. This ideal dimension finds its expression, for instance, in Wollstonecraft's conception of a "national education" in Chapter 12 of her *A Vindication of the Rights of Woman* (1792). There, she makes a plea for children – both girls and boys – not only to be educated in common – rather than under the supervision of a personal tutor, as was usual in the upper class at that time – but also to educate one another in learning together how to overcome problems and obstacles through cooperation on equal terms. Such an education aims at developing among these future adults an atmosphere of mutual friendship and cooperation, which is necessary not only for respecting each other's equal rights but also for making progress possible.[4] According to Wollstonecraft, this civil friendship belongs to human rights, whereas nowadays it is commonly viewed as separate from human rights. Thus, we have to keep in mind that Fichte, as well as the advocates for human rights during his time, did not clearly distinguish human rights in their extra-legal, merely moral dimension, on the one hand, from human rights in the legal dimension, on the other hand.

Admittedly, human rights partly entail a forward-looking, ideal dimension, which was formulated from the beginning of the history of human rights, for instance by Thomas Paine and Mary Wollstonecraft. Yet, unlike for some authors (for instance James Griffin), they are not to be understood as "manifesto rights" in a pejorative sense.[5] Instead, I mean that the human rights that are nowadays recognized and implemented in domestic and international law are not a closed, that is, entire and definitive, list of human rights, and that the list of human rights may keep extending in the future, as it has thus far. And, in fact, if one takes a historical look at the declarations of human rights, one observes that they gradually extended the list of rights; and, in this regard, one for instance usually speaks of

[3] When it comes to one's exercise of this right it is an imperfect duty, but it is a perfect duty that one respect this right.

[4] Wollstonecraft 1995: Ch. XII.

[5] Griffin 2008: 209.

three generations of human rights. Yet, these manifesto rights that still remain to be recognized in the future are all of a legal nature; that is, they could belong to a legal order, and not only to general moral principles. In this regard, whereas the "inalienable human right … to infinitely progress in this culture [of freedom]" cannot nowadays be considered as a human right in the legal sense, some rights that Fichte derives from it can qualify as human rights in a legal sense (*SW*, VI: 106). The "free inquiry into any possible object of thought, in any way, and indefinitely, is undoubtedly a human right" (*SW*, VI: 77), and "inquiring indefinitely is an inalienable human right" (cf. *SW*, VI: 77), writes Fichte, also mentioning the human right to communicate to others what one considers to be the truth (cf. *SW*, VI: 77). This corresponds to freedom of thought and freedom of opinion, which are considered, from the beginning, as human rights. This also corresponds to the fundamental right of freedom of sciences (*Wissenschaftsfreiheit*) in the current German *Fundamental Law* (Article 5 (3) GG), which is currently only a constitutional fundamental right (*Grundrecht*) in Germany, but might become in the future also a human right, because it has the features of a right and it protects fundamental interests of humankind.

Apart from the two conceptual elements of human rights, Fichte does not really define the concept of human right in the *Contribution*. More important for him in this work are two specific human rights: the human right of freedom of contract and the human right of subsistence.

Fichte considers only a very specific kind of free contract: the social contract. Unlike in his later *Foundations of Natural Right*, he addresses neither the structure of the social contract nor the substantial principles contained in the social contract; nor does he really inquire into the reasons for entering into the social contract. Whereas the *Foundations of Natural Right* does not handle how one moves from the state of nature to the social contract, and establishes a very demanding and restrictive procedure for leaving the social contract, the *Contribution* emphasizes the freedom to enter and leave the social contract at any time, with no other obligation than compensation for damages, whenever leaving the social contract damages others and the damage does not consist in the termination of the benefits resulting from a previous human rights violation (cf. *SW*, VI: 148, 160, 166, 170). Therefore, the focus adopted by the *Contribution* gives the impression of confirming the diagnosis made by Jeremy Bentham of the French *Declaration*, according to which it promotes insurrection against any government, however it may be. Nevertheless, this impression is not fully accurate. On the contrary, Fichte mentions an aspect of the role of the state authority that, in his (correct) view, admittedly does not support the thesis of the prohibition of all revolution, but is a strong argument in favor of state authority:

> But, one says, if the state did nothing, you could not count on the sanctity of the contracts that you, as a human being, may ever finalize (*schliessen*). Admittedly, if the other did not keep his word, you would have, according to natural right, the permission to coerce him to provide restitution for service and damages; but, you would not always be the stronger one. This, now, is the place of the state. It will help you recover your right, which you may nevertheless always consider as a human right, when someone violates it. The awe inspired by the state is the reason why your right is seldom violated. (*SW*, VI: 135)

Here, Fichte recognizes the traditional liberal role of the state as protector of natural rights, formulated for instance by Locke. But Fichte does not deal at all with a major part of the liberal tradition in regard to the protection of natural rights: all measures intended to protect citizens against the state's violation of fundamental rights, its arbitrary and abusive use of power. Consider, for instance, the protective role that parliamentarianism, division of powers, checks and balances, and such fundamental rights as the right to due process, and the protection granted by *habeas corpus* against arbitrary imprisonment plays in the liberal tradition. The only protection against state violations of human rights considered by Fichte's *Contribution* is the right of revolution, that is, something that is widely considered as an *ultima ratio*. We can also observe that at some places (e.g., *SW*, VI: 105), Fichte confuses the right to modify the constitution with the right of revolution, despite revolution being only a specific way of modifying a constitution.

Two fundamental, substantial interests of humankind are considered in the *Contribution* and protected by a human right: the aforementioned right to progress of knowledge and the right of subsistence, that is, to the means of self-conservation. Fichte derives this from the right to life:

> Each human being must live: this is his inalienable human right … This subsistence that is due to him is his property (*Eigenthum*) … and every time he eats, what he eats is his immediate property. (*SW*, VI: 178)

Now, the right to subsistence is not to be found in the French *Declaration*. It belongs to the second generation of human rights that was the object of controversies in the mid-nineteenth century and first recognized after the Second World War. Nor is the right of subsistence a focus of Wollstonecraft's and Paine's writings. However, unlike the *Foundations of*

Natural Right, the *Contribution* does not undertake the grounding of the right of subsistence. Still, one finds a fleeting mention of a point that will be at the core of the *Foundations of Natural Right* – the correlative duties to the rights of subsistence:

> Everyone must have what is indispensable … it is one's inalienable human right … As long as there remains even one person for whom, because of another, it is impossible to acquire what is indispensable through his own labor, the other's luxury must be mercilessly limited. (*SW*, VI: 188)

The correlative duty is the duty to exercise one's own labor with the aim toward subsistence, and the right to subsistence clearly enjoys priority over any other property right, even where property may fulfill the condition, that is, may have been acquired by labor, as required by Locke. But, here again, Fichte does not attempt to justify this assertion, nor does he explain whether other properties than the one of the means of subsistence are protected by some human rights to property.

The New Concept of Human Rights in the *Foundations of Natural Rights*

The word "human right" (*Menschenrecht*) very seldom occurs in the *Foundations of Natural Right* and in the *Doctrine of Right* (1812), but it does not fully disappear. However, conceptually speaking, in the *Foundations of Natural Right*, human rights are the individual rights included in Fichte's concept of right and cannot really be defined apart from this concept of right. Those rights are handled in the "Systematic application of the concept of right; or the doctrine of right," and especially in the "Applied natural right," so that at first sight human rights seem to be a subtopic of the concept of right. This impression is wrong. In order to understand why it is wrong, one has to keep in mind the systematic structure of Fichte's doctrine of right.

Fichte defines the concept of right in the following way:

> The relation between free beings that we have deduced (i.e. that each is to limit his freedom through the concept of the possibility of the other's freedom, under the condition that the latter likewise limit his freedom through the freedom of the former) is called the *relation of right*; and the formula that has now been established is the *principle of right*. (*FNR*, 49; *SW*, III: 52; see also *FNR*, 109; *SW*, III: 120)

This definition presupposes the concept of the freedom of an individual being in a twofold way. *First*, this definition includes the concept of freedom related to an individual free being, so that the formulation requires beginning with defining the latter. Thus, Fichte begins the "systematic application" with the "original right" (*Urrecht*) as "a mere *fiction*, but one that must necessarily be created for the sake of a science of right" (*FNR*, 102; *SW*, III: 102). The original right is a fiction because it cannot be real outside of the application of the concept of right. *Second*, this status as a fiction within the application of the concept of right does not imply that the original right has a lower foundation than the concept of right. In fact, whereas in the "First main division" the concept of right is deduced from the self-positing I in several steps, including intersubjectivity and recognition, the original right directly refers to the "First theorem" (§1) of the deduction and to its "Inference" (§2). Therefore, whereas human rights can be defined only within the concept of right, their foundation is to be found in the "original right" and in the "deduction of the concept of right." Rolf-Peter Horstmann writes:

> Why is there a theory of the original right, if it deals with contents of which already a conceptual determination of this concept shows that they cannot exist? Fichte provides no satisfying answer. He only asserts that an inquiry into original rights "must precede an investigation of rights within a commonwealth and must ground the later investigation," i.e. that the assumption of original rights "must necessarily be made for the sake of human rights." Unfortunately, Fichte does not provide any explicit foundations for these assertions.[6]

I disagree with Horstmann on this point, because the original right sets the requirements for human rights that are defined within the application of the concept of right. For this reason, Fichte writes:

> [I]t would be utterly impossible to reflect on rights merely as original rights, i.e. without considering the necessary limitations imposed by the rights of others. Nevertheless, an investigation into original rights must precede an investigation of rights within a commonwealth and must ground the latter investigation … An original right, therefore, is a mere *fiction*, but one that must necessarily be created for the sake of the science of right. (*FNR*, 101–2; *SW*, III: 111–12)

The original right presents a first formal characteristic of human rights: the *universality* of its bearer:

> The concept of freedom at issue here (which, as already stated above, has only formal meaning) yields the concept of original right, that is, of that

[6] Horstmann 2001: 115–16.

> right that should belong absolutely to every person as such. (*FNR*, 102; *SW*, III: 112–13)

Fichte defines the original right as follows:

> Original right is thus the absolute right of the person to be *only a cause* in the sensible world (and purely and simply never something caused). (*FNR* 103; *SW*, III: 113)

Fichte means absoluteness in a strong sense: "original right is an absolute and closed whole; every partial violation of it affects and influences the whole" (*FNR*, 108; *SW*, III: 119). Using the word "right," the *Foundations of Natural Right*, from the beginning – and unlike the *Contribution* – strictly separates the domains of morality and right. Fichte makes it clear that he is not referring to the issue of the freedom of the will, which is "beyond the bounds of the present investigation," because it "never enters the sensible world and cannot be restricted by anything within it," but that he is only addressing its phenomenal expression. The "person" is the external and legal expression of the I. Being only a cause means (i) that the will of the person *can* be coerced by other persons in the determination of her will, but the will should not be coerced, and (ii) that this will has an effect in the sensible world, yet under the limits of the laws of physics and natural sciences.[7] For these reasons, Fichte identifies the person with her body:

> The will of the person enters the realm of the sensible world only insofar as it is expressed in a determination of his body. Thus, in this realm the body of a free being is to be regarded as itself the final ground of its own determinations, and the free being – as appearance – is identical with the body. The body is the I's representative in the sensible world. (*FNR*, 103–4; *SW*, III: 113–14)

That original right is the body's right might seem to exclude, as a matter of principle, such human rights as freedom of thought and freedom of opinion. However, even the violation of those human rights is possible only through the body, for instance, by means either of threats against the integrity of the body or by hindering its actions. Also, torture is a means to break the will, thought, and opinion of the tortured person; and torture is exercised on the body.

The original right does not correspond to any concrete human right, not even the right to life, but at first sight it seems to include the human

[7] Therefore, Fichte talks of any "possible" effect" (*FNR*, 104; *SW*, III: 114).

right to physical integrity. Including the right to physical integrity without the right to life would contrast, for example, with the current German Fundamental Law, which asserts both fundamental rights: "Every person shall have the right to life and physical integrity" (Article 2 (2) GG). In fact, according to Fichte, the right to life is only a conditional right, as we will see. Fichte writes:

> There is no separate right to self-preservation ... Even if our end were more modest than self-preservation, other persons would still not be permitted to disturb our freedom, for they are not permitted to disturb it at all. (*FNR*, 108; *SW*, III: 119)

Just before this, Fichte asserts:

> Thus, original right includes:
>
> (1) The right to the continued existence of the absolute freedom and inviolability of the body (i.e. there should be absolutely nothing that exercises an immediate effect upon the body);
> (2) The right to the continued existence of our free influence within the entire sensible world. (*FNR*, 108; *SW*, III: 119)

Now, the prohibition of "anything that exercises an immediate effect upon the body" is not exactly the same as the current right to the body's integrity. In fact, forced blood tests on car drivers, the legal obligation to wear a helmet on motorcycles, custody in criminal investigations, DNA search for paternity, for example, exercise an immediate effect upon the body without constituting any violation of its integrity. A medical authority may also order without any consent an amputation that is necessary for survival, because in this case the right to life outweighs the right to bodily integrity. In such a case, there is a conflict of human rights, which contradicts the absoluteness of the alleged status of an original right granted to the Fichtean "inviolability of the body." Now, this contradiction between the subdivision of the original right and current human rights does not really exist since the original right cannot be a real right, but is explicitly only a fiction.

In its absoluteness, the "continued existence of our free influence within the entire sensible world" (*FNR*, 108; *SW*, III: 119) was obviously not possible except in a world with only one inhabitant, in which case no legal relation could apply. Thus, in its absoluteness, "the right to the continued existence of our free influence within the entire sensible world" remains a mere fiction. Waiving the absoluteness makes out of the fiction of the isolated individual's original rights a system of rights, including rights, correlative duties, and clear rules, including priority rules. In this system the human right of each individual is limited by the human right of all other individuals:

> Yet, it is supposed to be possible for the violator, by freely exercising his original right, to violate the rights of another. Therefore, if someone can violate a right by exercising his own original right, then original right must have a particular quantity that is determined by the law of right ... What quantity of freedom does the law of right determine for each person? (*FNR*, 109; *SW*, III: 120)

The equal limitation of freedoms or "equilibrium of right" (*FNR*, 109; *SW*, III: 120) is not handled in more detail in the "systematic application of the concept of right," the remaining part of this systematic application addressing the right of coercion and the organization of political powers. The "equilibrium of rights" is fully determined within the framework of the "civil contract" – or social contract – in the "civil legislation," which consists in a "property contract" (*FNR*, 183; *SW*, III: 210). The result is an exclusive "sphere" of action:

> [O]riginal right consists essentially in an ongoing reciprocal interaction, dependent only on the person's own will, between the person and the sensible world outside of him. In the property contract, a particular part of the sensible world is allocated exclusively to each individual as the sphere of his reciprocal interaction with it ... This sphere contains certain objects, as determined by the freedom that has been granted to him ... He acquires certain objects only for a particular use; and it is only from this use, and from what might hinder such use, that he has the right to exclude everyone else. The object of the property contract is a particular activity. (*FNR*, 183–4; *SW*, III: 210)

Obviously, what Fichte calls "property" is the entire set of all individual rights, and not only property right in the usual and narrower sense. Within that entire set of individual rights, Fichte first determines rights that *all* members of the social contract must claim and that should be provided to them. Looking from the perspective of human rights as they are conceived today, the status of these rights should correspond to the status of human rights. Yet, Fichte assigns another statute to human right and another location in his system of rights, which he characterizes as follows:

> [T]hat original human right which precedes all rightful contracts and which alone makes them possible: the right to every other human being's expectation to be able to enter into a rightful relation with him through contracts. (*FNR*, 333; *SW*, III: 384)

In fact, Fichte does not recognize any individual right, except in a positive legal system that results from a social contract. Fichte's view significantly diverges from Kant's formulation of the only human right recognized by the *Doctrine of Right* under the headline "There is only one innate right," although Kant and Fichte share almost the same concept of law as the mutual limitation of individual freedom:

> Freedom (independence from being constrained by another's choice), insofar as it can coexist with the freedom of every other in accordance with a universal law, is the only original right belonging to every man in virtue of his humanity. This principle of innate freedom already involves the following authorizations, which are not really distinct from it ... innate *equality*, ... hence a human being's quality of being *his own master* (*sui iuris*) as well as being a human being *beyond reproach* (*iusti*). (*MM*, 6: 237)

Whereas the unique human right is a right to freedom in Kant's *Doctrine of Right*, in Fichte's *Foundations of Natural Right*, it is a right to enter into a social contract. This conception expressed in the *Foundations of Natural Rights* still remains valid in Fichte's *Doctrine of Right* (1812):

> [T]he original human right that precedes all legal contracts and alone makes them possible ... the human right proper that belongs to the human being as a human being, the possibility to acquire rights. (*SW*, X: 650)

Consequently, in the *Foundations of Natural Right*, the "Outline of the right of nations and cosmopolitan right" also diverges from Kant's "cosmopolitan right," that is, according to Kant, a direct legal relationship between any state and any human being that is not its citizen. On the contrary, according to Fichte, an individual who is not a citizen does not enjoy any right toward a state on the mere basis that she is a human being. The rights that she enjoys result solely from the legal relationship between the state of which she is a citizen and the state that she is visiting. This means that all individual rights result either from a single social contract or from a combination of social contracts and international contracts. Hence, all individual rights – including the right to a limited sphere of action, that is, of free activity in the world – are "acquired rights," not "innate rights."

Fichte does not distinguish between two different issues, such that he misclassifies human rights. In fact, he confuses belonging to a legal system of rights and duties with belonging to a *positive* legal system. Under the influence of Bentham's critique and Hohfeld's classification of rights, nowadays human rights are conceived of as a system of rights and duties, as in the case of Fichte's *Foundations of Natural Right*, unlike in his *Contribution*.[8] Yet, human rights do not primarily draw their validity from a *positive* legal order, although they require positive legal recognition – in both domestic and international law – for their enforcement. In the *Foundations of Natural Right*, Fichte's assumption is that there is no system of rights and duties outside of a *positive* social contract. However, this does not imply that Fichte really abandons the idea of a universal right, which is included in the very concept of human rights. In fact, *all* human beings have the unique human right to enter into a social contract (this is similar to the "right of nationality" formulated by Article 15 of the *Universal Declaration of Human Rights*), so that, *indirectly*, that is, through a system of international treaties, every human being enjoys everywhere the *same rights* as those provided by Kant's cosmopolitan right in the *direct* relationship between a state and any foreigner.

In the following, by applying the same universal criterion of human rights, I examine whether there are further rights that belong to all human beings according to Fichte, even though he does not call them human rights.

Which Human Rights?

In the section devoted to the "civil or property contract," Fichte determines the content of the property right that he has previously defined. To this purpose, he examines the justification of property right, which lies in the protection of its objects, that is, of the freedom to subject objects in the world to one's own ends. His examination of the ends protected by property rights adopts a clearly universal perspective: "Now these ends can be quite varied ... The question is: can all of a citizen's possible ends be subordinated to one, single end?" (*FNR*, 184; *SW*, III: 211). Fichte answers this question with a teleological and fundamental anthropology that explores the features pertaining to all human beings. Let us put aside the teleological aspect of this fundamental anthropology provided by Fichte, that is, the reasons why Fichte sees an intention of nature in natural human dispositions. In fact, what matters for human rights in Fichte's *Foundations of Natural Rights* is only the list of the fundamental anthropological features on which the "possible ends" rely. These features are the following ones (my emphasis):

[8] Cf. Bentham 1973 and Hohfeld 2001.

[a] Nature has destined the human being … for **freedom**, i.e. for **activity**. (*FNR*, 184; *SW*, III: 211)

[b] If we assume that every human being wishes for something in the future, then nature would surely attain her end if she had arranged things so that **the possibility of any future** whatever for the human being *were* ***conditioned by present activity***. (*FNR*, 184; *SW*, III: 211)

[c] But since there could be human beings who did not wish for anything in the future … nature's arrangement would be a vicious circle. Therefore she had to unite both sides in some third thing within the present, namely **pain** … This pain is ***hunger*** **and** ***thirst***, and thus we find that the **need for nourishment alone** is the **original impetus** – and its satisfaction the ultimate end of all life and conduct. (*FNR*, 184–5; *SW*, III: 212)

From these universal features of human beings, Fichte draws the following conclusion pertaining to rights:

[1] And so we arrive at a more detailed description of the exclusive use of freedom that is granted to each individual in the property contract. To be able to live is the absolute, inalienable property of all human beings … A principle of all rational state constitutions is **that everyone ought to be able to live from his labor**. (*FNR*, 185; *SW*, III: 212)

[2] "We grant you the right to make such products," means the same as "We **obligate ourselves to buy** such products from you." (*FNR*, 185; *SW*, III: 213)

[3] As soon as someone suffers from need, that **portion** of other's property that would be required **to spare him from such need** no longer belongs to those others; rather, it rightfully belongs to the one in need. (*FNR*, 186; *SW*, III: 213)

The right to a profession that enables living from one's labor, and the right of subsistence in case one cannot exercise any such profession, are universal rights, connected to universal duties, and could thus be considered as defining a system of human rights, even though their enforcement depends on positive legislation.

The formulation of each of these two Fichtean human rights – property right to a profession and right to subsistence – already entails an obligation for the bearers (they must work), and the correlative duties to human rights are also clearly determined. By contrast, in earlier declarations as well as today, these human rights do not define specific addressees: the right to property, the right of free access to all professions, and the right of subsistence have many correlative duties and many potential addressees of those duties, even though in early modern times the first motivation of any declaration of human rights was to protect the citizens against absolute and arbitrary political power. Now, the complex questions of priority or subsidiarity among the addressees of correlative duties and the fact that the group of addressees potentially comprises all human beings and all institutions not only makes the implementation into a matter of complex and controversial interpretations but also makes it problematic to enforce human rights as much as would be possible. These weaknesses are absent from Fichte's human rights.

Another major difference between Fichtean human rights and our current human rights is that human rights as contained in the declarations of human rights grant *more formal freedom*, and at the same time *less real freedom* than Fichte's human rights. On the one hand, freedom of access to any profession and property right to use one's property as one wishes to allow more individual freedom to the owners and to those people who are competitive on the job market, but it does not provide the unemployed and persons without property any claim to either a property or a job. On the one hand, whereas our current human rights to free access to the profession, to property, and to subsistence are mostly conceived of as subjective rights, Fichte's human rights are defined out of duties, or more precisely out of the duty of activity.

However, in another respect, his foundation of human rights in the natural destination of human beings, that is, in activity, resembles many attempts of today's interpreters of human rights. In fact, both Fichte and the current philosophical theorists of human rights search for a *unique* foundation for all human rights. Such a project is problematic. Indeed, there are various human rights, and they protect or promote various fundamental interests. Each attempt to find a unique foundation for all human rights preferentially refers to some human rights, while neglecting others.

In the current discussion about human rights, a forerunner was Allen Gewirth's *Human Rights: Essays on Justification and Applications*.[9] His "transcendental" foundation of human rights justifies human rights as

[9] Gewirth 1982. Clarke 2014 rightly locates – along with the similarities between Fichte and Gewirth – the main difference between both authors in their founding of the concept of right as the condition for the intersubjective constitution of the individual self – "a reciprocal concept" in Fichte as opposed to Gewirth's "monological account of human agency." For this reason, whereas Gewirth "succeeds in showing only that each individual must raise a normative demand or right-claim," according to Clarke, Fichte demonstrates that this claim is "binding on other individuals" (Clarke 2014: 252f.).

being the condition of possibility for free agency.[10] In the current debate about the foundation of human rights, the transcendental foundation of human rights is the closest to Fichte's own foundation of human rights in free action in the world. It provides a plausible justification for such typical rights to freedom as the right of free movement, property right, freedom of thought and of opinion, and freedom of contracts. But how is it with the uncontroversial human right not to be tortured? Imagine a kind of torture that is particularly intense, but that does not impair at all the ability to act in the future, because it does not cause any physical or psychological damage in the future. And imagine that it is not intended to coerce the tortured person to any action. It just happens out of sadism. Like any other kind of torture, this kind of torture is prohibited by the human right not to be tortured (Article 4 of the *Universal Declaration of Human Rights*), because any deliberate infliction of pain must be duly justified. Since the Eighth Amendment to the US Constitution, punishments are not allowed to be either excessive or cruel, because, as argued by Cesare Beccaria,[11] this would inflict much pain while exceeding the amount of punishment needed for the prevention of crime. Now, admittedly, neither in Allen Gewirth's *Human Rights* nor in Fichte's conception of punishment as a "contract of expiation" for crime is there any punishment that would include torture, nor is there in their writings any permission to torture at all, even though some argue on the basis of Gewirth's thesis for allowing torture under extreme circumstances.[12] However, Fichte and Gewirth do not formulate a human right not to be tortured, nor do they adopt the adequate justification for such a right: protection against deliberate infliction of pain that is not necessary for protecting other human rights. There is yet another uncontroversial application of human rights that cannot find any justification in Fichte's *Foundations of Natural Right*. Persons suffering from either Alzheimer or dementia are no longer able to enjoy free action in the world, so that in their case the Fichtean justification for human rights does not apply. Yet, there is no controversy about their right to live and about their other human rights being recognized by the various declarations of human rights and being currently internationally considered as human rights.

[10] The use of the adjective "transcendental" refers – like in Kant – to the conditions of possibility of a universal activity.

[11] Beccaria 1995: Ch. 6.

[12] See, for instance, Levinson 2002.

Thus, Fichte's foundation for human rights is not an appropriate foundation for what human rights really are – without any controversy. This should be no surprise, since Fichte's purpose in the *Foundations of Natural Right* is not to inquire into what human rights really are, but to perform a deduction of right from the self-conscious – and thus free – I, and to apply it to right according to a contractual model.

Now, if we set aside Fichte's inappropriate, but unique foundation of all universal rights in the conditions for free action in the world, one can find in Fichte's *Foundations of Natural Right* an important inspiration for some current human rights. First of all, the right to live from one's labor finds some echo in Article 23 of the *Universal Declaration of Human Rights* (1948):

(1) Everyone has the right to work, to free choice of employment, to just and favorable conditions of work and to protection against unemployment.
(2) Everyone, without any discrimination, has the right to equal pay for equal work.
(3) Everyone who works has the right to just and favorable remuneration ensuring for himself and his family an existence worthy of human dignity, and supplemented, if necessary, by other means of social protection.

Admittedly, such aspects of Article 23 as the "free choice of employment" are not compatible with Fichte's view, but the majority is. Fichte's universal property right provides a real right to work, and thus protection against unemployment. In the remaining part of the civil contract, Fichte explains that the prizes of all goods should not be set by market value, but that the standard to be adopted by the political authority for setting the prizes is the amount of hours of work needed for producing each good. This may be seen as a possible interpretation for the "right to equal pay for equal work." In the same way, Fichte's right to a property that enables living from one's labor may also be seen as a possible interpretation of the "just and favourable remuneration ensuring for himself and his family an existence worthy of human dignity." Finally, Fichte's right of subsistence of those "who suffer of need" in spite of them being willing to work may be considered as a plausible interpretation of the right to work being "supplemented, if necessary, by other means of social protection." This similarity between Fichte and the *Universal Declaration of Human Rights* is remarkable for several reasons. *First*, it is not until the mid-nineteenth century that the question whether there is a human right to work or a human right of subsistence provided by the government became an issue in public and parliamentary debates, and the right to work is still a controversial issue. Kant ignores the right to work, and mentions the right of subsistence in a very short and minimalist way, although it is implicitly derived from Kant's unique human right:

> [T]he government is … authorized to constrain the wealthy to provide the means of sustenance to those who are unable to provide for even their most necessary natural needs. The wealthy have acquired an obligation to the commonwealth, since they owe their existence to an act of submitting to its protection and care, which they need in order to live; on this basis the state now bases its right to contribute what is theirs to maintaining their fellow citizens. (*MM*, 6: 326)

Second, unlike the right of subsistence or labor, the right to own property belongs from the beginning to all bills of rights and declarations of human rights, but it was always presented as a right separate from the right of labor or the right of subsistence (e.g., it is Article 17 of the *Universal Declaration of Human Rights*). Fichte makes out of those three human rights one single human right. There is also little doubt that in the *Foundations of Natural Right* property right as the right to a sphere of action also includes "the right to life, liberty and security of person" (Article 3), the prohibition of slavery (Article 4), the "right to marry and to found a family" (Article 16), and so on. In spite of the divergences between Fichte and the *Universal Declaration of Human Rights*, Fichte recognizes many of the human rights found in the *Declaration*, although they are not sufficiently differentiated from each other; and he does not provide an adequate justification for most human rights. Indeed, Fichte's purpose, not only in the *Foundations of Natural Right* but also in the *Contribution*, is not to develop the concept of human rights, but to elaborate political and legal institutions based on a contractual model.

Conclusion

Although several aspects of Fichte's philosophy of right, such as his concept of property, are original, interesting, and clearly argued, in my view, his approach to human rights faces a serious problem. His systematic deduction of right, his concept of a unique human right to enter into a legal system, and his concept of right as a sphere of action do not pay due attention to the existence of a diversity of fundamental human interests. Now, this diversity is at the very basis of human rights. Neither the declarations of human rights nor the bills of rights, nor international human rights law has ever been formulated as a single human right that would have been deduced from a unique justification or ground. Therefore, an adequate theory of human rights should inquire into the various fundamental interests protected or promoted by human rights, into the collision between human rights and the priority rules that apply to those collisions. Therefore, in spite of Fichte's undeniable and continued enthusiasm for the idea of human rights, neither Fichte nor German idealism in general seems to me to provide an appropriate approach, conception, and justification of human rights.

Bibliography

Aboab, Issac (trans.) (1655). *Sefer Sha'ar ha-shamayim* (Hebrew translation of Cohen de Herrera, *Puerto del Cielo*) (Amsterdam: Emanuel Benveniste).

Alexy, Robert (2002). *The Argument from Injustice: A Reply to Legal Positivism*, trans. Bonnie L. Paulson and Stanley L. Paulson (Oxford: Oxford University Press).

Alshekh, Moshe (1595). *Torat Moshe* (Belvedere: Yosef ben Yitzhak Ashkeloni).

Aristotle (1981). *On the Soul*, trans. Hippocrates G. Apostle (Grinell: Peripatetic Press).

Baier, Annette (1985). *Postures of the Mind: Essays on Mind and Morals* (Minneapolis: University of Minnesota Press).

Baum, Manfred (2013). "Freiheit und Recht bei Kant," in Stefano Bacin, Alfredo Ferrarin, Claudio La Rocca, and Margit Ruffing (eds.), *Kant und die Philosophie in weltbürgerlicher Absicht: Akten des XI. Kant-Kongresses 2010* (Berlin: DeGruyter).

Baur, Michael (2006). "Fichte's Impossible Contract," in Daniel Breazeale and Tom Rockmore (eds.), *Rights, Bodies and Recognition: New Essays on Fichte's Foundations of Natural Right* (Aldershot, Hampshire: Ashgate).

Beccaria, Cesare (1995). *Of Crimes and Punishments and Other Writings*, ed. Richard Bellamy (Cambridge: Cambridge University Press).

Beiser, Frederick (1987). *The Fate of Reason: German Philosophy from Kant to Fichte* (Cambridge, MA: Harvard University Press).

(2002). *German Idealism: The Struggle against Subjectivism 1781–1801* (Cambridge, MA: Harvard University Press).

ben Israel, Menasseh (1651). *Nishmat Ḥayyim* (Amsterdam: Samuel ben Israel Abrabanel Sueiro).

Bentham, Jeremy (1973). "A Critical Examination of the Declaration of Rights," in Bhikhu Parekh (ed.), *Bentham's Political Thought* (London: Croom Helm).

Berlin, Isaiah (1998). "Two Concepts of Liberty," in *The Proper Study of Mankind* (New York: Farrar, Straus and Giroux).

Bernstein, J. M. (2007). "Recognition and Embodiment," in Espen Hammer (ed.), *German Idealism: Contemporary Perspectives* (New York: Routledge).

(2010). "Recognition and Embodiment: Fichte's Materialism," in Hans-Christoph Schmidt am Busch and Christopher F. Zurn (eds.), *The*

Philosophy of Recognition: Historical and Contemporary Perspectives (Lanham, MD: Lexington Books).

Beyleveld, Deryck and Brownsword, Roger (1986). *Law as a Moral Judgment* (London: Sweet and Maxwell).

Bloch, Ernst (1987). *Natural Law and Human Dignity*, trans. Dennis Schmidt (Cambridge, MA: MIT Press).

Breazeale, Daniel (1999). "Ficthe's Abstract Realism," in Michael Baur and Daniel O. Dahlstrom (eds.), *The Emergence of German Idealism* (Washington, DC: Catholic University of America Press).

(2002). "Fichte's Philosophical Fictions," in Daniel Breazeale and Tom Rockmore (eds.), *New Essays on Fichte's Later Jena Wissenschaftslehre* (Evanston, IL: Northwestern University Press).

(2008). "The First-Person Standpoint of Fichte's Ethics," *Philosophy Today* 52(3–4): 270–81.

(2013a). "Circles and Grounds," in *Thinking through the Wissenschaftslehre: Themes from Fichte's Early Philosophy* (Oxford: Oxford University Press).

(2013b). "The Spirit of the Early *Wissenschaftslehre*," in *Thinking through the Wissenschaftslehre: Themes from Fichte's Early Philosophy* (Oxford: Oxford University Press).

(2013c). "The Divided Self and the Tasks of Philosophy," in *Thinking through the Wissenschaftslehre: Themes from Fichte's Early Philosophy* (Oxford: Oxford University Press).

(2013d). "Jumping the Transcendental Shark: Fichte's 'Argument of Belief' in Book III of *Die Bestimmung des Menschen* and the Transition from the Earlier to the Later *Wissenschaftslehre*," in Daniel Breazeale and Tom Rockmore (eds.), *Fichte's Vocation of Man: New Interpretive and Critical Essays* (Albany: State University of New York Press).

(2014). "Johann Gottlieb Fichte," *Stanford Encyclopaedia of Philosophy* (Spring 2014 Edition), Edward N. Zalta (ed.), http://plato.stanford.edu/archives/spr2014/entries/johann-fichte/.

Brucker, Johann (1762). *Historia Critica* (Leipzig: Bernhard Christoph Breitkopf).

Carman, Taylor (1999). "The Body in Husserl and Merleau-Ponty," *Philosophical Topics* 27(2): 205–26.

Cesa, Claudio (1992). *J.G. Fichte e l'idealismo trascendentale* (Bologna: Il Mulino).

Clarke, James Alexander (2009). "Fichte and Hegel on Recognition," *British Journal for the History of Philosophy* 17(2): 365–85.

(2011). "Hegel's Critique of Fichte in the 1802/03 Essay on Natural Right," *Inquiry* 54(3): 207–25.

(2014). "Fichte's Transcendental Justification of Human Rights," in Tom Rockmore and Daniel Breazeale (eds.) *Fichte and Transcendental Philosophy* (Basingstoke: Palgrave Macmillan).

Costello, Peter (2013). *Layers in Husserl's Phenomenology: On Meaning and Intersubjectivity* (Toronto: University of Toronto Press).

Crowe, Benjamin (2008). "Fichte's Fictions Revisited," *Inquiry* 51(3): 268–87.

Dahlstrom, Daniel. (2013). "The Self before Self-Consciousness: Hegel's Developmental Account," *Hegel Bulletin* 34(2): 135–58.

Darwall, Stephen (2005). "Fichte and the Second-Person Standpoint," in Karl Ameriks and Jürgen Stolzenberg (eds.), *Internationales Jahrbuch des Deutschen Idealismus/ International Yearbook of German Idealism.* Vol. 3 (Berlin: Walter de Gruyter).

(2006). *The Second-Person Standpoint: Morality, Respect, and Accountability* (Cambridge, MA: Harvard University Press).

De Pascale, Carla (1995). *Etica e diritto. La filosofia pratica di Fichte e le sue ascendenze kantiane* (Bologna: Il Mulino).

(2001). "Das Völkerrecht (Zweiter Anhang)," in Jean-Christophe Merle (ed.), *Johann Gottlieb Fichte: Grundlage des Naturrechts* (Berlin: Akademie).

Dewey, John (1916). *Democracy and Education* (New York: The Free Press).

Druet, Pierre-Philippe (1975). "La conversion de Fichte à la politique kantienne," *Revue de métaphysique et de morale* 80(1): 54–84.

Empiricus, Sextus (2000). *Outlines of Scepticism*, eds. Julia Annas and Jonathan Barnes (Cambridge: Cambridge University Press).

Erhard, Johann Benjamin (1970). "Apologie des Teufels," in Hellmut G. Haasis (ed.), *Über das Recht des Volkes zu einer Revolution und andere Schriften.* (Munich: C. Hanser).

(1970). *Über das Recht des Volks zu einer Revolution*, in Hellmut G. Haasis (ed.), *Über das Recht des Volks zu einer Revolutionund andere Schriften* (Munich: C. Hanser).

Estes, Yolanda (2006). "Fichte's Hypothetical Imperative: Morality, Right, and Philosophy in the Jena *Wissenschaftslehre*," in Daniel Breazeale and Tom Rockmore (eds.), *Rights, Bodies and Recognition: New Essays on Fichte's Foundations of Natural Right* (Aldershot, Hampshire: Ashgate).

Fano, Menahem Azariah de (1648). *Yonat Elem* (Amsterdam: Judah ben Mordecai and Samuel ben Moses ha-Levi).

Ferejohn, John (2001). "Pettit's Republic," *The Monist* 84(1): 77–97.

Ferry, Luc (1987). "The Distinction between Law and Ethics in the Early Philosophy of Fichte," *Philosophical Forum* 19(2–3): 182–96.

Feuerbach, Paul Johann Anselm (1796). *Kritik des natürlichen Rechts als Propädeutik zu einer Wissenschaft der natürlichen Rechte.* Altona, Hamburg: Verlagsgesellschaft.

Fichte, J. G. (1869). *The Science of Rights*, trans. A. E. Kroeger (Philadelphia: J. B. Lippincott).

Franks, Paul (2005). *All or Nothing: Systematicity, Transcendental Arguments, and Skepticism in German idealism* (Cambridge, MA: Harvard University Press).

(2008). "Ancient Skepticism, Modern Naturalism, and Nihilism in Hegel's Early Jena Writings," in Frederick Beiser (ed.), *The Cambridge Companion to Hegel and Nineteenth Century Philosophy* (Cambridge: Cambridge University Press).

(Forthcoming a). "Fichte's Position" in Günther Zöller (ed.), *The Cambridge Companion to Fichte* (Cambridge: Cambridge University Press).

(Forthcoming b). "Nothing Comes from Nothing: Judaism, the Orient, and Kabbalah in Hegel's Reception of Spinoza," in Michael Della Rocca (ed.), *The Oxford Handbook of Spinoza* (Oxford: Oxford University Press).

Freedman, Harry and Simon, Maurice (eds.) (1977). *The Midrash Rabbah*. 5 vols. (London: Soncino).

Füβer, Klaus (1999). "Farewell to 'Legal Positivism': The Separation Thesis Unravelling," in Robert P. George (ed.), *The Autonomy of Law: Essays on Legal Positivism* (Oxford: Oxford University Press).

Gadamer, Hans G. (1989). *Truth and Method*, trans. Joel Weinsheimer and Donald G. Marshall (New York: Continuum).

Gewirth, Alan (1982). *Human Rights. Essays on Justification and Applications* (Chicago: University of Chicago Press).

Gottlieb, Gabriel (2015). "Fichte's Deduction of the External World," *International Philosophical Quarterly* 55(2): 217–34.

Griffin, James (2008). *On Human Rights* (Oxford: Oxford University Press).

Hart, Herbert L. A. (1958). "Positivism and the Separation of Law and Morals," *Harvard Law Review* 71(4): 593–629.

(1961). *The Concept of Law* (Oxford: Oxford University Press).

(1982). *Essays on Bentham: Studies in Jurisprudence and Political Theory* (Oxford: Oxford University Press).

Haugeland, John (1998a). "Mind Embodied and Embedded," in *Having Thought*. Cambridge, MA: Harvard University Press.

Haugeland, John (1998b). "Truth and Rule-following," in *Having Thought*. Cambridge, MA: Harvard University Press.

Hegel, G. W. F. (1999). "On the Scientific Ways of Treating Natural Law," in Lawrence Dickey and H. B. Nisbet (eds.), *Political Writings* (New York: Cambridge University Press).

Henrich, Dieter (1966). "Fichtes ursprüngliche Einsicht," in Dieter Henrich and Hans Wagner (eds.), *Subjektivität und Metaphysik: Festschrift für Wolfgang Cramer* (Frankfurt: Klostermann).

(1982). "Fichte's Original Insight," in D. E. Christensen (ed.) and David Lachterman (trans.), *Contemporary German Philosophy*. Vol. 1 (University Park, PA: Penn State University Press).

(2009). "The Paradoxical Self-Relatedness of Consciousness," in *Between Kant and Hegel: Lectures on German idealism*. Cambridge, MA: Harvard University Press.

Herrera, Abraham Cohen de (2002). *Gate of Heaven* [*Puerto del Cielo*] (Leiden: Brill).

Hobbes, Thomas (1996). *Leviathan*, ed. Richard Tuck (Cambridge: Cambridge University Press).

(1997). *On the Citizen*, ed. Richard Tuck and Michael Silverthorne (Cambridge: Cambridge University Press).

Hohfeld, Wesley Newcomb (2001). *Fundamental Legal Conceptions as Applied in Judicial Reasoning* (Dartmouth: Ashgate).

Honneth, Axel. (1996). *The Struggle for Recognition: The Moral Grammar of Social Conflicts*. Cambridge, MA: MIT Press.

Honneth, Axel (2001). "Die transzendentale Notwendigkeit von Intersubjektivität (Zweiter Lehersatz: §3)", in Jean-Christophe Merle (ed.), *Johann Gottlieb Fichte: Grundlage des Naturrechts* (Berlin: Akademie).

Horowitz, Shabbetai Sheftel (1612). *Shefa Tal* (Hanau: Hans Jacoba Henna).

Horstmann, Rolf-Peter (2001). "Die Theorie des Urrechts (§§8–12)," in Jean-Christophe Merle (ed.), *Johann Gottlieb Fichte: Grundlage des Naturrechts* (Berlin: Akademie).

Hufeland, Gottlieb (1785). *Versuch über den Grundsatz des Naturrechts* (Leipzig: Göschen).

(1790). *Lehrsätze des Naturrechts und der damit verbundenen Wissenschaften* (Jena: Christian Heinrich Cuno's Erben).

Husserl, Edmund (1982). *Ideas Pertaining to a Pure Phenomenology and to a Phenomenological Psychology: First Book*, trans. Fred Kersten (Boston: Kluwer).

Idel, Moshe (1992). "On the Development of the Concept of ẓimẓum in Kabbalah and its Research," (Hebrew), *Jerusalem Studies in Jewish Thought* 10: 310–52.

Jacobi, Friedrich Heinrich (1994a). "Concerning the Doctrine of Spinoza in Letters to Herr Moses Mendelssohn," in George di Giovanni (ed. and trans.), *Main Philosophical Writings* (Kingston, ON and Montreal, QC: McGill-Queens University Press).

(1994b). "David Hume on Faith, or Idealism and Realism, A Dialogue," in George di Giovanni (ed. and trans.), *Main Philosophical Writings* (Kingston, ON and Montreal, QC: McGill-Queens University Press).

(1994c). "Edward Allwill's Collection of Letters," in George di Giovanni (ed. and trans.), *Main Philosophical Writings* (Kingston, ON and Montreal, QC: McGill-Queens University Press).

James, David (2010). "Fichte's Theory of Property," *European Journal of Political Theory* 9(2): 202–17.

(2011). *Fichte's Social and Political Philosophy: Property and Virtue* (Cambridge: Cambridge University Press).

(2015). *Fichte's Republic: Idealism, History and Nationalism* (Cambridge: Cambridge University Press).

Kant, Immanuel (1996). "On the Common Saying: That May be Correct in Theory, But it is of No Use in Practice," in Mary Gregor (ed. and trans.), *Practical Philosophy* (Cambridge: Cambridge University Press).

Kersting, Wolfgang (2001). "Die Unäbhangigkeit des Rechts von der Moral (Einleitung)," in Jean-Christophe Merle (ed.), *Johann Gottlieb Fichte: Grundlage des Naturrechts* (Berlin: Akademie Verlag).

Knorr von Rosenroth, Christian et al. (1677–84). *Kabbala Denudata seu doctrina Hebraeorum transcendentalis et metaphysica atque theological* (Sulzbach: Abraham Lichtentahler).

Kohn, Hans (1949). "The Paradox of Fichte's Nationalism," *Journal of the History of Ideas* 10(3): 319–43.

Kosch, Michelle (2013). "Formal Freedom in Fichte's System of Ethics," *International Yearbook of German Idealism* 9: 150–68.

Laudou, Christophe (2008). “Fichte, entre volonté générale et *Volkgeist*,” in Jean-Christophe Goddard and Jacinto Rivera de Rosales (eds.), *Fichte et la politique* (Monza: Polimetrica).

Levinson, Jerrold (2002). “Gewirth on Absolute Rights,” in G. W. Smith (ed.), *Critical Concepts in Political Theory* (London: Routledge).

Locke, John (1690). *The Second Treatise on Government* (London: Awnsham Churchill).

(1988). *The Second Treatise on Government*, ed. Peter Laslett (Cambridge: Cambridge University Press).

Maimon, Salomon (1792). *Lebensgeschichte* (Berlin: Friedrich Vieweg).

(1970). “Über die ersten Gründe des Naturrechts,” in Valerio Verra (ed.), *Gesammelte Werke*, VI, (Hildesheim: Olms).

Martin, Wayne (1997). “Pipe-dreams and Nonthoughts: The Problems with Things in Themselves,” in *Idealism and Objectivity: Understanding Fichte's Jena Project* (Stanford: Stanford University Press).

(2006). “Is Fichte a Social Contract Theorist?” in Daniel Breazeale and Tom Rockmore (eds.), *Rights, Bodies and Recognition: New Essays on Fichte's Foundations of Natural Right* (Aldershot, Hampshire: Ashgate).

(2015). “Fichtes transzendentale Phänomenologie des Tätigkeit,” in Jean-Christophe Merle and Andreas Schmidt (eds.), *Fichte's System der Sittenlehre: Ein kooperativer Kommentar* (Frankfurt: Vittorio Klostermann).

Maus, Ingeborg (2001). “Die Verfassung und ihre Garantie: das Ephorat (§§16, 17, und 21),” in Jean-Christophe Merle (ed.), *Johann Gottlieb Fichte: Grundlage des Naturrechts* (Berlin: Akademie).

Merle, Jean-Christophe (2001). “Eigentumsrecht (§§18–19),” in Jean-Christophe Merle (ed.), *Johann Gottlieb Fichte: Grundlage des Naturrechts* (Berlin: Akademie).

(2009). *German Idealism and the Concept of Punishment*. Cambridge: Cambridge University Press.

Merleau-Ponty, Maurice (2012). *Phenomenology of Perception*, trans. Donald A. Landes (New York: Routledge).

Merrill, Bruce (2006). “Fichte's Materialism,” in Daniel Breazeale and Tom Rockmore (eds.), *Rights, Bodies and Recognition: New Essays on Fichte's Foundations of Natural Right* (Aldershot, Hampshire: Ashgate).

Nagel, Thomas (1970). *The Possibility of Altruism* (Princeton: Princeton University Press).

Nance, Michael (2015). “Recognition, Freedom, and the Self in Fichte's *Foundations of Natural Right*,” *European Journal of Philosophy* 23(3): 608–32.

(n.d.) “Anarchy, Legitimacy, and Economic Planning in Fichte's Jena Political Philosophy” (unpublished ms).

Nease, Lon (2002). “The Severity of the Moral Law in Fichte's *Science of Ethics*,” in Daniel Breazeale and Tom Rockmore (eds.), *New Essays on Fichte's Later Jena Wissenschaftslehre* (Evanston, IL: Northwestern University Press).

Neuhouser, Frederick (1990). *Fichte's Theory of Subjectivity* (Cambridge: Cambridge University Press).

(1994). "Fichte and the Relationship between Right and Morality," in Daniel Breazeale and Tom Rockmore (eds.), *Fichte: Historical Contexts/ Contemporary Controversies* (Atlantic Highlands, NJ: Humanities Press).
(2001). "The Efficacy of the Rational Being," in Jean-Christophe Merle (ed.), *Johann Gottlieb Fichte: Grundlage des Naturrechts* (Berlin: Akademie Verlag).
(2013). "Rousseau's Critique of Economic Inequality," *Philosophy and Public Affairs* 41(3): 193–225.
Nomer, Nedim (2013). "Fichte's Separation Thesis," *Philosophical Forum* 44(3): 233–54.
Nozick, R. (1981). *Philosophical Explanations*. Cambridge, MA: Harvard University Press.
Nuzzo, Angelica (2006). "The Role of the Human Body in Fichte's *Grundlage des Naturrechts* (1796–97)," in Daniel Breazeale and Tom Rockmore (eds.), *Rights, Bodies and Recognition: New Essays on Fichte's Foundations of Natural Right* (Aldershot, Hampshire: Ashgate Publishing).
(2011). "Théorie de l'éthique et éthique appliquée chez Fichte: Sittenlehre ou Metaphysik der Sitten?" *Revue de Métaphysique et de Morale* 3: 319–33.
O'Neill, Onora (2007). "Experts, Practitioners, and Practical Judgment," *Journal of Moral Philosophy* 4(1): 154–66.
Panzieri, Efraim (1995). *Sefer ha-Derushim* (Jerusalem: Ahavat Shalom).
Parfit, Derek (2011). *On What Matters* (Oxford: Oxford University Press).
Pettit, Philip (1996). "Institutional Design and Rational Choice," in R. Goodin (ed.), *The Theory of Institutional Design* (Cambridge: Cambridge University Press).
Pettit, Philip (2012). "Freedom," in David Estlund (ed.), *The Oxford Handbook of Political Philosophy* (New York: Oxford University Press).
Philonenko, Alexis (1980). *La Liberté humaine dans la Philosophie de Fichte* (Paris: Vrin).
(1988). *Théorie et praxis dans la pensée morale et politique de Kant et de Fichte en 1793* (Paris: Vrin).
Rainbolt, George W. (2006). *The Concept of Rights* (Dordrecht: Springer).
Raz, Joseph (1999). *Practical Reasons and Norms* (Oxford: Oxford University Press).
Redding, Paul. (1996). *Hegel's Hermeneutics*. Ithaca: Cornell University Press.
Renaut, Alain (1986). *Le système du droit: Philosophie et droit dans la pensée de Fichte* (Paris: PUF).
Reuchlin, Johannes (1517). *De Arte Cabbalistica* (Hagenau: Thomas Anshelm.
Ritter, Joachim (ed.) (1971–84). *Historisches Wörterbuch der Philosophie*, vols. 1–6 (Darmstade: Wissenschaftliche Buchgesselschaft).
Rosenzweig, Franz (1979). *Briefe und Tagebücher II: 1918–29*, ed. Rachel Rosenzweig and Edith Rosenzweig-Scheinmann (Leiden: Martinus Nijhoff).
Russell, Bertrand (1945). *A History of Western Philosophy*. New York: Simon & Schuster.
Russon, John (2007). "The Spatiality of Self-Consciousness: Originary Passivity in Kant, Merleau-Ponty and Derrida," *Chiasmi International* 9: 219–32.
(2014). "Philosophy of Mind," in Michael Baur (ed.), *Hegel: Key Concepts* (New York: Routledge).

Sartre, Jean-Paul (1956). *Being and Nothingness* (New York: Philosophical Library).
Scheffler, Samuel (1994). *Human Morality* (Oxford: Oxford University Press).
Schelling, F. W. J. (1798). "Über die Weltseele," in K. F. A. Schelling (ed.), *Schellings sämtliche Werke*, Abtheilung I, Vol. 2 (Stuttgart: J. G. Cotta, 1856–61).
(1980). "New Deduction of Natural Right," in *The Unconditional in Human Knowledge. Four Early Essays (1794–1796)*, trans. Fritz Marti (Lewisburg, PA: Bucknell University Press).
Schmalz, Theodor (1792). *Das reine Naturrecht* (Königsberg: Friedrich Nicolovius).
Schmid, Carl Christian Erhard (1795). *Grundriss des Naturrechts* (Jena: Gabler).
Schneerson, Dov Ber (1820). *Ner Miẓvah ve-Torah Or* (Kopys: Yisrael ben Yitzhak Yafeh).
Scholem, Gershom (1978). *Kabbalah* (New York: Penguin).
Schottky, Richard (1995). *Untersuchungen zur Geschichte der staatsphilosophischen Vertragstheorie im 17. und 18. Jahrhundert (Hobbes – Locke – Rousseau – Fichte) mit einem Beitrag zum Problem der Gewaltenteilung bei Rousseau und Fichte* (Fichte-Studien-Supplementa 6) (Amsterdam: Rodopi).
Schulte, Christoph (2014). *Ẓimẓum* (Frankfurt am Main: Suhrkamp).
Scribner, S. (2002). "The 'Subtle Matter' of Intersubjectivity in the *Grundlage des Naturrechts*," in Daniel Breazeale and Tom Rockmore (eds.), *New Essays on Fichte's Later Jena Wissenschaftslehre* (Evanston, IL: Northwestern University Press).
Shapira, Kalman Kalonymous (1932). *Ḥovat ha-Talmidim* (Warsaw: Gross).
Siep, Ludwig (1979a). *Anerkennung als Prinzip der praktischen Philosophie* (Freiburg: Karl Alber).
(1979b). "Wandlungen in Fichtes Gesellschaftslehre," *Philosophische Rundschau* 26: 120–8.
(1992). "Einheit und Methode von Fichtes 'Grundlage des Naturrechts,'" in *Praktische Philosophie im Deutschen Idealismus* (Frankfurt am Main: Suhrkamp).
Spinoza, Baruch (1985). "Ethics," in *The Collected Writings of Spinoza: Volume 1*, trans. Edwin Curley (Princeton: Princeton University Press).
Stern, Robert (1993). "Introduction," in Robert Stern (ed.), *Transcendental Arguments: Problems and Prospects* (Oxford: Oxford University Press).
Tugendhat, Ernst (1993). *Vorlesungen über Ethik* (Frankfurt am Main: Suhrkamp).
Tully, James (1980). *A Discourse on Property: John Locke and his Adversaries* (Cambridge: Cambridge University Press).
Uleman, Jennifer (2004). "External Freedom in Kant's Doctrine of Right: Political, Metaphysical," *Philosophy and Phenomenological Research* 68: 578–601.
Valabregue-Perry, Sandra (2012). "The Concept of Infinity (Eyn Sof) and the Rise of Theosophical Kabbalah," *Jewish Quarterly Review* 102: 405–30.
Varden, Helga (2008). "Kant's Non-Voluntarist Conception of Political Obligation," *Kantian Review* 13: 1–45.
Vater, Michael (2006). "Schelling's Aphorisms on Natural Right: A Comparison with Fichte's *Grundlage des Naturrechts*," in Daniel Breazeale and Tom Rockmore (eds.), *Rights, Bodies and Recognition: New Essays on Fichte's Foundations of Natural Right* (Aldershot, Hampshire: Ashgate).

Verweyen, Hansjürgen (1975). *Recht und Sittlichkeit in J. G. Fichtes Gesellschaftslehre* (Freiburg: Alber).
Vital, Ḥaim (1784). *Ez Ḥaim*, ed. Meir Poppers (Koretz: Isaac Satanov).
Vital, Ḥaim (1999). *The Tree of Life: The Palace of Adam Kadmon*, Donald Wilder Menzi and Zwe Padeh (trans.) (Lanham, MD: Jason Aronson).
von Wright, Georg H. (1951). "Deontic Logic," *Mind* 60: 1–15.
Wachter, Johann Georg (1699). *Der Spinozismus im Jüdenthumb* (Amsterdam: Johann Wolters).
Waldron, Jeremy (1988). *The Right to Private Property* (Oxford: Clarendon).
(2002). *God, Locke and Equality: Christian Foundations in Locke's Political Thought* (Cambridge: Cambridge University Press).
Ware, Owen (2010). "Fichte's Voluntarism," *European Journal of Philosophy* 18: 262–82.
Wenar, Leif (2010). "Rights," in Edward N. Zalta (ed.), *Stanford Encyclopedia of Philosophy* (Fall 2010 edition), http://plato.stanford.edu/archives/fall/2010/entries/rights.
Williams, Robert (1992). *Recognition: Fichte and Hegel on the Other* (Albany: State University of New York Press).
(2002). "The Displacement of Recognition by Coercion in Fichte's *Grundlage des Naturrechts*," in Daniel Breazeale and Tom Rockmore (eds.), *New Essays on Fichte's Later Jena Wissenschaftslehre* (Evanston, IL: Northwestern University Press).
(2006). "Recognition, Right, and Social Contract," in Daniel Breazeale and Tom Rockmore (eds.), *Rights, Bodies and Recognition: New Essays on Fichte's Foundations of Natural Right* (Aldershot, Hampshire: Ashgate).
Wollstonecraft, Mary (1995). *A Vindication of the Rights of Men and A Vindication of the Rights of Women and Hints*, ed. Sylvana Tomaselli (Cambridge: Cambridge University Press).
Wood, Allen (1990). *Hegel's Ethical Thought* (Cambridge: Cambridge University Press).
(1991). "Fichte's Philosophical Revolution," *Philosophical Topics* 19(2): 1–28.
(2006). "Fichte's Intersubjective I," *Inquiry* 49(1): 71–6.
(2011). "Fichte's Absolute Freedom," *International Yearbook of German Idealism* 9: 100–29.
(2014). "Fichte's Absolute Freedom," reprint (with minor revisions) of the 2011 paper as Chapter 7 in *The Free Development of Each: Studies on Freedom, Right and Ethics in Classical German Philosophy* (Oxford: Oxford University Press).
(2016). *Fichte's Ethical Thoughts* (Oxford: Oxford University Press).
(Forthcoming). "Fichte's Philosophy of Right and Ethics," in Günter Zöller (ed.), *The Cambridge Companion to Fichte* (New York: Cambridge University Press).
Zalman of Liadi, Shneur (1797). *Tanya* (Slavuta: Shapira).
Zöller, Günter (1998). *Fichte's Transcendental Idealism: The Original Duplicity of Intelligence and Will* (Cambridge: Cambridge University Press).

Index

www.ingramcontent.com/pod-product-compliance
Ingram Content Group UK Ltd.
Pitfield, Milton Keynes, MK11 3LW, UK
UKHW020657150225
454996UK00023B/1023